Oliver Sacks

Musicophilia

Oliver Sacks is a practicing physician and the author of ten books, including *The Man Who Mistook His Wife for a Hat* and *Awakenings* (which inspired the Oscar-nominated film). He lives in New York City, where he is a professor of neurology and psychiatry at Columbia University Medical Center and Columbia's first Columbia University Artist. For more about his work, visit www.oliversacks.com.

"[Sacks] weaves neuroscience through a fascinating personal story, allowing us to think about brain functions and music in a bracing new light. . . . Human context is what makes good journalism, medical and otherwise. That's the art of Sacks's best essays." —*Salon*

"[Sacks's] lifelong love for music infuses the writing. . . . *Musicophilia* shows music can be more powerful (even dangerous) than most of us realize, and that defining it may be crucial to defining who we are." —*Pittsburgh Post-Gazette*

"Dr. Sacks writes not just as a doctor and a scientist but also as a humanist with a philosophical and literary bent. . . . [His] book not only contributes to our understanding of the elusive magic of music but also illuminates the strange workings, and misfirings, of the human mind." —*The New York Times*

"[Sacks's] ultimate gift to readers is a sustained sense of wonder at the enormous variability of individual human experience." —*The Oregonian*

"[These] persuasive essays about composers, patients, savants, and ordinary people . . . offer captivating variations on the central premise that human beings are 'exquisitely tuned' to the illuminating yet ultimately mysterious powers of music." —*Elle*

"Sacks spins one fascinating tale after another to show what happens when music and the brain mix it up." —*Newsweek*

"Evocative, thought-provoking and compassionate beyond measure, this is a book to cherish." —*The Washington Times*

Musicophilia

Musicophilia

Tales of Music and the Brain

Oliver Sacks

REVISED AND EXPANDED

VINTAGE CANADA

Published in Canada by Vintage Canada, a division of Random House of Canada
Limited, Toronto, in 2008, and simultaneously in the United States by Vintage Books,
a division of Random House, Inc., New York. Originally published in hardcover in
Canada by Alfred A. Knopf Canada, a division of Random House of Canada Limited,
Toronto, in 2007, and simultaneously in the United States by Alfred A. Knopf,
a division of Random House, Inc., New York. Distributed by Random House of
Canada Limited, Toronto.

Vintage Canada and colophon are registered trademarks of Random House
of Canada Limited.

Grateful acknowledgment is made to Hal Leonard Corporation for permission to
reprint an excerpt from "Music," words and music by Carole King, copyright © 1971
(renewed 1999) by Colgems-EMI Music Inc. All rights reserved. International
copyright secured. Reprinted by permission of Hal Leonard Corporation.

www.randomhouse.ca

Library and Archives Canada Cataloguing in Publication

Sacks, Oliver W.
Musicophilia : tales of music and the brain / Oliver Sacks.

Includes bibliographical references and index.
ISBN 978-0-676-97979-4

1. Music—Psychological aspects.   2. Music—Physiological aspects.   I. Title.

ML3830.S122 2008   781'.11   C2008-900333-0

Printed and bound in the United States of America

10 9 8 7 6 5 4 3 2 1

For Orrin Devinsky,
Ralph Siegel,
and Connie Tomaino

Contents

Part III: Memory, Movement, and Music

Part IV: Emotion, Identity, and Music

Preface

Whatanoddthingitistoseeanentirespecies—billions of people—playing with, listening to, meaningless tonal patterns, occupied and preoccupied for much of their time by what they call "music." This, at least, was one of the things about human beings that puzzled the highly cerebral alien beings, the Overlords, in Arthur C. Clarke's novel *Childhood's End*. Curiosity brings them down to the Earth's surface to attend a concert, they listen politely, and at the end, congratulate the composer on his "great ingenuity"—while still finding the entire business unintelligible. They cannot think what goes on in human beings when they make or listen to music, because nothing goes on with *them*. They themselves, as a species, lack music.

We may imagine the Overlords ruminating further, back in their spaceships. This thing called "music," they would have to concede, is in some way efficacious to humans, central to human life. Yet it has no concepts, makes no propositions; it lacks images, symbols, the stuff of language. It has no power of representation. It has no necessary relation to the world.

There are rare humans who, like the Overlords, may lack the neural apparatus for appreciating tones or melodies. But for virtually all of us, music has great power, whether or not we seek it out or think of ourselves as particularly "musical." This propensity to music—this "musicophilia"—shows itself in infancy, is manifest and central in every culture, and probably goes back to the very beginnings of our species. It may be developed or shaped by the cultures we live in, by the circumstances of life, or by the particular gifts or weaknesses we have as individuals—but it lies so deep in human nature that one is tempted to think of it as innate, much as E. O. Wilson regards "biophilia," our feeling for living things. (Perhaps musicophilia is a form of biophilia, since music itself feels almost like a living thing.)

While birdsong has obvious adaptive uses (in courtship, or aggression, or staking out territory, etc.), it is relatively fixed in structure and, to a large extent, hardwired into the avian nervous system (although there are a very few songbirds which seem to improvise, or sing duets). The origin of human music is less easy to understand. Darwin himself was evidently puzzled, as he wrote in *The Descent of Man:* "As neither the enjoyment nor the capacity of producing musical notes are faculties of the least use to man . . . they must be ranked among the most mysterious with which he is endowed." And, in our own time, Steven Pinker has referred to music as "auditory cheesecake," and asks: "What benefit could there be to diverting time and energy to making plinking noises? . . . As far as biological cause and effect are concerned, music is useless. . . . It could vanish from our species and the rest of our lifestyle would be virtually unchanged." While Pinker is very musical himself and would certainly feel his own life much impoverished by its absence, he does not believe that music, or any of the arts, are direct evolutionary adaptations. He proposes, in a 2007 article, that many of the arts may have no adaptive function at all. They may be by-products of two other traits: motivational systems that give us pleasure when we experience signals that correlate with adaptive outcomes (safety, sex, esteem, information-rich environments), and the technological know-how to create purified and concentrated doses of these signals.

Pinker (and others) feel that our musical powers—some of them, at least—are made possible by using, or recruiting, or co-opting brain systems that have already developed for other purposes. This might go with the fact that there is no single "music center" in the human brain, but the involvement of a dozen scattered networks throughout the brain. Stephen Jay Gould, who was the first to face the vexed question of nonadaptive changes squarely, speaks of "exaptations" in this regard, rather than adaptations—and he singles out music as a clear example as such an exaptation. (William James probably had something similar in mind when he wrote of our susceptibility to music and other aspects of "our higher aesthetic, moral and intellectual life" as having entered the mind "by the back stairs.")

Yet regardless of all this—the extent to which human musical powers and susceptibilities are hardwired or are a by-product of other powers and proclivities—music remains fundamental and central in every culture.

We humans are a musical species no less than a linguistic one. This takes many different forms. All of us (with very few exceptions) can perceive music, perceive tones, timbre, pitch intervals, melodic contours, harmony, and (perhaps most elementally) rhythm. We integrate all of these and "construct" music in our minds using many different parts of the brain. And to this largely unconscious structural appreciation of music is added an often intense and profound emotional reaction to music. "The inexpressible depth of music," Schopenhauer wrote, "so easy to understand and yet so inexplicable, is due to the fact that it reproduces all the emotions of our innermost being, but entirely without reality and remote from its pain. . . . Music expresses only the quintessence of life and of its events, never these themselves."

Listening to music is not just auditory and emotional, it is motoric as well: "We listen to music with our muscles," as Nietzsche wrote. We keep time to music, involuntarily, even if we are not consciously attending to it, and our faces and postures mirror the "narrative" of the melody, and the thoughts and feelings it provokes.

Much that occurs during the perception of music can also occur when music is "played in the mind." The imagining of music, even in relatively nonmusical people, tends to be remarkably faithful not only to the tune and feeling of the original but to its pitch and tempo. Underlying this is the extraordinary tenacity of musical memory, so that much of what is heard during one's early years may be "engraved" on the brain for the rest of one's life. Our auditory systems, our nervous systems, are indeed exquisitely tuned for music. How much this is due to the intrinsic characteristics of music itself—its complex sonic patterns woven in time, its logic, its momentum, its unbreakable sequences, its insistent rhythms and repetitions, the mysterious way in which it embodies emotion and "will"—and how much to special resonances, synchronizations, oscillations, mutual excitations, or feedbacks in the immensely complex, multilevel neural circuitry that underlies musical perception and replay, we do not yet know.

But this wonderful machinery—perhaps because it is so complex and highly developed—is vulnerable to various distortions, excesses, and breakdowns. The power to perceive (or imagine) music may be impaired with some brain lesions; there are many such forms of amusia. On the other hand, musical imagery may become excessive and uncontrollable, leading to incessant repetition of catchy tunes, or even musical hallucinations. In some people, music can provoke seizures. There are special neurological hazards, "disorders of skill," that may affect professional musicians. The normal association of intellectual and emotional may break down in some circumstances, so that one may perceive music accurately, but remain indifferent and unmoved by it or, conversely, be passionately moved, despite being unable to make any "sense" of what one is hearing. Some people—a surprisingly large number—"see" color or "taste" or "smell" or "feel" various sensations as they listen to music—though such synesthesia may be accounted a gift more than a symptom.

William James referred to our "susceptibility to music," and while music can affect all of us—calm us, animate us, comfort us, thrill us, or serve to organize and synchronize us at work or play—it may be especially powerful and have great therapeutic potential for patients with a variety of neurological conditions. Such people may respond powerfully and specifically to music (and, sometimes, to little else). Some of these patients have widespread cortical problems, whether from strokes or Alzheimer's or other causes of dementia; others have specific cortical syndromes—loss of language or movement functions, amnesias, or frontal-lobe syndromes. Some are retarded, some autistic; others have subcortical syndromes such as parkinsonism or other movement disorders. All of these conditions and many others can potentially respond to music and music therapy.

. . .

F OR ME, the first incitement to think and write about music
came in 1966, when I saw the profound effects of music on the
deeply parkinsonian patients I later wrote about in *Awakenings*.
And since then, in more ways than I could possibly imagine, I
have found music continually forcing itself on my attention,
showing me its effects on almost every aspect of brain function—
and life.

"Music" has always been one of the first things I look up in the
index of any new neurology or physiology textbook. But I could
find scarcely any mention of the subject until the 1977 publication of Macdonald Critchley and R. A. Henson's book *Music and
the Brain*, with its wealth of historical and clinical examples.
Perhaps one reason for the scarcity of musical case histories
is that physicians rarely ask their patients about mishaps of musical perception (whereas a linguistic problem, say, will immediately come to light). Another reason for this neglect is that
neurologists like to explain, to find putative mechanisms, as
well as to describe—and there was virtually no neuroscience of
music prior to the 1980s. This has all changed in the last
two decades with new technologies that allow us to see the living brain as people listen to, imagine, and even compose music.
There is now an enormous and rapidly growing body of work
on the neural underpinnings of musical perception and
imagery, and the complex and often bizarre disorders to which
these are prone. These new insights of neuroscience are exciting
beyond measure, but there is always a certain danger that the
simple art of observation may be lost, that clinical description
may become perfunctory, and the richness of the human context
ignored.

Clearly, both approaches are necessary, blending "old-fashioned" observation and description with the latest in technology, and I have tried to incorporate both of these approaches here. But above all, I have tried to listen to my patients and subjects, to imagine and enter their experiences—it is these which form the core of this book.

Part I

Haunted by Music

I

A Bolt from the Blue:
Sudden Musicophilia

Tony Cicoria was forty-two, very fit and robust, a former college football player who had become a well-regarded orthopedic surgeon in a small city in upstate New York. He was at a lakeside pavilion for a family gathering one fall afternoon. It was pleasant and breezy, but he noticed a few storm clouds in the distance; it looked like rain.

He went to a pay phone outside the pavilion to make a quick call to his mother (this was in 1994, before the age of cell phones). He still remembers every single second of what happened next: "I was talking to my mother on the phone. There was a little bit of rain, thunder in the distance. My mother hung up. The phone was a foot away from where I was standing when I got struck. I remember a flash of light coming out of the phone. It hit me in the face. Next thing I remember, I was flying backwards."

Then—he seemed to hesitate before telling me this—"I was flying forwards. Bewildered. I looked around. I saw my own body on the ground. I said to myself, 'Oh shit, I'm dead.' I saw people converging on the body. I saw a woman—she had been standing waiting to use the phone right behind me—position herself over my body, give it CPR. . . . I floated up the stairs—my conscious-ness came with me. I saw my kids, had the realization that they would be okay. Then I was surrounded by a bluish-white light . . . an enormous feeling of well-being and peace. The high-est and lowest points of my life raced by me. No emotion associ-ated with these . . . pure thought, pure ecstasy. I had the perception of accelerating, being drawn up . . . there was speed and direction. Then, as I was saying to myself, 'This is the most glorious feeling I have ever had'—SLAM! I was back."

Dr. Cicoria knew he was back in his own body because he had pain—pain from the burns on his face and his left foot, where the electrical charge had entered and exited his body—and, he real-ized, "only bodies have pain." He wanted to go back, he wanted to tell the woman to stop giving him CPR, to let him go; but it was too late—he was firmly back among the living. After a minute or two, when he could speak, he said, "It's okay—I'm a doctor!" The woman (she turned out to be an intensive-care-unit nurse) replied, "A few minutes ago, you weren't."

The police came and wanted to call an ambulance, but Cicoria refused. They took him home instead ("it seemed to take hours"), where he called his own doctor, a cardiologist. The car-diologist, when he saw him, thought Cicoria must have had a brief cardiac arrest, but could find nothing amiss with examina-tion or EKG. "With these things, you're alive or dead," the cardi-ologist remarked. He did not feel that Dr. Cicoria would suffer any further consequences of this bizarre accident.

Cicoria also consulted a neurologist—he was feeling sluggish (most unusual for him) and having some difficulties with his memory. He found himself forgetting the names of people he knew well. He was examined neurologically, had an EEG and an MRI. Again, nothing seemed amiss.

A couple of weeks later, when his energy returned, Dr. Cicoria went back to work. There were still some lingering memory problems—he occasionally forgot the names of rare diseases or surgical procedures—but all his surgical skills were unimpaired. In another two weeks, his memory problems disappeared, and that, he thought, was the end of the matter.

What then happened still fills Cicoria with amazement, even now, a dozen years later. Life had returned to normal, seemingly, when "suddenly, over two or three days, there was this insatiable desire to listen to piano music." This was completely out of keeping with anything in his past. He had had a few piano lessons as a boy, he said, "but no real interest." He did not have a piano in his house. What music he did listen to tended to be rock music.

With this sudden onset of craving for piano music, he began to buy recordings and became especially enamored of a Vladimir Ashkenazy recording of Chopin favorites—the *Military* Polonaise, the *Winter Wind* Étude, the *Black Key* Étude, the A-flat Major Polonaise, the B-flat Minor Scherzo. "I loved them all," Cicoria said. "I had the desire to play them. I ordered all the sheet music. At this point, one of our babysitters asked if she could store her piano in our house—so now, just when I craved one, a piano arrived, a nice little upright. It suited me fine. I could hardly read the music, could barely play, but I started to teach myself." It had been more than thirty years since the few piano lessons of his boyhood, and his fingers felt stiff and awkward.

And then, on the heels of this sudden desire for piano music, Cicoria started to hear music in his head. "The first time," he said, "it was in a dream. I was in a tux, onstage; I was playing something I had written. I woke up, startled, and the music was still in my head. I jumped out of bed, started trying to write down as much of it as I could remember. But I hardly knew how to notate what I heard." This was not surprising—he had never tried to write or notate music before. But whenever he sat down at the piano to work on the Chopin, his own music "would come and take me over. It had a very powerful presence."

I was not quite sure what to make of this peremptory music, which would intrude and overwhelm him. Was he having musical hallucinations? No, Dr. Cicoria said, they were not hallucinations—"inspiration" was a more apt word. The music was there, deep inside him—or somewhere—and all he had to do was let it come to him. "It's like a frequency, a radio band. If I open myself up, it comes. I want to say, 'It comes from heaven,' as Mozart said."

His music is ceaseless. "It never runs dry," he continued. "If anything, I have to turn it off."

Now he had to wrestle not just with learning to play the Chopin, but to give form to the music continually running in his head, trying it out on the piano, getting it on manuscript paper. "It was a terrible struggle," he said. "I would get up at four in the morning and play till I went to work, and when I got home from work I was at the piano all evening. My wife was not really pleased. I was possessed."

In the third month after being struck by lightning, then, Cicoria—once an easygoing, genial family man, almost indifferent to music—was inspired, even possessed, by music, and scarcely had time for anything else. It began to dawn on him that perhaps he had been "saved" for a special purpose. "I came to think," he said, "that the only reason I had been allowed to survive was the music." I asked him whether he had been a religious man before the lightning. He had been raised Catholic, he said, but had never been particularly observant; he had some "unorthodox" beliefs, too, such as in reincarnation.

He himself, he grew to think, had had a sort of reincarnation, had been transformed and given a special gift, a mission, to "tune in" to the music that he called, half metaphorically, "the music from heaven." This came, often, in "an absolute torrent" of notes with no breaks, no rests, between them, and he would have to give it shape and form. (As he said this, I thought of Caedmon, the seventh-century Anglo-Saxon poet, an uneducated goatherd who, it was said, had received the "art of song" in a dream one night, and spent the rest of his life praising God and creation in hymns and poems.)

Cicoria continued to work on his piano playing and his compositions. He got books on notation, and soon realized that he needed a music teacher. He would travel to concerts by his favorite performers but had nothing to do with musical friends or musical activities in his own town. This was a solitary pursuit, between himself and his muse.

I asked whether he had experienced other changes since the lightning strike—a new appreciation of art, perhaps, different taste in reading, new beliefs? Cicoria said he had become "very spiritual" since his near-death experience. He had started to read every book he could find about near-death experiences and about lightning strikes. And he had got "a whole library on Tesla," as well as anything on the terrible and beautiful power of high-voltage electricity. He thought he could sometimes feel "auras" of light or energy around people's bodies—he had never seen this before the lightning bolt.

Some years passed, and Cicoria's new life, his inspiration, never deserted him. He continued to work full-time as a surgeon, but his heart and mind now centered on music. He got divorced in 2004, and the same year had a fearful motorcycle accident. He had no memory of this, but his Harley was struck by another vehicle, and he was found in a ditch, unconscious and badly injured, with broken bones, a ruptured spleen, a perforated lung, cardiac contusions, and, despite his helmet, head injuries. In spite of all this, he made a complete recovery and was back at work in two months. Neither the accident nor his head injury nor his divorce seemed to have made any difference to his passion for playing and composing music.

I HAVE NEVER MET another person with a story like Tony Cicoria's, but I have occasionally had patients with a similar sudden onset of musical or artistic interests—including Salimah M., a research chemist. In her early forties, Salimah started to have brief periods, lasting a minute or less, in which she would get "a strange feeling"—sometimes a sense that she was on a beach that she had once known, while at the same time being perfectly conscious of her current surroundings and able to continue a conversation, or drive a car, or do whatever she had been doing. Occasionally these episodes were accompanied by a "sour taste" in the mouth. She noticed these strange occurrences, but did not think of them as having any neurological significance. It was only when she had a grand mal seizure in the summer of 2003 that she went to a neurologist and was given brain scans, which revealed a large tumor in her right temporal lobe—the cause of her peculiar episodes. The tumor, her doctors felt, was malignant (though it was probably an oligodendroglioma, of relatively low malignancy) and needed to be removed. Salimah wondered if she had been given a death sentence and was fearful of the operation and its possible consequences; she and her husband had been told that it might cause some "personality changes." But in any event, the surgery went well, most of the tumor was removed, and after a period of convalescence, Salimah was able to return to her work as a chemist.

Before the surgery, she had been a fairly reserved woman who would occasionally be annoyed or preoccupied by small things like dust or untidiness; her husband said she was sometimes "obsessive" about jobs that needed to be done around the house. But now, after the surgery, Salimah seemed unperturbed by such domestic matters. She had become, in the idiosyncratic words of her husband (English was not their first language), "a happy cat." She was, he declared, "a joyologist."

Salimah's new cheerfulness was apparent at work. She had worked in the same laboratory for fifteen years and had always been admired for her intelligence and dedication. But now, while losing none of this professional competence, she seemed a much warmer person, keenly sympathetic and interested in the lives and feelings of her co-workers. Where before, in a colleague's words, she had been "much more into herself," she now became the confidante and social center of the entire lab.

At home, too, she shed some of her Marie Curie–like, work-oriented personality. She permitted herself time off from her thinking, her equations, and became more interested in going to movies or parties, living it up a bit. And a new love, a new passion, entered her life. She had been "vaguely musical," in her own words, as a girl, had played the piano a little, but music had never played any great part in her life. Now it was different. She longed to hear music, to go to concerts, to listen to classical music on the radio or on CDs. She could be moved to rapture or tears by music which had carried "no special feeling" for her before. She became "addicted" to her car radio, which she would listen to while driving to work. A colleague who happened to pass her on the road to the lab said that the music on her radio was "incredibly loud"—he could hear it a quarter of a mile away. Salimah, in her convertible, was "entertaining the whole freeway."

Like Tony Cicoria, Salimah showed a drastic transformation from being only vaguely interested in music to being passionately excited by music and in continual need of it. And with both of them, there were other, more general changes, too—a surge of emotionality, as if emotions of every sort were being stimulated or released. In Salimah's words, "What happened after the surgery—I felt reborn. That changed my outlook on life and made me appreciate every minute of it."

COULD SOMEONE DEVELOP a "pure" musicophilia, without any accompanying changes in personality or behavior? In 2006 just such a situation was described by Rohrer, Smith, and Warren, in their striking case history of a woman in her mid-sixties who had intractable temporal lobe seizures with a right temporal lobe focus. After seven years, her seizures were finally brought under control by the anticonvulsant drug lamotrigine (LTG). Prior to starting on this medication, Rohrer and his colleagues wrote,

> she had always been indifferent to music, never listening to music for pleasure or attending concerts. This was in contrast to her husband and daughter, who played the piano and violin. . . . She was unmoved by the traditional Thai music she had heard at family and public events in Bangkok and by classical and popular genres of Western music after she moved to the United Kingdom. Indeed, she continued to avoid music where possible, and actively disliked certain musical timbres (for example, she would shut the door to

avoid hearing her husband playing piano music, and found choral singing "irritating").

This indifference to music changed abruptly when the patient was put on lamotrigine:

> Within several weeks of starting LTG, a profound change was noted in her appreciation of music. She sought out musical programmes on the radio and television, listened to classical music stations on the radio for many hours each day, and demanded to attend concerts. Her husband described how she had sat "transfixed" throughout *La Traviata* and became annoyed when other audience members talked during the performance. She now described listening to classical music as an extremely pleasant and emotion-charged experience. She did not sing or whistle, and no other changes were found in her behavior or personality. No evidence of thought disorder, hallucinations, or disturbed mood was seen.

While Rohrer et al. could not pinpoint the precise basis of their patient's musicophilia, they hazarded the suggestion that, during her years of incorrigible seizure activity, she might have developed an intensified functional connection between perceptual systems in the temporal lobes and parts of the limbic system involved in emotional response—a connection that only became apparent when her seizures were brought under control with medication. In the 1970s, David Bear suggested that such a sensory-limbic hyperconnection might be the basis for the emergence of the unexpected artistic, sexual, mystical, or religious feelings that sometimes occur in people with temporal lobe epilepsy. Could something similar have occurred with Tony Cicoria, too?

. . .

L AST SPRING, Cicoria took part in a ten-day music retreat for student musicians, gifted amateurs, and professionals. The camp doubles as a showroom for Erica vanderLinde Feidner, a concert pianist who also specializes in finding the perfect piano for each of her clients. Tony had just bought one of her pianos, a Bösendorfer grand, a unique prototype made in Vienna—she thought he had a remarkable instinct for picking out a piano with exactly the tone he wanted. It was, Cicoria felt, a good time, a good place, to make his debut as a musician.

He prepared two pieces for his concert: his first love, Chopin's B-flat Minor Scherzo; and his own first composition, which he called Rhapsody, Opus 1. His playing, and his story, electrified everyone at the retreat (many expressed the fantasy that they, too, might be struck by lightning). He played, said Erica, with "great passion, great brio"—and if not with supernatural genius, at least with creditable skill, an astounding feat for someone with virtually no musical background who had taught himself to play at forty-two.

W HAT DID I THINK, in the end, of his story, Dr. Cicoria asked me. Had I ever encountered anything similar? I asked him what he thought, and how he would interpret what had happened to him. He replied that as a medical man he was at a loss to explain these events, and he had to think of them in "spiritual" terms. I countered that, with no disrespect to the spiritual, I felt that even the most exalted states of mind, the most astounding transformations, must have some physical basis or at least some physiological correlate in neural activity.

At the time of his lightning strike, Dr. Cicoria had both a

near-death experience and an out-of-body experience. Many supernatural or mystical explanations have arisen to explain out-of-body experiences, but they have also been a topic of neurological investigation for a century or more. Such experiences seem to be relatively stereotyped in format: one seems to be no longer in one's own body but outside it, and, most commonly, looking down on oneself from eight or nine feet above (neurologists refer to this as "autoscopy"). One seems to see clearly the room and people and objects nearby, but from an aerial perspective. People who have had such experiences often describe vestibular sensations like "floating" or "flying." Out-of-body experiences can inspire fear or joy or a feeling of detachment, but they are usually described as intensely "real"—not at all like a dream or hallucination. They have been reported in many sorts of near-death experiences, as well as in temporal lobe seizures. There is some evidence that both the visuospatial and vestibular aspects of out-of-body experiences are related to disturbed function in the cerebral cortex, especially at the junctional region between the temporal and parietal lobes.[1]

But it was not just an out-of-body experience that Dr. Cicoria reported. He saw a bluish-white light, he saw his children, his life flashed past him, he had a sense of ecstasy, and, above all, he had a sense of something transcendental and enormously significant. What could be the neural basis of this? Similar near-death experiences have often been described by people who have been, or believed themselves to be, in great danger, whether they are involved in sudden accidents, struck by lightning, or, most commonly, revived after a cardiac arrest. All of these are

---

1. Orrin Devinsky et al. have described "autoscopic phenomena with seizures" in ten of their own patients and reviewed similar cases in the medical literature, while Olaf Blanke and his colleagues in Switzerland have been able to monitor the brain activity of epileptic patients actually undergoing out-of-body experiences.

situations not only fraught with terror but likely to cause a sudden drop in blood pressure and cerebral blood flow (and, if there is cardiac arrest, a deprivation of oxygen to the brain). There is likely to be intense emotional arousal and a surge of noradrenaline and other neurotransmitters in such states, whether the affect is one of terror or rapture. We have, as yet, little idea of the actual neural correlates of such experiences, but the alterations of consciousness and emotion that occur are very profound and must involve the emotional parts of the brain—the amygdala and brain-stem nuclei—as well as the cortex.[2]

While out-of-body experiences have the character of a perceptual illusion (albeit a complex and singular one), near-death experiences have all the hallmarks of mystical experience, as William James defines them—passivity, ineffability, transience, and a noetic quality. One is totally consumed by a near-death experience, swept up, almost literally, in a blaze (sometimes a tunnel or funnel) of light, and drawn towards a Beyond—beyond life, beyond space and time. There is a sense of a last look, a (greatly accelerated) farewell to things earthly, the places and people and events of one's life, and a sense of ecstasy or joy as one soars towards one's destination—an archetypal symbolism of death and transfiguration. Experiences like this are not easily dismissed by those who have been through them, and they may sometimes lead to a conversion or metanoia, a change of mind, that alters the direction and orientation of a life. One cannot suppose, any more than one can with out-of-body experiences, that such events are pure fancy; very similar features are emphasized in every account. Near-death experiences must also have a

---

2. Kevin Nelson and his colleagues at the University of Kentucky have published several neurological papers stressing the similarities between the dissociation, euphoria, and mystical feelings of near-death experiences and those of dreaming, REM sleep, and the hallucinatory states in the borderlands of sleep.

neurological basis of their own, one which profoundly alters consciousness itself.

What about Dr. Cicoria's remarkable access of musicality, his sudden musicophilia? Patients with degeneration of the front parts of the brain, so-called frontotemporal dementia, sometimes develop a startling emergence or release of musical talents and passions as they lose the powers of abstraction and language—but clearly this was not the case with Dr. Cicoria, who was articulate and highly competent in every way. In 1984, Daniel Jacome described a patient who had had a stroke damaging the left hemisphere of his brain and consequently developed "hypermusia" and "musicophilia," along with aphasia and other problems. But there was nothing to suggest that Tony Cicoria had experienced any significant brain damage, other than a very transient disturbance to his memory systems for a week or two after the lightning strike.

His situation did remind me a bit of Franco Magnani, the "memory artist" of whom I have written.[3] Franco had never thought of being a painter until he experienced a strange crisis or illness—perhaps a form of temporal lobe epilepsy—when he was thirty-one. He had nightly dreams of Pontito, the little Tuscan village where he was born; after he woke, these images remained intensely vivid, with a full depth and reality ("like holograms"). Franco was consumed by a need to make these images real, to paint them, and so he taught himself to paint, devoting every free minute to producing hundreds of views of Pontito.

Could Tony Cicoria's musical dreams, his musical inspirations, have been epileptic in nature? Such a question cannot be

---

3. Franco's story is related in "The Landscape of His Dreams," a chapter in *An Anthropologist on Mars*.

answered with a simple EEG such as Cicoria had following his accident, but would require special EEG monitoring over the course of many days.

And why was there such a delay in the development of his musicophilia? What was happening in the six or seven weeks that elapsed between his cardiac arrest and the rather sudden eruption of musicality? We know that there were temporary aftereffects—the confusional state that ensued for a few hours, and the disturbance of memory that lasted a couple of weeks. These could have been due to cerebral anoxia alone—for his brain must have been without adequate oxygen for a minute or more. One has to suspect, however, that Dr. Cicoria's apparent recovery a couple of weeks after these events was not as complete as it seemed, that there were other, unnoticed forms of brain damage, and that his brain was still reacting to the original insult and reorganizing itself during this time.

Dr. Cicoria feels that he is "a different person" now—musically, emotionally, psychologically, and spiritually. This was my impression, too, as I listened to his story and saw something of the new passions which had transformed him. Looking at him from a neurological vantage point, I felt that his brain must be very different now from what it was before his lightning strike or in the days immediately following this, when neurological tests showed nothing grossly amiss. Could we now, a dozen years later, define these changes, define the neurological basis of his musicophilia? Many new and far subtler tests of brain function have been developed since Cicoria had his injury in 1994, and he agreed that it would be interesting to investigate this further. But after a moment, he reconsidered, and said that perhaps it was best to let things be. His was a lucky strike, and the music, however it had come, was a blessing, a grace—not to be questioned.

Postscript

Since first publishing Tony Cicoria's story, I have received many letters from people who were *not* struck by lightning and seemed to have no special physical or psychological conditions, but, often to their great surprise—in their forties or fifties or even eighties—have found themselves with sudden or unexpected creative gifts or passions, either musical or artistic.

One correspondent, Grace M., described the rather sudden onset of her own musicality at the age of fifty-five. Shortly after returning from a vacation in Israel and Jordan, she started to hear song fragments in her head. She tried to record them "by drawing lines on paper"—she did not know formal musical notation. When this did not work, she bought a tape recorder and sang into it. Now, three years later, she has recorded more than thirty-three hundred fragments, and, arising from these, about four complete songs a month. Grace noted that while she has had popular tunes running through her head for as long as she can remember, it was only after her trip that she began hearing her own songs almost exclusively.

"I have never had any great ability in music," she wrote, "and do not have a great ear for it." Indeed, she wondered why someone like herself, apparently not too musical, should suddenly be filled with songs and song fragments. Somewhat diffidently, she has shown her songs to others, including professional musicians, and received favorable comments. "I never asked for, or expected, anything like this," she said. "I never in my life dreamed of being a song writer. . . . I had so little musical talent. I might as well have dreamed of being a supermodel."

She could not think of any physical reason for her sudden urge to write songs. "Unlike Dr. Cicoria," she wrote, "I have not been struck by lightning. I have not had any head injuries or been in any major accidents. I have never been ill enough to require hospitalization. I do not think I have temporal lobe seizures or frontotemporal dementia." She wondered, though, whether there might have been a psychological impetus, an "unlocking" of some sort, during her journey to Israel and Jordan. This was important to her as a religious person, but there were no special epiphanies or visions during her trip. (She does not believe she has a mission to share or spread her music; if anything, she is rather reticent about it. "I am not a performer or self-promoter by nature, and find this all a bit embarrassing," she wrote.)

Another correspondent, Eliza Bussey, also in her mid-fifties, wrote:

> Four years ago, at fifty, I walked by a music store, saw a folk harp sitting in the window, and came out two hours later with a two-thousand-dollar folk harp. That moment changed my life. My total world is now arranged around music and writing about music. Four years ago I could not read a note of music, and now I am studying classical harp at the Peabody Conservatory in Baltimore. I worked three twelve-hour overnights in the newsroom, trading in medical reporting for Iraq coverage, just so I could go to school on Thursdays and Fridays. I practice two or three hours a day (would do more if I could), and I can't describe the joy and wonder I have at finding this later in life. I have felt, for example, my brain and fingers trying to connect, to form new synapses, when [my teacher] gave me Handel's Passacale to play.

"I have been interested in getting an MRI," she added. "I know that my brain has dramatically changed."

2

A Strangely Familiar Feeling:
Musical Seizures

Jon S., a robust man of forty-five, had been in perfect health until January of 2006. His working week had just started; he was in the office on a Monday morning, and went to get something from the closet. Once he entered the closet, he suddenly heard music—"classical, melodic, quite nice, soothing . . . vaguely familiar. . . . It was a string instrument, a solo violin."

He immediately thought, "Where the hell is that music coming from?" There was an old, discarded electronic device in the closet, but this, though it had knobs, had no speakers. Confusedly, in a state of what he later called "suspended animation," he groped for the controls of the device to turn the music off. "Then," he says, "I went out." A colleague in the office who saw all this described Mr. S. as "slumped over, unresponsive," in the closet, though not convulsing.

Mr. S.'s next memory was of an emergency medical technician leaning over him, questioning him. He could not remember the date, but he remembered his name. He was taken to the emergency room of a local hospital, where he had another episode. "I was lying down, the doctor was checking me over, my wife was there . . . then I started to hear music again, and I said, 'It's happening again,' and then, very quickly, I was out of it."

He woke up in another room, where he realized he had bitten his tongue and cheeks and had intense pain in his legs. "They told me I had had a seizure—the full thing, with convulsions. . . . It all occurred much quicker than the first time."

Mr. S. had some tests and was put on an antiepileptic drug to protect him against further seizures. Since then, he has had more tests (none of which showed anything amiss—a situation not uncommon with temporal lobe epilepsy). Though no demonstrable lesion showed up on brain imaging, he mentioned that he had suffered a fairly severe head injury at the age of fifteen—a concussion, at least—and this may have produced slight scarring in the temporal lobes.

When I asked him to describe the music he heard just before his seizures, he tried to sing it but could not—he said he could not sing any music, even if he knew it well. He said he was not too musical, in any case, and that the sort of classical violin music he had "heard" before his seizure was not at all to his taste; it sounded "whiny, catlike." Usually he listens to pop music. Yet it seemed *familiar* somehow—perhaps he had heard it long ago, as a child?

I told him that if he ever did hear this music—on the radio, perhaps—he should note what it was and let me know. Mr. S. said that he would keep his ears open, but as we talked about it, he could not help wondering whether there was just a *feeling*, perhaps an illusion, of familiarity attached to the music, rather than an actual recollection of something he had once heard.

There was something evocative about it, but elusive, like the music heard in dreams. And there we left it. I wonder whether I will get a call from Mr. S. one day, saying, "I just heard it on the radio! It was a Bach suite for unaccompanied violin," or whether what he heard was a dreamlike construction or conflation which, for all its "familiarity," he will never identify.

HUGHLINGS JACKSON, writing in the 1870s, remarked upon the feeling of familiarity that is so often a feature of the aura which may precede a temporal lobe seizure. He spoke, too, of "dreamy states," "déjà vu," and "reminiscence." Such feelings of reminiscence, Jackson noted, may have no identifiable content whatever. Although some people lose consciousness during a seizure, others may remain perfectly aware of their surroundings yet also enter an odd, superimposed state in which they experience strange moods or feelings or visions or smells— or music. Hughlings Jackson referred to this situation as a "doubling of consciousness."

Eric Markowitz, a young musician and teacher, developed in his left temporal lobe an astrocytoma, a tumor of relatively low malignancy, which was operated on in 1993. It recurred ten years later, but was then considered inoperable due to its proximity to the speech areas of the temporal lobe. With the regrowth of his tumor, he has had repeated seizures, in which he does not lose consciousness but, as he wrote to me, "music explodes in my head for about two minutes. I love music; I've made my career around it, so it seems a bit ironic that music has also become my tormentor." Eric's seizures are not triggered by music, he emphasized, but music is invariably a part of them. As with Jon S., Eric's hallucinatory music seems very real to him, and hauntingly familiar:

> While I am unable to state exactly what song or songs I may be hearing during these aural seizures, I know they seem quite familiar to me—so familiar, in fact, that I am sometimes uncertain whether or not these songs are on a nearby stereo or in my brain. Once I become aware of that strange yet familiar confusion and realize it is in fact a seizure, I seem to try *not* to figure out what the music may be—indeed, if I could study it closely like a poem or piece of music, I would . . . but perhaps subconsciously I am afraid that if I pay too much attention to it, I may not be able to escape the song—like quicksand, or hypnosis.

Though Eric (unlike Jon S.) is quite musical, with an excellent musical memory and a highly trained ear, and though he has had more than a dozen such seizures, he is (like Mr. S.) completely unable to *recognize* his aural music.[1]

In the "strange yet familiar confusion" which is an integral part of his seizure experience, Eric finds it difficult to think

---

1. While epileptic music for some people seems intensely "familiar," but unidentifiable, it may be instantly recognizable for others. This was sometimes the case with the patients Wilder Penfield and his colleagues studied at the Montreal Neurological Institute over many years. Penfield gave detailed examples of at least ten of his patients who had temporal lobe seizures of a predominantly musical sort. The music they "heard" during their seizures was familiar—songs they had heard repeatedly on the radio or perhaps as Christmas carols or hymns or theme songs. In each of these cases, Penfield was able to find particular cortical points in a temporal lobe that, when electrically stimulated, caused the patients to hear their specific tunes, and when he was able to ablate these points, their seizures—and the hallucinatory tunes—ceased.

A retired pediatrician wrote to me about a nine-year-old boy referred to him for complex partial seizures—a familial condition, in this case. During his seizures, the boy heard music, and, remarkably, it was his mother "who first made the diagnosis, when she saw her son behaving strangely and whistling to himself the children's song, 'Pop Goes the Weasel'—this being the invariable auditory aura prior to her own seizures."

straight. His wife or friends, if they are present, may notice a "strange look" on his face. If he has a seizure while at work, he is usually able to "wing it" somehow, without his students realizing that anything is amiss.

There is a fundamental difference, Eric brings out, between his normal musical imagery and that of his seizures: "As a songwriter, I'm familiar with how melody and words seem to arrive out of nowhere . . . this is *intentional*, though—I sit with my guitar in the attic and work on completion of the song. My seizures, though, are beyond all this."

He went on to say that his epileptic music—seemingly contextless and meaningless, though hauntingly familiar—seemed to exert a frightening and almost dangerous spell on him, so that he was drawn deeper and deeper into it. And yet, he has also been so creatively stimulated by these musical auras that he has composed music inspired by them, trying to embody, or at least suggest, their mysterious and ineffable strange-but-familiar quality.

3

Fear of Music:
Musicogenic Epilepsy

In 1937 Macdonald Critchley, a superb observer of unusual neurological syndromes, described eleven patients he had seen with epileptic seizures *induced* by music, as well as extending his survey to cases reported by others. He entitled his pioneer article "Musicogenic Epilepsy" (though he indicated that he preferred the shorter and sweeter term "musicolepsia").

Some of Critchley's patients were musical, some were not. The type of music that could provoke their seizures varied a good deal from patient to patient. One specified classical music, another "old-time" or "reminiscent" melodies, while a third patient found that "a well-punctuated rhythm was for her the most dangerous feature in music." One of my own correspondents had seizures only in response to "modern, dissonant music," never in response to classical or romantic music (her husband, unfortunately, was partial to modern, dissonant music). Critchley observed how some patients responded only to particular instruments or noises. One such patient reacted only to "deep notes from a brass wind instrument"; this man was a radio operator on a large ocean liner but, continually convulsed by the sounds of its orchestra, had to transfer to a smaller ship with no orchestra. (One of my own patients with musicogenic seizures tells me that certain tones or notes can set him off. Their pitch is important: for example, a provocative G-sharp in one register may not be provocative in a higher or lower register. He is also very sensitive to timbre—a plucked guitar string is more apt to trigger a seizure than a strummed one.) Some of Critchley's patients responded only to particular melodies or songs.

The most striking case of all was that of an eminent nineteenth-century music critic, Nikonov, who had his first seizure at a performance of Meyerbeer's opera *The Prophet*. Thereafter, he became more and more sensitive to music, until finally almost any music, however soft, would send him into convulsions. ("The most noxious of all," remarked Critchley, "was the so-called 'musical' background of Wagner, which afforded an unrelieved and inescapable sound-procession.") Finally Nikonov, though so knowledgeable and passionate about music, had to relinquish his profession and avoid all contact with music. If he heard a brass band in the street, he would stop his ears and rush for the nearest doorway or side street. He developed a veritable phobia, a horror of music, and this he described in a pamphlet he titled *Fear of Music*.[1]

---

1. Musicogenic seizures do not have to be as devastating as they were for Nikonov; they may sometimes be pleasant and even stimulating. One young researcher described this to me in a letter:

> When listening to particular types of music I sometimes begin to feel an aura, which for me can be distinguished by either an intense wave of fear, disgust or pleasure, and then I will have a seizure. I particularly have this experience when listening to the music of Central Asia, but it has happened with several other types of music as well. I have to say that I enjoy the seizures with the pleasant auras, and I almost miss them while I am on medication, though the fearful ones I can certainly do without. I am a musician as well, and I believe it has been these pleasant auras that stimulated my interest in studying music.

Critchley had also published papers, a few years earlier, on seizures induced by nonmusical sounds—usually sounds of a monotonous type, such as a kettle on the boil, an airplane in flight, or machinery in a workshop. In some cases of musicogenic epilepsy, he thought, the particular quality of sound was all-important (as with the radio operator who could not tolerate the deep brass); but in others, the emotional impact of the music, and perhaps its associations, seemed more important.[2]

The types of seizure that might be provoked by music were quite varied, too. Some patients would have major convulsions, fall down unconscious, bite their tongues, be incontinent; others would have minor seizures, brief "absences" their friends might hardly notice. Many patients would have a complex temporal lobe type of seizure, as did one of Critchley's patients who said, "I have the feeling that I have been through it all before; as if I were going through a scene. It is the same on each occasion. People are there, dancing; I believe I am on a boat. The scene is not connected with any real place or event which I can recall."

Musicogenic epilepsy is generally considered to be very rare, but Critchley wondered if it might be notably more common than

2. The importance of purely sonic or musical attributes rather than emotional ones was discussed by David Poskanzer, Arthur Brown, and Henry Miller in their beautifully detailed description of a sixty-two-year-old man who repeatedly lost consciousness while listening to the radio, at exactly 8:59 p.m. On other occasions, he had seizures induced by the sound of church bells. It was realized, in retrospect, that the attacks caused by the radio were provoked by the sound of the Bow Church bells, which the BBC played just before the nine o'clock news. Using a variety of stimuli—recordings of different church bells, church bells played backwards organ and piano music—Poskanzer et al. were able to show that the seizures were induced only by tones that fell within a certain frequency range and had a strongly "bell-like" quality or timbre. The impact of the bell note, they observed, was lost if played backwards. The patient denied any emotional association with the Bow bells; it seemed simply that this series of tones of this particular frequency and timbre, played in this particular order, sufficed to trigger a seizure. (Poskanzer et al. also noted that their subject, once he had had a Bow bell seizure, would remain immune to such sounds for a week or so.)

supposed.[3] Many people, he thought, might start to get a queer feeling—disturbing, perhaps frightening—when they heard certain music, but then would immediately retreat from the music, turn it off, or block their ears, so that they did not progress to a full-blown seizure. He wondered, therefore, if abortive forms—*formes frustes*—of musical epilepsy might be relatively common. (This has certainly been my own impression, and I think there may also be similar *formes frustes* of photic epilepsy, when blinking lights or fluorescent lights may produce a peculiar discomfort without inducing a full-blown seizure.)

Working in an epilepsy clinic, I have seen a number of patients with seizures induced by music, and others who have musical auras associated with seizures—and occasionally both.[4] Both types of patient are prone to temporal lobe seizures, and most have temporal lobe abnormalities identifiable with EEG or brain imaging.

Among the patients I have seen recently is G.G., a young man who was in good health until June of 2005, when he had a severe attack of herpes encephalitis that started with a high fever and

---

Many people, it seems, may accept mild epileptic or other disturbances and not think to mention them to their doctors or anyone else. After reading this chapter, one correspondent, a neuroscientist, wrote to me of having "suffered seizures when the church bell rings during the consecration at Mass. . . . This doesn't bother me in the least," she added, "but now I'm wondering if I should mention it to my doctor." (She wondered, too, whether an EEG or brain scan could detect what she was experiencing.)

3. This was a topic that Critchley returned to again and again in his long career. In 1977, forty years after his pioneer paper on musicogenic epilepsy was published, he included two chapters on the subject in *Music and the Brain* (a book he edited with R. A. Henson).

4. I have also encountered patients whose seizures are alleviated or prevented by listening to music or—even more—by playing it. One such patient, with a very severe seizure disorder, wrote to me:

At 14, I had a grand mal of unknown origin. What followed was years of convulsing and depressing life. What saved me was the piano. Nothing could seize me while playing. Very recently, my psychologist asked me if I had ever had a seizure while playing. I hadn't thought about it before, but no, indeed, I never had.

generalized seizures; this was followed by a coma and then a severe amnesia. Remarkably, a year later, his amnesic problems had virtually cleared, but he remained highly seizure-prone, with occasional grand mal seizures and, much more commonly, complex partial seizures. Initially all of these were "spontaneous," but within a few weeks they started to occur almost exclusively in response to sound—"sudden, loud sounds, like ambulance sirens"—and, especially, music. Along with this G.G. developed a remarkable sensitivity to sound, becoming able to detect sounds too soft or distant for others to hear. He enjoyed this, and felt that his auditory world was "more alive, more vivid," but wondered, too, whether it played any part in his now-epileptic sensitivity to music and sound.

G.G.'s seizures may be provoked by a large range of music, from rock to classical (the first time I saw him, he played a Verdi aria on his cell phone; after about half a minute, this induced a complex partial seizure). He speaks of "romantic" music as being the most provocative, especially Frank Sinatra's songs ("He touches a chord in me"). He says that the music has to be "full of emotions, associations, nostalgia"; it is almost always music he has known from childhood or adolescence. It does not have to be loud to provoke a seizure—soft music may be equally effective—but he is in particular trouble in a noisy, music-permeated environment, so much so that he must wear earplugs most of the time.

His seizures start with or are preceded by a special state of intense, involuntary, almost forced attention or listening. In this already altered state, the music seems to grow more intense, to swell, to take possession of him, and at this point he cannot stop the process, cannot turn off the music or walk away from it. Beyond this point he retains no consciousness or memory, though various epileptic automatisms, like gasping and lip-smacking, ensue.

For G.G., music does not just provoke a seizure; it seems to constitute an essential *part* of the seizure, spreading (one imagines) from its initial perceptual locus to other temporal lobe systems, and occasionally to the motor cortex, as when he has generalized seizures. It is as if, at such times, the provocative music is itself transformed, becoming first an overwhelming psychic experience and then a seizure.

A NOTHER PATIENT, Silvia N., came to see me towards the end of 2005. Mrs. N. had developed a seizure disorder in her early thirties. Some of her seizures were of grand mal type, with convulsions and a total loss of consciousness. Others were of a more complex type in which there would be some doubling of consciousness. Sometimes her seizures seemed to be spontaneous or a reaction to stress, but most often they occurred in response to music. One day she was found unconscious on the floor, having had a convulsion. Her last memory before this was of listening to a CD of her favorite Neapolitan songs. No significance was ascribed to this at first, but when she had a similar seizure soon afterwards, also during the playing of Neapolitan songs, she started to wonder whether there could be a connection. She tested herself, cautiously, and found that listening to such songs, either live or on a recording, would now infallibly arouse a "peculiar" feeling, followed quickly by a seizure. No other music, though, had this effect.

She had loved the Neapolitan songs, which reminded her of her childhood. ("The old songs," she said, "they were always in the family; they always put them on.") She found them "very romantic, emotional . . . they had a meaning." But now that they triggered her seizures, she began to dread them. She became particularly apprehensive about weddings, coming as she did from a large Sicilian family, because such songs were always played at celebrations and family gatherings. "If the band started playing," Mrs. N. said, "I would run out. . . . I had half a minute or less to get away."

Though she sometimes had grand mal seizures in response to the songs, Mrs. N. more often experienced just a strange alteration of time and consciousness in which she would have a feeling of reminiscence—specifically, the feeling of being a teenager, or the reliving of scenes (some seemingly memories, others clearly fantasies) in which she was a teenager. She compared these to dreams and said she would "wake" from them as from a dream, but a dream in which she retained some consciousness, though little control. She was able, for instance, to hear what people around her were saying, but unable to respond—that doubling of consciousness which Hughlings Jackson called "mental diplopia." While most of her complex seizures referred to the past, she told me, on one occasion, "it was the future I saw. . . . I was up there, going to heaven. . . . My grandmother opened up the gates of heaven. 'It's not time,' she said—and then I came to."

Though Mrs. N. could avoid Neapolitan music most of the time, she also began to have seizures without music, and these grew more and more severe, finally becoming intractable. Medications were useless, and she sometimes had many seizures in a single day, so that daily life became virtually impossible. MRIs had shown both anatomical and electrical abnormalities in her left temporal lobe (probably from a head injury she had suffered as a teenager) and a virtually nonstop seizure focus associated with this, so early in 2003 she underwent brain surgery, a partial temporal lobectomy, to treat it.

The surgery eliminated not only the majority of her spontaneous seizures, but her highly specific vulnerability to Neapolitan songs as well, as she discovered almost by chance. "After the surgery, I was still afraid to listen to the type of song I had seizures with," she said, "but one day I was at a party, and they started to play the songs. I ran out into another room and closed the door. Then someone opened the door . . . I heard it like far away. It didn't bother me that much, so I tried to listen to it." Wondering if she was finally cured of her vulnerability to music, Mrs. N. went home ("it's safer there, you're not in front of five hundred people") and put some Neapolitan songs on her stereo. "I turned it up little by little, until it was really loud, and it didn't affect me."

So now Mrs. N. has lost her fear of music and can play her favorite Neapolitan songs without problem. She has also ceased to have her strange, complex, reminiscent seizures; it seems as though her surgery has put an end to both types of seizures—as Macdonald Critchley might have predicted.

Mrs. N. is delighted, of course, by her cure. But she is occasionally nostalgic, too, for some of her epileptic experiences— like the "gates of heaven," which seemed to take her to a place unlike anything she had ever experienced before.

4

Music on the Brain:
Imagery and Imagination

Heard melodies are sweet, but those unheard are sweeter.

—JOHN KEATS, *"Ode on a Grecian Urn"*

Music forms a significant and, on the whole, pleasant part of life for most of us—not only external music, music we hear with our ears, but internal music, music that plays in our heads. When Galton wrote on "mental imagery" in the 1880s, he concerned himself only with visual imagery and not at all with musical imagery. But a tally of one's friends will suffice to show that musical imagery has a range no less varied than the visual. There are some people who can scarcely hold a tune in their heads and others who can hear entire symphonies in their minds with a detail and vividness little short of actual perception.

I became aware of this huge variation early in life, for my parents stood at opposite ends of the spectrum. My mother had difficulty voluntarily calling any tune to mind, but my father seemed to have an entire orchestra in his head, ready to do his bidding. He always had two or three miniature orchestral scores stuffed in his pockets, and between seeing patients he might pull out a score and have a little internal concert. He did not need to put a record on the gramophone, for he could play a score almost as vividly in his mind, perhaps with different moods or interpretations, and sometimes improvisations of his own. His favorite bedtime reading was a dictionary of musical themes; he would turn over a few pages, almost at random, savoring this and that— and then, stimulated by the opening line of something, settle down to a favorite symphony or concerto, his own *kleine Nachtmusik,* as he called it.

Professional musicians, in general, possess what most of us would regard as remarkable powers of musical imagery. Many composers, indeed, do not compose initially or entirely at an instrument but in their minds. There is no more extraordinary example of this than Beethoven, who continued to compose (and whose compositions rose to greater and greater heights) years after he had become totally deaf. It is possible that his musical imagery was even intensified by deafness, for with the removal of normal auditory input, the auditory cortex may become hypersensitive, with heightened powers of musical imagery (and sometimes even auditory hallucinations). There is an analogous phenomenon in those who lose their sight; some people who become blind may have, paradoxically, heightened visual imagery. (Composers, especially composers of enormously intricate, architectonic music like Beethoven's, must also employ highly abstract forms of musical thought—and it might be said that it is especially such intellectual complexity that distinguishes Beethoven's later works.)

My own powers of musical imagery, and of musical perception, are much more limited. I cannot hear an entire orchestra in my head, at least under normal circumstances. What I do have, to some degree, is a pianist's imagery. With music I know well, such as Chopin's mazurkas, which I learned by heart sixty years ago and have continued to love ever since, I have only to glance at a score or think of a particular mazurka (an opus number will set me off) and the mazurka will start to play in my mind. I not only "hear" the music, but I "see" my hands on the keyboard before me, and "feel" them playing the piece—a virtual performance which, once started, seems to unfold or proceed by itself. Indeed, when I was learning the mazurkas, I found that I could practice them in my mind, and I often "heard" particular phrases or themes from the mazurkas playing by themselves. Even if it is involuntary and unconscious, going over passages mentally in this way is a crucial tool for all performers, and the imagination of playing can be almost as efficacious as the physical actuality. As one concert violinist, Cindy Foster, wrote to me:

> For many years I have, in the day of performance, had the program appear in my mind's ear unbidden and without effort. It has proved to be like a pre-dress rehearsal, and almost as useful as actually playing the pieces. It always feels like my mind has taken over the job of preparation without any effort or conscious directive from me.

Since the mid-1990s, studies carried out by Robert Zatorre and his colleagues, using increasingly sophisticated brain-imaging techniques, have shown that imagining music can indeed activate the auditory cortex almost as strongly as listening to it. Imagining music also stimulates the motor cortex, and conversely, imagining the action of playing music stimulates the auditory cortex. This, Zatorre and Halpern noted in a 2005 paper, "corresponds to reports from musicians that they can 'hear' their instrument during mental practice."

As Alvaro Pascual-Leone has observed, studies of regional cerebral blood flow

> [suggest that] mental simulation of movements activates some of the same central neural structures required for the performance of the actual movements. In so doing, mental practice alone seems to be sufficient to promote the modulation of neural circuits involved in the early stages of motor skill learning. This modulation not only results in marked improvement in performance, but also seems to place the subjects at an advantage for further skill learning with minimal physical practice. The combination of mental and physical practice [he adds] leads to greater performance improvement than does physical practice alone, a phenomenon for which our findings provide a physiological explanation.

Expectation and suggestion can greatly enhance musical imagery, even producing a quasi-perceptual experience. Jerome Bruner, a very musical friend, described to me how once, having put a favorite Mozart record on his turntable, he listened to it with great pleasure, and then went to turn it over to play the other side—only to find that he had never played it in the first place. Perhaps this is an extreme example of something we all experience occasionally with familiar music: thinking we hear music faintly when the radio has been turned off or a piece has come to an end, we wonder whether the music is still playing softly or we are simply imagining it.

Some inconclusive experiments were performed in the 1960s on what the researchers called "the 'White Christmas' effect."

When the then universally known Bing Crosby version of the song was played, some subjects "heard" it when the volume was turned down to near zero, or even when the experimenters announced they would play the song but never turned it on. Physiological confirmation of such "filling in" by involuntary musical imagery has recently been obtained by William Kelley and his colleagues at Dartmouth, who used functional MRI to scan the auditory cortex while their subjects listened to familiar and unfamiliar songs in which short segments had been replaced by gaps of silence. The silent gaps embedded in familiar songs were not consciously noticed by their subjects, but the researchers observed that these gaps "induced greater activation in the auditory association areas than did silent gaps embedded in unknown songs; this was true for gaps in songs with lyrics and without lyrics."[1]

Deliberate, conscious, voluntary mental imagery involves not only auditory and motor cortex, but regions of the frontal cortex involved in choosing and planning. Such deliberate mental imagery is clearly crucial to professional musicians.[2] The rest of us frequently call upon our musical imagery, too. Nevertheless, it seems to me that most of our musical imagery is not voluntarily commanded or summoned but comes to us apparently spontaneously. Sometimes it just pops into the mind; at other times it may play there quietly for a while without our even noticing it. And though voluntary musical imagery may not be

---

1. See David J. M. Kraemer et al., 2005.

2. Indeed, for any professional musician, voluntary imagery may dominate much of conscious and even subconscious life. Basically, any artist is always at work, even when he appears not to be. This is well brought out by Ned Rorem, in *Facing the Night:* "I'm never not working. Even as I sit here chatting of Kafka or cranberries, sodomy or softball, my mind is simultaneously glued to the piece I'm currently creating; the physical act of inserting the notes on a staff is merely a necessary afterthought."

But composers, like the rest of us, may have irrelevant imagery, too. The composer Joseph Horovitz tells me that he has a "twenty-four-hour classical Muzak" in his head; he enjoys this, but has to inhibit it when he comes to write his own highly original music.

easily available to the relatively unmusical, virtually everyone has involuntary musical imagery. "Every memory of my childhood has a soundtrack to it," one correspondent wrote to me; and she speaks for many of us here.

One sort of involuntary musical imagery is related to intense and repeated exposure to a particular piece or sort of music. I tend to fall in love with a certain composer or artist and to play their music over and over, almost exclusively, for weeks or months, until it is replaced with something else. In the past six months, I have had three such fixations, one after another. The first was on Janáček's opera *Jenufa*, after I had gone to hear a beautiful performance of this directed by Jonathan Miller; themes from *Jenufa* kept going through my mind, even entering my dreams, for two months, reinforced by my getting CDs of the opera and playing them constantly. Then I switched to a profoundly different experience after meeting Woody Geist, a patient who sang for me some of the music he performed with his a cappella jazz group, the Grunyons. This intrigued me, though I had never before been interested in this type of music; once again, I played his CD constantly, and *Jenufa* vanished from my mental concert hall, replaced by the Grunyons singing "Shooby Doin'." Most recently, I have turned to constant playing of recordings by Leon Fleisher, and his renditions of Beethoven, Chopin, Bach, Mozart, and Brahms have swept the Grunyons out of my head. If I ask what *Jenufa*, "Shooby Doin'," and Bach's Chromatic Fantasy and Fugue have in common, I would have to say nothing musically and probably nothing emotionally (beyond the pleasure they have all given me at different times). What they do share is the fact that I have bombarded my ears and brain with them, and the musical "circuits" or networks in my brain have been supersaturated, overcharged, with them. In such a supersaturated state, the brain seems ready to replay the music with no apparent external stimulus. Such replayings, curiously, seem to be almost as satisfying as listening to the actual music, and these involuntary concerts are rarely intrusive or uncontrollable (although they have the potential to be so).

In a sense, this type of musical imagery, triggered by overexposure, is the least personal, the least significant form of "music on the mind." We are on much richer, much more mysterious terrain when we consider tunes or musical fragments we have perhaps not heard or thought of in decades, that suddenly play in the mind for no apparent reason. No recent exposure, no repetition can explain such tunes, and it is almost impossible to avoid asking oneself, "Why this tune at this particular moment? What put it into my mind?" Sometimes the reason or association is obvious, or seems so.

As I write, in New York in mid-December, the city is full of Christmas trees and menorahs. I would be inclined to say, as an old Jewish atheist, that these things mean nothing to me, but Hanukkah songs are evoked in my mind whenever an image of a menorah impinges on my retina, even when I am not consciously aware of it. There must be more emotion, more meaning here than I allow, even if it is of a mostly sentimental and nostalgic kind.

But this December is also marked by a darker melody, or train of melodies, which forms an almost constant background to my thoughts. Even when I am hardly conscious of this, it produces a feeling of pain and grief. My brother is gravely ill, and this music, plucked out from ten thousand tunes by my unconscious, is Bach's *Capriccio on the Departure of a Most Beloved Brother*.

As I was dressing this morning after a swim, I was reminded, now I was on land again, of my painful, arthritic old knees—and I thought too about my friend Nick, who would be visiting that day. With this there suddenly popped into my head an old nurs-ery rhyme that was popular in my childhood but that I had prob-ably not heard (or thought about) for two-thirds of a century: "This Old Man," and, in particular, its refrain: "Knick-knack, paddy whack, give a dog a bone; / This old man came rolling home." Now I myself was an old man with painful knees who wanted to be rolled home—and Nick (punned as knick-knack) had entered into it, too.

Many of our musical associations are verbal, sometimes to the point of absurdity. Eating some smoked whitefish (which I adore) earlier in this Christmas season, I heard in my mind "O Come Let Us Adore Him." Now the hymn has become associated with whitefish for me.

Often such verbal associations are subconscious and only become explicit after the fact. One correspondent wrote to me about her husband, who, though well able to remember tunes, was unable to recall the words which went with them— nevertheless, like many people, he might make unconscious verbal associations to the lyrics. "For example," she related, "we could have been saying something like, 'Gee, it's getting dark really early these days,' and, a half-minute later, he would start whistling 'The Old Lamplighter'—a fairly obscure song which he has heard just a few times in his life. . . . Obviously, the lyrics are stored in his brain and linked to the music, but are somehow only retrievable through the music without the words!"

I recently spent several hours with a composer, grilling him about his musical imagery. He finally excused himself and went to the loo. On emerging, he told me that he had heard a song in his head—a song that had been popular forty years earlier but that, at first, he could not identify. He then recalled that the first line of the song was "Only five minutes more . . ." I accepted this as a hint from his unconscious, and made sure to keep him only five minutes more.

Sometimes there are deeper associations which I cannot fathom by myself—the deepest of these I seem to keep, as if by a sort of agreement with my unconscious, for sessions with my analyst, who is encyclopedically musical, and often able to identify the fragmentary and off-key sounds that are sometimes as much as I can reproduce.

In his book *The Haunting Melody: Psychoanalytic Experiences in Life and Music,* Theodor Reik wrote about the musical fragments or tunes that occur during the course of an analytical session:

> Melodies which run through your mind . . . may give the analyst a clue to the secret life of emotions that every one of us lives. . . . In this inward singing, the voice of an unknown self conveys not only passing moods and impulses, but sometimes a disavowed or denied wish, a longing and a drive we do not like to admit to ourselves. . . . Whatever secret message it carries, the incidental music accompanying our conscious thinking is never accidental.

And, of course, the greatest literary analysis of a musical association is that given by Proust, in his deciphering of "the little phrase" of Vinteuil's that runs through the entire structure of *Remembrance of Things Past.*

But why this incessant search for meaning or interpretation? It is not clear that any art cries out for this and, of all the arts, music surely the least—for while it is the most closely tied to the emotions, music is wholly abstract; it has no formal power of representation whatever. We may go to a play to learn about jealousy, betrayal, vengeance, love—but music, instrumental music, can tell us nothing about these. Music can have wonderful, formal, quasi-mathematical perfection, and it can have heartbreaking tenderness, poignancy, and beauty (Bach, of course, was a master at combining these). But it does not *have* to have any "meaning" whatever. One may recall music, give it the life of imagination (or even hallucination) simply because one likes it— this is reason enough. Or perhaps there may be no reason at all, as Rodolfo Llinás points out.

Llinás, a neuroscientist at New York University, is especially interested in the interactions of the cortex and the thalamus— which he postulates to underlie consciousness or "self"—and their interaction with the motor nuclei beneath the cortex, especially the basal ganglia, which he sees as crucial to the production of "action-patterns" (for walking, shaving, playing the violin, and so on). He calls the neural embodiments of these action-patterns "motor tapes." Llinás conceives of all mental activities—perceiving, remembering, and imagining no less than doing—as "motor." In his book *I of the Vortex*, he writes repeatedly of music, mostly of musical performance, but sometimes of that odd form of musical imagery when a song or tune suddenly pops into the mind:

> The neural processes underlying that which we call creativity have nothing to do with rationality. That is to say, if we look at how the brain generates creativity, we will see that it is not a rational process at all; creativity is not born out of reasoning.
>
> Let us think again of our motor tapes in the basal ganglia. I should like to suggest to you that these nuclei *do not* always wait for a tape to be called up for use by the thalamo-cortical system, the self. . . . In fact, the activity in the basal ganglia is running all the time, playing motor patterns

and snippets of motor patterns amongst and between themselves—and because of the odd, re-entrant inhibitory connectivity amongst and between these nuclei, they seem to act as a continuous, random, motor pattern noise generator. Here and there, a pattern or portion of a pattern escapes, without its apparent emotional counterpart, into the context of the thalamocortical system.

"And suddenly," Llinás concludes, "you hear a song in your head or out of seemingly nowhere find yourself anxious to play tennis. Things sometimes just come to us."

Anthony Storr, a psychiatrist, writes eloquently in *Music and the Mind* of his own musical imagery and wonders "what purpose is served by music running in the head unsummoned and perhaps unwanted?" He feels that such music generally has a positive effect: "It alleviates boredom, makes . . . movements more rhythmical, and reduces fatigue." It buoys the spirits, is intrinsically rewarding. Music drawn from memory, he writes, "has many of the same effects as real music coming from the external world." It has the additional bonus of drawing attention to otherwise overlooked or repressed thoughts, and in this way may serve a function similar to that of dreams. All in all, Storr concludes, spontaneous musical imagery is basically "beneficent" and "biologically adaptive."

Our susceptibility to musical imagery indeed requires exceedingly sensitive and refined systems for perceiving and remembering music, systems far beyond anything in any nonhuman primate. These systems, it seems, are as sensitive to stimulation from internal sources—memories, emotions, associations—as to external music. A tendency to spontaneous activity and repetition seems to be built into them in a way that has no analogue in other perceptual systems. I see my room, my furniture every day, but they do not re-present themselves as "pictures in the mind." Nor do I hear imaginary dog barks or traffic noises in the background of my mind, or smell aromas of imaginary meals cooking, even though I am exposed to such perceptions every day. I do have fragments of poetry and sudden phrases darting into my mind, but with nothing like the richness and range of my spontaneous musical imagery. Perhaps it is not just the nervous system, but music itself that has something very peculiar about it—its beat, its melodic contours, so different from those of speech, and its peculiarly direct connection to the emotions.

It really is a very odd business that all of us, to varying degrees, have music in our heads. If Arthur C. Clarke's Overlords were puzzled when they landed on Earth and observed how much energy our species puts into making and listening to music, they would have been stupefied when they realized that, even in the absence of external sources, most of us are incessantly playing music in our heads.

5

Brainworms, Sticky Music, and Catchy Tunes

Music is playing inside my head
Over and over and over again
. . . There's no end . . .

—CAROLE KING

Sometimes normal musical imagery crosses a line and becomes, so to speak, pathological, as when a certain fragment of music repeats itself incessantly, sometimes maddeningly, for days on end. These repetitions—often a short, well-defined phrase or theme of three or four bars—are apt to go on for hours or days, circling in the mind, before fading away. This endless repetition and the fact that the music in question may be irrelevant or trivial, not to one's taste, or even hateful, suggest a coercive process, that the music has entered and subverted a part of the brain, forcing it to fire repetitively and autonomously (as may happen with a tic or a seizure).

Many people are set off by the theme music of a film or television show or an advertisement. This is not coincidental, for such music is designed, in the terms of the music industry, to "hook" the listener, to be "catchy" or "sticky," to bore its way, like an earwig, into the ear or mind; hence the term "earworms"—though one might be inclined to call them "brainworms" instead. (One newsmagazine, in 1987, defined them, half facetiously, as "cognitively infectious musical agents.")

A friend of mine, Nick Younes, described to me how he had been fixated on the song "Love and Marriage," a tune written by James Van Heusen.[1] A single hearing of this song—a Frank Sinatra rendition used as the theme song of the television show *Married . . . with Children*—was enough to hook Nick. He "got trapped inside the tempo of the song," and it ran in his mind almost constantly for ten days. With incessant repetition, it soon lost its charm, its lilt, its musicality, and its meaning. It interfered with his schoolwork, his thinking, his peace of mind, his sleep. He tried to stop it in a number of ways, all to no avail: "I jumped up and down. I counted to a hundred. I splashed water on my face. I tried talking loudly to myself, plugging my ears." Finally it faded away—but as he told me this story, it returned and went on to haunt him again for several hours.[2]

---

1. An earlier generation will remember the tune of "Love and Marriage" as the Campbell's soup advertisement "Soup and Sandwich." Van Heusen was a master of the catchy tune and wrote dozens of (literally) unforgettable songs—including "High Hopes," "Only the Lonely," and "Come Fly with Me"—for Bing Crosby, Frank Sinatra, and others. Many of these have been adapted for television or advertising theme songs.

2. Since the original publication of *Musicophilia*, many people have written to me about ways of dealing with a brainworm—such as consciously singing or playing it to the end of the song, so that it is no longer a fragment circling round and round, incapable of resolution; or displacing it by singing or listening to another tune (though this may only become another brainworm in turn).

Musical imagery, especially if it is repetitive and intrusive, may have a motor component, a subvocal "humming" or singing of which the person may be unaware, but which

Though the term "earworm" was first used in the 1980s (as a literal translation of the German *Ohrwurm*), the concept is far from new.[3] Nicolas Slonimsky, a composer and musicologist, was deliberately inventing musical forms or phrases that could hook the mind and force it to mimicry and repetition, as early as the 1920s. And in 1876, Mark Twain wrote a short story ("A Literary Nightmare," subsequently retitled "Punch, Brothers, Punch!") in which the narrator is rendered helpless after encountering some "jingling rhymes":

> They took instant and entire possession of me. All through breakfast they went waltzing through my brain. . . . I fought hard for an hour, but it was useless. My head kept humming. . . . I drifted downtown, and presently discovered that my feet were keeping time to that relentless jingle. . . . [I] jingled all through the evening, went to bed, rolled, tossed, and jingled all night long.

---

still may exact a toll. "At the end of a bad music-loop day," wrote one correspondent, "my throat is as uncomfortable as it might have been had I sung all day." David Wise, another correspondent, found that using progressive relaxation techniques to relax the "muscular correlates to the hearing of music involving the tightening and movement of the speech apparatus . . . associated with auditory thinking" was efficacious in stopping annoying brainworms. While some of these methods seem to work for some people, most others have found, like Nick Younes, no cure.

3. Jeremy Scratcherd, a scholarly musician who has studied the folk genres of Northumberland and Scotland, informs me that

> Examination of early folk music manuscripts reveals many examples of various tunes to which have been attributed the title "The piper's maggot." These were perceived to be tunes which got into the musician's head to irritate and gnaw at the sufferer—like a maggot in a decaying apple. There is one such tune in the [1888] *Northumbrian Minstrelsy.* . . . The earliest collection of pipe music was penned in 1733 by another Northumbrian, William Dixon, and this along with other Scottish collections suggests that the "maggot" most probably appeared in the early 18th century. Interesting that despite the disparity of time the metaphor has remained much the same!

Two days later, the narrator meets an old friend, a pastor, and inadvertently "infects" him with the jingle; the pastor, in turn, inadvertently infects his entire congregation.

What is happening, psychologically and neurologically, when a tune or a jingle takes possession of one like this? What are the characteristics that make a tune or a song "dangerous" or "infectious" in this way? Is it some oddity of sound, of timbre or rhythm or melody? Is it repetition? Or is it arousal of special emotional resonances or associations?

My own earliest brainworms can be reactivated by the act of thinking about them, even though they go back more than sixty years. Many of them seemed to have a very distinctive musical shape, a tonal or melodic oddness that may have played a part in imprinting them on my mind. And they had meaning and emotion, too, for they were usually Jewish songs and litanies associated with a sense of heritage and history, a feeling of family warmth and togetherness. One favorite song, sung after the meal on Seder nights, was "Had Gadya" (Aramaic for "one little goat"). This was an accumulating and repetitive song, and one that must have been sung (in its Hebrew version) many times in our Orthodox household. The additions, which became longer and longer with each verse, were sung with a mournful emphasis ending with a plaintive fourth. This little phrase of six notes in a minor key would be sung (I counted!) forty-six times in the course of the song, and this repetition hammered it into my head. It would haunt me and pop into my mind dozens of times a day throughout the eight days of Passover, then slowly diminish until the next year. Did the qualities of repetition and simplicity or that odd, incongruous fourth perhaps act as neural facilitators, setting up a circuit (for it felt like this) that reexcited itself automatically? Or did the grim humor of the song or its solemn, liturgical context play a significant part, too?

Yet it seems to make little difference whether catchy songs have lyrics or not—the wordless themes of *Mission: Impossible* or Beethoven's Fifth can be just as irresistible as an advertising jingle in which the words are almost inseparable from the music (as in Alka-Seltzer's "Plop, plop, fizz, fizz" or Kit Kat's "Gimme a break, gimme a break . . .").

For those with certain neurological conditions, brainworms or allied phenomena—the echoic or automatic or compulsive repetition of tones or words—may take on additional force. Rose R., one of the post-encephalitic parkinsonian patients I described in *Awakenings*, told me how during her frozen states she had often been "confined," as she put it, in "a musical paddock"—seven pairs of notes (the fourteen notes of "Povero Rigoletto") which would repeat themselves irresistibly in her mind. She also spoke of these forming "a musical quadrangle" whose four sides she would have to perambulate, mentally, endlessly. This might go on for hours on end, and did so at intervals throughout the entire forty-three years of her illness, prior to her being "awakened" by L-dopa.

Milder forms of this may occur in ordinary Parkinson's disease. One correspondent described how, as she became parkinsonian, she became subject to "repetitive, irritating little melodies or rhythms" in her head, to which she "compulsively" moved her fingers and toes. (Fortunately, this woman, a gifted musician with relatively mild parkinsonism, could usually "turn these melodies into Bach and Mozart" and play them mentally to completion, transforming them from brainworms to the sort of healthy musical imagery she had enjoyed prior to the parkinsonism.)

The phenomenon of brainworms seems similar, too, to the way in which people with autism or Tourette's syndrome or obsessive-compulsive disorder may become hooked by a sound or a word or a noise and repeat it, or echo it, aloud or to themselves, for weeks at a time. This was very striking with Carl Bennett, the surgeon with

Tourette's syndrome whom I described in *An Anthropologist on Mars.* "One cannot always find sense in these words," he said. "Often it is just the sound that attracts me. Any odd sound, any odd name, may start repeating itself, get me going. I get hung up with a word for two or three months. Then, one morning, it's gone, and there's another one in its place." But while the involuntary repetition of movements, sounds, or words tends to occur in people with Tourette's or OCD or damage to the frontal lobes of the brain, the automatic or compulsive internal repetition of musical phrases is almost universal—the clearest sign of the overwhelming, and at times helpless, sensitivity of our brains to music.

There may be a continuum here between the pathological and the normal, for while brainworms may appear suddenly, fullblown, taking instant and entire possession of one, they may also develop by a sort of contraction, from previously normal musical imagery. I have lately been enjoying mental replays of Beethoven's Third and Fourth Piano Concertos, as recorded by Leon Fleisher in the 1960s. These "replays" tend to last ten or fifteen minutes and to consist of entire movements. They come, unbidden but always welcome, two or three times a day. But on one very tense and insomniac night, they changed character, so that I heard only a single rapid run on the piano (near the beginning of the Third Piano Concerto), lasting ten or fifteen seconds and repeated hundreds of times. It was as if the music was now trapped in a sort of loop, a tight neural circuit from which it could not escape. Towards morning, mercifully, the looping ceased, and I was able to enjoy entire movements once again.[4]

---

4. The duration of such loops is generally about fifteen to twenty seconds, and this is similar to the duration of the visual loops or cycles which occur in a rare condition called palinopsia, where a short scene—a person walking across a room, for example, seen a few seconds before—may be repeated before the inner eye again and again. That a similar periodicity of cycling occurs in both visual and auditory realms suggests that some physiological constant, perhaps related to working memory, may underlie both.

Brainworms are usually stereotyped and invariant in character. They tend to have a certain life expectancy, going full blast for hours or days and then dying away, apart from occasional afterspurts. But even when they have apparently faded, they tend to lie in wait; a heightened sensitivity remains, so that a noise, an association, a reference to them is apt to set them off again, sometimes years later. And they are nearly always fragmentary. These are all qualities that epileptologists might find familiar, for they are strongly reminiscent of the behavior of a small, sudden-onset seizure focus, erupting and convulsing, then subsiding, but always ready to reignite.

Certain drugs seem to exacerbate earworms. One composer and music teacher wrote to me that when she was put on lamotrigine for a mild bipolar disorder, she developed a severe, at times intolerable increase in earworms. After she discovered an article (by David Kemp et al.) about the increase of intrusive, repetitive musical phrases (as well as verbal phrases or numerical repetitions) associated with lamotrigine, she stopped the medication (under her physician's supervision). Her earworms subsided somewhat but have remained at a much higher level than before. She does not know whether they will ever return to their original, moderate level: "I worry," she wrote, "that somehow these pathways in my brain have become so potentiated that I will be having these earworms for the rest of my life."

Some of my correspondents compare brainworms to visual afterimages, and as someone who is prone to both, I feel their similarity, too. (We are using "afterimage" in a special sense here, to denote a much more prolonged effect than the fleeting afterimages we all have for a few seconds following, for instance, exposure to a bright light.) After reading EEGs intently for several hours, I may have to stop because I start to see EEG squiggles all over the walls and ceiling. After driving all day, I may see fields and hedgerows and trees moving past me in a steady stream, keeping me awake at night. After a day on a boat, I feel the rocking for hours after I am back on dry land. And astronauts, returning from a week spent in the near-zero-gravity conditions of space, need several days to regain their "earth legs" once again. All of these are simple sensory effects, persistent activations in low-level sensory systems, due to sensory overstimulation. Brainworms, by contrast, are perceptual constructions, created at a much higher level in the brain. And yet both reflect the fact that certain stimuli, from EEG lines to music to obsessive thoughts, can set off persistent activities in the brain.

There are attributes of musical imagery and musical memory that have no equivalents in the visual sphere, and this may cast light on the fundamentally different way in which the brain treats music and vision.[5] This peculiarity of music may arise in part because we have to *construct* a visual world for ourselves, and a selective and personal character therefore infuses our visual memories from the start—whereas we are given pieces of music already constructed. A visual or social scene can be constructed or reconstructed in a hundred different ways, but the

---

5. And yet an earworm may also, more rarely, include a visual aspect, especially for those musicians who automatically visualize a score as they are hearing or imagining music. One of my correspondents, a French horn player, finds that when her brain is occupied by a brainworm,

> reading, writing, and doing spatial tasks like arithmetic are all disturbed by it. My brain seems to be pretty well taken up with processing the [brainworm] in various ways, mainly spatial and kinesthetic: I ponder the relative sizes of the intervals between the notes, I see them laid out in space, I consider the layout of the harmonic structure that they are a part of, I feel the fingerings in my hand, and the muscular movements required to play them, although I don't actually act these out. It's not a particularly intellectual activity; it's rather careless and I don't put any intentional effort into it; it just happens. . . .
>
> I should mention that these unbidden [brainworms] never interfere with physical activity or with activities that don't require visual thought, like engaging in normal conversation.

recall of a musical piece has to be close to the original. We do, of course, listen selectively, with differing interpretations and emotions, but the basic musical characteristics of a piece—its tempo, its rhythm, its melodic contours, even its timbre and pitch—tend to be preserved with remarkable accuracy.

It is this fidelity—this almost defenseless engraving of music on the brain—which plays a crucial part in predisposing us to certain excesses, or pathologies, of musical imagery and memory, excesses that may even occur in relatively unmusical people.

There are, of course, inherent tendencies to repetition in music itself. Our poetry, our ballads, our songs are full of repetition. Every piece of classical music has its repeat marks or variations on a theme, and our greatest composers are masters of repetition; nursery rhymes and the little chants and songs we use to teach young children have choruses and refrains. We are attracted to repetition, even as adults; we want the stimulus and the reward again and again, and in music we get it. Perhaps, therefore, we should not be surprised, should not complain if the balance sometimes shifts too far and our musical sensitivity becomes a vulnerability.

Is it possible that earworms are, to some extent, a modern phenomenon, at least a phenomenon not only more clearly recognized, but vastly more common now than ever before? Although earworms have no doubt existed since our forebears first blew tunes on bone flutes or beat tattoos on fallen logs, it is significant that the term has come into common use only in the past few decades.[6] When Mark Twain was writing in the 1870s, there was

---

6. It may be that brainworms, even if maladaptive in our own music-saturated modern culture, stem from an adaptation that was crucial in earlier hunter-gatherer days: replaying the sounds of animals moving or other significant sounds again and again, until their recognition was assured—as one correspondent, Alan Geist, has suggested to me:

  I discovered, by accident, that after five or six continuous days in the woods without hearing any music of any kind, I spontaneously start replaying the sounds that

plenty of music to be had, but it was not ubiquitous. One had to seek out other people to hear (and participate in) singing—at church, family gatherings, parties. To hear instrumental music, unless one had a piano or other instrument at home, one would have to go to church or to a concert. With recording and broadcasting and films, all this changed radically. Suddenly music was everywhere for the asking, and this has increased by orders of magnitude in the last couple of decades, so that we are now enveloped by a ceaseless musical bombardment whether we want it or not.

Half of us are plugged into iPods, immersed in daylong concerts of our own choosing, virtually oblivious to the environment—and for those who are not plugged in, there is nonstop music, unavoidable and often of deafening intensity, in restaurants, bars, shops, and gyms. This barrage of music puts a certain strain on our exquisitely sensitive auditory systems, which cannot be overloaded without dire consequences. One such consequence is the ever-increasing prevalence of serious hearing loss, even among young people, and particularly among musicians. Another is the omnipresence of annoyingly catchy tunes, the brainworms that arrive unbidden and leave only in their own time—catchy tunes that may, in fact, be nothing more than advertisements for toothpaste but are, neurologically, completely irresistible.

I hear around me, mainly birds. The local wildlife becomes "the song stuck in my head." . . . [Perhaps in more primitive times] a traveling human could more readily recognize familiar areas by adding his memory of sounds to the visual clues that told him where he was. . . . And by rehearsing those sounds, he was more likely to commit them to long-term memory.

6

Musical Hallucinations

In December of 2002, I was consulted by Sheryl C., an intelligent and friendly woman of seventy. Mrs. C. had had progressive nerve deafness for more than fifteen years, and now had profound hearing loss on both sides. Until a few months earlier, she had managed to get by with lip-reading and the use of sophisticated hearing aids, but then her hearing had suddenly deteriorated further. Her otolaryngologist suggested a trial of prednisone. Mrs. C. took a gradually rising dose of this for a week, and during this time she felt fine. But then, she said, "on the seventh or eighth day—I was up to sixty milligrams by then—I woke up in the night with dreadful noises. Terrible, horrific, like trolley cars, bells clanging. I covered my ears, but it made no difference. It was so loud, I wanted to run out of the house." Her first thought, indeed, was that a fire engine had stopped outside the house, but when she went to the window and looked out, the street was completely empty. It was only then that she realized that the noise was in her head, that she was hallucinating for the first time in her life.

After about an hour, this clangor was replaced by music: tunes from *The Sound of Music* and part of "Michael, Row Your Boat Ashore"—three or four bars of one or the other, repeating themselves with deafening intensity in her mind. "I was well aware that there was no orchestra playing, that it was *me*," she emphasized. "I was afraid I was going mad."

Mrs. C.'s physician suggested that she taper off the prednisone, and a few days later the neurologist whom she had now consulted suggested a trial of Valium. Mrs. C.'s hearing, meanwhile, had returned to its previous level, but neither this nor the Valium nor the tapering of the prednisone had any effect at all on her hallucinations. Her "music" continued to be extremely loud and intrusive, stopping only when she was "intellectually engaged," as in conversation or in playing bridge. Her hallucinatory repertoire increased somewhat but remained fairly limited and stereotyped, confined mostly to Christmas carols, songs from musicals, and patriotic songs. All of these were songs she knew well—musically gifted and a good pianist, she had often played them in her college days and at parties.

I asked her why she spoke of musical "hallucinations" rather than musical "imagery."

"They are completely unlike each other!" she exclaimed. "They are as different as thinking of music and actually hearing it." Her hallucinations, she emphasized, were unlike anything she had ever experienced before. They tended to be fragmentary—a few bars of this, a few bars of that—and to switch at random, sometimes even in mid-bar, as if broken records were being turned on and off in her brain. All of this was quite unlike her normal, coherent, and usually "obedient" imagery—though it did have a little resemblance, she granted, to the catchy tunes that she, like everyone, sometimes heard in her head. But unlike catchy tunes, and unlike anything in her normal imagery, the hallucinations had the startling quality of actual perception.

At one point, sick of carols and popular songs, Mrs. C. had tried to replace the hallucinations by practicing a Chopin étude on the piano. "*That* stayed in my mind a couple of days," she said. "And one of the notes, that high F, played over and over again." She started to fear that all of her hallucinations would become like this—two or three notes, or perhaps a single note, high, piercing, unbearably loud, "like the high A Schumann heard at the end of his life."[1] Mrs. C. was fond of Charles Ives, and another worry she had was that she might have "an Ives hallucination." (Ives's compositions often contain two or more simultaneous melodies, sometimes completely different in character.) She had never yet heard two hallucinatory tunes simultaneously, but she started to fear that she would.

She was not kept awake by her musical hallucinations or prone to musical dreams, and when she awoke in the morning, there would be an inner silence for a few seconds, during which she would wonder what the "tune du jour" was going to be.

When I examined Mrs. C. neurologically, I found nothing amiss. She had had EEG and MRI studies to rule out epilepsy or brain lesions, and these had been normal. The only abnormality was her rather loud and poorly modulated voice, a consequence of her deafness and impaired auditory feedback. She needed to look at me when I spoke, so that she could lip-read. She seemed

---

1. Robert Jourdain, in *Music, the Brain, and Ecstasy*, cites Clara Schumann's diaries describing how her husband heard "music that is so glorious, and with instruments sounding more wonderful than one ever hears on earth." One of his friends reported that Schumann "unburdened himself about a strange phenomenon . . . the inner hearing of wondrously beautiful pieces of music, fully formed and complete! The sound is like distant brasses, underscored by the most magnificent harmonies."

Schumann probably had a manic-depressive or schizo-affective disorder, as well as, towards the end of his life, neurosyphilis. And, as Peter Ostwald brings out in his study of the composer, *Schumann: Music and Madness*, in Schumann's final breakdown, the hallucinations that he had sometimes been able to command and use in his creative days now overwhelmed him, degenerating first into "angelic," then into "demonic" music, and finally into a single, "terrible" note, an A, which played ceaselessly day and night, with unbearable intensity.

neurologically and psychiatrically normal, though understandably upset by the feeling that something was going on inside her that was beyond her control. She had been upset, too, by the idea that these hallucinations might be a sign of mental illness.

"But why only music?" Mrs. C. asked me. "If these were psychotic, wouldn't I be hearing voices, too?"

Her hallucinations, I replied, were not psychotic but neurological, so-called "release" hallucinations. Given her deafness, the auditory part of the brain, deprived of its usual input, had started to generate a spontaneous activity of its own, and this took the form of musical hallucinations, mostly musical memories from her earlier life. The brain needed to stay incessantly active, and if it was not getting its usual stimulation, whether auditory or visual, it would create its own stimulation in the form of hallucinations. Perhaps the prednisone or the sudden decline in hearing for which it was given had pushed her over some threshold, so that release hallucinations suddenly appeared.

I added that brain imaging had recently shown that the "hearing" of musical hallucinations was associated with striking activity in several parts of the brain: the temporal lobes, the frontal lobes, the basal ganglia, and the cerebellum—all parts of the brain normally activated in the perception of "real" music. So, in this sense, I concluded to Mrs. C., her hallucinations were not imaginary, not psychotic, but real and physiological.

"That's very interesting," said Mrs. C., "but rather academic. What can you do to *stop* my hallucinations? Do I have to live with them forever? It's a dreadful way to live!"

I said we had no "cure" for musical hallucinations, but perhaps we could make them less intrusive. We agreed to start a trial of gabapentin (Neurontin), a drug that was developed as an antiepileptic but is sometimes useful in damping down abnormal brain activity, whether epileptic or not.

The gabapentin, Mrs. C. reported at her next appointment, actually exacerbated her condition and had added a loud tinnitus, a ringing of the ears, to the musical hallucinations. Despite this, she was considerably reassured. She knew now that there was a physiological basis for her hallucinations, that she was not going mad, and she was learning to adapt to them.

What did upset her was when she heard fragments repeated again and again. She instanced hearing snatches of "America the Beautiful" ten times in six minutes (her husband had timed this), and parts of "O Come, All Ye Faithful" nineteen and a half times in ten minutes. On one occasion, the iterating fragment was reduced to just two notes.[2] "If I can hear a whole verse, I'm very happy," she said.

Mrs. C. was now finding that though certain tunes seemed to repeat themselves at random, suggestion and environment and context played an increasing part in stimulating or shaping her hallucinations. Thus, once as she was approaching a church, she heard a huge rendering of "O Come, All Ye Faithful" and thought at first that it was coming from the church. After baking a French apple cake, she hallucinated bits of "Frère Jacques" the next day.

There was one more medication that I felt might be worth a trial: quetiapine (Seroquel), which had been successfully used in one case to treat musical hallucinations.[3] Though we only knew of this single report, the potential side effects of quetiapine were minimal, and Mrs. C. agreed to try a small dose. But it had no clear effect.

---

2. Diana Deutsch, at the University of California–San Diego, has received letters from many people with musical hallucinations and has been struck by how commonly these hallucinations contract over time into shorter and shorter musical phrases, sometimes only a note or two. These experiences may have analogies with those of phantom limbs, which characteristically shrink or "telescope" over time—thus a phantom arm may be reduced to a clawlike hand seemingly attached to one's shoulder.

3. This case was reported by R. R. David and H. H. Fernandez of Brown University.

Mrs. C. had been trying, in the meantime, to enlarge her hallucinatory repertoire, feeling that if she did not make a conscious effort it would contract to three or four endlessly repeated songs. One hallucinatory addition was "Ol' Man River" sung with extreme slowness, almost a parody of the song. She did not think she had ever heard the song performed in this "ludicrous" way, so this was not so much a "recording" from the past as a memory that had been revamped, recategorized in a humorous way. This, then, represented a further degree of control, not merely switching from one hallucination to another, but modifying one creatively, if involuntarily. And though she could not stop the music, she could sometimes switch it now by an effort of will. She no longer felt so helpless, so passive, so put upon; she had a greater sense of control. "I still hear music all day long," she said, "but either it has become softer or I'm handling it better. I haven't been getting as upset."

Mrs. C. had been thinking about a cochlear implant for her deafness for years but had postponed this when the musical hallucinations began. Then she learned that one surgeon in New York had performed a cochlear implant in a severely hard-of-hearing patient with musical hallucinations and found that it not only provided good hearing, but had eliminated the musical hallucinations. Mrs. C. was excited by this news and decided to go ahead.

After her implant had been inserted and, a month later, activated, I phoned Mrs. C. to see how she was doing. I found her very excited and voluble over the phone. "I'm terrific! I hear every word you say! The implant is the best decision I ever made in my life."

I saw Mrs. C. again two months after her implant was activated. Her voice before had been loud and unmodulated, but now that she could hear herself speak, she spoke in a normal, well-modulated voice, with all the subtle tones and overtones that were absent before. She was able to look around the room as we spoke, where previously her eyes had always been fixed on my lips and face. She was manifestly thrilled with this development. When I asked how she was, she responded, "Very, very well. I can hear my grandchildren, I can distinguish male from female voices on the telephone. . . . It's made a world of difference."

Unfortunately, there was a downside, too: she could no longer enjoy music. It sounded crude, and with the relative pitch-insensitivity of her implant, she could hardly detect the tonal intervals that are the building blocks of music.

Nor had Mrs. C. observed any change in the hallucinations. "My 'music'—I don't think the increasing stimulation from the implant will make any difference. It's *my* music, now. It's like I have a circuit in my head. I think I am landed with it forever."[4]

Though Mrs. C. still spoke of the hallucinating part of herself as a mechanism, an "it," she no longer saw it as wholly alien— she was trying, she said, to reach an amicable relation, a reconciliation, with it.

D WIGHT MAMLOK was a cultivated man of seventy-five with mild high-frequency deafness who came to see me in 1999. He told me how he had first started to "hear music"—very

---

4. Michael Chorost's experience following a cochlear implant was very different, as he described in his book *Rebuilt: How Becoming Part Computer Made Me More Human:*

  A week or two after activation, the mad orchestra has dismissed most of its play-ers. The implant masks the auditory hallucinations the way the sun blanks out the stars. When I take off the headpiece, I still hear the soft roar of a distant crowd. But no longer a jet engine, or a restaurant with a thousand patrons, or jazz drum-mers on speed.

  It's as if my auditory cortex has been angrily saying to me, "If you won't give me sound, then I'm just going to make it up." Which it proceeded to do, endlessly, in inverse proportion to the loss. But now that it is being gorged with all it can take, it is happy again, and it has shut up.

  The first night I realize that, I take off my clothes and go to sleep in a deep, blessed silence.

loud and in minute detail—ten years earlier, on a flight from New York to California. It seemed to have been stimulated by the drone of the plane engine, to be an elaboration of this—and, indeed, the music ceased when he got off the plane. But thereafter, every plane trip had a similar musical accompaniment for him. He found this odd, mildly intriguing, sometimes entertaining, and occasionally irritating but gave it no further thought.

The pattern changed when he flew to California in the summer of 1999, for this time the music continued when he got off the plane. It had been going on almost nonstop for three months when he first came to see me. It tended to start with a humming noise, which then "differentiated" into music. The music varied in loudness; it was at its loudest when he was in a very noisy environment, such as a subway train. He found the music difficult to bear, for it was incessant, uncontrollable, and obtrusive, dominating or interrupting daytime activities and keeping him awake for hours at night. If he woke from deep sleep, it came on within minutes or seconds. And though his music was exacerbated by background noise, he had found, like Sheryl C., that it might be lessened or even go away if he paid attention to something else—if he went to a concert, watched television, engaged in animated conversation or some other activity.

When I asked Mr. Mamlok what his internal music was like, he exclaimed, angrily, that it was "tonal" and "corny." I found this choice of adjectives intriguing and asked him why he used them. His wife, he explained, was a composer of atonal music, and his own tastes were for Schoenberg and other atonal masters, though he was fond of classical and, especially, chamber music, too. But the music he hallucinated was nothing like this. It started, he said, with a German Christmas song (he immediately hummed this) and then other Christmas songs and lullabies; these were followed by marches, especially the Nazi marching songs he had heard growing up in Hamburg in the 1930s. These songs were particularly distressing to him, for he was Jewish and had lived in terror of the Hitlerjugend, the belligerent gangs who had roamed the streets looking for Jews. The marching songs lasted for a month or so (as had the lullabies that preceded them) and then "dispersed," he said. After that, he started to hear bits of Tchaikovsky's Fifth Symphony—this was not to his taste either. "Too noisy . . . emotional . . . rhapsodic."

We decided to try using gabapentin, and at a dose of 300 milligrams three times a day, Mr. Mamlok reported that his musical hallucinations had greatly diminished—they hardly occurred at all spontaneously, though they might still be evoked by an external noise, such as the clatter of his typewriter. At this point, he wrote to me, "the medicine has done wonders for me. The very annoying 'music' in my head is virtually gone. . . . My life has changed in a truly significant way."

After two months, however, the music started to escape from the control of the gabapentin, and Mr. Mamlok's hallucinations became intrusive again, though not as much so as before the medication. (He could not tolerate larger doses of gabapentin, because they caused excessive sedation.)

Five years later, Mr. Mamlok still has music in his head, though he has learned to live with it, as he puts it. His hearing has declined further and he now wears hearing aids, but these have made no difference to the musical hallucinations. He occasionally takes gabapentin if he finds himself in an exceptionally noisy environment. But the best remedy, he has discovered, is listening to real music, which, for him, displaces the hallucinations—at least for a while.

.   .   .

JOHN C., an eminent composer in his sixties with no deafness or significant health problems, came to see me because, as he put it, he had "an iPod" in his head which played music, mostly popular tunes from his childhood or adolescence. It was music he had no taste for but which he had been exposed to when growing up. He found it intrusive and annoying. Though it was inhibited when he was listening to music, reading, or conversing, it was apt to return the moment he was not otherwise engaged. He sometimes said, "Stop!" to himself (or even aloud), and the internal music would stop for thirty or forty seconds but then resume.

John never thought his "iPod" was anything external, but he did feel that its behavior was quite unlike the normal imagery (voluntary or involuntary) which was so much a part of his mind and which was especially active when he was composing. The "iPod" seemed to go on by itself—irrelevantly, spontaneously, relentlessly, and repetitively. It could be quite disturbing at night.

John's own compositions are particularly complex and intricate, both intellectually and musically, and he said that he had always struggled to compose them. He wondered whether, with the "iPod" in his brain, he was taking "the easy way out," indulging secondhand tunes from the past instead of wrestling with new musical ideas. (This interpretation seemed unlikely to me, because though he had worked creatively all his life, he had only had the "iPod" for six or seven years.)

Interestingly, though the music he hallucinated was usually vocal or orchestral in origin, it was instantly and automatically transcribed into piano music, often in a different key. He would find his hands physically "playing" these transcriptions "almost by themselves." He felt that there were two processes involved here: the refluxing of old songs, "musical information from the memory banks," and then an active reprocessing by his composer's (and pianist's) brain.

.   .   .

M Y INTEREST IN musical hallucinations goes back more than thirty years. In 1970, my mother had an uncanny experience at the age of seventy-five. She was still practicing as a surgeon, with no hearing or cognitive impairment, but she described to me how one night she had suddenly started to hear patriotic songs from the Boer War playing incessantly in her mind. She was amazed by this, for she had not thought of these songs at all for nearly seventy years and doubted if they had ever held much significance for her. She was struck by the accuracy of this replaying, for normally she could not keep a tune in her head. The songs faded after a couple of weeks. My mother, who had had some neurological training herself, felt that there must have been some organic cause for this eruption of long-forgotten songs: perhaps a small, otherwise asymptomatic stroke, or perhaps the use of reserpine to control her blood pressure.

Something similar happened with Rose R., one of the post-encephalitic patients I described in *Awakenings*. This lady, whom I had put on L-dopa in 1969, reanimating her after decades in a "frozen" state, immediately requested a tape recorder, and in the course of a few days she recorded innumerable salacious songs from her youth in the music halls of the 1920s. No one was more astonished by this than Rose herself. "It's amazing," she said. "I can't understand it. I haven't heard or thought of these things for more than forty years. I never knew I still had them. But now they keep running through my mind." Rose was in a neurologically excited state at this time, and when the L-dopa dosage was reduced she instantly "forgot" all these early musical memories and was never again able to recall a single line of the songs she had recorded.

Neither Rose nor my mother had used the term "hallucination." Perhaps they realized, straightaway, that there was no external source for their music; perhaps their experiences were not so much hallucinatory as a very vivid and forced musical imagery, unprecedented and astonishing to them. And their experiences were, in any case, transient.

Some years later, I wrote about two of my nursing home patients, Mrs. O'C. and Mrs. O'M., who had very striking musical hallucinations.[5] Mrs. O'M. would "hear" three songs in rapid succession: "Easter Parade," "The Battle Hymn of the Republic," and "Good Night, Sweet Jesus."

"I came to hate them," she said. "It was like some crazy neighbor continually putting on the same record."

Mrs. O'C., mildly deaf at eighty-eight, dreamt of Irish songs one night and woke to find the songs still playing, so loud and clear she thought that a radio had been left on. Virtually continuous for seventy-two hours, the songs then became fainter and more broken up. They ceased entirely after a few weeks.

My account of Mrs. O'C. and Mrs. O'M., when it was published in 1985, seemed to have a wide resonance, and a number of people, after reading it, wrote in to the widely syndicated newspaper column "Dear Abby," to report that they, too, had experienced such hallucinations. "Abby" in turn asked me to comment on the condition in her column. I did this in 1986, stressing the benign, nonpsychotic nature of such hallucinations—and was surprised by the volume of mail that soon flooded in. Scores of people wrote to me, many of them giving very detailed accounts of their own musical hallucinations. This sudden influx of reports made me think that the experience must be much more common than I had thought—or than the medical profession had recognized. In the twenty years since, I have

---

5. This essay, "Reminiscence," is included in *The Man Who Mistook His Wife for a Hat.*

continued to receive frequent letters on the subject, and to see this condition in a number of my own patients.

As early as 1894, W. S. Colman, a physician, published his observations on "Hallucinations in the Sane, Associated with Local Organic Disease of the Sensory Organs, Etc." in the *British Medical Journal*. But notwithstanding this and other sporadic reports, musical hallucinations were considered to be very rare, and there was scarcely any systematic attention to them in the medical literature until 1975 or so.[6]

Wilder Penfield and his colleagues at the Montreal Neurological Institute had written famously in the 1950s and early '60s of "experiential seizures," in which patients with temporal lobe epilepsy might hear old songs or tunes from the past (though here the songs were paroxysmal, not continuous, and were often accompanied by visual or other hallucinations). Many neurologists of my generation were strongly influenced by Penfield's reports, and when I wrote about Mrs. O'C. and Mrs. O'M., I attributed their phantom music to some sort of seizure activity.

But by 1986, the torrent of letters I received showed me that temporal lobe epilepsy was only one of many possible causes of musical hallucination and, indeed, a very rare one.

THERE ARE MANY different factors that may predispose one to musical hallucinations, but their phenomena are remarkably unvarying. Whether the provocative factors are

---

6. In 1975, Norman Geschwind and his colleagues published a seminal paper which alerted neurologists to this underreported syndrome (see Ross, Jossman, et al.). In the last decade or two, there has been increasing attention to musical hallucination in the medical literature, and in the early 1990s, G. E. Berrios published two exhaustive reviews of the literature. The most extensive clinical study of musical hallucinations in a single population to date is that of Nick Warner and Victor Aziz, who in 2005 published the results of a fifteen-year study of the incidence, phenomenology, and ecology of musical hallucinations in older people in southern Wales.

peripheral (such as hearing impairment) or central (such as seizures or strokes), there seems to be a final common path, a cerebral mechanism common to all of them. Most of my patients and correspondents emphasize that the music they "hear" seems at first to have an external origin—a nearby radio or television, a neighbor putting on a record, a band outside the window, whatever—and it is only when no such external source can be found that patients are compelled to infer that the music is being generated by their brain. They do not speak of themselves "imagining" the music, but of some strange, autonomous mechanism set off in the brain. They speak of "tapes," "circuits," "radios," or "recordings" in their brains; one of my correspondents called it his "intracranial jukebox."

The hallucinations are sometimes of great intensity ("This problem is so intense it is wrecking my life," wrote one woman), yet many of my correspondents are reluctant to speak of their musical hallucinations, fearing that they will be seen as crazy— "I can't tell people, because God knows what they would think," one person wrote. "I have never told anyone," wrote another, "afraid they would lock me in a mental ward."[7] Others, while

---

7. In twenty-five years of working at a state psychiatric hospital, I encountered many schizophrenic patients who reported hearing voices, but very few who acknowledged hearing music. There was only a single patient, Angel C., who heard both, and he clearly differentiated them. He had heard "voices" addressed to him, accusing, threatening, cajoling, or commanding, since his first psychotic break, at the age of eighteen. He had only started hearing "music," by contrast, in his mid-thirties, when he had become somewhat deaf. He was not frightened by the music, though he was "puzzled"—whereas the "command" hallucinations he was subject to were charged with terror and threat. The musical hallucinations started with "a confused murmur," as of a crowd, and then differentiated into music—music he liked. "I used to put on Spanish records," he said. "Now it is like I am listening to them again, but there's no record." There were sometimes other noises interleaved with the music—the "murmuring" which he heard at the start, noises "like jetliners going overhead," and "factory noises" resembling sewing machines.

Yukio Izumi et al., studying a patient with both verbal and musical hallucinations, found "clearly different" patterns of regional blood flow in the brain, "possibly reflecting the different causes of the two types of hallucinations."

Occasionally, however, the two types may be coalesced or conflated. In one schizophrenic patient, the lyrics of songs underwent strange transformations, so that they

acknowledging their experiences, are embarrassed by the use of the term "hallucination" and say they would be much more at ease with these unusual experiences, much readier to acknowledge them, if they could use a different word for them.

And yet while musical hallucinations all share certain features—their apparent exteriority, their incessancy, their fragmentary and repetitive character, their involuntary and intrusive nature—their particulars can vary widely. So too can their role in people's lives—whether they assume importance or relevance, become part of a personal repertoire, or remain alien, fragmentary, and meaningless. Each person, consciously or unconsciously, finds their own way of responding to this mental intrusion.

GORDON B., a seventy-nine-year-old professional violinist in Australia, had fractured his right eardrum as a child, and subsequently had progressive hearing loss following mumps in adulthood. He wrote to me about his musical hallucinations:

> About 1980, I noticed the first signs of tinnitus, which manifested itself as a constant high note, an F-natural. The tinnitus changed pitch several times during the next few years and became more disturbing. By this time, I was suffering quite a substantial hearing loss and distortion of sounds in my right ear. In November 2001, during a two-hour train trip, the sound of the diesel engine started up the most horrific grinding in my

---

carried psychotic commands and messages of every sort. He felt that these were being beamed into his head from outer space. Another patient, psychotically depressed following the death of her father from a heart attack, kept hearing a dreadful transformation of the words (but not the music) of "Twinkle, Twinkle, Little Star"—she called this "The Heart Attack Song."

head, which lasted for some hours after I left the train. For the next few weeks I heard constant grinding noises.[8]

"The following day," he wrote, "the grinding was replaced by the sound of music, which has since been with me twenty-four hours a day, rather like an endless CD. . . . All other sounds, the grinding, the tinnitus, disappeared."[9]

For the most part, these hallucinations are "musical wallpaper, meaningless musical phrases and patterns." But sometimes they are based on the music he is currently studying and creatively transformed from this—a Bach violin solo he is working on may turn into "a hallucination played by a superb orchestra, and when this happens, it goes on to play variations on the themes." His musical hallucinations, he pointed out, "cover the full gamut of moods and emotions . . . the rhythmic patterns depend on my state of mind at the time. If I'm relaxed . . . [they are] very gentle and discreet. . . . During the day the musical

---

8. Tinnitus sometimes precedes or accompanies musical hallucinations but often occurs on its own. Sometimes it has a tonal quality, as with Gordon B.'s high F-natural; often it resembles a hissing or ringing sound. The ringing or whistling or hissing of tinnitus, like musical hallucinations, seems to come from the outside. When I first developed tinnitus a few years ago, I thought that it was steam escaping from a radiator in my apartment, and only when it "followed" me out into the street did I realize that the sound was generated by my own brain. Tinnitus, like musical hallucinations, can sometimes be so loud as to make it difficult to hear people's voices.

9. For Gordon, as with Sheryl C., a mechanical noise was replaced by music. Was this the brain imposing order on disorder? Something similar seemed to happen with Michael Chorost when, over a few hours, he moved from a severe hearing loss to total deafness—and, with this, the immediate onset of musical hallucinations. In his book *Rebuilt* he describes how each day now started with noise and ended with music:

Grotesquely, I am not living in the silent world that I might have expected. That would at least be familiar, for I had always been able to take my hearing aids out and experience near-total silence. Now I hear a thunderous river, now a jet engine, now a restaurant with a thousand patrons all talking at once. The sound is unending and overwhelming.

. . . But there are consolations. In the evenings the rumbles and bells soften. They become grand, sonorous and deep. I hear a vast organ playing a slowly evolving dirge without a time or a beat. It has the solemn grandeur of an aurora . . . it fits the occasion, for my ears are dying. But they are playing superbly at their own funeral.

hallucinations can get loud and remorseless and very violent, often with tympani beating an insistent rhythm underneath."

Other, nonmusical sounds may influence the musical hallucinations: "Whenever I mow the lawns, for example, I get a motif starting up in my head which I recognize as only ever happening when the mower is on. . . . It's evident that the sound of the mower stimulated my brain to select precisely that composition." Sometimes reading the title of a song would cause him to hallucinate the song.

In another letter he said, "My brain makes up patterns which go on incessantly for hours on end, even while I am playing the violin." This comment intrigued me, as it was a striking example of how two quite different processes—the conscious playing of music and a separate and autonomous musical hallucination—can proceed simultaneously. It was a triumph of will and concentration that Gordon could continue to play and even perform under these circumstances, so effectively, he reported, that "my cellist wife, for instance, wouldn't know I had any problems. . . . Perhaps," he wrote, "my concentration on what I'm currently playing mutes the musical hallucinations." But in a less active context, such as listening to a concert rather than performing, he has found that "the music in my head just about equalled the sounds coming from the platform. This stopped me from attending any more concerts."

Like several other hallucinators, he found that although he could not stop the musical hallucinations, he could often change them:

> I can change the music at will by simply thinking of the theme of another musical composition, whereupon for a few moments I will have several themes running in my head until the new one which I have selected takes over completely.

These hallucinatory performances, he noted, are "always perfect in terms of accuracy and tonal quality, and never suffer from any of the distortion which my ears are subject to."[10]

Gordon, trying to account for his hallucinations, wrote that before concerts he would find himself "mentally rehearsing" the passage he had just worked out, to see if he could find better ways of fingering or bowing, and that imagining different ways of playing might cause the music to go round and round in his mind. He wondered whether this "obsessive" mental rehearsal predisposed him to hallucinations. But there were absolute differences, he felt, between his rehearsal imagery and the involuntary musical hallucinations.

Gordon had consulted several neurologists. He had had MRI and CT scans of his brain and twenty-four-hour EEG monitoring, all of which were normal. Hearing aids had not reduced his musical hallucinations (though they had greatly improved his hearing), nor had acupuncture or various drugs, including clonazepam, risperidone, and Stelazine. His musical hallucinations were keeping him awake at night. Did I have any other ideas? he

---

10. One of my nursing home patients, Margaret H., had hearing problems for several years—severe deafness in the right ear and moderate deafness in the left, both increasing. Her complaints, however, were less of impaired hearing than of "recruitment"—exaggerated and abnormal sensitivity to sounds. She complained of "an unpleasant emphasis which makes certain voices almost unbearable." A year later, she said, "I go to the chapel, but the sound of the organ and the singing mount and mount, stay in my head, until they are unbearable." At this point, she started to wear earplugs; she refused hearing aids, feeling that they might further accentuate the unpleasant amplification and distortion of sounds.

But Margaret H. did not have any musical hallucinations until one morning five years later, when she woke up and heard a voice singing the chorus of "My Darling Clementine" over and over again. She said that this would start up as "an endearing soft melody, but then it gets jazzed up, loud and jazzy, noisy, not tender at all. I almost like it, but then it gets rough-like, not melodic." For a couple of days, she was convinced that Father O'Brien, the patient next door, was continually playing an old Sinatra record.

Mrs. H.'s hallucinations have the same qualities of mounting amplification and distortion and discomfort as her earlier auditory phenomena. In this way, she is unlike Gordon B. and others, whose musical hallucinations are not distorted (even though their hearing of real music may be).

asked. I suggested that he speak to his physician about quetiapine, which had helped some patients, and he wrote back to me, excitedly, a few days later:

> I wanted to let you know that on the fourth night after starting the medication, about three in the morning, I lay awake for two hours with no music in my head! It was incredible—the first break I have had in four years. Although the music returned the following day, it has been generally more subdued. It looks promising.

A year later Gordon wrote to say that he continued to take a small dose of quetiapine before bed, which damped down the musical hallucinations enough for him to sleep. He does not take quetiapine during the day—it makes him too drowsy—but he continues to practice the violin through his hallucinations. "You could say," he summarized, "I have learned to live with them by now, I suppose."

M OST OF MY PATIENTS and correspondents with musical hallucinations have had hearing loss, in many cases severe. Many but not all of them have also had some sort of "noise in the ear"—rumbling, hissing, or other forms of tinnitus, or, paradoxically, recruitment—an abnormal and often unpleasant loudness of certain voices or noises. Sometimes additional factors seem to push the person over a critical limit—an illness, or surgery, or a further decrement in hearing.

That said, about a fifth of my correspondents have no significant hearing loss—and only about 2 percent of those who do have hearing loss develop musical hallucinations (but given the number of aging people with advancing deafness, this means, potentially, hundreds of thousands of people are candidates for musical hallucinations). A majority of my correspondents are elderly, and there is a considerable overlap between the elderly and the hard of hearing. So while neither age nor hearing loss alone is sufficient to cause auditory hallucinations, the conjunction of an aging brain with hearing impairment or other factors may push a frail balance of inhibition and excitation towards a pathological activation of the auditory and musical systems of the brain.[11]

Some of my correspondents and patients, however, are neither elderly nor hard of hearing; one was a boy of nine.

There are very few documented cases of musical hallucinations in younger children—though it is not clear whether this represents the actual rarity of such hallucinations in children or their unwillingness or inability to speak of them. But Michael B. had very clear musical hallucinations.[12] His parents said that these were con-

---

11. While the musical hallucinations associated with deafness are commoner in older people, they can start at any age and may last a lifetime. This is brought out by a letter from Mildred Forman, a now-elderly lady who became deaf as a young adult:

> I am a post-lingually deafened woman and I have lived for many years with continuous musical hallucinations. They have been present since very close to the beginning of my hearing loss, more than sixty years ago. . . . I only recall melodies that I heard when I could hear. . . . My inner "iPod" never plays a tune that I cannot recognize and name. . . . Before losing my hearing I played the piano. I can still read music, and when I look at a page of notes I can imagine in my mind what they would sound like. But the songs that I read and have never actually heard are not stored in the database, and I forget them after a short interval. This leads me to believe that what once traveled into the musical section of my database via my auditory nerve remains embedded in it, but what now enters via my optic nerve is quickly erased.

12. Most of my patients are adults, but Michael's case and a number of letters I have received since first publishing *Musicophilia* have made me wonder whether musical (or other) hallucinations may be more common in children than we acknowledge. One correspondent, Steven L. Rosenhaus, an eminent composer, wrote to me to say:

> I have also had only one musical hallucination in my life, the memory of which was recalled only in reading this chapter. I was young, maybe four or five. I was already very musical; my parents have told me that I was one of those precocious kids who sang, in tune, before learning to speak (around age two). I woke up on one Christmas morning clearly hearing "The Little Drummer Boy" in the original (Ray Conniff chorus) arrangement. I called my mother into the room to find out

stant, "unrelenting, from morning to night. . . . He hears one song after another. When he gets tired or stressed out, the music gets louder and distorted." Michael first complained of this when he was seven, saying, "I'm hearing music in my head. . . . I have to check the radio to see if it's really on." But it seems likely that he first experienced it even earlier, for when he was five, while traveling in the car he would sometimes scream, cover his ears, and ask for the radio to be turned off—when it was not on.

Michael could not turn his musical hallucinations down or off, though he could suppress or replace them to some extent by hearing or playing familiar music, or by the use of a white-noise generator, especially at night. But as soon as he woke in the morning, he said, the music turned itself on. It can become almost unbearably loud if he is under pressure—he may scream at such times and seems to be in what his mother calls "acoustic agony." He cries, "Take it out of my head. Take it away!" (This reminded me of a story that Robert Jourdain relates about Tchaikovsky as a child, who was reportedly once found weeping in bed, saying, "This music! It is here in my head. Save me from it!")

For Michael, there is never any holiday from the music, his mother stresses. "He has never been able to enjoy the beauty of a quiet sunset, take a silent walk in the woods, quietly reflect, or read a book without hearing a band playing in the background."

---

where the music was coming from, to which she said "I don't hear anything." I recall saying that I did, and that it was still going on. I don't remember her reaction (I can only imagine what it might have been at that point), although I do remember her telling me I was dreaming. I think the music stopped soon after that.

Another correspondent, Louis Klonsky, wrote about a strange musical incident when he was seven or eight years old, growing up in the Bronx. He remembered watching the Frank Sinatra movie *A Hole in the Head* and being "entranced" by the song "High Hopes":

One night soon after seeing the movie, I woke up and couldn't fall back asleep for a long while and, for the only time in my life, could hear the song being "played" outside my apartment window—pretty tricky as we were on the fourth floor. The next day I asked my mother about it, and of course she told me I must have been dreaming. Until I read your book, I didn't realize these types of hallucinations could occur.

But he has recently started taking drugs to reduce cortical, and specifically musical, excitability, and he is beginning to show some response to this medication, though his music remains overwhelming. His mother recently wrote to me, "Last evening, Michael was very happy because his internal music stopped for about fifteen seconds. This has never happened before."[13]

BESIDES PEOPLE who are tortured by loud and intrusive musical hallucinations, there are others whose musical hallucinations are so soft, so easily disregarded, that they may feel these are not worth seeking treatment for. Such was the case with Joseph D., an eighty-two-year-old retired orthopedist. He was moderately deaf and had given up playing his Steinway a few years earlier, because it sounded "tinny" with his hearing aids and "washed out" without them. He had also, in his increasing deafness, been "banging" on the piano—"My wife kept yelling at me, 'You'll break the piano!'" The onset of tinnitus ("like steam coming out of a radiator") started two years before he came to see me, and this was followed by a low humming sound ("I thought it was the refrigerator or something in the kitchen").

About a year later, he started to hear "collections of notes, scales up and down, little twists and turns of two or three notes." These would come on suddenly, repeat themselves for hours, and then disappear just as suddenly. Then, a few weeks later, he heard

---

13. Three years later, Michael's mother gave me the following update:

Michael, who is now twelve and in seventh grade, continues to hear nonstop music. He seems to be better able to cope with it, unless he is under stress at school. Then he gets migraines where the music gets very loud and jumbled up, as if someone were changing the dial between radio stations. Thankfully, these episodes have dramatically decreased in frequency this year. Interestingly when Michael hears music, his brain automatically records it and he can recall or play a piece even years later as if he just heard it. He loves to compose his own music, and he has perfect pitch.

musical passages (which he recognized as themes from the Beethoven violin concerto) repeated again and again. He never heard the entire concerto, just this medley of themes. He could not specify hearing the sound of a piano or an orchestra—"It is only melody," he said. He could not banish this by force of will, but it was usually quite soft, easily disregarded or overcome by external sound; it would disappear if he was physically or mentally engaged.

Dr. D. was struck by the fact that, though his perception of real music was now distorted or washed out because of his hearing loss, his hallucinations were clear, vivid, and undistorted (he had tested this, at one point, by humming into a tape recorder along with his hallucination and then comparing the tape to an original recording—the two coincided exactly in pitch and tempo). Humming itself can produce a sort of echo, a repetition, in his mind.

I asked him whether he ever got pleasure from his musical hallucinations, and he said, emphatically, "No!"

Dr. D. was getting used to his hallucinations, which were mercifully mild. "At first I thought I was falling apart," he said, "but now I just regard it as baggage. As you get older, you accumulate baggage." Nevertheless, he was glad the baggage was only these relatively soft hallucinations.

W HEN I SPOKE, a few years ago, to a class of perhaps twenty college undergraduates and inquired whether any of them had ever experienced musical hallucinations, I was astonished when three of them said that they had. Two told me rather similar stories of how, playing different sports, they were each briefly knocked unconscious and, upon recovering consciousness, "heard music" for a minute or two—music which they felt came from an external source, perhaps the public-address system, or maybe another student with a radio. A third student told me how he lost consciousness and had a seizure during a karate match when his opponent immobilized him in a too-tight neck hold. Coming around after this, he heard "sweet music," which seemed to come from outside him, for a couple of minutes.

Several correspondents have told me about musical hallucinations that occur only when they are in a particular position, usually recumbent. One was a ninety-year-old man described by his physician as healthy and with a "brilliant" memory. When guests at his ninetieth-birthday party toasted him with "Happy Birthday to You" (in English, though both he and they were German), he continued to hear this song, but only when recumbent. It would last for three or four minutes, stop for a while, then restart. He could neither stop it nor provoke it himself, and it never occurred while he was sitting or standing. His physician was struck by certain EEG changes in the right temporal region that were seen only when the patient was lying down.

A thirty-three-year-old man also experienced musical hallucinations only when recumbent: "Just the movement of lying down on my bed would trigger them, and in a fraction of a second the music appeared. . . . But if I tried to stand up or even sit up, or even to raise my head slightly, the music would disappear." His hallucinations were always songs, sometimes sung by individual voices, sometimes by a choir—he called them "my little radio." This correspondent ended his letter by saying that he had heard about the case of Shostakovich, but that unlike him, he did not have any fragments of metal in his head.[14]

---

14. In a 1983 *New York Times* article, Donal Henahan wrote about Shostakovich's brain injury. Though there was no evidence to support this, Henahan noted, it was rumored that the composer had been hit by German shrapnel during the siege of Leningrad, and that some years later an X-ray showed a metal fragment lodged in the auditory area of his brain.

Strokes, transient ischemic attacks, and cerebral aneurysms or malformations can all lead to musical hallucinations,
but these tend to die down with the subsiding or treatment of
the pathology, whereas the majority of musical hallucinations
are very persistent, though they may fade a little over the
years.[15]

A wide range of medications (some that affect the ear itself, like
aspirin and quinine, and others that affect the central nervous
system, like propranolol and imipramine) may cause transient

Henahan relates that

Shostakovich, however, was reluctant to have the metal removed and no wonder:
Since the fragment had been there, he said, each time he leaned his head to one
side he could hear music. His head was filled with melodies—different each
time—which he then made use of when composing. Moving his head back level
immediately stopped the music.

I have since been told by Nora Klein, a student of Shostakovich's history and music,
that the shrapnel story is "a bit of nonsense that got printed somewhere during the war. . . .
In fact, Shostakovich never spent a moment up on a roof while enemy planes were flying
overhead; he was busy composing the first movements of his Seventh Symphony." Spreading such fabrications, Dr. Klein added, was "a popular pastime of Soviet bureaucrats."

15. A fellow neurologist, Dr. John Carlson, described to me a patient of his, P.C., who had
experienced vivid musical hallucinations after a temporal lobe stroke. Mrs. C., now in her
nineties, is a gifted and musical woman who has written more than six hundred poems
and many hymns, and she had kept a diary about her strange experiences. For more than
two weeks, she was convinced that a neighbor was playing a tape recorder loudly and
incessantly, at all hours. Then she began to realize that this was not so:

March 17—Kevin stood in the hallway with me, and I said, "I wonder why Theresa
   keeps playing those same songs. It bothers me. In fact, it's driving me crazy."
Kevin said, "I don't hear anything." I wonder if his hearing is going bad?
March 19—I finally called Theresa on the phone. She is NOT playing music, and I
   can't tell where it's coming from.
March 23—This music I keep hearing is slowly driving me out of my head. . . . I
   couldn't sleep for hours. . . . Now I'm hearing "Silent Night," "Away in a
   Manger," "Little Brown Church," and back to "Sun of My Soul." Christmas in
   March??
Each song is in perfect pitch and rhythm and will not stop till the entire song has
   been completed. Can it be my EARS? My MIND?

In April, Mrs. C. went to see Dr. Carlson for a neurological evaluation, which included an
MRI and an EEG. The MRI indicated that she had suffered strokes in both temporal lobes (the
one on the right side was more acute and recent). Her musical hallucinations largely subsided
after three or four months, though two years later, she would still have one on occasion.

musical hallucinations, as can certain metabolic abnormalities, epileptic conditions, or migraine auras.[16]

In most cases of musical hallucination, there is a sudden onset of symptoms; then the hallucinatory repertoire expands, becoming louder, more insistent, more intrusive—and the hallucinations may continue even if one can identify and remove the predisposing cause. The hallucinations have become autonomous, self-stimulating, self-perpetuating. At this point, they are almost impossible to stop or inhibit, though some people may be able to shift them to another tune in the "jukebox," provided it has some similarity of rhythm, melody, or theme. Along with this stickiness or stubbornness, there may develop an extreme susceptibility to new musical inputs, so that whatever is heard is instantly replayed. This sort of instant reproduction has some resemblance to our reaction to catchy tunes, but the experience for someone with musical hallucinations is not mere imagery, but often physically loud, as-if-heard "actual" music.

These qualities of ignition, kindling, and self-perpetuation are epilepsy-like characteristics (though similar physiological qualities are also characteristic of migraine and of Tourette's syndrome).[17] They suggest some form of persistent, uninhibitable spreading electrical excitement in the musical networks of the brain. Perhaps it is not coincidental that drugs like gabapentin (originally designed as an antiepileptic) are sometimes also useful for musical hallucinations.

---

16. In his 1957 autobiographical novel *The Ordeal of Gilbert Pinfold*, Evelyn Waugh describes a toxic delirium, or psychosis, induced by very large doses of chloral hydrate, admixed with alcohol and opiates. While on a cruise to calm his nerves, Pinfold has auditory hallucinations of all sorts—noises, voices, and, especially, music.

17. Victorian physicians used the vivid term "brainstorms" to apply not only to epilepsies but to migraines, hallucinations, tics, nightmares, manias, and excitements of all kinds. (Gowers spoke of these and other "hyperphysiological" states as being in "the borderland" of epilepsy.)

. . .

HALLUCINATIONS OF MANY SORTS, including musical ones, may also occur if the senses and the perceptual systems of the brain have too little stimulation. The circumstances have to be extreme—such sensory deprivation is not likely to occur in ordinary life, but it may occur if one is immersed for days on end in deep stillness and silence. David Oppenheim was a professional clarinet player and a university dean when he wrote to me in 1988. He was sixty-six, with some mild high-frequency hearing loss. A few years earlier, he wrote, he had spent a week at a monastery retreat deep in the woods, where he took part in a sesshin, an intense meditation practice of nine or more hours a day. After two or three days of this, he started to hear faint music, which he took to be people singing around a distant campfire. The following year he returned, and once again he heard the distant singing, but soon the music got louder and more specific. "At its height the music is quite loud," he wrote. "It is repetitive and orchestral in nature. It is all slow passages from Dvořák and Wagner. . . . The presence of this musical track makes the meditation impossible."

> I can summon up Dvořák, Wagner, or anyone else, when not in meditation, but I don't "hear" them. . . . In the sesshin version, I *hear* them.
>
> There is obsessive repetition of the same musical material, over and over for days at a time. . . . The "inner" musician cannot be stopped or shut up, but he *can* be controlled and manipulated. . . . I was successful in banishing the "Pilgrims' Chorus" from *Tannhäuser* by changing it into the slow movement from Mozart's lovely Symphony 25 in A major, because they start out with the same intervals.

Not all of his hallucinations were of familiar music—some of it he "composed"; but, he added, "I don't compose at all in my everyday life. I used the word to indicate that at least one of the pieces that played in my head was not Dvořák or Wagner, but new music that I was somehow making up."

I have heard similar accounts from some of my friends. Jerome Bruner tells me that when he sailed the Atlantic solo and there were calm days with little to do, he sometimes "heard" classical music "stealing across the water."

Michael Sundue, a botanist, wrote to me about his own experience as a novice sailor:

> I was twenty-four years old, working as a member of a crew that was hired to deliver a sailboat. We were at sea for a total of twenty-two days. It was very boring. After the first three days, I had read every book that I brought with me. There was nothing to do for entertainment except to watch the clouds and take naps. For days and days, there was no wind, so we simply puttered along at a few knots by running the engine while the sails luffed. I would lie on my back on the deck or on a bench in a cabin and stare out through the Plexiglas window. It was during these long days of complete inactivity that I had several musical hallucinations.
>
> Two of the hallucinations began from the monotonous and ever-present sounds that were generated by the boat itself. These were the buzzing of the reefer (the small refrigerator), and the whistling sound of the rigging in the wind. Each of these sounds transformed into never-ending instrumental solos. The transformation into music was such that the original sound and its source were forgotten, and I lay there in my lethargic state for long stretches of time just listening to what sounded like stunning and beautiful compositions. Only after

enjoying each of these in a sort of daydream-like state did I figure out what the sources of noise were. The instrumental sounds themselves were interesting in that they were not anything I typically listened to for enjoyment. The buzzing noise of the reefer to me sounded like a virtuoso heavy metal guitar solo, an onslaught of high-pitched strings played quickly through a distorting amplifier. The whistling sound of the rigging took on the form of highland Scottish bagpipes with a set of drones and a melody line. The sounds of both of these types of music are familiar to me, but neither are things that I would generally play on my home stereo.

Around the same time, I would also hear my father's voice call my name. As far as I know, there was no sound which triggered this. (At one point, I also had a visual hallucination of a shark's fin emerging from the water. It took no time at all for my companions to discredit my claim that I had seen a shark. They laughed at me. I think from their reaction that seeing sharks was a very common reaction for inexperienced sailors to have.)

A LTHOUGH COLMAN, in 1894, wrote specifically about "Hallucinations in the Sane, associated with local organic disease of the sensory organs, etc.," the impression has long remained both in the popular mind and among physicians, too, that "hallucinations" mean psychosis—or gross organic disease of the brain.[18] The reluctance to observe the common phenomenon of "hallucinations in the sane" before the 1970s was perhaps influenced by the fact that there was no theory of how such hallu-

---

18. A comprehensive and rich examination of auditory hallucinations in both sane and schizophrenic people is given by Daniel B. Smith in his book *Muses, Madmen, and Prophets: Rethinking the History, Science, and Meaning of Auditory Hallucinations.*

cinations could occur until 1967, when Jerzy Konorski, a Polish neurophysiologist, devoted several pages of his *Integrative Activity of the Brain* to the "physiological basis of hallucinations." Konorski inverted the question "Why do hallucinations occur?" to "Why do hallucinations not occur all the time? What constrains them?" He conceived a dynamic system which, he wrote, "can generate perceptions, images, and hallucinations . . . the mechanism producing hallucinations is built into our brains, but it can be thrown into operation only in some exceptional conditions." Konorski brought together evidence—weak in the 1960s, but overwhelming now—that there are not only afferent connections going from the sense organs to the brain, but "retro" connections going in the other direction. Such retro connections may be sparse compared to the afferent connections, and may not be activated under normal circumstances. But they provide, Konorski felt, the essential anatomical and physiological means by which hallucinations can be generated. What, then, normally prevents this from happening? The crucial factor, Konorski suggested, is the sensory input from eyes, ears, and other sense organs, which normally inhibits any backflow of activity from the highest parts of the cortex to the periphery. But if there is a critical deficiency of input from the sense organs, this will facilitate a backflow, producing hallucinations physiologically and subjectively indistinguishable from perceptions. (There is normally no such reduction of input in conditions of silence or darkness, because "off-units" fire up and produce continuous activity.)

Konorski's theory provided a simple and beautiful explanation for what soon came to be called "release" hallucinations associated with "de-afferentation." Such an explanation now seems obvious, almost tautological—but it required originality and audacity to propose it in the 1960s.

There is now good evidence from brain-imaging studies to

support Konorski's idea. In 2000, Timothy Griffiths published a detailed and pioneering report on the neural basis of musical hallucinations; he was able to show, using PET scans, that musical hallucinations were associated with a widespread activation of the same neural networks that are normally activated during the perception of actual music.

I N 1995 I received a vivid letter from June B., a charming and creative woman of seventy, telling me of her musical hallucinations:

> This first started last November when I was visiting my sister and brother-in-law one night. After turning off the TV and preparing to retire, I started hearing "Amazing Grace." It was being sung by a choir, over and over again. I checked with my sister to see if they had some church service on TV, but they had Monday night football, or some such. So I went onto the deck overlooking the water. The music followed me. I looked down on the quiet coastline and the few houses with lights and realized that the music couldn't possibly be coming from anywhere in that area. It had to be in my head.

Mrs. B. enclosed her "play list," which included "Amazing Grace," "The Battle Hymn of the Republic," Beethoven's "Ode to Joy," the drinking song from *La Traviata*, "A-Tisket, A-Tasket," and "a really dreary version" of "We Three Kings of Orient Are."

"One night," Mrs. B. wrote, "I heard a splendidly solemn rendition of 'Old Macdonald Had a Farm,' followed by thunderous applause. At that moment I decided that, as I was obviously completely bonkers, I'd better have the matter looked into."

Mrs. B. described how she had tests for Lyme disease (she had read that this could cause musical hallucinations), brainstem-evoked audiometry, an EEG, and an MRI. During her EEG, she heard "The Bells of St. Mary's"—but nothing abnormal showed. She had no signs of hearing loss.

Her musical hallucinations tended to occur during quiet moments, especially when she went to bed. "I can never turn the music on or off, but I can sometimes change the melody—not to just anything I want to hear, but to something that has already been programmed. Sometimes the songs overlap, I can't stand another minute, so I turn on WQXR and go to sleep by some real music.[19]

"I'm very fortunate," Mrs. B. concluded, "that my music isn't all that loud. . . . If it were, I'd really go crazy. It takes over in quiet moments. Any audio distractions—conversation, radio, TV—effectively drown out whatever I'm hearing. You observe that I seem to get on with my new addition 'amiably.' Well, I can cope okay, but it can be very annoying. . . . When I wake up at 5 a.m. and can't get back to sleep, I don't appreciate having a chorus reminding me that 'the old gray mare ain't what she used to be.' This is not a joke. It really did happen, and I might have thought it amusing if it hadn't kept singing the same refrain over and over again."

A decade after she first wrote to me, I met with Mrs. B., and I asked her whether, after so many years, her hallucinated music had become "important" in her life, in either a positive or a negative way. "If it went away," I asked, "would you be pleased or would you miss it?"

"Miss it," she answered at once. "I would miss the music. You see, it is now a part of me."

---

19. I asked her later whether she had other, simpler hallucinations. Sometimes just "ding, dong, ding, dong," she replied, the "dong" a fifth lower than the "ding," maddeningly repeated hundreds of times.

. . .

WHILE THERE IS no doubt of the physiological basis of musical hallucinations, one has to wonder to what extent other (let us call them "psychological") factors may enter into the initial "selection" of the hallucinations and their subsequent evolution and role. I wondered about such factors when I wrote in 1985 about Mrs. O'C. and Mrs. O'M.; Wilder Penfield, too, had wondered whether there was any sense or significance in the songs or scenes evoked in "experiential seizures" but had decided there was not. The selection of hallucinatory music, he had concluded, was "quite at random, except that there is some evidence of cortical conditioning." Rodolfo Llinás, similarly, has written of the incessant activity in the nuclei of the basal ganglia, and how they "seem to act as a continuous, random motor pattern noise generator." When a pattern or fragment might escape now and then and thrust into consciousness a song or a few bars of music, Llinás felt this was purely abstract and "without its apparent emotional counterpart." But something may start randomly—a tic, for example, bursting out of overexcited basal ganglia—and then *acquire* associations and meaning.

One may use the word "random" with regard to the effects of a low-level mishap in the basal ganglia—in the involuntary movement called chorea, for example. There is no personal element in chorea; it is wholly an automatism—it does not, for the most part, even make its way to consciousness and may be more visible to others than to the patient himself. But "random" is a word one would hesitate to use in regard to *experiences*, whether these are perceptual, imaginary, or hallucinatory. Musical hallucinations draw upon the musical experience and memories of a lifetime, and the importance that particular sorts of music have for the individual must surely play a major role. The sheer weight of exposure may also play a significant part, even overriding personal taste—the vast majority of musical hallucinations tend to take the form of popular songs or theme music (and, in an earlier generation, hymns and patriotic songs), even in professional musicians or very sophisticated listeners.[20] Musical hallucinations tend to reflect the tastes of the times more than the tastes of the individual.

Some people—a few—come to enjoy their musical hallucinations; many are tormented by them; most, sooner or later, reach some kind of accommodation or understanding with them. This may sometimes take the form of direct interaction, as in a charming case history published by Timothy Miller and T. W. Crosby. Their patient, an elderly deaf lady, "awoke one morning hearing a gospel quartet singing an old hymn she remembered from childhood days." Once she had ascertained that the music was not coming from a radio or television, she rather calmly accepted that it was coming "from inside my head." The choir's repertoire of hymns increased: "the music was generally pleasing, and the patient often enjoyed singing along with the quartet. . . . She also found that she could teach the quartet new songs by thinking of a few lines, and the quartet would supply any forgotten words or verses." Miller and Crosby observed that a year later the hallucinations were unchanged, adding that their patient had "adjusted well to her hallucinations and views them as a 'cross' she must bear." Yet "bearing a cross" may not carry a wholly negative connotation; it can also be a sign of favor, of election. I recently had occasion to see a remarkable old lady,

---

20. This is not always the case, as with one accomplished cellist, Daniel Stern. Stern had a prodigious musical memory, and his hallucinatory music, as he became increasingly hard of hearing, consisted almost entirely of cello concertos or other pieces for strings which he had played professionally, and which he heard in their entirety. Stern, also a novelist, wrote of musical hallucinations in his novella "Fabrikant's Way."

a pastor who developed musical hallucinations—mostly of hymns—as she became hard of hearing. She came to see her hallucinations as "a gift" and has "trained" them to a considerable extent, so that they occur while she is in church or at prayer, but not at mealtimes, for instance. She has incorporated her musical hallucinations into a deeply felt religious context.

Such personal influences are fully allowed—indeed required—in Konorski's model, and in Llinás's, too. Fragmentary music patterns may be emitted or released from the basal ganglia as "raw" music, without any emotional coloring or associations—music which is, in this sense, meaningless. But these musical fragments make their way to the thalamocortical systems that underlie consciousness and self, and there they are elaborated and clothed with meaning and feeling and associations of all sorts. By the time such fragments reach consciousness, meaning and feeling have already been attached.

PERHAPS THE MOST intensive analysis of musical hallucinations and their shaping by personal experience and feeling, their continuing interaction with the mind and personality, has been pursued by the eminent psychoanalyst Leo Rangell. For Rangell, musical hallucinations have been the subject of continuing self-study that has lasted now for more than a decade.

Dr. Rangell first wrote to me about his musical hallucinations in 1996.[21] He was eighty-two, and had had a second bypass surgery a few months before:

> Immediately upon awakening, in the ICU, I heard singing, which made me say to my children, "Hey, there's a rabbi

---

21. Rangell, now in his ninety-third year, continues to practice as a psychoanalyst and is writing a book about his musical hallucinations.

school out there." It sounded to me like an old rabbi who . . . was teaching young rabbi students how to sing, and perform their things. I told my family the rabbi must work late, even midnight, since I heard the music then too. My kids looked at each other, and said amusedly and tolerantly: "There's no rabbi school out there."

I of course soon began to know this was me. This gave me both relief and concern. . . . The music must have been continuous, but I paid little or no attention to it for large blocks of time, especially during the busy hospital routines. When I left the hospital, after six days . . . the "rabbi" followed me. He was now outside my windows at home, towards the hills; or was he in the canyon? On my first plane trip a few weeks later, he came with me.

Rangell had hoped that these musical hallucinations—perhaps, he thought, a product of the anesthesia, or the morphine he had received after surgery—would go away with time. He had also experienced "copious cognitive distortions, which every bypass patient I know has had"—but these had quickly cleared up.[22]

After six months, however, he feared they were becoming permanent. During the day, he could often push the music aside when otherwise absorbed, but at night, the musical hallucinations kept him awake ("I feel quite ragged from lack of sleep," he wrote).

Dr. Rangell did have a significant hearing loss. "I have had nerve deafness for many years now, familial. The musical hallucinosis is related, I feel, to the hyperacusis that goes with the hypo-hearing. The internal, central auditory pathways must

---

22. He had a vague memory, too, that fifteen years earlier, with his first bypass surgery, he had heard "the same sober songs and chanting," but these had disappeared. ("I cannot vouch for this recollection," he wrote, "but it gave me hope.")

overwork and enhance sounds." He speculated that this over-activity of auditory brain pathways might at first be based on external rhythms of wind, traffic, or humming motors or on internal rhythms of breath or heartbeat—and that "the mind then converts these to music or song, establishing control over it. Passivity is overcome by activity."

Dr. Rangell felt that his internal music reflected his moods and circumstances. At first, in the hospital, the songs varied; they were sometimes funereal, elegiac, rabbinical, sometimes lilting and happy ("Oo la la, oo la la" alternating with "oy vey, oy vey, oy vey, vey, vey"—later he realized these were to the same tune). When he was due to come home from the hospital, he began to hear "When Johnny Comes Marching Home Again," and then "jaunty, jolly ones" like "Alouette, gentille alouette."

"When there is no official song that comes on by itself," he continued, "my brain-mind makes one up—the rhythmic sounds are put to music, often with nonsense words—maybe the last words someone said, or I read or heard or thought." This phenomenon, he felt, was related to creativity, like dreams.

I continued to correspond with Dr. Rangell, and in 2003 he wrote:

> I have lived with this thing now for almost eight years. The symptom is always there. One senses it is 24/7 . . . [but] to say that it is always with me does not mean that I am always aware of it—that would indeed send me to a loony house. It is part of me in that it is there whenever I think about it. Or whenever my mind is not occupied, that is, attending to something.
>
> But I can bring the tunes on in the most effortless way. I have but to think about one bar of music or one word of a

lyric and the total work rushes in and gets going. It is like the most sensitive remote control. It then stays as long as "it" wishes—or as long as I let it. . . .

It is like a radio with only a turn-on key.

Rangell has lived with his musical hallucinations for more than ten years now, and increasingly, they seem less meaningless, less random to him. The songs are all from his younger years, and "they can be categorized," he wrote:

They are romantic, or poignant, or tragic, or celebratory, about love, or make me cry—everything. All bring memories. . . . Many are of my wife . . . she passed away seven years ago, a year and a half after this began. . . .

They are structurally like a dream. They have a precipitating stimulus, relate to affects, bring back thoughts automatically whether I want to or not, are cognitive as well, have a substructure if I want to pursue them. . . .

Sometimes when the music stopped, I would find myself humming the tune I had just wished would please stop. I found I missed it. . . . Every psychoanalyst knows that in every symptom (and this is a symptom), behind every defense is a wish. . . . The songs that come to the surface . . . carry urges, hopes, wishes. Romantic, sexual, moral, aggressive wishes, as well as urges for action and mastery. They are in fact what brought [my musical hallucinations] to their final shape, neutralizing and replacing the original interfering noise. Complain as I will, the song is welcome, at least partially so.

Summarizing his experiences in a long article published online in the *Huffington Post*, Rangell wrote:

I consider myself a kind of living laboratory, an experiment in nature through an auditory prism. . . . I have been living at the edge. But a very special edge, the border between the brain and the mind. From here the vistas are wide, in several directions. The fields over which these experiences roam cover neurologic, otologic, and psychoanalytic realms, converging into a unique symptomatic combination of them all, lived and experienced not on a controlled couch but on the stage of an ongoing life.

Part II

A Range of Musicality

7

Sense and Sensibility:
A Range of Musicality

We often speak of people as having or not having "a good ear." A good ear means, as a start, having an accurate perception of pitch and rhythm. We know that Mozart had a wonderful "ear" and, of course, he was a sublime artist. We take it that all good musicians must have a decent "ear," even if not one of Mozartian caliber—but is a good ear sufficient?

This comes up in Rebecca West's partly autobiographical novel *The Fountain Overflows*, a story of life in a musical family, with a mother who is a professional musician (like West's own mother), an intellectually brilliant but unmusical father, and three children—two of whom, like their mother, are deeply musical. The best ear, however, belongs to the "unmusical" child, Cordelia. She, in her sister's words,

> had a true ear, indeed she had absolute pitch, which neither
> Mamma, nor Mary, nor I had . . . and she had supple fingers,

she could bend them right back to the wrist, and she could read anything at sight. But Mamma's face crumpled, first with rage, and then, just in time, with pity, every time she heard Cordelia laying the bow over the strings. Her tone was horribly greasy, and her phrasing always sounded like a stupid grown-up explaining something to a child. Also she did not know good music from bad, as we did, as we had always done.

It was not Cordelia's fault that she was unmusical. Mamma had often explained that to us. . . . [She] had taken her inheritance from Papa.

An opposite situation is described in Somerset Maugham's story "The Alien Corn." Here the elegant young son of a newly ennobled family, being groomed for a gentleman's life of hunting and shooting, develops, to his family's dismay, a passionate desire to be a pianist. A compromise is reached, in which the young man goes to Germany to study music, with the understanding that he will return to England after two years and submit himself to the opinion of a professional pianist.

When the time comes, George, newly returned from Munich, takes his place at the piano. Lea Makart, a famous pianist, has come down for the day, and all the family is gathered around. George throws himself into the music, playing Chopin "with a great deal of brio." But something is amiss, as the narrator observes:

I wish I knew music well enough to give an exact description of his playing. It had strength, and a youthful exuberance, but I felt that he missed what is to me the peculiar charm of Chopin, the tenderness, the nervous melancholy, the wistful gaiety and the slightly faded romance that reminds me always of an Early Victorian keepsake. And again I had the vague sensation, so slight that it almost escaped me, that the two hands did not quite synchronise. I looked at Ferdy and saw him give his sister a look of faint surprise. Muriel's eyes were fixed on the pianist, but presently she dropped them and for the rest of the time stared at the floor. His father looked at him too, and his eyes were steadfast, but unless I was much mistaken he went pale and his face betrayed something like dismay. Music was in the blood of all of them, all their lives they had heard the greatest pianists in the world, and they judged with instinctive precision. The only person whose face betrayed no emotion was Lea Makart. She listened very attentively. She was as still as an image in a niche.

Finally, Makart delivered her judgment:

> "If I thought you had in you the makings of an artist I shouldn't hesitate to beseech you to give up everything for art's sake. Art is the only thing that matters. In comparison with art, wealth and rank and power are not worth a straw. . . . Of course I can see that you've worked very hard. Don't think it's been wasted. It will always be a pleasure to you to be able to play the piano and it will enable you to appreciate great playing as no ordinary person can hope to do."

But George had neither the hands nor the ear, she continued, to become a first-rate pianist, "not in a thousand years."

George and Cordelia are both incurably deficient in their musicality, though in quite different ways. George has drive, energy, dedication, a passionate feeling for music, but he lacks some basic neurological competence—his "ear" is deficient. Cordelia, on the other hand, has a perfect ear, but one has the feeling that she will never "get" musical phrasing, will never improve her "greasy" tone, never be able to tell good music from bad, because she is profoundly deficient (although she does not realize it) in musical sensibility and taste.

Does musical sensibility—"musicality" in the most general sense—also demand a specific neurological potential? Most of us can hope that there may be some harmony, some alignment, between our desires and our powers and our opportunities, but there will always be those like George whose abilities do not match their desires, and those like Cordelia who seem to have every talent except the most important one: judgment or taste. No one has all the talents, cognitively or emotionally. Even Tchaikovsky was keenly aware that his great fertility in melody was not matched by a comparable grasp of musical structure— but he had no desire to be a great architectonic composer like Beethoven; he was perfectly happy to be a great melodic one.[1]

Many of the patients or correspondents I describe in this book are conscious of musical misalignments of one sort or another. The "musical" parts of their brains are not entirely at their service, and may indeed seem to have a will of their own. This is the case, for example, with musical hallucinations, which are imposed upon, and not sought by, those who have them—and are thus quite different from the musical imagery or imagination one feels to be one's own. On the performance side, this is what happens with musician's dystonia, when the fingers refuse to obey one's will and curl up or show a "will" of their own. In such

---

1. One might put the emphasis the other way around, as Stravinsky did in his *Poetics of Music*, in a discussion of Beethoven and Bellini: "Beethoven amassed a patrimony for music that seems to be solely the result of obstinate labor. Bellini inherited melody without having even so much as asked for it, as if Heaven had said to him, 'I shall give you the one thing Beethoven lacks.'"

circumstances, a part of the brain is at odds with one's intentionality, one's self.

Even if there is no misalignment of a gross sort, where mind and brain are in conflict with one another, musicality, like other gifts, can create its own problems. I think here of the eminent composer Tobias Picker, who also, as it happens, has Tourette's syndrome. Soon after I met him he told me that he had "a congenital disorder" that had "bullied" him all his life. I assumed that he was talking about his Tourette's, but he said no—the congenital disorder was his great musicality. He had, it seemed, been born with this; he had recognized and tapped out tunes in the first years of life and had started to play the piano and compose at four. By the age of seven, he could reproduce long and elaborate pieces of music after a single hearing and constantly found himself "overwhelmed" by musical emotion. He said that it was understood, practically from the start, that he would be a musician, and that he had little chance of doing anything else, because his musicality was all consuming. He would not, I think, have had it any other way, but he sometimes felt that his musicality controlled him, rather than the other way around. Many artists and performers, no doubt, have the same feeling at times—but with music (as with mathematics) such abilities can be especially precocious and may determine one's life from a very early age.

Listening to Picker's music, watching him play or compose, I have the feeling that he has a special brain, a musician's brain, very different from my own. It is a brain that works differently and has connections, whole fields of activity that mine lacks. It is difficult to know how much such differences may be "congenital," as Picker puts it, and how much they are the result of training—a tricky question, since Picker, like many musicians, began intensive musical training in early childhood.

With the development of brain imaging in the 1990s, it became possible to actually visualize the brains of musicians and to compare them with those of nonmusicians. Using MRI morphometry, Gottfried Schlaug at Harvard and his colleagues made careful comparisons of the sizes of various brain structures. In 1995, they published a paper showing that the corpus callosum, the great commissure that connects the two hemispheres of the brain, is enlarged in professional musicians and that a part of the auditory cortex, the planum temporale, has an asymmetric enlargement in musicians with absolute pitch. Schlaug et al. went on to show increased volumes of gray matter in motor, auditory, and visuospatial areas of the cortex, as well as in the cerebellum.[2] Anatomists today would be hard put to identify the brain of a visual artist, a writer, or a mathematician—but they could recognize the brain of a professional musician without a moment's hesitation.[3]

How much, Schlaug wondered, are these differences a reflection of innate predisposition and how much an effect of early musical training? One does not, of course, know what distinguishes the brains of musically gifted four-year-olds before they start musical training, but the effects of such training, Schlaug and his colleagues showed, are very great: the anatomical

---

2. See, for example, Gaser and Schlaug's 2003 paper and Hutchinson, Lee, Gaab, and Schlaug, 2003.

3. Nina Kraus and her colleagues (see Musacchia et al.), struck by these changes in the auditory, visual, motor, and cerebellar regions of musicians' brains, wondered whether basic sensory mechanisms at the brain-stem level might also be enhanced in musicians. They found that there was indeed a difference: "Musicians had earlier and larger brain-stem responses than non-musician controls to both speech and music stimuli . . . evident as early as ten milliseconds after acoustic onset." This enhancement, they found, is "strongly correlated with length of musical practice."

Such functional changes in the brain stem of musicians may not seem as spectacular as the grossly visible enlargements of corpus callosum and cortex and cerebellum, but they are no less remarkable, for one would scarcely have thought that experience and training could affect so basic a sensory mechanism.

changes they observed with musicians' brains were strongly correlated with the age at which musical training began and with the intensity of practice and rehearsal.

Alvaro Pascual-Leone at Harvard has shown how rapidly the brain responds to musical training. Using five-finger piano exercises as a training test, he has demonstrated that the motor cortex can show changes within minutes of practicing such sequences. Measurements of regional blood flow in different parts of the brain, moreover, have shown increased activity in the basal ganglia and the cerebellum, as well as various areas of the cerebral cortex—not only with physical practice, but with mental practice alone.

There is clearly a wide range of musical talent, but there is much to suggest there is an innate musicality in virtually everyone. This has been shown most clearly by the use of the Suzuki method to train young children, entirely by ear and by imitation, to play the violin. Virtually all hearing children respond to such training.[4]

Can even a brief exposure to classical music stimulate or enhance mathematical, verbal, and visuospatial abilities in children? In the early 1990s Frances Rauscher and her colleagues at the University of California at Irvine designed a series of studies to see whether listening to music could modify nonmusical cognitive powers. They published several careful articles, in which they reported that listening to Mozart (compared to listening to "relaxation" music or silence) did temporarily enhance abstract spatial reasoning. The Mozart effect, as this was dubbed, not only aroused scientific controversy but excited intense journalistic attention and, perhaps unavoidably, exaggerated claims beyond anything intimated in the researchers' original modest reports.

---

4. Even profoundly deaf people may have innate musicality. Deaf people often love music and are very responsive to rhythm, which they feel as vibration, not as sound. The acclaimed percussionist Evelyn Glennie has been profoundly deaf since the age of twelve.

The validity of such a Mozart effect has been disputed by Schellenberg and others, but what is beyond dispute is the effect of intensive early musical training on the young, plastic brain. Takako Fujioka and her colleagues, using magnetoencephalography to examine auditory evoked potentials in the brain, have recorded striking changes in the left hemisphere of children who have had only a single year of violin training, compared to children with no training.[5]

The implication of all this for early education is clear. Although a teaspoon of Mozart may not make a child a better mathematician, there is little doubt that regular exposure to music, and especially active participation in music, may stimulate development of many different areas of the brain—areas which have to work together to listen to or perform music. For the vast majority of students, music can be every bit as important educationally as reading or writing.

Can musical competence be seen as a universal human potential in the same way as linguistic competence? There is exposure to language in every household, and virtually all children develop linguistic competence (in a Chomskian sense) by the age of four or five.[6] This may not be the case with regard to music, since some households may be almost devoid of music, and musical potential, like other potentials, needs stimulation to develop fully. In the

---

5. It is not always easy or possible for children to receive musical training, especially in the United States, where music instruction is being eliminated from many public schools. Tod Machover, a composer and leading designer of new technology for music, seeks to address this problem by "democratizing" music, making it accessible to anyone. Machover and his colleagues at MIT's Media Lab have developed not only the Brain Opera, the Toy Symphony, and the popular video game Guitar Hero, but Hyperinstruments, Hyperscore, and other interactive systems used by professional musicians from Joshua Bell, Yo-Yo Ma, and Peter Gabriel to the Ying Quartet and the London Sinfonietta.

6. There are very few exceptions here—some children with autism and some with congenital aphasia. But for the most part, even children with marked neurological or developmental problems acquire functional language.

absence of encouragement or stimulation, musical talents may not develop. But while there is a fairly well-defined critical period for language acquisition in the first years of life, this is much less so for music. To be languageless at the age of six or seven is a catastrophe (it is only likely to occur in the case of deaf children given no effective access to either Sign or speech), but to be musicless at the same age does not necessarily predict a musicless future. My friend Gerry Marks grew up with very little exposure to music. His parents never went to concerts and rarely listened to music on the radio; there were no instruments or books on music in the house. Gerry was puzzled when classmates talked about music, and he wondered why they were so interested in it. "I had a tin ear," he recalled. "I could not sing a tune, I could not tell if others sang in tune, and I could not distinguish one note from another." A precocious child, Gerry was passionate about astronomy, and he seemed all set for a life of science—without music.

But when he was fourteen, he became fascinated by acoustics, especially the physics of vibrating strings. He read about this and did experiments in the school lab, but, increasingly, craved a stringed instrument for himself. His parents gave him a guitar for his fifteenth birthday, and he soon taught himself to play. The sounds of the guitar and the feeling of plucked strings excited him, and he learned rapidly—by the time he was seventeen, he came in third in a contest for "the most musical" in his senior class in high school. (His high-school friend Stephen Jay Gould, musical from infancy, came in second.) Gerry went on to major in music at college, where he supported himself by teaching guitar and banjo. A passion for music has been central to his life ever since.

Nevertheless, there are limits imposed by nature. Having absolute pitch, for example, is highly dependent on early musical training, but such training cannot, by itself, guarantee absolute pitch. Nor, as Cordelia shows, can the presence of absolute pitch guarantee that there will be other, higher musical gifts. Cordelia's planum temporale was no doubt well developed, but perhaps she was a bit lacking in prefrontal cortex, in judgment. George, on the other hand, while doubtless well endowed in those areas of the brain involved in emotional reaction to music, may have been lacking in other areas.

The examples of George and Cordelia introduce a theme that will be echoed and explored in many of the clinical case histories that follow: that what one calls musicality comprises a great range of skills and receptivities, from the most elementary perceptions of pitch and tempo to the highest aspects of musical intelligence and sensibility, and that, in principle, all of these are dissociable one from another. All of us, indeed, are stronger in some aspects of musicality, weaker in others, and so have some kinship to both Cordelia and George.

8

Things Fall Apart:
Amusia and Dysharmonia

We take our senses for granted. We feel we are given the visual world, for example, complete with depth, color, movement, form, and meaning all perfectly matched and synchronous. Given this seeming unity, it may not occur to us that there are many different elements composing a single visual scene, and that all of these have to be separately analyzed and then put together. This composite nature of visual perception may be more apparent to an artist or a photographer; or it may *become* apparent when, due to some damage or failure of development, one element or another is defective or lost. The perception of color has its own neural basis, and so, too, have the perception of depth, motion, form, and so on. But even if all of these preliminary perceptions are working, there may be difficulty synthesizing them into a visual scene or object with meaning. Someone with such a higher-order defect here—a visual agnosia, for example—may be able to copy a picture or paint a scene so that others can recognize it, but they themselves cannot.

It is similar with hearing and with the special complexities of music. There are many elements involved, all concerned with the perception, decoding, and synthesis of sound and time, and thus there are many forms of amusia—A. L. Benton (in his chapter on the amusias in Critchley and Henson's *Music and the Brain*) distinguishes "receptive" from "interpretive" or "performance" amusia, and identifies more than a dozen varieties.

There are forms of rhythm deafness, slight or profound, congenital or acquired. Che Guevara was famously rhythm-deaf; he might be seen dancing a mambo while the orchestra was playing a tango (he also had considerable tone deafness). But, especially after a left-hemisphere stroke, one can develop profound forms of rhythm deafness *without* tone deafness (just as, after some right-hemisphere strokes, a patient may develop tone deafness without rhythm deafness). In general, though, forms of rhythm deafness are rarely total, because rhythm is represented widely in the brain.

There are also cultural forms of rhythm deafness. Thus, as Erin Hannon and Sandra Trehub have reported, infants at six months can readily detect all rhythmic variations, but by twelve months their range has narrowed, albeit sharpened. They can now more easily detect the types of rhythms to which they have previously been exposed; they learn and internalize a set of rhythms for their culture. Adults find it harder still to perceive "foreign" rhythmic distinctions.

Having been raised on Western classical music, I have no difficulty with its relatively simple rhythms and time signatures, but I get confused by the more complex rhythms of tangos or mambos—to say nothing of the syncopations and polyrhythms of jazz or African music. Culture and exposure determine some of one's tonal sensitivities as well. Thus someone like myself may find the diatonic scale more "natural" and more orienting than the twenty-two-note scales of Hindu music. But there does not seem to be any innate neurological preference for particular types of music, any more than there are for particular languages. The only indispensable elements of music are discrete tones and rhythmic organization.

Many of us are unable to sing or whistle in tune, though usually we are very conscious of this—we do not have an "amusia."[1] But true tone deafness is present in perhaps five percent of the population, and people with such an amusia can veer off key without realizing it, or be unable to recognize off-key singing by others.

Sometimes tone deafness can be quite gross. I used to attend a small temple that employed a cantor who could hit jarringly wrong notes, sometimes a third of an octave away from where he should have been. He particularly fancied himself as a cantillator, and would embark on elaborate tonal excursions of a sort that require a very good ear, but he would get completely lost in these. When I complained discreetly to the rabbi one day about the cantor's singing, I was told that he was a man of exemplary piety, and that he did his best. I said I had no doubt of this,

---

1. Steven Mithen has addressed the question of whether anyone can learn to sing—using himself as a test subject. "My research [had] persuaded me that musicality is deeply embedded in the human genome, with far more ancient evolutionary roots than spoken language," he wrote in a charming and candid 2008 article in *New Scientist*. "Yet here I was, unable to carry a tune or match a rhythm." He went on to describe how he had been so "humiliated" by being forced to sing in front of his class at school that he had avoided participating in anything musical for more than thirty-five years. He resolved to see whether, with a year of singing lessons, he could improve his tone, pitch, and rhythm—and to document this process with functional MRIs.

Mithen's singing did improve—not spectacularly, but substantially—and fMRI showed heightened activity in the inferior frontal gyrus and in two areas of the superior temporal gyrus (more on the right side). These changes reflected his improved ability to control pitch, project his voice, and convey musical phrasing. There was also a lessening of activity in certain areas, as what had at first required conscious effort became increasingly automatic.

but that one could not have a tone-deaf cantor; this was, to anyone musical, akin to having a clumsy surgeon.[2]

Those with gross tone deafness can still enjoy music and enjoy singing. Amusia in its absolute sense—total amusia—is another matter, for here tones are not recognized as tones, and music, therefore, is not experienced as music.

Some of the classic cases in the neurological literature describe this. Henri Hécaen and Martin L. Albert noted that for such people, "melodies lose their musical quality, and may acquire a non-musical, disagreeable character." They described one man, a former singer, who "complained of hearing 'a screeching car' whenever he heard music."

I found these descriptions almost unimaginable, until I experienced amusia myself on two occasions, both in 1974. On the first, I was driving along the Bronx River Parkway, listening to a Chopin ballade on the radio, when a strange alteration of the music occurred. The beautiful piano tones started to lose their pitch and their character and were reduced, within a couple of minutes, to a sort of toneless banging with an unpleasant metallic reverberation, as if the ballade were being played with a hammer on sheet metal. Though I had lost all sense of melody, I had no impairment of rhythmic sense and I could still recognize the ballade by its rhythmic structure. A few minutes later, just as the piece was ending, normal tonality returned. Greatly puzzled by all this, when I got home I phoned the radio station and asked

2. Florence Foster Jenkins, a coloratura who attracted a sell-out audience to Carnegie Hall in her time, considered herself a great singer and attempted the most difficult operatic arias, arias that required a flawless ear as well as an extraordinary vocal range. But she would sing notes that were excruciatingly wrong, flat, even screechy, without (apparently) realizing that she was doing so. Her sense of rhythm was also terrible—but audiences continued to flock to her concerts, which always featured great theatrics and many costume changes. Whether her fans were devoted to her in spite of her lack of musicality or because of it is not clear.

them if this had been some sort of experiment or joke. They said no, of course not, and suggested that I get my radio checked.

A few weeks later I had a similar episode while playing a Chopin mazurka on my piano. There was again a profound loss of tone, and the music seemed to decompose into a disconcerting racket, along with an unpleasant metallic reverberation. But this time it was accompanied by a brilliant, scintillating zigzag expanding in half of my visual field—I had often experienced such zigzags during attacks of migraine. Now, it was evident, I was experiencing an amusia as part of a migraine aura. Still, when I went downstairs and spoke to my landlord, I found that my voice and his voice sounded perfectly normal. It was only music, and not speech or sound in general, that was so strangely affected.[3]

My experience, like most of those described in the neurological literature, was of an *acquired* amusia—one that I found startling and frightening but also fascinating. Were there, I wondered, people with congenital amusia of an equally extreme degree? I was startled to find the following passage in Nabokov's autobiography, *Speak, Memory*:

> Music, I regret to say, affects me merely as an arbitrary succession of more or less irritating sounds. . . . The concert piano and all wind instruments bore me in small doses and flay me in larger ones.

I do not know what to make of this, for Nabokov is such a jester, such an ironist, that one is never sure whether to take him seriously. But it is conceivable, at least, that in the Pandora's box

---

3. In 2000, Piccirilli, Sciarma, and Luzzi described the sudden onset of amusia in a young musician with a stroke. "I can't hear any musicality," he complained. "All the notes sound the same." Speech, in contrast, sounded normal to him; his sense of rhythm, too, was intact.

of his multitudinous gifts there was, along with these, perhaps, a profound amusia.[4]

I had met the French neurologist François Lhermitte, who once told me that when he heard music, he could say only that it was "The Marseillaise" or that it was not—his ability to recognize melodies stopped there.[5] He did not seem distressed by this, nor had he ever had the impulse to investigate its neural basis— it was simply the way he was, and had always been. I should have asked him *how* he recognized "The Marseillaise": Was it by its rhythm or the sound of a particular instrument? By the behavior or attention of other people around him? And what did it actually sound like to him? I wondered when and how he had discovered his amusia, and what effect, if any, it had had on his life. But we had only a few minutes together, and conversation veered to other topics. I would not meet another person with complete congenital amusia for another twenty years, and only then through the kindness of my colleague Isabelle Peretz, a pioneer in the study of neuroscience and music.

In late 2006, Peretz introduced me to D.L., an intelligent, young-looking seventy-six-year-old woman who has never "heard" music, though she seems to hear, recognize, remember, and enjoy other sounds and speech without difficulty. Mrs. L. recollected that when she was in kindergarten, children were asked to sing their names, as in "My name is Mary Adams." She could not do this and did not know what was meant by "singing"; nor could she perceive what the other children were doing. In second or third grade, she said, there was a music-appreciation

---

4. Nabokov's son Dmitri has remarked, I am told, that his father could not in fact recognize any music. (He has also written of both his parents' synesthesia in the introduction to a forthcoming book by Richard Cytowic and David Eagleman.)

5. Daniel Levitin points out that Ulysses S. Grant was "said to be tone-deaf, and claimed to know only two songs. He reported, 'One is Yankee Doodle and the other is not.'"

class in which five pieces, including the *William Tell* Overture, were played. "I could never tell which piece was being played," she said. When her father heard of this, he got a Victrola and records of the five pieces. "He played them again and again," she said, "but it didn't help." He also got her a little toy piano or xylophone that could be played by numbers, and she learned in this way to play "Mary Had a Little Lamb" and "Frère Jacques"— while having no sense that she was producing anything but "noise." If others played these songs, she could not tell whether they made mistakes, but if she herself made a mistake, she would *feel* this, she said, "in my fingers—not by hearing."

She came from a very musical family—everyone played an instrument—and her mother would always ask her, "Why don't you like music the way the other girls do?" A family friend who was a learning specialist tested her with pitches. D.L. was asked to stand up if a note was higher than another, or to sit down if it was lower. But this too failed: "I could not tell if one note was higher than the other," she said.

D.L. was told as a little girl that her voice was monotonous when she recited poetry, and one teacher set herself to tutor her in inflections and intonations, to read dramatically. This, apparently, was successful, for I could not detect anything abnormal in her speech. Indeed, she now spoke warmly of Byron and Sir Walter Scott, and when I asked her to, she recited "The Lay of the Last Minstrel" with expression and feeling. She enjoyed poetry readings and going to the theater. She had no difficulty recognizing people's voices, nor did she have difficulty recognizing all sorts of sounds around her: water running, wind blowing, cars hooting, dogs barking.[6]

D.L. loved tap dancing as a girl, was very good at it, and could

---

6. The fact that most people with congenital amusia are virtually normal in their speech perceptions and patterns, while profoundly disabled in musical perception, is very startling. Can speech and music be that tonally different? Ayotte et al. at first thought that the

tap-dance on skates. She said she was "a street kid," and liked to perform with other kids on the street. She seemed, therefore, to have a good sense of rhythm in her body (and now likes rhythmic aerobics), but if there was a musical accompaniment, this would throw her off and interfere with her dancing. When I tapped a simple rhythm with my pencil, like the opening of Beethoven's Fifth or a bit of Morse code, Mrs. L. could easily imitate it. But if the rhythm was embedded in a complex melody, she had much more trouble, and the rhythm tended to be lost in the overall noisy confusion she heard.

During junior high school, D.L. developed a liking for war songs (this was in the mid-1940s). "I recognized them because of their words," she said. "Anything with words is okay." Her father, newly encouraged, bought records of war songs, but, she remembered, "if an orchestra was in the background it drove me crazy, like sounds coming from all different directions, overwhelming noise."

People often ask Mrs. L. what she hears when music is played, and she answers, "If you were in my kitchen and threw all the pots and pans on the floor, that's what I hear!" Later, she said that she was "very sensitive to high notes" and that if she went to an opera, "it all sounded like screaming.

"I couldn't recognize 'The Star-Spangled Banner,'" Mrs. L. said, "I had to wait until others stood up." She also failed to recognize "Happy Birthday to You," even though when she became a teacher, she would play a recording of it "at least thirty times a year, when any of my students had a birthday."

---

ability of amusic people to perceive the intonations of speech might be because speech was less exacting than music in its requirements for fine pitch discrimination. But Patel, Foxton, and Griffiths have shown that if intonation contours are extracted from speech, amusic individuals have severe difficulties discriminating these. It is clear, therefore, that other factors, such as the recognition of words, syllables, and sentence structure, must play a crucial part in allowing severely tone-deaf people to speak and understand nuances of speech almost normally. Peretz and her colleagues are beginning to study whether this is also the case for speakers of more tonally dependent languages such as Chinese.

When she was in college, a professor did some hearing tests on all of his students, and told D.L. that she had "impossible results"—he wondered if she could, in fact, perceive music. Around this time, she started going out with boyfriends. "I went to all these musicals," she told me, including *Oklahoma!* ("my father managed to cough up enough for a ninety-cent seat"). She would sit through these musicals—they were not too bad, she said, if only one person was singing, as long as it was not too high.

She mentioned that when her mother had a stroke and was admitted to a nursing home, all sorts of activities, but especially music, delighted and calmed her. But Mrs. L. said that if *she* were in the same position, music would make her worse, drive her mad.

Seven or eight years ago, Mrs. L. saw an article in the *New York Times* about Isabelle Peretz's work on amusia, and she said to her husband, "That's what I have!" Although she had never thought of her problem as "psychological" or "emotional," as her mother seemed to, she had not explicitly thought of it as "neurological." Excitedly, she wrote to Peretz, and in her subsequent meeting with Peretz and Krista Hyde, she was reassured that the condition was "real," not in her mind—and that others had it as well. She got in touch with other amusic people, and feels that now, with a bona fide "condition," she can excuse herself from going to musical events. (She wishes that a diagnosis of amusia had been made when she was seven rather than seventy— this might have saved her from a lifetime of being bored or excruciated by concerts, to which she went only out of politeness.)[7]

---

7. The first extended description of amusia in the medical literature was an 1878 paper by Grant Allen in the journal *Mind*:

> Not a few men and women are incapable of distinguishing in consciousness between the sounds of any two tones lying within the compass of about half an octave (or even more) from one another. Upon this abnormality I have ventured to bestow the name of Note-Deafness.

In 2002 Ayotte, Peretz, and Hyde published a paper, "Congenital Amusia: A Group Study of Adults Afflicted with a Music-Specific Disorder," in the journal *Brain*, based on their investigation of eleven subjects. Most of them had normal perception of speech and environmental sounds, but the majority were profoundly impaired in recognizing melodies and in pitch discrimination, unable to distinguish between adjacent tones and semitones. Without these basic building blocks, there can be no sense of a tonal center or key, no sense of scale or melody or harmony—any more than, in a spoken language, one can have words without syllables.[8]

Allen's lengthy paper included a superb case study of a young man whom he had "abundant opportunities of observing and experimenting upon"—the sort of detailed case study that established experimental neurology and psychology in the latter part of the nineteenth century.

But Charles Lamb provided a literary description of amusia even earlier, in "A Chapter on Ears," in his 1823 *Essays of Elia:*

> I even think that *sentimentally* I am disposed to harmony. But *organically* I am incapable of a tune. I have been practicing *"God Save the King"* all my life; whistling and humming it over to myself in solitary corners; and am not yet arrived, they tell me, within many quavers of it. . . . Scientifically I could never be made to understand (yet I have taken some pains) what a note in music is; or how one note should differ from another. Much less in voices can I distinguish a soprano from a tenor. . . . To music [the ear] cannot be passive. It will strive—mine at least will—'spite of its inaptitude, to thrid the maze; like an unskilled eye painfully poring upon hieroglyphics. I have sat through an Italian Opera, till, for sheer pain, and inexplicable anguish, I have rushed out into the noisiest places of the crowded streets. I lace myself with sounds, which I was not obliged to follow . . . I take refuge in the unpretending assemblage of honest common-life sounds;—and the purgatory of the Enraged Musician becomes my paradise. . . . Above all, those insufferable concertos, and pieces of music, as they are called, do plague and embitter my apprehension.—Words are something; but to be exposed to an endless battery of mere sounds . . .

8. Someone with a cochlear implant, which is only capable of reproducing a limited range of tones, has, in effect, a technologically induced amusia, as Mrs. L. has a neurologically based one. Cochlear implants replace the 3,500 inner hair cells of a normal ear with just 16 or 24 electrodes. While speech is understandable with such poor frequency resolution, music suffers. In 1995, with his cochlear implants, Michael Chorost compared his experience of music to "walking colorblind in an art museum." It is difficult to add more electrodes, because they short each other out if placed too close together in the wet environment of the body. However, software programming can be used to create *virtual* electrodes in between the physical ones, giving a 16-electrode implant the equivalent of

. . .

W HEN MRS. L. compared the sound of music to that of pots and pans being thrown around the kitchen, I was puzzled, for it seemed to me that pitch discrimination alone, however defective, would not produce such an experience. It was as if the whole character, the timbre, of musical notes was being radically undermined.

(Timbre is the particular quality or acoustic richness of a sound produced by an instrument or a voice, independent of its pitch or loudness—it is what distinguishes a middle C played on a piano from the same note played on a saxophone. The timbre of a sound is influenced by all sorts of factors, including the frequencies of harmonics or overtones and the onset, rise, and decay of acoustic waveforms. The ability to maintain a sense of timbre constancy is a multileveled and extremely complex process in the auditory brain that may have some analogies with color constancy— indeed, the language of color is often applied to timbre, which is sometimes referred to as "sound color" or "tone color.")

I had a similar impression reading Hécaen and Albert's case history of the man for whom music was transformed into the sound of "a screeching car," and with my own experience of a Chopin ballade sounding as if it were being banged out on a sheet of steel. And Robert Silvers has written to me of how Joseph Alsop, the journalist, "used to tell me that the music I admired, or indeed any music, for him was something like the sound of a horse-drawn carriage passing over cobbled streets." These cases,

---

121 electrodes. With new software, Chorost reported that he went from being able to distinguish between tones 70 hertz apart—equivalent to three or four semitones in the middle frequency range—to tones 30 hertz apart. While this is still poorer than the resolution of a normal ear, it significantly improved his ability to enjoy music. Technological amusia can therefore be addressed by uniquely technological means. (See Chorost's fascinating memoir, *Rebuilt: How Becoming Part Computer Made Me More Human,* and an article he wrote for *Wired,* "My Bionic Quest for *Boléro.*")

like D.L.'s, differed somewhat from the cases of pure pitch amusia described by Ayotte et al. in 2002.

The term "dystimbria" is beginning to be used to denote such experiences, and to be recognized as a distinct form of amusia that may coexist with defective pitch discrimination or occur on its own. Timothy Griffiths, A. R. Jennings, and Jason Warren recently reported the striking case of a forty-two-year-old man who, after suffering a right-hemisphere stroke, experienced dystimbria without any alteration of pitch perception. Mrs. L., it would seem, has both congenital dystimbria and impairments of pitch perception.

One might think, too, that a gross dystimbria for musical notes would make speech sound very different, and perhaps unintelligible. But this was not the case with Mrs. L. (Indeed, Belin, Zatorre, and their colleagues have found "voice-selective" areas in the auditory cortex that are anatomically separate from the areas involved in the perception of musical timbre.)

I asked Mrs. L. how she felt about her failure to "get" music. Was she ever curious or wistful about what others were feeling? She replied that she had been curious as a child: "If I had a wish, it would be to hear music as others heard it." But she no longer gives this much thought. She cannot perceive or imagine what others are enjoying so much, but she has many other interests and does not think of herself as "defective" or as missing an essential part of life—she is simply the way she is, and always has been.[9]

---

9. Later, reflecting on this, Mrs. L. brought up a passage that had struck her, from my book *The Island of the Colorblind.* I had described a totally, congenitally colorblind friend who had said, "As a kid, I used to think it would be nice to see colors. . . . I suppose it might open up a new world, as if one were tone-deaf and suddenly become able to hear melodies. It would probably be a very interesting thing, but it would be confusing."

Mrs. L. was intrigued by this, and said, "If I were to hear melodies, by some miracle, would I also be confused? Would I have to learn what melody *is* first? How would I know what I was hearing?"

In 1990, Isabelle Peretz and her colleagues in Montreal devised a special battery of tests for evaluating amusia, and they have been able, in many cases, to identify the broad neural correlates of certain types of amusia. They feel that there are two basic categories of musical perception, one involving the recognition of melodies, the other the perception of rhythm or time intervals. Impairments of melody usually go with right-hemisphere lesions, but representation of rhythm is much more widespread and robust and involves not only the left hemisphere, but many subcortical systems in the basal ganglia, the cerebellum, and other areas.[10] There are many further distinctions; thus some individuals can appreciate rhythm but not meter, and others have the reverse problem.

There are yet other forms of amusia, all probably with their own specific neural bases. There may be an impairment of the

---

Never having been able to "get" music is one thing, but losing the ability to hear it may affect one very deeply, especially if music has been central to one's life. This was brought out by one correspondent, Sara Bell Drescher. "Music was my life, my joy, my raison d'etre," she wrote, but, in her fifties, she lost most of her hearing from Ménière's disease. It was, she noted,

> the beginning of the end of my life as I knew it. Within six months I had lost many decibels and within a year, I could not hear music. . . . I could discriminate speech only with very strong hearing aids and only imperfectly, but the range of music completed eluded me. . . . Although a severe hearing loss keeps me from engaging in many other activities, it is the loss of music that leaves a gigantic hole in my life. . . . Nothing, nothing else fulfills the joy of a life with music.

10. The neurosurgeons Stephen Russell and John Golfinos have written about several patients of theirs, including a young professional singer who developed a glioma of the primary auditory cortex (Heschl's gyrus) on the right side. Surgery to remove this resulted in a difficulty with pitch discrimination so profound that this patient found she could neither sing nor recognize any melodies, including "Happy Birthday to You." These difficulties were transient, however, and in three weeks she recovered her previous ability to sing and recognize music. Whether this was due to tissue recovery or cerebral plasticity is not known. They stress that comparable amusias are not seen with tumors of the left Heschl's gyrus.

It has recently been shown that patients with congenital amusia have diminished development of an area of the white matter in the right inferior frontal gyrus, an area known to be involved in musical pitch encoding and melodic pitch memory. (See Hyde, Zatorre, et al., 2006.)

ability to perceive dissonance (the discordant sound produced by a major second, for example), something that is normally recognized and reacted to even by infants. Gosselin, Samson, and others in Peretz's lab have reported that loss of this ability (and nothing else) may occur with particular types of neurological lesion. They tested a number of subjects in discriminating dissonant from nondissonant music and found that only those with extensive damage to an area involved in emotional judgments, the parahippocampal cortex, were affected. Such subjects were able to judge consonant music to be pleasant, and to judge music as happy or sad, but they did not show the normal response to dissonant music, which they rated as "slightly pleasant."

(In a quite different category—for it has nothing to do with the cognitive aspects of appreciating music—there can be a partial or total loss of the feeling or emotions normally evoked by music, even though perception of music is unimpaired. This too has its own specific neural basis, and is discussed further in chapter 24, "Seduction and Indifference.")

In most cases, an inability to hear melodies is the consequence of very poor pitch discrimination and a distorted perception of musical tones. But some people may lose the ability to recognize melodies even though they can hear and discriminate the component tones perfectly. This is a higher-order problem—a "tune deafness" or "amelodia" analogous to the losing of sentence structure or meaning, perhaps, though words themselves are intact. Such a person hears a sequence of notes, but the sequence seems arbitrary, seems to have no logic or purpose, makes no musical sense. "What such amusics seem to be lacking," wrote Ayotte et al., "is the knowledge and procedures required for mapping pitches and musical scales."

In a recent letter, my friend Lawrence Weschler wrote:

I have an excellent sense of rhythm, and yet I am almost completely amusical in another sense. The missing element for me is the ability to hear the relations between notes and hence aurally to appreciate their interactions and interweavings. If you were to play two relatively close notes on the piano, say within an octave, I would likely not be able to tell you whether one was higher than the other—whether, say, in any given sequence of notes you had gone up and up and then down and down and then up . . . or the reverse.

Curiously, I have a relatively good sense of melody, or rather melodic memory, in that I can, tape-recorder-like, hum back a tune or even take to whistling or humming it with relative fidelity, days or weeks after being exposed to it. But I couldn't even tell you in my own humming if a particular melodic trill were going up or down. I have always been this way.

A somewhat similar description comes from a correspondent, Carleen Franz:

When listening to music in a higher register, particularly a soprano voice or a violin, I experience pain. There is a series of rapidly popping noises in my ears that drown out any other sounds and this is quite uncomfortable. I get the same sensation when I hear an infant cry. Music often makes me feel irritable, and reminds me of scratching sounds. I occasionally hear a single line of melody in my head, but I have no idea what you mean by hearing an orchestra or symphony. Although I had years of music lessons as a child, I cannot match pitch and often cannot tell if one pitch is higher or lower than another. I've never been able to understand why anyone would buy a CD or go to a concert. Although I regularly go to concerts in which my husband or daughter perform, it has nothing to do with a desire to hear the music. The association of music and emotion is a mystery to me. I never realized that music can make people feel different things—I thought music was described as happy or sad because of the tempo or title. Reading your book made me realize for the first time that maybe I am missing something.

Some years ago my colleague Steven Sparr told me of a patient of his, Professor B., a greatly gifted musician who had played double bass with the New York Philharmonic under Toscanini, and was the author of a major textbook in musical appreciation and a close friend of Arnold Schoenberg's. "Now, at 91," Sparr wrote, Professor B., "still articulate, vibrant and very much intellectually alive, had had a stroke that left him suddenly unable to discern a tune as simple as 'Happy Birthday.'" His perception of pitch and rhythm was perfectly intact; it was only their synthesis into melody that was gone.

Yet Professor B. was admitted to the hospital with weakness of the left side, and on the day of admission had hallucinations of a choir singing. He was unable to identify Handel's *Messiah* (played to him on the bedside music channel) or "Happy Birthday" (hummed to him by Dr. Sparr). Professor B. did not recognize either piece of music, but he did not acknowledge any problem, maintaining that his difficulties were due to "poor fidelity of the recording equipment" and that Dr. Sparr's humming was mere "pseudovocalization."

Professor B. could immediately get a melody by reading its notation. His musical imagery was intact—and he could hum a melody himself quite accurately. His problem was wholly one of auditory processing, an inability to hold an auditory sequence of notes in memory.

While there have been many accounts of such melody deafness coming on after a head injury or stroke, I had not heard of a harmony deafness—until I met Rachael Y.

R ACHAEL Y. WAS a gifted composer and performer in her early forties when she came to see me a few years ago. She had been a passenger in a car that had skidded off the road and into a tree; she suffered severe head and spine injuries and was paralyzed in her legs and right arm. She lay in a coma for some days, followed by a twilight state for several weeks, before finally emerging into consciousness. She then discovered that though her intelligence and powers of language were intact, something extraordinary had happened to her perception of music, and she described this in a letter:

> There is "before" the accident and there is "after" the accident. So many things changed, so many things are different. Some changes are easier to take than others. The most difficult one is the enormous change in my musical abilities and in the perception of music.
>
> I cannot remember all my musical abilities, but I do remember the fluency and easiness, the "no effort" feeling in anything I tried to do musically.
>
> Listening to music was a complex process of quick analysis of form, harmony, melody, key, historical period, instrumentation. . . . Listening was linear and horizontal at the same time. . . . It was all at the tip of my fingers, at the tip of my ears.
>
> And then came the blow to my head that changed everything. Perfect pitch disappeared. I still hear and differentiate pitches, but am no longer able to recognize them with name

and place in the musical space. I do hear, but in a way I hear too much. I absorb everything equally, to a degree that becomes at times a real torture. How does one listen with no filtering system?

Symbolically the first piece I desperately wanted to listen to after I regained enough discernment was Beethoven's opus 131. A four-voice, complicated string quartet that is very emotional and abstract. It is not an easy piece, either to listen to or to analyze. I have no idea how I even remembered that there was such a piece, at a time when I hardly remembered my name.

When the music arrived, I listened to the first solo phrase of the first violin again and again, not really being able to connect its two parts. When I listened to the rest of the movement, I heard four separate voices, four thin, sharp laser beams, beaming to four different directions.

Today, almost eight years after the accident, I still hear the four laser beams equally . . . four intense voices. And when I listen to an orchestra I hear twenty intense laser voices. It is extremely difficult to integrate all these different voices into some entity that makes sense.

In his letter referring her to me, Rachael's physician described her "agonizing experience of hearing all music as discrete, contrapuntal lines, being unable to hold on to the harmonic sense of chordal passages. Thus, where listening was linear, vertical and horizontal at the same time, now it was horizontal only." Her major complaint, when she first came to see me, was of this dysharmonia, her inability to integrate different voices and instruments.

But she had other problems, too. The injury had rendered her deaf in the right ear; she did not realize this at first, but wondered later whether it played a part in her altered perceptions of music. And though she noted the disappearance of absolute pitch right away, she was even more disabled by the undermining of her sense of *relative* pitch, her representation of tonal space. Now she had to rely on literal enaction: "I can remember a pitch only because I remember how it feels to sing it. Just start the process of singing, and there it is."[11]

Rachael found that if she had a score in front of her, it could at least provide a visual and conceptual representation of harmony, though this could not by itself supply the missing perception, "any more than a menu can provide a meal," she said. But it served to "frame" a piece, to prevent the music from "spreading all over the place." Playing the piano, and not just listening, she discovered, would also help to "integrate musical information . . . demands both a tactile and an intellectual understanding . . . contributes to the ability of quickly switching attention between the different musical elements, and thereby helped integrate them into a musical piece." But this "formal integration," as she called it, was still very limited.

There are many levels in the brain at which perceptions of music are integrated and many levels, therefore, at which integration may fail or be compromised. In addition to her difficulties with musical integration, Rachael experienced a similar problem with other sounds, to some extent. Her auditory environment was split sometimes into discrete and unconnected elements: street sounds, domestic sounds, or the sounds of animals, for example,

---

11. This reminded me of John Hull, a man whose book *Touching the Rock* describes how he lost his sight during middle age, and with it his once-vivid visual imagery. He could no longer visualize the numeral 3, unless he traced it in the air with a finger. He had to make use of an enactive or procedural memory in place of the iconic one he had lost.

might suddenly stand out and preempt her attention because they were isolated, not integrated into the normal auditory background or landscape. Neurologists refer to this as simultagnosia, and it is more often visual than auditory.[12] For Rachael, this simultagnosia meant that she had to build up a picture of her auditory environment in a much more conscious and deliberate, item-by-item way than the rest of us do. And yet, paradoxically, this had some advantages, as it forced her to experience previously overlooked sounds with a supernormal attention and intensity.

Playing the piano had been impossible in the months following her injury, when her right hand was still almost paralyzed. But she taught herself, in these months, to use her left hand for writing and all else. Remarkably, she also took up painting at this time, using her left hand. "I never painted before the accident," she told me.

> When I was still wheelchair bound and my right hand was in
> a splint, I taught myself to write with my left hand, to make
> needlepoint works. . . . It was not an option to let injury dic-
> tate my life. I was dying to play, make music. . . . I bought a
> piano and got the shock of my life. Yet the burning creative
> urge did not stop and I turned to painting. . . . I had to open
> the color tubes with my teeth and left hand, and my very
> first painting ever, a 24-by-36-inch canvas, was painted only
> with the left hand.

---

12. Something analogous to a transient simultagnosia may occur with intoxication from cannabis or hallucinogens. One may find oneself in a kaleidoscope of intense sensations, with isolated colors, shapes, smells, sounds, textures, and tastes standing out with startling distinctness, their connections with each other diminished or lost. Anthony Storr, in *Music and the Mind*, describes listening to Mozart after taking mescaline:

> I was conscious of the throbbing, vibrant quality of the sounds which reached me;
> of the bite of bow upon string; of a direct appeal to my emotions. In contrast,
> appreciation of form was greatly impaired. Each time a theme was repeated, it
> came as a surprise. The themes might be individually entrancing, but their rela-
> tion with one another had disappeared.

With time and physical therapy, her right hand became stronger, and Rachael found herself slowly able to play the piano again with both hands. When I visited her a few months after our initial meeting, I found her working on a Beethoven bagatelle, a Mozart sonata, Schumann's *Forest Scenes,* a Bach three-part invention, and Dvořák's *Slavonic Dances for Four Hands* (this last she would play with her piano teacher, whom she visited weekly). Rachael told me that she had experienced a distinct improvement in her powers to integrate the "horizontals" of music. She had recently been to a performance of three short Monteverdi operas. At first, she said, she delighted in the music, experiencing it for the first time since her accident as harmony, as integration. After a few minutes, however, it became difficult: "It was a great cognitive effort to hold the strands together." And then the music burst apart, becoming a chaos of different voices:

> At the beginning I enjoyed it very much, but then I was caught up in a fragmented music environment. . . . It became a challenge, and gradually a torture. . . . And Monteverdi is a good example, because he is so contrapuntally complicated, but at the same time uses a very small orchestra, with no more than three vocal parts at the same time.

I was reminded here of my patient Virgil, who had been virtually blind all his life and then, at the age of fifty, had gained sight following eye surgery.[13] But his new sight was very limited and fragile (in large part because, with very limited early vision, his brain had never developed robust visual cognitive systems). So vision was taxing for him, and when he shaved, for example, he could see and recognize his face in the mirror at first, but after a

---

13. Virgil is described in "To See and Not See," in *An Anthropologist on Mars.*

few minutes, he would have to struggle to hold on to a recognizable visual world. Finally, he would give up and shave by touch,
because the visual image of his face had decomposed into unrec-
ognizable fragments.

Rachael had, in fact, also developed some visual problems
following the accident, peculiar problems of visual synthesis—
though, with typical resourcefulness, she had managed to turn
these to creative use. She had, to some degree, a difficulty in synthesizing the elements of an entire scene at a glance, a visual
simultagnosia analogous to her auditory one. Thus she would
notice one thing, then another, then a third; her attention would
be commandeered successively by different elements, and she
could piece the scene together as a whole only slowly and with
difficulty, in an intellectual rather than a perceptual way. Her
paintings and collages made use of this weakness and, indeed,
turned it into a strength, disassembling the visual world and
reassembling it in new ways.

Though her apartment is now hung with her many paintings
and collages, Rachael has not been able to write music since her
accident in 1993. The chief reason for this is another sort of amusia, a lack of musical imagery. Before the accident, she used to
compose in her head, without a piano, straight onto manuscript
paper. But now, she says, she cannot "hear" what she is writing.
She once had the most vivid musical imagery, and as soon as she
looked at a score—her own or another composer's—she could
hear the music in her mind with full orchestral or choral complexity. This musical imagery has been virtually extinguished by
her injury, and that makes it difficult for her to transcribe what
she has just improvised, for as soon as she reaches for her manuscript paper, in the seconds it takes her to put pen in hand, the
music she has just played evaporates from her mind. With the
difficulty in imagery comes a difficulty in working memory, and

this makes it impossible for her to retain what she has just composed. "This is the major loss," she told me. "I need a mediator between me and the printed page." A crucial breakthrough thus came for her in 2006, when she found a young collaborator and learned with him to use a music-processing computer. The computer can hold in its memory what she cannot hold in her own, and Rachael can now explore the themes that she has created on the piano and transform them into notation or into the voices of different instruments. She can achieve a continuity with her own compositions, and orchestrate or develop them, with the help of her collaborator and her computer.

Rachael has now embarked on her first large-scale composition since her accident thirteen years ago. She has decided to take a string quartet, one of the last works she wrote before her accident, to disassemble it and reassemble it in a new way—as she says, to "cut it into the wind, collect the parts, and put it together in a new form." She wants to incorporate the ambient sounds which she is now so conscious of, "to weave sounds together that are not meant to be musical," to compose a new sort of music. Against the background of this, she herself will improvise by breathing, singing, and playing a variety of instruments (her worktable, when I visited her, contained an alto recorder, a Chinese jade flute, a Syrian flute, plumber's brass tubing, bells and drums, and an assortment of wooden rhythm instruments). The sound, the music, will be interwoven with projections of visual forms and patterns provided by photographs she has taken.

She played for me, on her computer, a small sample of the finished piece, which starts with "Breathing . . . a darkness." Though she agrees with Stravinsky that music does not represent anything but itself, when she composed this opening, her mind was full of the idea of coma and near death, a time when, for days, the sound of her own breathing, amplified by a respirator, was almost the only sound she heard. This opening passage is followed by "incoherent fragments, a shattered world," as she puts it, representing her own broken awareness at a time when "nothing made sense." There are agitated, strongly rhythmic pizzicatos at this point, and unexpected sounds of all sorts. Then comes a strongly melodic passage, her recomposing a world, and finally darkness and breathing again—but "a free breathing," she says, representing "reconciliation, acceptance."

Rachael thinks of this new piece, to some extent, as autobiographic, a "rediscovery of identity." And when it is performed next month, it will be her coming out, her first return to the world of musical composition and performance, the public world, in thirteen years.

9

Papa Blows His Nose in G:
Absolute Pitch

People with absolute pitch can immediately, unthinkingly tell the pitch of any note, without either reflection or comparison with an external standard. They can do this not only with any note they hear, but with any note they imagine or hear in their heads. Indeed, Gordon B., a professional violinist who wrote to me about tinnitus, or ringing in his ears, remarked matter-of-factly that his tinnitus was "a high F-natural." He did not realize, I think, that saying this was in any way unusual; but of the millions of people with tinnitus, probably not one in ten thousand could say what pitch their tinnitus has.

The precision of absolute pitch varies, but it is estimated that most people with it can identify upwards of seventy tones in the middle region of the auditory range, and each of these seventy tones has, for them, a unique and characteristic quality that distinguishes it absolutely from any other note.

The Oxford Companion to Music was a sort of *Arabian Nights* for me as a boy, an inexhaustible source of musical stories, and it

gives many charming examples of absolute pitch. Sir Frederick
Ouseley, a former professor of music at Oxford, for example,
"was all his life remarkable for his sense of absolute pitch. At
five he was able to remark, 'Only think, Papa blows his nose in
G.' He would say that it thundered in G or that the wind was
whistling in D, or that the clock (with a two-note chime) struck
in B minor, and when the assertion was tested it would invariably be found correct." For most of us, such an ability to recognize an exact pitch seems uncanny, almost like another sense, a
sense we can never hope to possess, such as infrared or X-ray
vision; but for those who are born with absolute pitch, it seems
perfectly normal.

The Finnish entomologist Olavi Sotavalta, an expert on the
sounds of insects in flight, was greatly assisted in his studies by
having absolute pitch—for the sound pitch of an insect in flight
is produced by the frequency of its wingbeats. Not content with
musical notation, Sotavalta was able to estimate very exact frequencies by ear. The sound pitch made by the moth *Plusia
gamma* approximates a low F-sharp, but Sotavalta could estimate it more precisely as having a frequency of 46 cycles per second. Such an ability, of course, requires not only a remarkable
ear, but a knowledge of the scales and frequencies with which
pitch can be correlated.

Yet such a correlation, though immensely impressive, deflects
attention from the real wonder of absolute pitch: to those with
absolute pitch, every tone, every key seems qualitatively different, each possessing its own "flavor" or "feel," its own character.
Those who have absolute pitch often compare it to color—they
"hear" G-sharpness as instantly and automatically as we "see"
blue. (Indeed, the word "chroma" is sometimes used in musical
theory.)

While absolute pitch may sound like a delicious extra sense, allowing one to instantly sing or notate any music at its correct pitch, it may cause problems, too. One such problem occurs with the inconstant tuning of musical instruments. Thus the seven-year-old Mozart, comparing his own little violin to that of his friend Schactner, said, "If you have not altered the tuning of your violin since I last played on it, it is half a quarter of a tone flatter than mine here." (So it is related in *The Oxford Companion to Music*; there are many tales about Mozart's ear, some no doubt apocryphal.) When the composer Michael Torke encountered my own ancient piano, which—still having its original nineteenth-century strings—is not tuned up to the 440 cycles per second standard of modern pianos, he instantly remarked that it was a third of a tone flat. Such an overall sharpness or flatness would not be noticed by someone without absolute pitch, but it can be distressing and even disabling to those who do have it. *The Oxford Companion to Music* again gives many examples, including one of an eminent pianist who, playing the *Moonlight* Sonata (a piece which "every schoolgirl plays"), got through it only "with the greatest difficulty" because the piano was tuned to a pitch he was not accustomed to, and he "experienced the distress of playing the piece in one key and hearing it in another."

When people with absolute pitch "hear a familiar piece of music played in the wrong key," Daniel Levitin and Susan Rogers write, "they often become agitated or disturbed. . . . To get a sense of what it is like, imagine going to the produce market and finding that, because of a temporary disorder of visual processing, the bananas all appear orange, the lettuce yellow and the apples purple."

Transposing music from one key to another, though effortless for some musicians, can be difficult for others. But it can be especially challenging for those with absolute pitch, for whom each key has its own unique character, and the key in which one has always heard a piece is likely to be felt as the only right one. Transposing a piece of music, for someone with absolute pitch, can be analogous to painting a picture with all the wrong colors.[1]

Another difficulty was mentioned to me by the neurologist and musician Steven Frucht, who himself has absolute pitch. He sometimes experiences a certain difficulty in hearing intervals or harmonies because he is so conscious of the chroma of the notes that compose them. If, for example, one plays a C on the piano and the F-sharp above this, he might be so conscious of the C-ness of the C and the F-sharpness of the F-sharp that he fails to notice that they form a tritone, a dissonance which makes most people wince.[2]

Absolute pitch is not necessarily of much importance even to musicians—Mozart had it, but Wagner and Schumann lacked it. But for anyone who has it, the loss of absolute pitch may be felt as a severe privation. This sense of loss was clearly brought out by one of my patients, Frank V., a composer who suffered brain damage from the rupture of an aneurysm of the anterior communicat-

---

1. For Mozart, then, a piece written in a specific key would have its own unique character, and the piece would scarcely be the same work if transposed to another key. And as one correspondent, Steve Salemson, asks:

What about the fact that the A=440 of today's orchestras is approximately a half-tone higher than the A of Mozart's orchestra? Does that mean that Mozart's Symphony No. 40, in G-minor, is nowadays heard in what would have been to Mozart G-sharp minor?

2. The tritone—an augmented fourth (or, in jazz parlance, a flatted fifth)—is a difficult interval to sing and has often been regarded as having an ugly, uncanny, or even diabolical quality. Its use was forbidden in early ecclesiastical music, and early theorists called it *diabolus in musica* ("the devil in music"). But Tartini used it, for this very reason, in his *Devil's Trill* Sonata for violin. (And, as Steve Salemson reminds me, "Leonard Bernstein used the 'devil in music' most effectively and repeatedly in his song "Maria" from *West Side Story*.")

Though the raw tritone sounds so harsh, it is easily filled out with another tritone to form a diminished seventh chord. And this, the *Oxford Companion to Music* notes, "has a luscious effect. . . . The chord is indeed the most Protean in all harmony. In England the nickname has been given it of 'The Clapham Junction of Harmony'—from a railway station in London where so many lines join that once arrived there one can take a train for almost anywhere else."

ing artery. Frank was highly gifted musically, and had been musically trained since the age of four. He had had absolute pitch as long as he could recall, but now, he said, "it is gone, or it has certainly been eroded." Since absolute pitch was of advantage to him as a musician, he felt its "erosion" keenly. Originally, he said, he perceived pitches instantly, absolutely, as he perceived colors—no "mental process" was involved, no inference, no reference to other pitches or intervals or scales. This form of absolute pitch had vanished completely; it was, he said, as if he had become "colorblind" in this regard. But as he convalesced from his brain injury, he found that he still possessed reliable pitch memories of certain pieces and certain instruments, and he could use these reference points to infer other pitches—though this, in comparison to his "instant" absolute pitch, was a slower process.

It was also, subjectively, entirely different, for previously every note and every key had had a distinctive flavor for him, a character uniquely its own. Now all of this was gone, and there was no longer any real difference, for him, between one key and another.[3]

---

3. Absolute pitch can shift with age, and this has often been a problem for older musicians. Marc Damashek, a piano tuner, wrote to me about such a problem:

When I was four, my older sister discovered that I had perfect pitch—could instantly identify any note across the keyboard without looking. . . . I've been surprised (and disturbed) to find that my perceived piano pitch has shifted upwards by perhaps 150 cents [a semitone and a half]. . . . Now when I hear a recorded piece or a live performance, my best guess at what note is being played is consistently, absurdly high.

Damashek relates that he cannot easily compensate for this because "I'm always so firmly convinced that the note I'm hearing is the one that I've always called by its correct name: it still sounds like an F, damn it, but it's an E-flat!"

In general, as Patrick Baron, a musician and piano tuner, has written to me, "older piano tuners tend to tune the highest treble octaves quite sharp, and the last three or four notes incredibly sharp (sometimes more than a semitone). . . . Perhaps there is some sort of atrophy of the basilar membrane or a stiffening of the hair cells which causes this, rather than a template shift."

Other conditions may cause a temporary or permanent shift of absolute pitch, including strokes, head injuries, and brain infections. One correspondent told me that his absolute pitch shifted a semitone during an attack of multiple sclerosis and remained slightly off thereafter.

. . .

IT SEEMS CURIOUS, in a way, that absolute pitch is so rare (it is estimated as occurring in less than one person in ten thousand). Why don't all of us hear "G-sharpness" as automatically as we see blue or smell a rose? "The real question concerning absolute pitch," wrote Diana Deutsch et al. in 2004, ". . . is not why some people possess it, but rather why it is not universal. It is as though most people have a syndrome with respect to the labeling of pitches which is like color anomia, in which the patient can recognize colors, and discriminate between them, but cannot associate them with verbal labels."

Deutsch speaks here from personal experience as well. As she wrote to me in a recent letter:

> My realization that I had absolute pitch—and that this was unusual—came in the form of a great surprise when I discovered, at age 4, that other people had difficulty naming notes out of context. I still remember vividly my shock at discovering that when I played a note on the piano, others had to see what key was being struck in order to name it. . . .
>
> To give you a sense of how strange a lack of absolute pitch appears to those of us who have it, take color naming as an analogy. Suppose you showed someone a red object and asked him to name the color. And suppose he answered, "I can recognize the color, and I can discriminate it from other colors, but I just can't name it." Then you juxtaposed a blue object and named its color, and he responded, "OK, since the second color is blue, the first one must be red." I believe that most people would find this process rather bizarre. Yet from the perspective of someone with absolute pitch this is precisely how most people name pitches—they evaluate the

relationship between the pitch to be named and another pitch whose name they already know. . . . When I hear a musical note and identify its pitch, much more happens than simply placing its pitch on a point (or in a region) along a continuum. Suppose I hear an F-sharp sounded on the piano. I obtain a strong sense of familiarity for "F-sharpness"—like the sense one gets when one recognizes a familiar face. The pitch is bundled in with other attributes of the note—its timbre (very importantly), its loudness, and so on. I believe that, at least for some people with absolute pitch, notes are perceived and remembered in a way that is far more concrete than for those who do not possess this faculty.

Absolute pitch is of special interest because it exemplifies a whole other realm of perception, of qualia, something which most of us cannot even begin to imagine; because it is an isolated ability with little inherent connection to musicality or anything else; and because it shows how genes and experience can interact in its production.

It has long been clear anecdotally that absolute pitch is commoner in musicians than in the general public, and this has been confirmed by large-scale studies. Among musicians, absolute pitch is commoner in those who have had musical training from an early age. But the correlation does not always hold: many gifted musicians fail to develop absolute pitch, despite intensive early training. It is commoner in certain families—but is this because of a genetic component or because some families provide a richer musical environment? There is a striking association of absolute pitch with early blindness (some studies estimate that about 50 percent of children born blind or blinded in infancy have absolute pitch).

One of the most intriguing correlations occurs between

absolute pitch and linguistic background. For the past few years, Diana Deutsch and her colleagues have studied such correlations in greater detail, and they observed in a 2006 paper that "native speakers of Vietnamese and Mandarin show very precise absolute pitch in reading lists of words"; most of these subjects showed variation of a quarter tone or less. Deutsch et al. have also showed very dramatic differences in the incidence of absolute pitch in two populations of first-year music students: one at the Eastman School of Music in Rochester, New York, and the other at the Central Conservatory of Music in Beijing. "For students who had begun musical training between ages 4 and 5," they wrote, "approximately 60% of the Chinese students met the criterion for absolute pitch, while only about 14% of the US nontone language speakers met the criterion." For those who had begun musical training at age six or seven, the numbers in both groups were correspondingly lower, about 55 percent and 6 percent. And for students who had begun musical training later still, at age eight or nine, "roughly 42% of the Chinese students met the criterion while none of the US nontone language speakers did so." There were no differences between genders in either group.

This striking discrepancy led Deutsch et al. to conjecture that "if given the opportunity, infants can acquire AP as a feature of speech, which can then carry over to music." For speakers of a nontonal language such as English, they felt, "the acquisition of AP during music training is analogous to learning the tones of a second language." They observed that there was a critical period for the development of absolute pitch, before the age of eight or so—roughly the same age at which children find it much more difficult to learn the phonemes of another language (and thus to speak a second language with a native accent). Deutsch et al. suggested, therefore, that all infants might have the potential for acquiring absolute pitch, which could perhaps be "realized by enabling infants to associate pitches with verbal labels during the critical period" for language acquisition. (They did not exclude the possibility, nonetheless, that genetic differences might be important, too.)

The neural correlates of absolute pitch have been illuminated by comparing the brains of musicians with and without absolute pitch using a refined form of structural brain imaging (MRI morphometry), and by functional imaging of the brain as subjects identify musical tones and intervals. A 1995 paper by Gottfried Schlaug and his colleagues showed that in musicians with absolute pitch (but not musicians without), there was an exaggerated asymmetry between the volumes of the right and left planum temporale, structures in the brain that are important for the perception of speech and music. Similar asymmetries in the size and activity of the planum temporale have been shown in other people with absolute pitch.[4]

Absolute pitch is not just a matter of pitch perception. People with absolute pitch must be able not only to perceive precise pitch differences, but to label them, to line them up with the notes or names of a musical scale. It is this ability which Frank V. lost with the frontal lobe damage caused by the rupture of his cerebral aneurysm. The additional cerebral mechanisms required to correlate pitch and label are in the frontal lobes, and this, too, can be seen in functional MRI studies; thus, if someone with absolute pitch is asked to name tones or intervals, MRIs will show focal activation in certain associative areas of the frontal cortex. In those with relative pitch, this region is activated only when naming intervals.

---

4. Such asymmetries are not seen, interestingly, in blind subjects with absolute pitch, where there may be radical reorganizations of the brain, with parts of the visual cortex being recruited for the detection of pitch, as well as a variety of other auditory and tactile perceptions.

While such categorical labeling is learned by all people with absolute pitch, it is not clear that this excludes a prior *categorical* perception of pitch that is not dependent on association and learning. And the insistence of many with absolute pitch on the unique perceptual qualities of every pitch—its "color" or "chroma"—suggests that before the learning of categorical labels, there may be a purely perceptual categorization.

Jenny Saffran and Gregory Griepentrog at the University of Wisconsin compared eight-month-old infants to adults with and without musical training in a learning test of tone sequences. The infants, they found, relied much more heavily on absolute pitch cues; the adults, on relative pitch cues. This suggested to them that absolute pitch may be universal and highly adaptive in infancy but becomes maladaptive later and is therefore lost. "Infants limited to grouping melodies by perfect pitches," they pointed out, "would never discover that the songs they hear are the same when sung in different keys or that words spoken at different fundamental frequencies are the same." In particular, they argued, the development of language necessitates the inhibition of absolute pitch, and only unusual conditions enable it to be retained. (The acquisition of a tonal language may be one of the "unusual conditions" that lead to the retention and perhaps heightening of absolute pitch.)

Deutsch and her colleagues, in their 2006 paper, suggested that their work not only has "implications for the issues of modularity in the processing of speech and music . . . [but] of the evolutionary origin" of both. In particular, they see absolute pitch, whatever its subsequent vicissitudes, as having been crucial to the origins of both speech and music. In his book *The Singing Neanderthals: The Origins of Music, Language, Mind and Body*, Steven Mithen takes this idea further, suggesting that music and language have a common origin, and that a sort of combined

protomusic-cum-protolanguage was characteristic of the Nean-
derthal mind.[5] This sort of singing language of meanings, without individual words as we understand them, he calls Hmmm
(for holistic-mimetic-musical-multimodal)—and it depended,
he speculates, on a conglomeration of isolated skills, including
mimetic abilities and absolute pitch.

With the development of "a compositional language and syn-
tactic rules," Mithen writes, "allowing an infinite number of
things to be said, in contrast to the limited number of phrases that
Hmmm allowed . . . the brains of infants and children would have
developed in a new fashion, one consequence of which would have
been the loss of perfect pitch in the majority of individuals, and a
diminution of musical abilities." We have little evidence as yet for
this audacious hypothesis, but it is a tantalizing one.

I was once told of an isolated valley somewhere in the Pacific
where all the inhabitants have absolute pitch. I like to imagine
that such a place is populated by an ancient tribe that has
remained in the state of Mithen's Neanderthals, with a host of
exquisite mimetic abilities and communicating in a protolanguage
as musical as it is lexical. But I suspect that the Valley of Absolute
Pitch does not exist, except as a lovely, Edenic metaphor, or perhaps some sort of collective memory of a more musical past.

---

5. Though intriguingly elaborated by Mithen, this idea is not new. Jean-Jacques Rousseau
(who was a composer as well as a philosopher) suggested in his "Essai sur l'Origine des
Langues" that in primitive society, speech and song were not distinct from each other. For
Rousseau, primitive languages were "melodic and poetic rather than practical or prosaic,"
as Maurice Cranston wrote, and were not so much uttered as chanted or sung.

A somewhat different thought was expressed by Proust in *Remembrance of Things
Past*. Swann, sitting in a musical salon, is transported by a musical phrase and, irritated
by the "insignificant chatter around him," wonders

whether music might not be the unique example of what might have been—if the
invention of language, the formation of words, the analysis of ideas had not
intervened—the means of communication between souls. It is like a possibility
that has come to nothing; humanity has developed along other lines.

10

Pitch Imperfect:
Cochlear Amusia

Untune that string
And hark, what discord follows!

—SHAKESPEARE, *Troilus and Cressida*

Darwin saw the eye as a miracle of evolution; the ear, in its way, is just as complex and beautiful. The path taken by sound vibrations, from their entrance into the external ear canals, through the eardrums on either side to the tiny bones, the ossicles, of the middle ear, to the snail-shaped cochlea, was first worked out in the seventeenth century. It was suggested then that sounds were transmitted by the ear, becoming amplified in the cochlea "as in a musical instrument." A century later, it was discovered that the tapered shape of the cochlear spiral was differentially tuned to the range of audible frequencies, receptive to high sounds at its base, low sounds at its apex. By 1700 it was realized that the cochlea was filled with fluid and lined with a membrane that was conceived as a series of vibrating strings, a resonator. In 1851, Alfonso Corti, an Italian physiologist, discovered the complex sensory structure that we now call the organ of Corti, lying on the basilar membrane of the cochlea and containing about thirty-five hundred inner hair cells, the ultimate auditory receptors. A youthful ear can hear ten octaves of sound, spanning a range from about thirty to twelve thousand vibrations a second. The average ear can distinguish sounds a seventeenth of a tone apart. From top to bottom, we hear about fourteen hundred discriminable tones.

Unlike the eye, the organ of Corti is well protected from accidental injury; it is lodged deep in the head, encased in the petrous bone, the densest in the body, and floats in fluid to absorb accidental vibrations. But protected as it is from gross injuries, the organ of Corti, with its delicate hair cells, is highly vulnerable in other ways—vulnerable, as a start, to loud noise (every ambulance siren or garbage truck exacts a cost, to say nothing of airplanes, rock concerts, blaring iPods, and the like). The hair cells are vulnerable, too, to the effects of age and hereditary cochlear deafness.[1]

Jacob L., a distinguished composer in his late sixties, came to consult me in 2003. His problems had started, he said, about three months earlier. "I hadn't been playing or composing much for a month," he said, "and then I suddenly noticed the upper register of the piano I was playing was grossly out of tune. Terribly sharp . . . detuned." In particular, these notes were sharpened, subjectively, by a quarter of a tone or so for the first octave and a semitone or so for the next octave up. When Jacob

---

1. Such problems can be expected to increase exponentially for people who play iPods or other music at too-loud levels. It is said that more than fifteen percent of young people now have significant hearing impairments. Listening to music in an already-noisy environment, using it to drown out other noise, almost guarantees that it will be destroying hair cells.

complained of this, his host, the owner of the piano, was surprised, and said that his piano had just been tuned and that everyone else had found it fine. Puzzled, Jacob returned home and
tested his hearing on his electronic synthesizer, which is always
exactly in tune. To his dismay, he found the same sharpening in
the upper octaves here.

He arranged to visit the audiologist he had been seeing for
the last six or seven years (because of a hearing loss in the
upper ranges). The audiologist was struck, as Jacob himself had
been, by the correspondence between his hearing loss and his
hearing distortion, both starting at around 2,000 hertz (nearly
three octaves above middle C), and the fact that his left ear sharpened sound more than his right (the difference was almost a
major third at the top of the piano keyboard). This sharpening,
Jacob said, was "not strictly linear." One note might be scarcely
sharpened, while notes on either side of it would be markedly
sharpened—and there were also variations from day to day.
There was, in addition, one strange anomaly: the E-natural ten
notes above middle C, not in the hearing-impaired range, was
flattened by almost a quarter tone, but no such flattening
occurred with the notes to either side.

While there was a certain consistency, a certain logic in the
sharpening of notes in the affected range, Jacob was very
struck by the isolated flattening of the E. "It shows how sharply
tuned the organ of Corti is," he said. "A few hair cells out,
the hair cells on either side in good shape, and you get one flattened note in the midst of normality—like one bad string on a
piano."

He was also conscious of what he called "contextual correction," an odd phenomenon that made him wonder whether his
problem was, in fact, located in his brain rather than his ears. If,
say, there was only a flute or piccolo above a bass, it sounded

strikingly out of tune, but when there was orchestral richness, a continuum of tones and pitches, the distortion was scarcely noticeable. Why, if it was only a question of a few hair cells, should this correction occur? Was there something happening with him neurologically, too?

These distortions were very distressing to Jacob—and disabling. He found it problematic, under the circumstances, to conduct his own music, for he would think some of the instruments were out of tune or that the players were hitting the wrong notes when they were not. It was not as easy, either, to compose, which he tended to do at his piano. I suggested, half seriously, that he get his piano or synthesizer mistuned to exactly the degree needed to counterbalance his perceptual distortions—this way it would sound normal to him, even if it sounded out of tune to everybody else. (Neither of us was quite certain of the logic of this, whether it would help him to compose or only exacerbate the problem.) I also wondered if his hearing aids could be purposely mistuned—but he had already discussed this with his audiologist, who felt that the erratic and unpredictable character of his distortions would make any such effort impossible.

While Jacob had managed very well when he had experienced only high-end hearing loss—stronger hearing aids had compensated for this—he had become worried when the distortions began, fearing that they might put an end to his conducting, to say nothing of undermining the pleasure of simply listening to music. But in the three months since the distortions had started, he had made some accommodations—for instance, he would work out high passages on the keyboard below the distorting range, then notate the music in the correct range. This allowed him to continue composing effectively.

He could do this because his musical imagery and memory

were intact. He knew how music—his own music and others'—
should sound. It was only his *perception* of music that was
distorted.[2] It was Jacob's ears, and not his brain, that had suffered
damage. But what exactly was happening in Jacob's brain?

People have compared the cochlea, the spiral organ, to a
stringed instrument, differentially tuned to the frequency of
notes; but such metaphors need to be extended to the brain as
well, for it is here that the cochlea's output, all eight or ten
octaves of audible sound, are mapped tonotopically onto the auditory cortex. Cortical mappings are dynamic, and can change as
circumstances alter. Many of us have experienced this, getting a
new pair of glasses or a new hearing aid. At first the new glasses
or hearing aids seem intolerable, distorting—but within days or
hours, our brain adapts to them, and we can make full use of our
now optically or acoustically improved senses. It is similar with
the brain's mapping of the body image, which adapts quite rapidly
if there are changes in the sensory input or the use of the body.
Thus if a finger, for example, is immobilized or lost, its cortical
representation will become smaller or disappear entirely, the representations of other parts of the hand expanding to fill its place.
If, conversely, the finger is used a great deal, its cortical representation will enlarge, as happens with the Braille-reading index finger in a blind person, or the fingers of a string player's left hand.

One might expect something similar to happen with the mapping of tones from a damaged cochlea. If high-frequency notes
are no longer clearly transmitted, their cortical representations

2. In this way, he differed radically from Mr. I., the painter who became totally unable to
see color because of damage to the color-constructing areas of his visual cortex. Mr. I.
became not only unable to perceive colors, but unable to imagine or see them in his
mind's eye. Had Mr. I.'s damage been to the color-sensitive cells in his retina, rather than
to the visual areas of his brain, he would still have been able to imagine and remember
color. Mr. I.'s story, "The Case of the Colorblind Painter," was published in *An Anthropologist on Mars.*

shrink, become narrow and compressed. But such changes are not fixed or static, and a rich and varied tonal input can serve to reexpand the representations, at least while the stimulus lasts, as Jacob had found out for himself.[3] And when we pay attention to or focus on a sound, this too temporarily enlarges its cortical representation, and it becomes sharper and clearer, at least for a second or two. Could such a concentration or focus allow Jacob to correct his misperception of tones? He thought about this, and said yes: when he was aware of distortions, he could indeed sometimes diminish them by an effort of will—the danger, he said, was that he might be unaware of them. He compared this sort of voluntary alteration to the way in which one might "will" oneself to see a particular aspect of a visual illusion, such as the face-vase illusion.

Was this explicable wholly in terms of the dynamic mapping of tones in the cortex and the ability to enlarge or shift these in relation to circumstances? Jacob felt his perception changing as he pulled a note in and as it escaped him once again. Could he actually be retuning his cochlea, if only for a second or two?

What might seem a preposterous notion has gained support

---

3. The power of context is equally clear in the visual sphere. The retina, like the cochlea, is mapped systematically on the cerebral cortex, and damage to it (or edema beneath it) can cause strange distortions of vision, sometimes a warping of horizontal and vertical lines, as if one is looking through a fish-eye lens. These distortions may be very noticeable if one glances at individual objects: a rectangular picture frame may appear both curved and trapezoidal, or a cup or saucer bizarrely deformed. But these distortions diminish or disappear if one looks at a landscape or a rich visual scene—for context helps the cortex normalize its retinal mappings.

In such a situation, some rectification may also be possible using other senses. A straight-edged windowsill, for example, may *look* wavy due to retinal deformation, but if one draws a finger slowly across the windowsill, the visual distortions disappear when the finger tells the brain that the edge is straight—but the distortions will then reappear behind the finger once it has passed. Visual concentration alone is much less effective. Seeing a triangle bulge in a non-Euclidean way, as if inscribed on a curved surface, one cannot force it, using knowledge or willpower, to reassume its proper shape. Bits of retinal image, it seems, cannot be retuned as easily as pitch distortions from a damaged cochlea.

from recent work demonstrating that there are massive efferent connections (the olivocochlear bundles) going from the brain to the cochlea and thence to the outer hair cells. The outer hair cells serve, among other things, to calibrate or "tune" the inner hair cells, and they have an exclusively efferent nerve supply; they do not transmit nerve impulses *to* the brain, they get orders *from* the brain. Thus one has to see the brain and ear as forming a single functional system, a two-way system, with the ability not only to modify the representation of sounds in the cortex but to modulate the output of the cochlea itself. The power of attention—to pick out a tiny but significant sound in our environment, to home in on a single soft voice in the ambient din of a crowded restaurant—is very remarkable and seems to depend on this ability to modulate cochlear function, as well as on purely cerebral mechanisms.

The ability of the mind and brain to exercise efferent control over the cochlea can be heightened by training and musical activities, and is (as Christophe Micheyl et al. have shown) particularly powerful in musicians. In Jacob's case, of course, this ability is constantly in training, as he has to confront and control his pitch distortions every day.

Discovering that he had at least some voluntary control made Jacob feel less helpless, less the victim of an inexorable deterioration, and more hopeful. Could he hope for a longer-lasting improvement? Could his musician's brain, with its vivid and accurate memory of pitch, its exact and detailed knowledge of how things should sound—could this musical brain not compensate for and transcend the aberrations of a damaged cochlea?

But a year later, he reported that his distortions were "worse, more erratic . . . some notes have a greater pitch shift, sometimes as much as a minor third or more." He said that if he played a note repeatedly it might shift its pitch, but if it began off pitch, he could sometimes "pull it in," at least for a while. He used the term "audio illusion" for the two notes, the "true" and the "phantom," or distorted, one, and spoke of how they might interweave and alternate with each other like a moiré pattern or the two aspects of an ambiguous figure. This shifting or alternation was much more obvious now that the tonal disparities had increased from a quarter tone to a full tone or more. The range of distortion, too, was "creeping down." "The two highest octaves," he said, "are more and more useless to me."

Jacob's cochlear function, it was clear, was still deteriorating, but he continued to play and compose in a lower register. "You work with the ears you have," he said wryly, "not the ears you want." Though Jacob was an affable man, it was nonetheless evident that the last year had been a difficult one. He had trouble rehearsing his own compositions, which he could not hear in reality as clearly as he heard them in his mind's ear. He could not listen to music in the higher ranges and experience it without distortions, though he could still enjoy Bach cello suites, for instance, which stay in a lower register. Overall, he was finding that "music doesn't sound as delicious as it used to" and lacked the "glorious, spacious resonance" it once had. Jacob's father, also a musician, had become very deaf as he grew older. Would Jacob, finally, like Beethoven, be unable to hear any music at all, except in his own mind?

ONE OF JACOB'S CONCERNS, on his first visit to me, was that he had never met or heard of anyone else with a condition like this. Nor, apparently, had any of the otologists or audiologists he had consulted. Surely, he thought, he could not be "unique." This set us both thinking, wondering whether, in fact, pitch distortions might be relatively common in people with advancing hearing loss.[4]

Such changes might go unnoticed by a nonmusician; and professional musicians might be loath to admit, publicly at least, that their hearing was "off." In early 2004, Jacob sent me a clipping from the *New York Times* ("The Shushing of the Symphony," by James Oestereich), detailing the hearing problems in musicians caused by the ever-increasing decibel level of the modern orchestra. He highlighted an excerpt of this that had leapt off the page:

> The problem of hearing loss, stemming both from the player's own instrument and from those of others, is a real one among classical musicians worldwide. Hearing loss may manifest itself as a decreased ability to perceive high frequencies or slight changes in pitch. . . . But as pervasive as hearing loss may be, it's rarely discussed. Performers are reluctant to mention it, or any other work-related ailment, for fear of losing their standing in the field of their employability.

---

4. A few months later I was to learn that such distortions could arise in a *temporary* fashion and were not uncommon. My friend Patrick Baron, the piano tuner, told me that once he had experienced temporary deafness, more severe on one side than the other, after being exposed to a very loud noise. He found it

> difficult, if not impossible, to tune the two highest C-sharps on the piano. They seemed to have no center to the pitch. . . . There seemed to be a hole in my hearing apparatus at that particular pitch (family of pitches: i.e., two frequencies an octave apart). It was at least six months and maybe as much as a year during which I was forced to rely on an electronic tuning device specifically for those two C-sharps. There were times when my inability seemed to drift to adjacent notes— ballooning, as it were, to include a larger area of two or three half steps, but generally it was just the C-sharps.

Baron's experience seems to indicate that there may be very focal detunings of hair cells, or short stretches of the organ of Corti, which may come and go in a few weeks or months.

"So there it is," Jacob concluded, "a confirmation of both pitch distortion as an adjunct symptom to the hearing loss, and of our suspicion that the malady is usually a guarded secret. . . . I will, of course, continue accepting and accommodating just as I have for many months . . . but it's of considerable intellectual and psychological comfort to learn . . . that, as far as this particular malady is concerned, I'm indeed part of a large club after all."

I was moved by Jacob's philosophical attitude, his acceptance of the increasing loss of a power so crucial to his life and his art. I was intrigued, too, by his ability sometimes to rectify the pitches he heard, briefly, by attention or will, by a rich musical context, and, in more general terms, by musical *activity*. With these he could fight against the distortions, using the brain's power and plasticity to compensate for his damaged cochleas—up to a certain point. But I was greatly surprised when, three years after his initial visit, Jacob sent me the following letter:

> I want to share some wonderful news which I haven't disclosed to you sooner because I wanted to make sure it was really happening and wasn't a chimera or something temporary that would soon reverse itself. My condition has significantly improved, to the point where on some days it is close to normal! Let me be more specific.
>
> I was hired a few months ago to write a score for a large string orchestra and several solo instruments, which largely called for semi-dissonant twelve-tone techniques and the use of the full orchestral range. . . . In short, the most difficult kind of music for me to compose with my cochlear amusia. But I just plunged ahead . . . I even capably conducted the recording sessions, with my longtime music producer in the

recording booth checking for pitch problems, wrong notes, making sure the balance was correct, etc. During the sessions I did have the expected problems accurately hearing some of the high passages, but when they sounded "funny" I knew that my producer was hearing them correctly and checking everything. . . . Anyway, the score came out wonderfully.

To my disbelief, in the weeks immediately following all this, I started to notice, as I worked at the piano or synthesizer, that my amusia was ameliorating. Not consistently—some days it was worse again, some days better—some tonal areas better than others, then a different set of anomalies the next day, or even next moment!—but generally improving. Sometimes I would check it first thing in the morning, and it was almost normal at first, but within a few seconds it would jump back to the aberrant norm. But then I would try to "correct" it with an effort of will and/or by playing the same note an octave or two lower to help pull it back in to accuracy, and I found I could do this more and more often. This nonlinear but generally improving process has continued now for almost two months.

This improvement seemed to start happening right after I was composing, producing, conducting, and trying to hear—both in my inner and outer ears—harmonically and texturally complex music with an extremely wide tonal range. Perhaps it was like doing extensive musico-neurological calisthenics, and I was gradually strengthening whatever mechanism of will exists in the old gray matter that can be focused on this problem. . . . It may be worth mentioning that during these last four or five months I've been very busy with other musical projects as well. . . . I first started noticing the distortions after and during a period of relatively little compositional activity; and now they have abated after a period of very intense and varied compositional activity.[5]

Jacob, of course, is overjoyed at this change, which promises to reopen a once-closing door, expanding his musical life and his enjoyment of music to the full again. And I, as a neurologist, am filled with wonder that the retuning in his musician's brain has been able to counterbalance the patchy and inconstant output from his aging cochleas, that through intensive musical activity, attention, and will, Jacob's brain has literally reshaped itself.[6]

---

5. What Jacob discovered in himself has similarities to a phenomenon reported in experimental animals by Arnaud Noreña and Jos Eggermont in 2005. They found that cats exposed to "noise trauma" and then raised for a few weeks in a quiet environment developed not only hearing loss but distorted tonotopic maps in the primary auditory cortex. (They would have complained of pitch distortion, were they able to.) If, however, the cats were exposed to an enriched acoustic environment for several weeks following exposure to noise trauma, their hearing loss was less severe, and distortions in their auditory cortical mapping did not occur.

6. After the original publication of Jacob's story, I received a letter from a violinist who, like Jacob, experienced advancing pitch distortion in both ears. In addition, he had diplacusis, an intolerable clashing of auditory input as each ear perceived a different pitch—the auditory equivalent of double vision. (Given the discrepancy between his two ears, it is rather surprising that Jacob did not, apparently, experience this particular symptom.) As the violinist's problem grew worse, playing became more and more difficult and listening to music more and more excruciating. But then, like Jacob, he started to have a spontaneous resolution of his problems:

It must be ten or perhaps twelve years ago when I first noticed that something had gone seriously awry. I have played chamber or chamber orchestral music, especially string quartets, for most of my life. I had been in the habit of tuning by holding the A tuning fork to my left ear. One day, for no particular reason, I held it to the right ear also, with a rather daunting result: left A, right B-flat. For a while the brain seemed to cope (interestingly) but eventually tuning became a real problem. . . .

I had assumed that, sadly, my afflication was irreversible . . . however, for some time now I have (incredulously) observed a progressive reversal. I can hear straightforward diatonic music—Mozart, Beethoven orchestral works and even chamber music—quite comfortably in tune, though transitions even there are still confusing. I can almost sing along in tune and have even dared to join some long-suffering friends in (not too demanding) chamber music. Most convincing of all, both ears now hear the tuning fork at the same pitch. Admittedly, there is still much room for improvement, but you will understand what a boost to morale this has been.

II

In Living Stereo:
Why We Have Two Ears

In 1996 I began corresponding with a Norwegian physician, Dr. Jorgen Jorgensen, who had written to tell me that his appreciation of music had been altered suddenly and radically when he lost all hearing in the right ear, after removal of an acoustic neuroma in the sensory nerve. "The perception of the specific qualities of music—pitch, timbre—did not change," he wrote. "However, my emotional reception of music was impaired. It was curiously flat and two-dimensional." Mahler's music, in particular, had once had a "shattering" effect on him. But when he went to a concert soon after his surgery and heard Mahler's Seventh Symphony, it sounded "hopelessly flat and lifeless."

After six months or more, he began to adapt to this:

> I gained a pseudostereo effect, which although it cannot have been as it used to be, gave me ample compensation. The music was not stereo, but it was all the same broad and rich. So, in the opening funeral march of Mahler's Fifth, after

the trumpet announces the gloomy depth of a funeral procession, the full orchestra fortissimo, I was almost lifted out of the chair.

"This may be my own psychological adjustment to the loss," Dr. Jorgensen added, "[but] our brain is a wonderful instrument. Hearing fibres may have crossed in the corpus callosum to receive input from my functioning left ear. . . . I also believe my left ear is better than should be expected from a seventy-year-old."

When we listen to music, as Daniel Levitin has written, "we are actually perceiving multiple attributes or 'dimensions.'" Among these he includes tone, pitch, timbre, loudness, tempo, rhythm, and contour (the overall shape, the up and down of melodies). One speaks of an amusia when the perception of some or all of these qualities is impaired, but Dr. Jorgensen was not amusic in this sense. His perception in the unaffected left ear was normal.

Levitin goes on to speak of two other dimensions. Spatial location, he writes, is "the perception of how distant the source is from us, in combination with how large a room or hall the music is in . . . it distinguishes the spaciousness of singing in a large concert hall from the sound of singing in your shower." And reverberation, he writes, "has an underappreciated role in communicating emotion and creating an overall pleasing sound."

It was precisely these qualities that Dr. Jorgensen missed when he lost the ability to hear in stereo. When he went to a concert, he found that it lacked spaciousness, voluminousness, richness, resonance—and this rendered the music "flat and lifeless."

I was struck here by the analogy to the experience of those who lose the use of one eye, and with this their ability to see depth stereoscopically.[1] The resonances of losing stereoscopy

---

1. I have described such a case at length in my essay "Stereo Sue."

can be unexpectedly far-reaching, causing not only a problem in judging depth and distance, but a "flattening" of the whole visual world, a flattening that is both perceptual and emotional. People in this situation speak of feeling "disconnected," of a difficulty in relating themselves not only spatially but emotionally to what they are seeing. The return of binocular vision, if this occurs, can thus give great pleasure and relief, as the world once again seems visually and emotionally rich. Yet even if there is no restoration of binocular vision, there may be a slow change, an adaptation analogous to what Dr. Jorgensen described—the development of a pseudostereo effect.

It is important to emphasize the word "pseudostereo." Genuine stereo perception, either visual or auditory, depends on the brain's ability to infer depth and distance (and such qualities as rotundity, spaciousness, and voluminousness) from the disparities between what is transmitted by the two individual eyes or ears—a spatial disparity in the case of the eyes, a temporal disparity in the case of the ears. Tiny differences are involved here, spatial disparities of a few arc seconds with vision, or of microseconds with hearing. This allows some animals, especially nocturnal predators like owls, to construct a veritable sound map of the environment. We humans are not up to this standard, but we nevertheless use binaural disparities, no less than visual cues, for orienting ourselves, for judging or forming impressions of what lies around us. It is stereophony that allows concertgoers to enjoy the full complexity and acoustic splendor of an orchestra or a choir performing in a concert hall designed to make listening as rich, subtle, and three-dimensional as possible—an experience we try to re-create, as best we can, with two earphones, or stereo speakers, or surround sound. We tend to take our stereo world for granted, and it requires a mishap like Dr. Jorgensen's to bring home, starkly and suddenly, the huge but often overlooked importance of having two ears.

No genuine stereo perception is possible if one has lost an eye or an ear. But as Dr. Jorgensen observed, a remarkable degree of adjustment or adaptation can occur, and this depends on a variety of factors. One of these is the increased ability to make judgments using one eye or ear, a heightened use of monocular or monaural cues. Monocular cues include perspective, occlusion, and motion parallax (the shifting appearance of the visual world as we move through it), and monaural cues are perhaps analogous to these, though there are also special mechanisms peculiar to hearing. The diffusion of sound with distance can be perceived monoaurally as well as binaurally, and the shape of the external ear, the pinna, provides valuable cues about both the direction and the asymmetries of sound reaching it.

If one has lost stereoscopy or stereophony, one must, in effect, recalibrate one's environment, one's spatial world—and movement here is especially important, even relatively small but very informative movements of the head. Edward O. Wilson describes in his autobiography, *Naturalist,* how he lost an eye in childhood but nonetheless is able to judge distances and depths with great accuracy. When I met him I was struck by a curious nodding of the head, and took this to be a habit or a tic. But he said it was nothing of the sort—it was a strategy designed to give his remaining eye alternating perspectives (such as normally the two eyes would receive), and this, he felt, combined with his memories of true stereopsis, could give him a sort of simulacrum of stereo vision. He said that he adopted these head movements after observing similar movements in animals (like birds and reptiles, for instance) whose visual fields have very little overlap. Dr. Jorgensen did not mention any comparable head movements in himself—they would not be too popular in a concert hall—but such movements might well help one construct a richer, more diverse soundscape.

There are other cues that stem from the complex nature of sounds and the vicissitudes of sound waves as they bounce off objects and surfaces around one. Such reverberation can provide an enormous amount of information even to a single ear, and this, as Daniel Levitin has remarked, has an essential role in communicating emotion and pleasure. It is for this reason that acoustical engineering is a major science and art. If a concert hall or lecture hall is badly designed, sounds may be "killed," voices and music seem "dead." Through centuries of experience, the builders of churches and auditoriums have become remarkably adept at making their buildings sing.

Dr. Jorgensen says that he believes his good ear is "better than should be expected from a seventy-year-old." One's ear, one's cochlea, cannot improve as one gets older, but as Jacob L. clearly demonstrated, the brain itself can improve its ability to make use of whatever auditory information it has. This is the power of cerebral plasticity. Whether or not "hearing fibres may have crossed in the corpus callosum" to the other ear, as Jorgensen suggests, is questionable—but there most assuredly have been significant changes in his brain as he has adapted to life with one ear. New connections must have been made, new areas recruited (and a sufficiently subtle brain-imaging technique might be able to demonstrate such changes). It seems probable, too—for vision and hearing normally complement each other and tend to compensate for each other if one is impaired—that Dr. Jorgensen, consciously or unconsciously, is using vision and visual data to map the position of instruments in the orchestra and the dimensions, spaciousness, and contours of the concert hall, as a way of reinforcing a sense of auditory space.

Perception is never purely in the present—it has to draw on experience of the past; this is why Gerald M. Edelman speaks of "the remembered present." We all have detailed memories of how things have previously looked and sounded, and these memories are recalled and admixed with every new perception. Such perceptions must be especially powerful in a strongly musical person, a habitual concertgoer like Dr. Jorgensen, and imagery is surely recruited to complement one's perceptions, especially if perceptual input is limited. "Every act of perception," Edelman writes, "is to some degree an act of creation, and every act of memory is to some degree an act of imagination." In this way the brain's experience and knowledge are called upon, as well as its adaptability and resilience. What is remarkable in Dr. Jorgensen's case, at least, is that, after such a severe loss, with no possibility of function being restored in the ordinary sense, there has nonetheless been a significant *reconstruction* of function, so that much of what seemed irretrievably lost is now available to him again. Though it took some months, he has, against all expectation, been able to recover in large measure what was most important to him: the richness, the resonance, and the emotional power of music.

DR. JORGENSEN'S ACCOUNT was the first I had received of the effects of sudden deafness on one side, but since he wrote to me, I have found that his experience is far from unusual. One friend of mine, Howard Brandston, related to me how, twenty years ago, he had an attack of sudden vertigo, followed by an almost complete loss of hearing in his right ear. "I could still hear sounds on that side," he said, "but could not unscramble words or distinguish tonal differences." He continued:

> The following week I had concert tickets but the musical performance sounded flat, lifeless, and without the harmonious quality I loved. Yes, I could recognize the music, but

instead of the uplifting emotional experience I was anticipating, I became so depressed that tears came to my eyes.

There were other problems, too. Howard was an avid hunter, and
on his first deer-hunting trip after his hearing loss, he found that
his ability to locate sounds was severely undermined:

> Standing absolutely still, I could hear the scurry of the chip-
> munk, the foraging of the squirrel, but the ability I formerly
> had to pinpoint the location of these sounds was now lost to
> me. I began to realize that if I wished to be a successful
> hunter, I would have to learn to compensate for the sensory
> handicap.

After several months, Howard discovered many ways to compensate for his hearing loss on one side. He would alternate
between analyzing a scene visually and auditorily, trying to meld
the two perceptual inputs. "After a while," he said, "I no longer
had to close my eyes if I kept scanning the scene by moving my
head in a side-to-side motion, with a very slight up-and-down
wave motion. After quite a while I began to feel comfortable
enough to go dangerous game hunting again. Now I was search-
ing for sounds that were familiar to me."[2]

In a concert hall, Howard learned to turn his head slightly, "as
if I was looking at the instruments that would be playing at that
moment—to the left for the violins and slightly to the right for
the bass and percussion." The sense of touch, as well as that of

---

2. Composer, ethnomusicologist, and virtual reality pioneer Jaron Lanier is concerned
with designing virtual reality with the greatest possible visual and auditory fidelity. He
stresses that micromovements of the head (movements of a few millimeters, or tiny rota-
tions), performed automatically and unconsciously in fractions of a second, occur even in
those with perfect binaural hearing and are, indeed, necessary for precise sound location.
The scanning head movements that Brandston describes (and which most of those who
lose an eye or an ear develop) seem to be, at least in part, an amplification of these normally tiny micromovements of the head.

sight, was crucial in helping him reconstruct a sense of musical space. He experimented with his stereo's subwoofer, which, he said, "made me most aware of the tactile physical nature of the sounds I was listening to." In his trophy room, which he had designed to be a perfect listening environment for his high-end stereo, he would use the power of the subwoofer to help him "round up" memories and images of sound and space. Perhaps all of us, unconsciously, use visual and tactile cues along with auditory ones to create the fullness of musical perception. With these and doubtless many other accommodations, both conscious and unconscious, Howard now gets a pseudostereo effect, as Dr. Jorgensen does, and he enjoys music once again.

Postscript

In November of 2007, I was contacted by Nick Coleman, an English music critic, who had read my account of Dr. Jorgensen. He told me of how his own hearing and especially his perception of music had drastically changed since he had suddenly lost the hearing in one ear a few months before. Music had been central in Coleman's life, and now, with the loss of stereophony, he found himself deprived of not only the fullness and spaciousness of music but its emotional resonance, too. He subsequently wrote at length about this experience in the *Guardian:*

> I imagine that if you like music at all then it has, in your head, some kind of third dimension to it, a dimension suggesting volume as well as surface, depth of field as well as texture. Speaking for myself, I used to hear "buildings" whenever I heard music—three-dimensional forms of architectural substance and tension. I did not "see" these

buildings in the classic synaesthetic way so much as sense them in my sensorium. These forms had "floors," "walls," "roofs," "windows," "cellars." They expressed volume. They were constructed out of interlinked surfaces which depended on each other for coherence. Music to me has always been a handsome three-dimensional container, a vessel, as real in its way as a scout hut or a cathedral or a ship, with an inside and an outside and subdivided internal spaces. I'm absolutely certain that this "architecture" had everything to do with why music has always exerted such an emotional hold over me. . . .

I've always kept quiet about this architecture business, partly . . . because I'd never been entirely confident that "architecture" was what I really meant. Maybe "hearing music architecturally" was just me being inarticulate.

But I am confident now. "Architecturally" was precisely right. What I hear now when I listen to music is a flat, two-dimensional representation: flat as in literally flat, like a sheet of paper with lines on it. Where I used to get buildings, I now only get architectural drawings. I can interpret what the drawings show but I don't get the actual structure: I can't enter music and I can't perceive its inner spaces. I've never got much of an emotional hit from technical drawings. This is what really hurts: I no longer respond to music emotionally.

Six months after his hearing loss, though Coleman had experienced some adaptation or recovery as far as balance and vestibular function was concerned, music, he wrote, "is still perceived flatly in a sliver of space." He has learned how to "read" it, laboriously, in a new way, and feels capable, therefore, of analyzing it and making esthetic judgements, even though he continues to feel "nothing much" at the emotional level. But these are still early days, and Coleman is fervently hopeful that music will one day snap back into three-dimensional space and give him back his musical architecture. Encouraged by Dr. Jorgensen's experience, Coleman makes himself listen to music every day, fighting to hear it as he used to. He still has the memory, the imagination, of what it was like to hear with two ears.

12

Two Thousand Operas:
Musical Savants

The first adult musical savant I met was a retarded man who had been admitted to a nursing home where I worked.[1] Martin had been normal at birth, but at the age of three he contracted meningitis, which caused seizures and a spastic weakness of his limbs and voice. It also affected his intelligence and personality, so that he became impulsive, "odd," and unable to keep up with his classmates at school. But along with these problems, he developed curious powers: he became fascinated by music, would listen to it intently, and would then sing the melodies he had heard or play them on the piano, as best he could with his spastic limbs and voice. He was greatly encouraged in this by his father, who was a professional opera singer.

Along with his musical abilities, Martin also developed a prodigious rote memory. Once he was fitted with glasses for the

---

1. I first described Martin in "A Walking Grove," a chapter in *The Man Who Mistook His Wife for a Hat.*

very severe visual problems he had been born with, he became an avid reader, retaining (though often not understanding) everything he read. And this, like his musical memory, was auditory—whatever he read he heard in his mind's ear, sometimes in his father's voice. As some people may be said to have a photographic memory, Martin had a phonographic one.

Though solitary in his habits, Martin was able to live independently and to do simple, unskilled work. His only pleasure, seemingly, was to sing in church choirs; he could not be a solo singer with his hoarse, spastic voice. But by the time he was sixty-one, his increasing physical disabilities (arthritis and heart disease among them) brought him to the nursing home.

When I met him in 1984, he told me that he knew more than two thousand operas, as well as the *Messiah*, the *Christmas Oratorio*, and all of Bach's cantatas. I brought along scores of some of these, and tested him as best I could; I found I was unable to fault him. And it was not just the melodies that he remembered. He had learned, from listening to performances, what every instrument played, what every voice sang. When I played him a piece by Debussy that he had never heard, he was able to repeat it, almost flawlessly, on the piano. He then transposed it into different keys and extemporized on it a little, in a Debussyan way. He could grasp the rules and the conventions of any music he heard, even if it was unfamiliar or not to his taste. This was musicianship of a high order, in a man who was otherwise so mentally impoverished.

What was the origin of Martin's musical powers? He had an intensely musical father, and musical ability is often inherited, as with the seven generations of the Bach family. He was born into and grew up in a musical household. Was this enough, or did his auditory and potentially musical powers also gain strength from the poorness of his vision? (Darold Treffert, in his remarkable book on savantism, *Extraordinary People*, notes that more than a third of all musical savants are blind or have very poor vision.) Martin was born with very severe visual problems, but this was not recognized and corrected until he was almost three, so in these early years he must have been nearly blind and dependent on hearing to orient him and make sense of the world. Or was it the meningitis, which, while stripping him of some of his cortical controls and higher powers, also stimulated or released previously unsuspected savant powers?

The term "idiot savant" was introduced in 1887 by Langdon Down, a London physician, in reference to "feebleminded" children who had special and sometimes remarkable "faculties." Among these were exceptional powers of calculation, drawing, mechanical aptitude, and, above all, of remembering, playing, and sometimes composing music. Musicality is the most common and perhaps the most dramatic form of savant talent, for it readily comes to public notice and commands attention. The case of Blind Tom, an American slave who exhibited prodigious musical powers from an early age, attracted worldwide attention in the 1860s.[2] Darold Treffert devoted a large part of *Extraordinary People* to musical savants, and Leon K. Miller wrote an entire book about a single musical savant, Eddie.[3] Detailed studies of savant talents and especially of musical savant skills have been

---

2. Savants are not "idiots" or necessarily retarded at all, but they are almost always autistic. Autism was not recognized as an entity until the 1940s, and we now realize that the majority of savants are autistic; indeed, it is estimated that more than ten percent of those with classical autism have savant talents. Contemporary accounts of Blind Tom (including one by the French physician Édouard Séguin, who saw Blind Tom in concert) strongly suggest that he had many of the mannerisms and stereotypies common to autistic people.

The pianist John Davis has recorded much of Blind Tom's music and written about him in several articles; he is currently working on a book about Blind Tom and his times.

3. Miller's book, *Musical Savants: Exceptional Skill in the Mentally Retarded*, demands comparison with *The Psychology of a Musical Prodigy*, Geza Révész's classic study of the Hungarian musical prodigy Erwin Nyiregyházi. Nyiregyházi, unlike Eddie, was not a savant (he had an exceptionally wide-ranging and articulate intelligence), but in musical terms the two musically gifted boys were very comparable.

carried out by Beate Hermelin and others in London, and these confirm that such skills depend on the recognition (which may be implicit and unconscious) of essential musical structures and rules, as is the case with normal musical skills. The anomaly is not in the skill itself, but in its isolation—its unusual and sometimes prodigious development in a mind that may otherwise be markedly underdeveloped in verbal and abstract thought.

One teacher wrote to me about a student who had mild retardation, hydrocephalus, and seizures, in addition to his autism:

> He cannot tie his shoes, he cannot add three plus two, but he can play you a movement of a Beethoven symphony and can transpose it to any key. He seems to have a rich understanding of the "grammar" of conventional harmony. I have been having him listen to more complex harmonies (including Debussy, the Berg piano sonata, the opening of *Tristan*, and the Ligeti piano études), and he can improvise now using any of these harmonic "languages." . . . He has a tremendous love of music . . . and when he is playing well (which is not always), his playing is extraordinarily beautiful and moving.

Stephen Wiltshire, an autistic English prodigy, is widely known as a visual savant; he can produce amazingly detailed drawings of complex buildings and even whole cityscapes, sometimes after a single glance.[4] He is able to hold these images in his mind, with little loss or distortion, for years on end. When he went to school at the age of six, his teacher commented that his drawings were the most "unchildlike drawings I have ever seen."

Adam Ockelford has written a book-length study, *In the Key of Genius*, about Derek Paravicini, a blind musical savant.

4. I have described Stephen's visual and musical powers at length in *An Anthropologist on Mars*, in the chapter called "Prodigies."

Stephen is also a musical savant. Savant abilities usually appear before the age of ten, and this is especially so of musical savant talents. Yet when Stephen's mentor, Margaret Hewson, phoned me to say, "Stephen has erupted musical powers—*huge* powers!" he was already sixteen. Like Martin, Stephen had absolute pitch and could instantly reproduce complex chords, play melodies he had never heard before, even if they were several minutes long, and transpose them easily into different keys. He also showed powers of improvisation. It is unclear why Stephen's musical gifts seemed to appear relatively late. It seems likely that he had great musical potential from an early age, but, perhaps due to his own passivity and the focus of others on his visual gifts, this was not noticed. Perhaps, too, adolescence had an effect, as Stephen suddenly became fixated on Stevie Wonder and Tom Jones at this point, and loved to mimic their movements and mannerisms along with their music.

I T I S A CHARACTERISTIC—indeed, the defining characteristic—of savant syndromes that there is a heightening of certain powers along with an impairment or poor development of other powers.[5] The powers that are heightened in savant skills are always of a concrete sort, whereas those that are impaired are abstract and often linguistic—and there have been many speculations as to how such a conjunction of strength and weakness may come about.

It has been known for a century and a half that there is a relative

---

5. While the term "savant syndrome" is used to refer to individuals who exhibit savant talents in a context of retardation or low-functioning autism, savant abilities, especially calculating talents, may be present in people of high general intelligence, too. (Steven B. Smith discusses this in his book *The Great Mental Calculators*.) Some great mathematicians have had savant calculating powers—Gauss was a famous example—but many others have not. Calculating ability has some resemblance, in this way, to absolute pitch, which may be present as part of a "syndrome," but can also occur in people of normal intelligence.

(but not absolute) specialization in the functions of the two sides of the brain, with the development of abstract and verbal powers being especially associated with the left, or dominant, cerebral hemisphere and perceptual skills with the right. This hemispheric asymmetry is very pronounced in humans (and present in a lesser degree in primates and some other mammals) and is observable even in utero. In the fetus, and perhaps the very young child, the situation is reversed, for the right hemisphere develops earlier and more quickly than the left, allowing perceptual functions to be established in the first days and weeks of life. The left hemisphere takes longer to develop, but continues to change in fundamental ways after birth. And as it develops and acquires its own (largely conceptual and linguistic) powers, it starts to suppress or inhibit some of the (perceptual) functions of the right hemisphere.

The functional (and perhaps immunological) immaturity of the left hemisphere in utero and during infancy makes it unusually susceptible to damage, and if such damage occurs—so Geschwind and Galaburda have hypothesized—there may be a compensatory overdevelopment of the right hemisphere, an actual enlargement made possible by neuronal migration. This may reverse the normal course of events and produce an anomalous right-hemisphere dominance instead of the usual left-hemisphere dominance.[6]

Shifts to right-hemisphere dominance can also occur after

---

6. In addition to the insults or injuries that may damage the left hemisphere in utero, at birth, or in early childhood, there is a physiological correlate of early hemispheric asymmetry with the exposure to testosterone in utero. Testosterone slows the development of the left hemisphere in utero, and while both male and female fetuses are exposed to this, male fetuses are exposed to much greater amounts. There is indeed a striking preponderance of males over females (and an increase in left-handedness) in many congenital syndromes, including autism, savant syndrome, Tourette's syndrome, and dyslexia. This, Geschwind speculated, may reflect the testosterone effect.

And yet, as Leon Miller cautions: "Most musical savants are male, visually impaired, and have a history of language disorder, yet this combination of factors does not ensure the appearance of savant skill. . . . These characteristics may be present in someone who

birth, at least in the first five years of life, if the left hemisphere is damaged. (Geschwind's interest in this phenomenon was ignited in part by the remarkable fact that a left hemispherectomy—a drastic procedure sometimes performed for intractable epilepsy, in which the entire left hemisphere is removed—does not render a young child permanently languageless but is followed by the development of language functions in the right hemisphere.) It seems quite possible that something like this happened with the three-year-old Martin, following his meningitis. Such hemispheric shifts may also occur, though to a lesser degree, in adults who have predominantly left-sided damage to the brain.

Savantlike talents may sometimes emerge in later life. There are several anecdotal descriptions of such an emergence following brain injuries, strokes, tumors, and frontotemporal dementia, especially if the damage is confined initially to the left temporal lobe. Clive Wearing, described in chapter 15, had a herpes encephalitis infection affecting especially his left frontal and temporal regions and, in addition to his devastating amnesia, developed a savantlike speed of calculation and punning.

The rapidity with which savant talents may emerge in such circumstances suggests a disinhibition or release of right-hemisphere functions from an inhibition or suppression normally exerted by the left temporal lobe.

In 1999, Allan Snyder and D. J. Mitchell inverted the usual question of why savant talents are so rare and asked instead: why don't we *all* have savant talents? They suggested that the mechanism for such skills might reside in all of us in early life but that as the brain matures, they are inhibited, at least from conscious awareness.

---

is unexceptional in any area." (Miller goes on to consider other factors—obsessional tendencies, special opportunities, right-hemisphere dominance, genetic predisposition, etc.—but concludes that no single factor is adequate to explain or predict the appearance of savant skills.)

They theorized that savants might have "privileged access to lower levels of information not available through introspection." Subsequently they started to test this theory experimentally using transcranial magnetic stimulation (TMS), which now allows a brief and virtually instantaneous way of inhibiting physiological functions in different parts of the brain. Using normal volunteers, they applied TMS to the left temporal lobe for a few minutes, in a stimulation designed to inhibit the abstract and conceptual thought governed by this area of the brain and, they hoped, to allow a transient release of perceptual functions in the right hemisphere. These experiments have produced modest but suggestive results, seemingly improving skills like drawing, calculating, and proofreading for a few minutes. (Bossomaier and Snyder are also investigating whether absolute pitch can be released by TMS.)[7]

Similar techniques have been used by Robyn Young and her colleagues, who found in one study that they could duplicate the release effect but only in five out of seventeen subjects. They concluded that "these mechanisms are *not* available to everyone and individuals may differ in either their ability to access these mechanisms or even whether they possess such a mechanism." Whether or not this is the case, it certainly seems that a sizeable minority, perhaps thirty percent, of "normal" adults may

---

7. Something perhaps analogous happened to me in 1965, when, like a certain number of medical students and residents at the time, I was taking massive doses of amphetamines. For a period of two weeks, I found myself in possession of a number of extraordinary skills I normally lacked. (I published an account of this, "The Dog Beneath the Skin," which focused on the heightening of smell, in *The Man Who Mistook His Wife for a Hat.*)

I could not only recognize everyone I knew by smell, but could hold very accurate and stable visual images in my mind and trace them on paper, as with a camera lucida. My powers of musical memory and transcription were greatly increased, and I could replay complex melodies on my piano after a single hearing. My enjoyment of these newfound powers and the world of greatly heightened sensation that went with them was mitigated, however, by finding that my abstract thinking was extremely compromised. When, decades later, I read of Bruce Miller's patients and of Allan Snyder's experiments, I wondered whether the amphetamines might have caused a transient temporal lobe disinhibition and a release of "savant" powers.

have latent or suppressed savant potentials which may be released to some degree by techniques such as TMS. This is not entirely surprising, given that various pathological conditions—frontotemporal dementia, dominant-hemisphere strokes, certain head injuries and infections—may lead on occasion to the appearance of savantlike abilities.

One must infer that there are, in many individuals, at least, very concrete eidetic and mnemonic powers which are normally hidden, but which may surface or be released under exceptional conditions. The existence of such potentials is only intelligible in evolutionary and developmental terms, as early forms of perception and cognition which once had adaptive value but are now suppressed and superseded by other forms.[8]

Darold Treffert, who has studied dozens of people with savant powers, both congenital and acquired, emphasizes that there are no "instant" savants, no easy path to savantism. Special mechanisms, whether they are universal or not, may be necessary but not sufficient for savantism. All savants spend years developing and honing their skills, sometimes obsessively and sometimes drawn on by the pleasure of exercising a special skill—a pleasure perhaps heightened by its contrast with their own overall intellectual impairments, or by the recognition and rewards their powers may bring. Being a savant is a way of life, a whole organization of personality, even though it may be built on a single mechanism or skill.

---

8. Ongoing work by Tetsuro Matsuzawa and his colleagues in Kyoto on the numerical memory span of chimpanzees may provide an example of such a "primitive" ability. In a paper with Nobuyuki Kawai, Matsuzawa showed that Ai, a young chimpanzee, could remember a sequence of at least five numbers, more than a preschool child; and at a recent symposium in Chicago on "The Mind of the Chimpanzee," he showed how Ai, with further training, had developed powers of working memory beyond that of most adult humans. He suggested that "our common ancestors might have had immediate memory, but in the course of evolution, they lost this and acquired languagelike skills." (See Kawai and Matsuzawa, 2000, and a news report on the symposium in *Science*, by Jon Cohen.)

13

An Auditory World:
Music and Blindness

When I was growing up in London in the 1930s, I especially enjoyed the visits of Enrico, the piano tuner, who would come every few months to tune our pianos. We had an upright and a grand, and since everyone in the family played, they were always getting out of tune. Once when Enrico was ill, a substitute tuner came—a tuner who, to my amazement, got around without a white stick and could apparently see normally. Up to that point, I had assumed that, like Enrico, all piano tuners were blind.

I thought of this years later in regard to my friend Jerome Bruner, for in addition to his many other gifts, he is immensely sensitive to music and possesses extraordinary powers of musical memory and imagery. When I asked him about these, he said that he did not come from a musical family but that he was born with congenital cataracts, not operated on until he was two. He was functionally blind in his first two years, seeing only light and shadow and some movement before his cataracts were removed—and this, he thought, forced him to focus on sounds of all sorts, especially voices and music. This special sensitivity to the auditory has stayed with him all his life.

It was similar with Martin, my musical savant patient, who wore thick pebble glasses like Jerry Bruner; Martin had been born with very severe farsightedness, more than twenty diopters, which was not diagnosed and corrected until he was almost three. He too must have been functionally blind as an infant, before he had glasses. Did this play a part in making him a musical savant?

THE IMAGE OF the blind musician or the blind poet has an almost mythic resonance, as if the gods have given the gifts of music or poetry in compensation for the sense they have taken away. Blind musicians and bards have played a special role in many cultures, as wandering minstrels, court performers, religious cantors. "In Gaelic culture," John Purser tells me, "a considerable number of harpers and pipers were named as blind—'dall,' smallpox, being frequently the cause." These included Ruairidh Dall O'Cathan, Ruairidh Dall Morrison, Blind Denis Hempson, and many others. Purser remarks that

> their blindness is not presented with any suggestion of handicap, inferiority, or even dependence. These men are not shown with a servant boy carrying the harp on his back (though they were often dependent upon a servant), they are not depicted with a stick feeling their way through the world, they are not shown as mendicants begging for a living: on the contrary, such figures are shown with dignity and even with a sense that they possess an inner vision appropriate to their status as bardic musicians.

For centuries, there was a tradition of blind church organists in Europe. There are many blind musicians, especially (though not exclusively) in the world of gospel, blues, and jazz—Stevie Wonder, Ray Charles, Art Tatum, José Feliciano, Rahsaan Roland Kirk, and Doc Watson are only a few. Many such artists, indeed, have "Blind" added to their names almost as an honorific: Blind Lemon Jefferson, the Blind Boys of Alabama, Blind Willie McTell, Blind Willie Johnson.

The channeling of blind people into musical performance is partly a social phenomenon, since the blind were perceived as being cut off from many other occupations. But social forces here are matched by strong internal forces. Blind children are often precociously verbal and develop unusual verbal memories; many of them are similarly drawn to music and motivated to make it central to their lives. Children who lack a visual world will naturally discover or create a rich world of touch and sound.[1]

At least there are many anecdotes to suggest this, but Adam Ockelford has moved beyond these casual observations to systematic studies in the last twenty years or so. Ockelford has worked as a music teacher at a school for the blind, and is now

---

1. A friend of Mozart's (he greatly admired her and dedicated a piano concerto to her) was the pianist and composer Maria Theresia von Paradis. Blind since early childhood, von Paradis was attuned to an auditory and especially a musical world; she was famous for her almost-Mozartian ear and musical memory. At the age of eighteen, she gained a little vision during a period of treatment by the famous Franz Anton Mesmer, but this led to a sharp decline in her musical perception, memory, and piano playing. Mesmer's treatments came to an end when he left Paris, and with this von Paradis's rudiments of vision faded. She was not entirely sorry, for she then enjoyed a complete reimmersion in the world of sound and music, and the return of her brilliant career.

Indeed, we all sometimes block out the visual world to focus on another sense. My father was fond of improvising, thinking, at the piano. He would get into a sort of reverie and play with a dreamy look, his eyes closed, as if translating straight to the keyboard what he was hearing in his mind. And he would often close his eyes to listen to a record or the radio. He would always say that he could hear music better when his eyes were closed—he could exclude visual sensations and immerse himself fully in an auditory world.

director of education at the Royal National Institute of the Blind in London. He has been especially concerned with a rare congenital condition, septo-optic dysplasia, which leads to visual impairment, sometimes relatively mild but often profound. Working with Linda Pring, Graham Welch, and Darold Treffert, he compared thirty-two families of children with this condition to an equal number of control families. Half of the children with SOD had no vision or could perceive only light or movement (they were ranked as "blind"); the other half were "partially sighted." Ockelford et al. noted that there was far more interest in music among the blind and the partially sighted than among the fully sighted. One mother, speaking of her seven-year-old blind daughter, said, "Her music is always with her. If there is not music playing, she is singing. She listens to music while in the car, while falling asleep, and loves to play the piano and any other instrument."

Though the partially sighted children also showed a heightened interest in music, exceptional musical abilities were observed only in the blind children—abilities that surfaced spontaneously, without any formal teaching. Thus it was not SOD as such but the degree of blindness, the fact of not having a significant visual world, that played a key role in stimulating the musical propensities and abilities of the blind children.

In various other studies, Ockelford found that 40 to 60 percent of the blind children he taught had absolute pitch, and a recent study by Hamilton, Pascual-Leone, and Schlaug also found that 60 percent of blind musicians had absolute pitch, as opposed to perhaps 10 percent among sighted musicians. In normally sighted musicians, early musical training (before the age of six or eight) is crucial in the development or maintenance of absolute pitch—but in these blind musicians, absolute pitch was common even when musical training had been started relatively late, sometimes as late as adolescence.

A third or more of the human cortex is concerned with vision, and if visual input is suddenly lost, very extensive reorganizations and remappings may occur in the cerebral cortex, with the development, sometimes, of intermodal sensations of all sorts. There is much evidence, from Pascual-Leone and his colleagues as well as others,[2] to show that in those born blind or early blinded, the massive visual cortex, far from remaining functionless, is reallocated to other sensory inputs, especially hearing and touch, and becomes specialized for the processing of these.[3] Even when blindness begins later in life, such reallocation can occur. Nadine Gaab et al., in their study of one late-blinded musician with absolute pitch, were able to show extensive activation of both visual-association areas while he listened to music.

Frédéric Gougoux, Robert Zatorre, and others in Montreal have shown that "blind people are better than sighted controls at judging the direction of pitch change between sounds, even when the speed of change is ten times faster than that perceived by controls—but only if they became blind at an early age." A tenfold difference here is extraordinary—one does not usually encounter a whole order of magnitude difference in a basic perceptual capacity.

The exact neural correlates underlying musical skills in the blind have not yet been fully defined, but are being intensively studied in Montreal and elsewhere.

In the meantime, we have only the iconic image of the blind musician, the large numbers of blind musicians in the world, descriptions of the frequent musicality of blind children, and personal memoirs. One of the most beautiful of these is the

---

2. See, for instance, Amedi, Merabet, Bermpohl, and Pascual-Leone, 2005.

3. People with congenital or acquired blindness may be able to form fairly accurate and detailed auditory maps of their immediate environment. The acquisition of such a power was beautifully described by John Hull in his book *Touching the Rock*.

autobiography of Jacques Lusseyran, a writer and hero of the French Resistance who was gifted musically and played the cello as a boy even before being blinded at the age of seven. In his memoir, *And There Was Light*, he emphasized the immense importance of music for him after he lost his sight:

> The first concert hall I ever entered, when I was eight years old, meant more to me in the space of a minute than all the fabled kingdoms. . . . Going into the hall was the first step in a love story. The tuning of the instruments was my engagement. . . . I wept with gratitude every time the orchestra began to sing. A world of sounds for a blind man, what sudden grace! . . . For a blind person music is nourishment. . . . He needs to receive it, to have it administered at intervals like food. . . . Music was made for blind people.

14

The Key of Clear Green: Synesthesia and Music

For centuries, humans have searched for a relationship between music and color. Newton thought that the spectrum had seven discrete colors, corresponding in some unknown but simple way to the seven notes of the diatonic scale. "Color organs" and similar instruments, in which each note would be accompanied by a specific color, go back to the early eighteenth century. And there are no less than eighteen densely packed columns on "Colour and Music" in *The Oxford Companion to Music*. For most of us, the association of color and music is at the level of metaphor. "Like" and "as if" are the hallmarks of such metaphors. But for some people one sensory experience may instantly and automatically provoke another. For a true synesthete, there is no "as if"—simply an instant conjoining of sensations. This may involve any of the senses—for example, one person may perceive individual letters or days of the week as having their own particular colors; another may feel that every color has its own peculiar smell, or every musical interval its own taste.[1]

One of the first systematic accounts of synesthesia (as this was dubbed in the 1890s) was provided by Francis Galton in his classic 1883 *Inquiries into Human Faculty and Its Development*—an eccentric and wide-ranging book which included his discovery of the individuality of fingerprints, his use of composite photography, and, most notoriously, his thoughts on eugenics.[2] Galton's studies of "mental imagery" started with an inquiry into people's abilities to visualize scenes, faces, and so on in vivid, veridical detail, and then proceeded to their imagery of numbers. Some of Galton's subjects, to his astonishment, said they invariably "saw" particular numerals—whether they were actually looking at them or even imagining them—in a particular color, always the same color. Though Galton at first thought of this as no more than an "association," he soon became convinced that it was a physiological phenomenon, a specific and innate faculty of mind with some kinship to mental imagery but more fixed, more stereotyped and automatic in nature, and, in contrast to other

---

1. At the end of the nineteenth century, the novelist Joris-Karl Huysmans wrote of every liqueur as "corresponding" in taste to a musical instrument—dry curaçao like a clarinet, kümmel like an oboe, crème de menthe like a flute, and so on—but he was at pains to point out later that these were only analogies. A similar pseudosynesthetic metaphor was used by Evelyn Waugh in *Brideshead Revisited*, when Anthony Blanche enthuses about "real green chartreuse . . . there are five distinct tastes as it trickles over the tongue. It is like swallowing a spectrum."

2. Synesthesia made its way into literature much earlier, when the German Romantic composer-writer E.T.A. Hoffmann described one of his heroes, Johannes Kreisler, as "the little man in a coat the color of C-sharp minor with an E-major-colored collar." This seems too specific to be a metaphor, and suggests that Hoffmann himself had color-music synesthesia or was well acquainted with the phenomenon.

Paul Herruer, a correspondent in Groningen, raises another possibility:

In the eighteenth and nineteenth centuries there was a tendency to associate the various keys with certain characteristics. . . . E-major was considered a sparkling or even flashing tonality. In contrast, C-sharp minor was described as a melancholy one, a bit sad. So Hoffmann could also have used a sort of for-musicians-only set of metaphors to evoke a drab coat with a contrasting (upstanding?) collar.

forms of mental imagery, virtually impossible to influence by consciousness or will.

Until recently, I had rarely had occasion, as a neurologist, to see anyone with synesthesia—for synesthesia is not something that brings patients to neurologists. Some estimate the incidence of synesthesia to be about one in two thousand, but it may be considerably more common, since most people who have it do not consider it to be a "condition." They have always been this way, and they assume, until they learn to the contrary, that what they experience is perfectly normal and usual, that everyone experiences fusions of different senses as they do. Thus I have recently discovered, simply by asking, that several patients whom I have been seeing for other conditions, sometimes for years, are in fact synesthetes as well. They had simply never thought to mention it, and I had never asked.

For many years, the only patient I knew to be a synesthete was a painter who suddenly became totally colorblind following a head injury.[3] He lost not only the ability to perceive or even imagine color, but also the automatic seeing of color with music which he had had all his life. Though this was, in a sense, the least of his losses, it was nevertheless a significant one, for music had always been "enriched," as he put it, by the colors that accompanied it.

This persuaded me that synesthesia was a physiological phenomenon, dependent on the integrity of certain areas of the cortex and the connections between them—in his case, between specific areas in the visual cortex needed to construct the perception or imagery of color. The destruction of these areas in this man had left him unable to experience *any* color, including "colored" music.

---

3. I described this case, "The Case of the Colorblind Painter," in *An Anthropologist on Mars*.

Of all the different forms of synesthesia, musical synesthesia—especially color effects experienced while listening to or thinking of music—is one of the most common, and perhaps the most dramatic. We do not know if it is more common in musicians or musical people, but musicians are, of course, more likely to be aware of it, and many of the people who have recently described their musical synesthesias to me have been musicians.[4]

T HE EMINENT contemporary composer Michael Torke has been deeply influenced by experiences with colored music. Torke showed striking musical gifts at an early age, and when he was five he was given a piano, and a piano teacher. "I was already a composer at five," he says—his teacher would divide pieces into sections, and Michael would rearrange the sections in different orders as he played.

One day he remarked to his teacher, "I love that blue piece."

His teacher was not sure she had heard correctly: "Blue?"

"Yes," said Michael, "the piece in D major . . . D major is blue."

"Not for me," the teacher replied. She was puzzled, and

---

4. There are many other forms of synesthesia which may or may not include music. One correspondent sent me a fascinating description of her daughter's synesthesia:

I recently discovered my 16-year-old daughter has synesthesia. (The quotes below are hers.) Letters, numbers and words have colors, textures and gender, sometimes personalities: "P: a very deep black with a purple undertone, blotchy, and sometimes feels like a stuffy nose. Male."

"The number 4 is a bright acid-yellow and 5 is crayola-blue. Together they *should* make 8, which is a bright green, but instead they *really* make 9, which is wet-dirt-brown. It has *never* made sense to me. Algebra is what makes X turn brown, too. Letters least of all should be brought into that mess."

Music and sounds in general evoke colors and shapes: "A high-pitched whine is like someone took a needle dipped in yellow highlighter ink and scratched a line above me."

Sometimes taste is involved: "The name Samantha tastes like bubble gum."

Michael, too, for he assumed that *everyone* saw colors associated with musical keys. When he began to realize that not everyone shared this synesthesia, he had difficulty imagining what that would be like. He thought it would amount to "a sort of blindness."

Michael has had this kind of key synesthesia—seeing fixed colors associated with the playing of music, scales, arpeggios, anything with a key signature—as far back as he can remember. He has always had absolute pitch, too, as far as he knows. This in itself makes musical keys absolutely distinctive for him: G-sharp minor, for example, has a different "flavor" from G minor, he says, in the same way that major and minor keys have different qualities for the rest of us. Indeed, he says, he cannot imagine having key synesthesia without having absolute pitch. Each key, each mode, for him, *looks* as distinctive (and as "characteristic") as it sounds.

The colors have been constant and fixed since his earliest years, and they appear spontaneously. No effort of will or imagination can change them. They seem completely natural to him, and preordained. The colors are highly specific. G minor, for example, is not just "yellow," but "ochre" or "gamboge." D minor is "like flint, graphite"; F minor is "earthy, ashy." He struggles to find the right word, as he would struggle to find the right paint or crayon.

The colors of major and minor keys are always related (for instance, G minor is a subdued yellow ochre, G major bright yellow), but otherwise he is hard put to find any system or rule by which the colors of particular keys might be predicted. At one time, he wondered whether the colors had been suggested by actual associations when he was very young—a toy piano, perhaps, with each key a different color—but he has no clear memories of any such thing. He feels, in any case, that there are far too many color associations (twenty-four for the major and minor keys, another half dozen for the modes, as a start) to make such an explanation likely. Moreover, some keys seem to have strange hues which he can hardly describe, and which he has almost never seen in the world about him.[5]

When I asked Michael in what sense he "saw" his colors, he spoke of their luminosity. The colors had a sort of transparent, luminous brilliance, he said, "like a screen" before him, but they in no way occluded or altered his normal vision. What would happen, I asked, if he saw a D-major "blue" while looking at a yellow wall—would he see green? No, he replied; his synesthetic colors were wholly inward and never confused with external colors. Yet subjectively, they were very intense and "real."

The colors he sees with musical keys have been absolutely fixed and consistent for forty years or more, and he wonders whether they were present at birth, or determined when he was a newborn. Others have tested the accuracy and consistency of his color-key associations over time, and they have not changed.

He sees no colors associated with isolated notes or different pitches. Nor will he see color if, say, a fifth is played—for a fifth, as such, is ambiguous, not associated with a particular key. There needs to be a major or minor triad or a succession of notes sufficient to indicate the basic key signature. "Everything goes back to the tonic," he says. Context, however, is also important;

---

5. V. S. Ramachandran and E. M. Hubbard (in their 2001 *PRSL* paper) described a partially colorblind man with letter-color synesthesia who said that when synesthetically stimulated, he saw colors he had never seen with his eyes—he called these "Martian colors." Ramachandran and Hubbard subsequently found that "the Martian color effect" might occur in noncolorblind synesthetes as well. "We attribute this," they wrote in a 2003 paper, "to the fact that the colours evoked by cross-activation in the fusiform [gyrus] 'bypass' earlier stages of colour-processing, and therefore may confer an unusual ('Martian') tint to the colours evoked. This . . . suggests that the qualia—the subjective experience of the colour-sensation—depends not merely on the final stages of processing, but on the total pattern of neural activity, including the earlier stages."

thus Brahms's Second Symphony is in D major (blue), but one movement is in G minor (ochre). This movement will still be blue if played in the context of the whole symphony, but it may be ochre if he reads, plays, or imagines it separately.

He particularly liked Mozart and Vivaldi as a boy, above all for their use of keys, which, he says, was "pure, narrow . . . they used a simpler palette." Later, in adolescence, he became enamored of Chopin, Schumann, the Romantic composers—though, with their convoluted modulations, they made special demands on his synesthesia.

Michael does not have any color associations with musical pattern or texture, rhythm, instruments, composers, mood, or emotion—only with key. He does, however, have other sorts of nonmusical synesthesia. For him, letters, numbers, and days of the week all have their own particular colors, and a peculiar topography or landscape as well.[6]

I asked Michael what role, if any, his musical synesthesia played in his creative life, whether it took his thinking and imagination in unexpected directions.[7] There was an explicit connection, he answered, between color and key in the first orchestral

---

6. Monday is green, Tuesday whitish-yellow—the "terrain" here, as he calls it, ascends and turns to the right. Wednesday is magenta, "almost old-brick color," Thursday a deep, almost indigo purple, Friday, almost the highest point of the terrain, a birch color, Saturday "drops down, to a dark, murky brown." Sunday is black.

Numbers have a landscape, too. "At 20, they take a sharp turn to the right, at 100 a sharp turn to the left." For Michael, the idea of numbers is as important as their form; thus, he says, "a Roman VII will be as gold as an Arabic 7 . . . or perhaps slightly less so." The ones, tens, and hundreds often share similar colors, so that where 4 is "dark green," the 40s are "forest green," the 400s a fainter green, and so on.

As soon as any reference is made to the date, its color-topographic correlate jumps into Michael's mind. Sunday, July 9, 1933, for example, would instantly generate the chromatic equivalent of day, date, month, and year, spatially coordinated. This sort of synesthesia, he finds, has some use as a mnemonic device.

7. Certain composers—Rimsky-Korsakov, Scriabin, Messiaen, and others—are said to have had key-color synesthesia; *The Oxford Companion to Music* even includes a table contrasting Rimsky-Korsakov's and Scriabin's "colors." But these may have represented a conscious symbolism rather than actual synesthesia.

music he wrote, a series of five pieces called *Color Music* in which each piece explored the musical possibilities of a single key—and thus a single color. The first of these pieces was entitled "Ecstatic Orange"; the others were "Bright Blue Music," "Green," "Purple," and "Ash." But apart from these early pieces, Michael has never again made explicit use of his key synesthesia in his work—a remarkable and ever-expanding range of music which now includes operas, ballets, and symphonic pieces. He is frequently asked whether synesthesia has made much difference to his life, especially as a professional musician. He says, "For me, at least, it's no big deal." For him, it is normal and completely unremarkable.

D AVID CALDWELL, another composer, also has musical synesthesia, but of a distinctly different sort. When I mentioned Michael's equation of yellow with G major to him, he exclaimed, "That seems wrong to me!" So too was Michael's green for E major, and indeed most of Michael's colors (although, David said, he could see the "logic" of some of them). Every synesthete has his own color correspondences.[8]

Color-key association goes both ways for David; seeing a piece of transparent golden-yellow glass on my windowsill put him in mind of B-flat major. ("Something clear and golden about that key," he said. Was it, he wondered, the color of brass? Trumpets,

---

8. The sense of "wrongness" can be so intense as to produce physical symptoms. One correspondent wrote:

> I have been reading your book and have just started the chapter on synesthesia, but could read no further than the third page because the person you cite defined D major as blue. I couldn't believe my reaction at a person not feeling the same color as I do for D (vermilion red)—it actually made me feel slightly dizzy and nauseous. I have never discussed with other synesthetes their perceptions, so I was shocked at my reaction.

he said, are B-flat instruments, and a lot of brass music is written in this key.) He is not sure what determines his particular colors: Have they arisen from experience, by conventional association? Are they arbitrary? Have they any "meaning"?

While David does not have perfect pitch, he has excellent relative pitch. He remembers accurately the pitch of many songs and many instruments, and can immediately infer from this what key any piece is played in. Each key, he says, "has its own quality"—and each key also has its own individual color.

David feels that the color of music is central to his musical sensibility and musical thought, for it is not just keys that have distinctive colors; musical themes, patterns, ideas, and moods have colors too, as do particular instruments and parts for them. Synesthetic colors accompany every stage of his musical thinking; his groping for "the underlying structure of things" is facilitated by color, and he knows he is on course, that he is achieving his goal, when the synesthetic colors seem right. Color flavors and enriches and, above all, clarifies his musical thinking. But it is difficult to pin down or systematize his correspondences. When I asked him to make a chart of his synesthetic colors, he thought for a few days and then wrote to me:

> The more I've tried to fill in the blanks on my chart, the more tenuous the connections have seemed. Michael's connections are so fixed, and don't seem to involve intellectual or emotional consideration. Mine, on the other hand, have a lot to do with how I *feel* about keys and how I use them in composing and playing music.

Gian Beeli, Michaela Esslen, and Lutz Jäncke, researchers in Zurich, have described a professional musician with both music-color and music-taste synesthesia: "Whenever she hears a specific musical interval, she automatically experiences a taste on her tongue that is consistently linked to that musical interval." In a 2005 article in *Nature*, they detailed her associations:

Minor second	Sour
Major second	Bitter
Minor third	Salty
Major third	Sweet
Fourth	(Mown grass)
Tritone	(Disgust)
Fifth	Pure water
Minor sixth	Cream
Major sixth	Low-fat cream
Minor seventh	Bitter
Major seventh	Sour
Octave	No taste

Any auditory uncertainty as to what musical interval she is hearing is immediately compensated for by its "taste," for her musical-synesthetic tastes are instantaneous, automatic, and always correct. I have also heard of violinists who make use of synesthesia to tune their instruments, and piano tuners who find it useful in their work.

CHRISTINE LEAHY, a writer, visual artist, and guitar player, has strong synesthesia for letters, numbers, and days of the week, as well as a strong, though less specific, color synesthesia for music. Her letter chromesthesia is especially strong, and if a word begins with a "red" letter, for example, its redness may spread to involve the whole word.[9]

Christine does not have absolute pitch and cannot perceive any intrinsic difference between different keys. But the color concomitants of letters also apply to the letters of the musical scale, so that if she knows that a particular note is D, it will elicit a sensation of greenness as vivid as that of the letter *D*. This synesthesia applies also to the sound of the note. She described the following color sensations when tuning her guitar, bringing a string down from E (blue) to D (green): "Rich, saturated blue . . . blue fading out, it seems grainier . . . a textured and unsaturated green . . . a smooth, pure, rich green."

I asked about what happened, visually, with the semitone, the E-flat, between E and D, and she said, "Nothing; it's a blank." None of the sharps or flats have color concomitants for her, though she perceives them and plays them without any difficulty. When she plays a diatonic scale—the scale of C major— she sees a "rainbow" of colors in spectral order, each color "dissolving" into the next. But when she plays a chromatic scale, the colors are interrupted by a series of "blanks." She ascribes this to the fact that when she was very young, she learned the alphabet by means of colored letter magnets on the refrigerator. These were organized in groups of seven (A to G, H to N, etc.), their colors corresponding to the seven colors of the rainbow, but

---

9. Thus when she looks at a page in a book, she is apt to see it as a polychromatic mosaic, the larger colored pieces formed by words, the smaller ones by individual letters. This chromesthesia has no relation to the meaning of words, or to her ability to understand them, but it does depend on the familiarity of letters. She saw a page of German as richly colored, although this is a language she does not understand. But when I showed her a page of Korean, she saw no colors at all, until some of the Korean letters, in her mind, assumed a slight resemblance to English ones; then isolated points of color appeared on the page.

there was nothing, of course, corresponding to sharps or flats in these letters.[10]

She regards her musical synesthesia as an enhancement or enrichment of music, even though it may have initially had a linguistic rather than a musical origin. She was aghast when I told her the story of the colorblind painter and how he had lost his musical synesthesia when he became colorblind. She would be "stricken," she said, if she were to lose hers—it would be "like losing a sense."

PATRICK EHLEN is a psychologist and songwriter who has very extensive synesthesia—not only to music but to sounds of all sorts, from musical instruments to car horns, voices, animal noises, thunder—so that the world of sound is continuously transformed into a flowing world of colors and shapes. He also has color synesthesia to letters, numbers, and days of the week. He remembers how his first-grade teacher, seeing him staring into space, asked what he was looking at. He replied that he was "counting the colors till Friday." The whole class burst into laughter, and thereafter he kept such matters to himself.

It was only when he was eighteen, in a chance conversation with a fellow student, that he heard the term "synesthesia"— and realized that what he had always had, and had always taken for granted, was in fact "a condition." His curiosity aroused, he began reading about synesthesia, and thought about writing his dissertation on the subject. He feels that his synesthesia moved him to become a psychologist, though his professional work has

---

10. When I asked Christine how her synesthesia affected her reading and writing, she said that though she was perhaps a slow reader because of the varied colors of letters and words, this allowed her to "savor" words in a special way, a way unavailable to ordinary people. She is fond of certain words because of their color (blues and greens are especially to her liking), and she feels this may incline her subconsciously to use them in her writing.

been in other realms—speech, discourse, linguistics—and not in synesthesia.

Some of his synesthetic correspondences are of mnemonic use to him (thus when someone said that 9/11 was a Monday, he could instantly and with assurance say that it was not, for Tuesday is yellow for him, and 9/11 is yellow too).[11] But it is the musical synesthesia which plays a vital part in his sensibility and his creative life.

Patrick does not experience, like Michael Torke, a fixed relation between color and key (this seems to be a relatively rare form of musical synesthesia, perhaps because it demands absolute pitch, too). Synesthesia, for Patrick, is evoked by virtually every other aspect of music: its rhythm and tempo, the shapes of melodies, their modulation into different keys, the richness of harmonies, the timbre of different instruments, and, especially, the overall character and mood of what he is hearing. Listening to music for Patrick is immensely enhanced—never occluded or distracted—by the rich stream of visual sensations that accompany it.

But it is in composing, above all, that he values his synesthesia. Patrick has songs, fragments of songs, and ideas for songs

---

11. Many synesthetes find their powers of memory made more reliable, matrixed by their synesthesia. But occasionally the reverse may happen, as Susan Foster-Cohen wrote to me in an e-mail she titled "The treachery of synaesthesia."

I quite often misremember dates because my synaesthesia betrays me. 1 is white, 2 is green, 3 is yellow, 7 is blue, and so on. Friday is a sort of russet brown, Wednesday is scrambled egg yellow (a little darker than 3, but not by much), and Tuesday is a blue that is quite close to 7. So, here's the problem: Wednesday 3rd is easy: two yellows. Wednesday 7th is harder because it's a yellow and a blue and so is Tuesday 3rd. So was my appointment on Wednesday 7th or Tuesday 3rd?

And when numbers are combined, it's the same. 17 is made up of white for the 1 and blue for the seven. 71 has the same combination of colours. Someone tells me there are 648 and I remember, or rather recall, 486. Well, the colours are the same: orange, green and red. I have to use quite distinct executive function abilities to determine whether 400 or so would be more likely than 600 and such.

continually running through his head, and his synesthesia is crucial for their realization, an integral part of the creative process. The very concept of music, for him, is infused with the visual. Color is not "added" to music, it is integral to it. He only wishes that others could share this totality, and he tries to suggest it, he says, as fully as he can, in his own songs.

SUE B., another synesthete, seems to experience musical synesthesia not so much with color as with light, shape, and position. She describes her experience this way:

> I always see images when I hear music, but I do not associate specific colors with particular musical keys or musical intervals. I wish that I could say that a minor third is always a blue-green color, but I do not distinguish the intervals all that well. My musical skills are pretty modest. When I hear music, I see little circles or vertical bars of light getting brighter, whiter, or more silvery for higher pitches and turning a lovely, deep maroon for the lower pitches. A run up the scale will produce a succession of increasingly brighter spots or vertical bars moving upward, while a trill, like in a Mozart piano sonata, will produce a flicker. High distinct notes on a violin evoke sharp bright lines, while notes played with vibrato seem to shimmer. Several stringed instruments playing together evoke overlapping, parallel bars or, depending on the melody, spirals of light of different shades shimmering together. Sounds made by brass instruments produce a fan-like image. High notes are positioned slightly in front of my body, at head level, and toward the right, while bass notes are located deep in the center of my abdomen. A chord will envelop me.

. . .

T HE HISTORY OF scientific interest in synesthesia has gone through many vicissitudes. In the early nineteenth century, when Keats and Shelley and other poets used extravagant inter-sensory images and metaphors, it seemed that synesthesia was no more than a poetic or imaginative conceit. Then came a series of careful psychological studies in the 1860s and 1870s, culminating in Galton's *Inquiries into Human Faculty and Its Development* in 1883. These served to legitimate the phenomenon and were soon followed by the introduction of the word "synesthesia." Towards the end of the nineteenth century, with Rimbaud and the Symbolist poets, the notion of synesthesia again seemed a poetic conceit, and it ceased to be regarded as a subject for scientific investigation.[12] This changed yet again in the last third of the twentieth century, as John Harrison details in his excellent book *Synaesthesia: The Strangest Thing*. In the 1980s, Richard Cytowic made the first neurophysiological studies of synesthetic subjects—studies that, for all their technical limitations, seemed to show a genuine activation of different sensory areas in the brain (e.g., auditory and visual) coincident with synesthetic experiences. In 1989, he published a pioneering text, *Synesthesia: A Union of the Senses*, and this was followed by a popular exploration of the subject in 1993, *The Man Who Tasted Shapes*. Current techniques of functional brain imaging now give unequivocal evidence for the simultaneous activation or

---

12. A striking exception was *The Mind of a Mnemonist*, A. R. Luria's 1968 study of a synesthetic memorizer. For Luria's subject, Shereshevsky, "there was no distinct line, as there is for others of us, separating vision from hearing, or hearing from a sense of touch or taste." Every word or image Shereshevsky heard or saw, every perception, instantly gave rise to an explosion of synesthetic equivalences—and these were held in mind, precisely, indelibly, and relentlessly for the rest of his life.

coactivation of two or more sensory areas of the cerebral cortex in synesthetes, just as Cytowic's work had predicted.

While Cytowic was investigating synesthesia in the United States, Simon Baron-Cohen and John Harrison were opening up the subject in England, and in 1997 they published a review volume, *Synaesthesia: Classic and Contemporary Readings.*

Galton believed that genuine synesthesia was strongly familial, and Harrison and Baron-Cohen noted that a third of their subjects reported close relatives who also had synesthesia. Nabokov, in his autobiography, *Speak, Memory,* wrote of how as a child he saw all the letters of the alphabet as having distinct colors and was deeply upset when he was given a box of colored letters and found that nearly all of them were the "wrong" color. His mother, also a synesthete, agreed with him that the colors were wrong, but not on what they should be. (Nabokov's wife, too, was a synesthete, as is their son.)

While synesthesia has been regarded as quite rare, affecting perhaps one person in two thousand, and to have a strong gender preference (with a female to male ratio of about six to one), a recent study by Julia Simner, Jamie Ward, and their colleagues has brought both of these suppositions into question. Using a random population of almost seventeen hundred subjects, and objective tests to separate genuine from pseudosynesthesia, they found that one person in twenty-three had some kind of synesthesia—most commonly for colored days—and that there was no significant gender difference.[13]

Prior to 1999, there were no objective psychological tests for

---

13. Synesthesia literally means a fusion of the senses, and it is classically described as a purely sensory phenomenon. But it is becoming clear that there are conceptual forms of synesthesia, too. For Michael Torke, the *idea* of seven is golden—whether this is an Arabic 7 or a Roman VII. Some people have an instant and automatic conjoining of other categorical characteristics—for example, they may see certain days of the week as male or female, or certain numbers as "mean" or "kind." This constitutes a sort of "higher"

synesthesia. But in the past few years, V. S. Ramachandran and E. M. Hubbard have brought great experimental ingenuity to the testing of this. In order to distinguish true synesthesia from pseudosynesthesia, for example, they have devised tests that only a genuine synesthete can "pass." One such test (described in their 2001 paper in the *Journal of Consciousness Studies*) presents the subject with a medley of rather similar-looking 2's and 5's, all printed in black. The ordinary person would be hard put to distinguish these at a glance, but a color-number synesthete can distinguish them easily by their different "colors."

Functional brain imaging has now confirmed that there is activation of visual areas (especially color-processing areas) in synesthetes when they "see" colors in response to speech or music.[14] There is little room for doubt, anymore, as to the physiological as well as the psychological reality of synesthesia.

Synesthesia seems to go with an unusual degree of cross-activation between what, in most of us, are functionally independent areas of the sensory cortex—such cross-activation could be based on an anatomical excess of neural connections between different areas of the brain. There is some evidence that such "hyperconnectivity" is indeed present in primates and other mammals during fetal development and early infancy, but is reduced or "pruned" within a few weeks or months after birth. There have not been equivalent anatomical studies in human infants, but as Daphne Maurer of McMaster University notes, behavioral observations of infants suggest "that the newborn's senses are not well differentiated, but are instead intermingled in a synaesthetic confusion."

---

synesthesia, a union of ideas rather than sensations. For such synesthetes, these are not whims or fancies but fixed, irresistible, and lifelong correspondences. Such conceptual forms of synesthesia are being investigated especially by Julia Simner and her colleagues, and by V. S. Ramachandran.

14. See, for example, Paulescu, Harrison, et al.

Perhaps, as Baron-Cohen and Harrison write, "we might all be colored-hearing synesthetes until we lose connections between these two areas somewhere about three months of age." In normal development, according to this theory, a synesthetic "confusion" gives way in a few months, with cortical maturation, to a clearer distinction and segregation of the senses, and this in turn makes possible the proper cross-matching of perceptions which is needed for the full recognition of an external world and its contents—the sort of cross-matching which ensures that the look, the feel, the taste, and the crunch of a Granny Smith apple all go together. In those individuals with synesthesia, it is supposed, a genetic abnormality prevents complete deletion of this early hyperconnectivity, so that a larger or smaller remnant of this persists in adult life.

Synesthesia seems to be commoner in children. As early as 1883, the same year that Galton's book was published, the eminent psychologist Stanley Hall described music-color synesthesia in 40 percent of children interviewed—a figure which may err on the high side. But a variety of more recent studies agree that synesthesia is a good deal commoner in childhood and tends to disappear at adolescence. Whether this goes with hormonal changes or cerebral reorganizations, which are both occurring at this time, or with a movement to more abstract forms of thinking is unclear.

While synesthesia usually appears very early in life, there are rare situations which may provoke its appearance later in life—for example, it can occur transiently during temporal lobe seizures or under the influence of hallucinogens.

But the only significant cause of permanent acquired synesthesia is blindness. The loss of vision, especially early in life, may lead, paradoxically, to heightened visual imagery and all sorts of intersensory connections and synesthesias. The rapidity with which synesthesia can follow blindness would scarcely allow the formation of new anatomical connections in the brain and suggests instead a release phenomenon, the removal of an inhibition normally imposed by a fully functioning visual system. In this way, synesthesia following blindness would be analogous to the visual hallucinations (Charles Bonnet syndrome) often associated with increasing visual impairment or the musical hallucinations sometimes associated with increasing deafness.

Within weeks of losing his sight, Jacques Lusseyran developed a synesthesia so intense as to replace the actual perception of music, thus preventing him from becoming a musician, as he had intended:

> I had no sooner made a sound on the A string, or D or G or C, than I no longer heard it. I looked at it. Tones, chords, melodies, rhythms, each was immediately transformed into pictures, curves, lines, shapes, landscapes, and most of all colors. . . . At concerts, for me, the orchestra was like a painter. It flooded me with all the colors of the rainbow. If the violin came in by itself, I was suddenly filled with gold and fire, and with red so bright that I could not remember having seen it on any object. When it was the oboe's turn, a clear green ran all through me, so cool that I seemed to feel the breath of night. . . . I *saw* music too much to be able to speak its language.[15]

Similarly, V. S. Ramachandran, in *A Brief Tour of Human Consciousness*, described one patient who felt himself "invaded" by

---

15. Complex neurological reactions to blindness, including Lusseyran's, are explored further in my 2003 article "The Mind's Eye."

intrusive synesthesia after becoming blind at the age of forty. When his patient touched objects or read Braille, Ramachandran wrote, "his mind would conjure up vivid visual images, including flashes of light, pulsating hallucinations or sometimes the actual shape of the object he was touching." These confusing sensations were "often irrelevant and always irrevocable and intrusive . . . a spurious and distracting nuisance," and greatly interfered with every aspect of life.[16]

There is a world of difference, of course, between acquiring a condition later in life and being born with it. For Lusseyran, who acquired it in mid-childhood, color-music synesthesia, though beautiful, was intrusive and prevented him from enjoying music. But for those born with color-music synesthesia, it is different.

There is a wide range in people's attitudes to congenital synesthesia, the importance it may have for them, and the role it may play in their lives. This is evident even in the small sample of individuals I have described. Michael Torke, while he has a very strong and specific musical synesthesia, which at one time influenced both his musical sensibilities and his compositions, has

---

16. Even those with congenital synesthesia may occasionally appreciate a break from it. This was brought out by Kjersti Beth, a young woman with perfect pitch and key-color synesthesia. There are times, however, when she wishes to hear music alone, without any attendant visual sensations, and this is possible for her when she goes to rock concerts: "The distortion of heavy metal essentially disables my perfect pitch. . . . I go to a metal concert . . . and enjoy the music because I don't 'see' it."

Another correspondent, Liz Adams, reports a wide range of synesthetic experiences, in which words or names are conjoined with images involving color and texture and sometimes movement. She experiences a "physical taste from certain colors, bitterness from purple, and unbearable tingling from certain shades of yellow on the acid side." She has, like Ramachandran's patient, experienced colors "outside of the visible spectrum." And, she adds,

> visual images create noise for me. It's literally deafening to be among clutter, like being in the middle of a brass band. I can't hear conversation over it, and I need uncluttered surfaces in order to hear properly. I used to do collaborative art, and the other artist's studio was a welter of objects and to me, noise. I had to escape at regular intervals to regain my poise from the jumble of material and the racket it set up for me.

come to think over time that "it is no big deal." David Caldwell and Patrick Ehlen, on the other hand, feel that their synesthesia continues to be central to their musical identity and plays a most active part in their process of composing. But for all of them, synesthesia is natural, almost an extra sense—so much so that such questions as "What is it like?" or "What does it mean to you?" are as unanswerable as asking "What is it like to be alive? What is it like to be *you?*"

Part III

Memory, Movement, and Music

15

In the Moment:
Music and Amnesia

*You are the music
while the music lasts.*

—T. S. ELIOT, *The Four Quartets*

In January 1985, his wife records, Clive Wearing, an eminent English musician and musicologist in his mid-forties, was reading "The Lost Mariner," a piece I had written about a patient with severe amnesia. My patient, Jimmie, I wrote, was "isolated in a single moment of being, with a moat or lacuna of forgetting all round him. . . . He is a man without a past (or future), stuck in a constantly changing, meaningless moment."[1]

"Clive and I," Deborah Wearing wrote in her memoir, *Forever*

---

1. Jimmie's story, "The Lost Mariner," was published in *The Man Who Mistook His Wife for a Hat*.

Today, "could not get this story out of our heads and talked about it for days." They had no way of knowing that they were, as Deborah put it, "staring into a mirror of our own future."

Two months later, Clive himself was struck by a devastating brain infection, a herpes encephalitis, affecting especially the parts of his brain concerned with memory; and he was left in a state far worse even than that of the patient I had described. Jimmie had a memory span of about half a minute; with Clive, it was only a few seconds. New events and experiences were effaced almost instantly, as Deborah wrote:

> His ability to perceive what he saw and heard was unimpaired. But he did not seem to be able to retain any impression of anything for more than a blink.[2] Indeed, if he did blink, his eyelids parted to reveal a new scene. The view before the blink was utterly forgotten. Each blink, each glance away and back, brought him an entirely new view. I tried to imagine how it was for him. . . . Something akin to a film with bad continuity, the glass half empty, then full, the cigarette suddenly longer, the actor's hair now tousled, now smooth. But this was real life, a room changing in ways that were physically impossible.

In addition to this inability to preserve new memories, Clive had a devastating retrograde amnesia, a deletion of virtually his entire past.

When he was filmed in 1986 for Jonathan Miller's extraordinary BBC documentary, *Prisoner of Consciousness*, Clive showed

---

2. At this point, early in his illness, it was very difficult for Clive to fix his mind on anything—his attention was volatile and darted to and fro. Now that his state is more settled, Clive is more readily able to maintain a conversation or to remember a string of digits or a sentence or two of what he reads—so the title of a recent documentary about him, *The Man with the Seven Second Memory* (Granada Television, 2005), is probably nearer the mark.

a desperate aloneness, fear, and bewilderment. He was acutely, continually, agonizingly conscious that something bizarre, something terrible, was the matter. His constantly repeated complaint, however, was not of a faulty memory, but of being deprived, in some uncanny and terrible way, of all experience, deprived of consciousness and life itself. As Deborah wrote,

> It was as if every waking moment was the first waking moment. Clive was under the constant impression that he had just emerged from unconsciousness because he had no evidence in his own mind of ever being awake before. . . . "I haven't heard anything, seen anything, touched anything, smelled anything," he would say. "It's like being dead."

Desperate to hold on to something, to gain some purchase, Clive started to keep a journal, first on scraps of paper, then in a notebook. But his journal entries consisted, essentially, of the statements "I am awake" or "I am conscious," entered again and again every few minutes. He would write: "2.10 pm: this time properly awake. . . . 2.14 pm: this time finally awake. . . . 2.35 pm: this time completely awake," along with negations of these statements: "At 9.40 pm I awoke for the first time, despite my previous claims." This in turn was crossed out, followed by "I was fully conscious at 10.35 pm, and awake for the first time in many, many weeks." This in turn was canceled out by the next entry.[3]

This dreadful journal, almost void of any other content but

---

3. I had suggested to my patient Jimmie that he keep a diary, but these attempts were foiled, at first, by his continually losing the diary. Even when we were able to organize a way for him to find his notebook every day, keeping it always in the same place by his bedside, this too failed, for he dutifully kept his journal but had no recollection of his earlier entries in it. He recognized his own writing and was always astounded to find that he had written something the day before.

these passionate assertions and denials, intending to affirm existence and continuity but forever contradicting them, was filled
anew each day, and soon mounted to hundreds of almost identical
pages. It was a terrifying and poignant testament to Clive's mental state, his lostness, in the years that followed his amnesia—
a state that Deborah, in Miller's film, called "a never-ending
agony."

Mr. Thompson, another profoundly amnesic patient I knew,
dealt with his abysses of amnesia by fluent confabulations.[4] He
was wholly immersed in his quick-fire inventions and had no
insight into what was happening; so far as he was concerned,
there was nothing the matter. He would confidently identify or
misidentify me as a friend of his, a customer in his delicatessen,
a kosher butcher, another doctor—as a dozen different people in
the course of a few minutes. This sort of confabulation was not
one of conscious fabrication. It was, rather, a strategy, a desperate
attempt—unconscious and almost automatic—to provide a sort
of continuity, a narrative continuity, when memory, and thus
experience, was being snatched away every instant.

Though one cannot have direct knowledge of one's own amnesia, there may be ways to infer it: from the expressions on
people's faces when one has repeated something half a dozen
times, when one looks down at one's coffee cup and finds that it
is empty, when one looks at one's diary and sees entries in one's
own handwriting. Lacking memory, lacking direct experiential
knowledge, amnesiacs have to make hypotheses and inferences,
and they usually make plausible ones. They can infer that they
have been doing *something*, been *somewhere*, even though
they cannot recollect what they have been doing or where. Yet

---

4. I originally described Mr. Thompson in "A Matter of Identity," a chapter in *The Man
Who Mistook His Wife for a Hat.*

Clive, rather than making plausible guesses, always came to the conclusion that he had just been "awakened," that he had been "dead." This seemed to me a reflection of the almost instantaneous effacement of perception for Clive—thought itself was almost impossible within this tiny window of time. Indeed, Clive once said to Deborah, "I am completely incapable of thinking."

At the beginning of his illness, Clive would sometimes be confounded at the bizarre things he experienced. Deborah wrote of how, coming in one day, she saw him

> holding something in the palm of one hand, and repeatedly covering and uncovering it with the other hand as if he were a magician practising a disappearing trick. He was holding a chocolate. He could feel the chocolate unmoving in his left palm, and yet every time he lifted his hand he told me it revealed a brand new chocolate.
>
> "Look!" he said. "It's new!" He couldn't take his eyes off it.
>
> "It's the same chocolate," I said gently.
>
> "No . . . look! It's changed. It wasn't like that before . . ."
> He covered and uncovered the chocolate every couple of seconds, lifting and looking.
>
> "Look! It's different again! How do they do it?"

Within months Clive's confusion gave way to the agony, the desperation, that are so clear in Miller's film. This, in turn, was succeeded by a deep depression, as it came upon him—if only in sudden, intense, and immediately forgotten moments—that his former life was over, that he was incorrigibly disabled, and that the rest of his life would be spent in institutions.

As the months passed without any real improvement, the hope

of significant recovery became fainter and fainter, and towards the
end of 1985 Clive was moved to a room in a chronic psychiatric
unit—a room he was to occupy for the next six and a half years,
but which he was never able to recognize as his own. A young psychologist saw Clive for a period of time in 1990 and kept a verbatim record of everything he said, and this caught the grim mood
that had taken hold. Clive said at one point, "Can you imagine
one night five years long? No dreaming, no waking, no touch, no
taste, no smell, no sight, no sound, no hearing, nothing at all. It's
like being dead. I came to the conclusion that I was dead."

The only times of feeling alive were when Deborah visited
him. But the moment she left, he was desperate once again and
by the time she got home, ten or fifteen minutes later, she would
find repeated messages from him on her answering machine:
"Please come and see me, darling—it's been ages since I've seen
you. Please fly here at the speed of light."

To imagine the future was no more possible for Clive than to
remember the past—both were engulfed by the onslaught of
amnesia. Yet at some level, Clive could not be unaware of the
sort of place he was in, and the likelihood that the rest of his life,
his endless night, would be spent in such a place.

But then, seven years after his illness, after huge efforts made
by Deborah, Clive was moved to a small country residence for the
brain-injured, much more congenial than a hospital. Here he was
one of only a handful of patients, and in constant contact with a
dedicated staff who treated him as an individual and respected his
intelligence and talents. He was taken off most of his heavy tran-
quilizers, and seemed to enjoy his walks around the village and
gardens near the home, the spaciousness, the fresh food.

For the first eight or nine years in this new home, Deborah
told me, "Clive was calmer and sometimes jolly, a bit more content, but often with angry outbursts still, unpredictable, with-

drawn, spending most of his time in his room alone." But gradually, in the last six or seven years, Clive has become more sociable, more talkative. Conversation (though of a "scripted" sort) has come to fill what had been before empty, solitary, and desperate days.

THOUGH I HAD corresponded with Deborah since Clive first became ill, it was only twenty years later that I met Clive in person. And he was so changed from the haunted, agonized man I had seen in Miller's 1986 film that I was scarcely prepared for the dapper, bubbling figure who opened the door when Deborah and I went to visit him in the summer of 2005. He had been reminded of our visit just before we arrived, and he flung his arms around Deborah the moment she entered.

Deborah introduced me: "This is Dr. Sacks," and Clive immediately said, "You doctors work twenty-four hours a day, don't you? You're always in demand." We went up to his room, which contained an electric organ console and a piano piled high with music. Some of the scores, I noted, were transcriptions of Orlandus Lassus, the Renaissance composer whose works Clive had edited. I saw Clive's journal by the washstand—he has now filled up scores of volumes, and the current one is always kept in this exact location. Next to it was an etymological dictionary with dozens of reference slips of different colors stuck between the pages and a large, handsome volume, *The 100 Most Beautiful Cathedrals in the World*. A Canaletto print hung on the wall, and I asked Clive if he had ever been to Venice. No, he said (but Deborah told me they had visited several times before his illness). Looking at the print, Clive pointed out the dome of a church: "Look at it," he said, "see how it soars—like an angel!"

When I asked Deborah whether Clive knew about her memoir,

she told me that she had shown it to him twice before, but that he had instantly forgotten. I had my own heavily annotated copy with me, and asked Deborah to show it to him again.

"You've written a book!" he cried, astonished. "Well done! Congratulations!" He peered at the cover. "All by you? Good heavens!" Excited, he jumped for joy. Deborah showed him the dedication page ("For my Clive"). "Dedicated to me?" He hugged her. This scene was repeated several times within a few minutes, with almost exactly the same astonishment, the same expressions of delight and joy each time.

Clive and Deborah are still very much in love with each other, despite his amnesia (indeed, the subtitle of Deborah's book is *A Memoir of Love and Amnesia*). He greeted her several times as if she had just arrived. It must be an extraordinary situation, I thought, both maddening and flattering, to be seen always as new, as a gift, a blessing.

Clive had, in the meantime, addressed me as "Your Highness" and inquired at intervals, "Been at Buckingham Palace? . . . Are you the prime minister? . . . Are you from the U.N.?" He laughed when I answered, "Just the U.S." This joking or jesting was of a somewhat waggish, stereotyped nature and highly repetitive. Clive had no idea who I was, little idea who anyone was, but this bonhomie allowed him to make contact, to keep a conversation going. I suspected he had some damage to his frontal lobes, too— such jokiness (neurologists speak here of *Witzelsucht,* joking disease), like his impulsiveness and chattiness, could go with a weakening of the usual, social frontal lobe inhibitions.

He was excited at the notion of going out for lunch, lunch with Deborah. "Isn't she a wonderful woman?" he kept asking me. "Doesn't she have marvelous kisses?" I said yes, I was sure she had.

As we drove to the restaurant, Clive, with great speed and fluency, invented words for the letters on the license plates of passing cars: JCK was Japanese Clever Kid; NKR was New King of Russia; and BDH (Deborah's car) was British Daft Hospital, then Blessed Dutch Hospital. *Forever Today*, Deborah's book, immediately became "Three-Ever Today," "Two-Ever Today," "One-Ever Today." This incontinent punning and rhyming and clanging was virtually instantaneous, occurring with a speed no normal person could match. It resembled Tourettic or savantlike speed, the speed of the preconscious, undelayed by reflection.

When we arrived at the restaurant, Clive did all the license plates in the parking lot and then, elaborately, with a bow and a flourish, let Deborah enter: "Ladies first!" He looked at me with some uncertainty as I followed them to the table: "Are you joining us, too?"

When I offered him the wine list, he looked it over and exclaimed: "Good God! Australian wine! New Zealand wine! The colonies are producing something original—how exciting!" This partly indicated his retrograde amnesia—he is still in the 1960s (if he is anywhere), when Australian and New Zealand wines were almost unheard of in England. "The colonies," however, was part of his compulsive waggery and parody.

At lunch he talked about Cambridge—he had been at Clare College, but had often gone next door to King's, for their famous choir. He spoke of how after Cambridge, in 1968, he joined the London Sinfonietta, where they played modern music, though he was already attracted to the Renaissance and Lassus. He was the chorus master there, and he reminisced that singers could not talk during coffee breaks; they had to save their voices ("It was often misunderstood by the instrumentalists, seemed standoffish to them"). These all sounded like genuine memories. But they could, equally, have reflected his knowing *about* these events, rather than actual memories of them—expressions of "semantic" memory rather than "event" or "episodic" memory.

Then he spoke of the Second World War (he was born in 1938) and how they would go to bomb shelters and play chess or cards there. He said that he remembered the doodlebugs: "There were more bombs in Birmingham than in London." Was it possible that these were genuine memories? He would only have been six or seven, at most. Or was he confabulating or simply, as we all do, repeating stories he had been told as a child?

At one point, he talked about pollution and how dirty petrol engines were. When I told him I had a hybrid with an electric motor as well as a combustion engine, he was astounded, as if something he had read about as a theoretical possibility had, far sooner than he had imagined, become a reality.

In her remarkable book, so tender, yet so tough-minded and realistic, Deborah wrote about the change which had so struck me: that Clive was now "garrulous and outgoing . . . could talk the hind legs off a donkey." There were certain themes he tended to stick to, she said, favorite subjects (electricity, the Tube, stars and planets, Queen Victoria, words and etymologies), which would all be brought up again and again:

"Have they found life on Mars yet?"

"No, darling, but they think there might have been water . . ."

"Really? Isn't it amazing that the sun goes on burning? Where does it get all that fuel? It doesn't get any smaller. And it doesn't move. We move round the sun. How can it keep on burning for millions of years? And the earth stays the same temperature. It's so finely balanced."

"They say it's getting warmer now, love. They call it global warming."

"No! Why's that?"

"Because of the pollution. We've been emitting gases into the atmosphere. And puncturing the ozone layer."

"OH NO!! That could be disastrous!"

"People are already getting more cancers."

"Oh, aren't people stupid! Do you know the average IQ is only 100? That's terribly low, isn't it? One hundred. It's no wonder the world's in such a mess."

"Cleverness isn't everything . . ."

"Well, no . . ."

"It's better to be good-hearted than clever."

"Yes, you've got a point."

"And you don't have to be clever to be wise."

"No, that's true."

Clive's scripts were repeated with great frequency, sometimes three or four times in one phone call. He stuck to subjects he felt he knew something about, where he would be on safe ground, even if here and there something apocryphal crept in. . . . These small areas of repartee acted as stepping stones on which he could move through the present. They enabled him to engage with others.

I would put it even more strongly and use a phrase that Deborah used in another connection, when she wrote of Clive being poised upon "a tiny platform . . . above the abyss." Clive's loquacity, his almost compulsive need to talk and keep conversations going, served to maintain a precarious platform, and when he came to a stop, the abyss was there, waiting to engulf him. This, indeed, is what happened when we went to a supermarket and he got separated briefly from Deborah. He suddenly exclaimed, "I'm conscious now . . . never saw a human being before . . . for thirty years . . . it's like death!" He looked very angry and distressed.

Deborah said the staff calls these grim monologues his "deads"—
they make a note of how many he has in a day or a week and gauge
his state of mind by their number.

Deborah thinks that repetition has slightly dulled the very
real pain that goes with this agonized but stereotyped complaint,
but when he says such things, she will distract him immediately.
Once she has done this, there seems to be no lingering mood—an
advantage of his amnesia. And, indeed, once we were back in the
car, Clive was off on his license plates again.

B ACK IN HIS ROOM, I spotted the two volumes of Bach's
Forty-eight Preludes and Fugues on top of the piano and
asked Clive if he would play one of them. He said that he had
never played any of them before, but then he played Prelude 9 in
E major and said as he played, "I remember this one." He remembers almost nothing unless he is actually doing it; then it may
come to him. He inserted a tiny, charming improvisation at one
point, and did a sort of Chico Marx ending, with a huge down-
ward scale. With his great musicality and his playfulness, he can
easily improvise, joke, play with any piece of music.[5]

---

5. Some readers have expressed surprise that someone with a dense amnesia like Clive's
should be able to be playful or to improvise. Would not the performance of an amnesiac be
fixed in tempo, dynamics, phrasing, etc.? But spontaneity, improvisation, experiment, and
exploration are built into the mind of any creative musician (Mozart, it is said, could
hardly play a piece of music—his own or anyone else's—*without* improvising, fiddling
with it a bit), and these qualities are evident even in the musical hallucinations Clive has
had for years.

Deborah wrote about this in a 1995 article coauthored with the psychologist Barbara
Wilson:

He hears what he thinks is a tape of himself playing in the distance. He refers to
this in his diaries as a "master tape." . . . If asked to sing what he can hear—a
sound only ever heard in the distance—he picks the tune up in the middle and is
puzzled that no one else hears it. Half an hour later when asked to sing what he
can hear it is usually the same tune but sometimes sung in a different style as if it
were replaying in variations.

His eye fell on the book about cathedrals, and he talked about cathedral bells—did I know how many combinations there could be with eight bells? "Eight by seven by six by five by four by three by two by one," he rattled off. "Factorial eight." And then, without pause: "That's forty thousand." (I worked it out laboriously: it is 40,320.)

I asked him about prime ministers. Tony Blair? Never heard of him. John Major? No. Margaret Thatcher? Vaguely familiar. Harold Macmillan, Harold Wilson: ditto. (But earlier in the day, he had seen a car with JMV plates and instantly said, "John Major Vehicle"—showing that he had an *implicit* memory of Major's name.) Deborah wrote of how he could not remember *her* name, "but one day someone asked him to say his full name, and he said, 'Clive David Deborah Wearing—funny name that. I don't know why my parents called me that.'" He has gained other implicit memories, too, slowly picking up new knowledge, like the layout of his residence. He can go alone now to the bathroom, the dining room, the kitchen—but if he stops and thinks en route, he is lost. Though he could not describe his residence, Deborah tells me that he unclasps his seat belt as they draw near and offers to get out and open the gate. Later, when he makes her coffee, he knows where the cups, the milk, and the sugar are kept. (He cannot *say* where they are, but he can go to them; he has actions, but few facts, at his disposal.)

I decided to widen the testing and asked Clive to tell me the names of all the composers he knew. He said, "Handel, Bach, Beethoven, Berg, Mozart, Lassus." That was it. Deborah told me that at first, when asked this question, he would omit Lassus, his favorite composer. This seemed appalling for someone who had been not only a musician but an encyclopedic musicologist. Perhaps it reflected the shortness of his attention and recent immediate memory—perhaps he thought that he had in fact given us dozens of names. So I asked him other questions on a variety of topics that he would have been knowledgeable about in his earlier days. Again, there was a paucity of information in his replies and sometimes something close to a blank. I started to feel that I had been beguiled, in a sense, by Clive's easy, nonchalant, fluent conversation into thinking that he still had a great deal of general information at his disposal, despite the loss of memory for events. Given his intelligence, ingenuity, and humor, it was easy to think this on meeting him for the first time. But repeated conversations rapidly exposed the limits of his knowledge. As Deborah writes in her book, Clive "stuck to subjects he knew something about" and used these islands of knowledge as "stepping stones" in his conversation. Clearly Clive's general knowledge, or semantic memory, was greatly affected, too— though not as catastrophically as his episodic memory.[6]

Yet semantic memory of this sort, even if completely intact, is not of much use in the absence of explicit, episodic memory. Clive is safe enough in the confines of his residence, for instance, but he would be hopelessly lost if he were to go out alone. Lawrence Weiskrantz comments on the need for both sorts of memory in his book *Consciousness Lost and Found*:

> The amnesic patient can think about material in the immediate present . . . he can also think about items in his semantic memory, his general knowledge. . . . But thinking for successful everyday adaptation requires not only factual knowledge, but the ability to recall it on the right occasion, to relate it to other occasions, indeed the ability to reminisce.

---

6. This erosion of semantic memory in Clive's case was emphasized in a 1995 paper by Barbara Wilson, A. D. Baddeley, and Narinder Kapur, and also in a 1995 chapter by Barbara Wilson and Deborah Wearing.

This uselessness of semantic memory unaccompanied by episodic memory is also brought out by Umberto Eco in his novel *The Mysterious Flame of Queen Loana*, where the narrator, an antiquarian bookseller and polymath, is a man of Eco-like intelligence and erudition. Though amnesic from a stroke, he retains the poetry he has read, the many languages he knows, his encyclopedic memory of facts; but he is nonetheless helpless and disoriented (and recovers from this only because the effects of his stroke are transient).

It is similar, in a way, with Clive. His semantic memory, while of little help in organizing his life, does have a crucial social role; it allows him to engage in conversation (though it is occasionally more monologue than conversation). Thus, Deborah wrote, "he would string all his subjects together in a row, and the other person simply needed to nod or mumble." By moving rapidly from one thought to another, Clive managed to secure a sort of continuity, to hold the thread of consciousness and attention intact—albeit precariously, for the thoughts were held together, on the whole, by superficial associations. Clive's verbosity made him a little odd, a little too much at times, but it was highly adaptive—it enabled him to reenter the world of human discourse.

In the 1986 BBC film Deborah quoted Proust's description of waking from a heavy sleep, not knowing at first where he was, or who he was. He had only "the most rudimentary sense of existence, such as may lurk and flicker in the depths of an animal's consciousness" until memory came back to him, "like a rope let down from heaven to draw me up out of the abyss of not-being, from which I could never have escaped by myself"—this gave him back his personal consciousness and identity. No rope from heaven, no autobiographical memory will ever come down in this way to Clive.

. . .

FROM THE START there have been, for Clive, two realities of immense importance. The first of these is Deborah, whose presence and love for him have made life tolerable, at least intermittently, in the twenty or more years since his illness.

Clive's amnesia not only destroyed his ability to retain new memories, it deleted almost all of his earlier memories, including those of the years when he met and fell in love with Deborah—he told Deborah, when she questioned him, that he had never heard of John Lennon or John F. Kennedy. Though he always recognized his own children, Deborah told me, "he would be surprised at their height and amazed to hear he is a grandfather. He asked his younger son what O-level exams he was doing in 2005, more than twenty years after Edmund left school." Yet somehow he always recognized Deborah as his wife when she visited and felt moored by her presence, lost without her. He would rush to the door when he heard her voice, and embrace her with passionate, desperate fervor. Having no idea how long she had been away—since anything not in his immediate field of perception and attention would be lost, forgotten, within seconds—he seemed to feel that she, too, had been lost in the abyss of time, and so her "return" from the abyss seemed nothing short of miraculous.

"Clive was constantly surrounded by strangers in a strange place," Deborah wrote,

> with no knowledge of where he was or what had happened to him. To catch sight of me was always a massive relief—to know that he was not alone, that I still cared, that I loved him, that I was there. Clive was terrified all the time. But I

was his life, I was his lifeline. Every time he saw me, he would run to me, fall on me, sobbing, clinging.

How, why, when he recognized no one else with any consistency, did Clive recognize Deborah? There are clearly many sorts of memory, and emotional memory is one of the deepest and least understood.

Neal J. Cohen has written about the famous experiment of Édouard Claparède, a Swiss physician, in 1911:

> Upon shaking hands with a patient with Korsakoff syndrome [the condition which caused my patient Jimmie's severe amnesia], Claparède pricked her finger with a pin hidden in his hand. Subsequently, whenever he again attempted to shake the patient's hand, she promptly withdrew it. When he questioned her about this behavior, she replied, "Isn't it allowed to withdraw one's hand?" and "Perhaps there is a pin hidden in your hand," and finally, "Sometimes pins are hidden in hands." Thus the patient learned the appropriate response based on previous experience, but she never seemed to attribute her behavior to the personal memory of some previously experienced event.

For Claparède's patient, some sort of memory of the pain, an implicit and emotional memory, persisted. It seems certain, likewise, that in the first two years of life, even though one retains no explicit memories (Freud called this infantile amnesia), deep emotional memories or associations are nevertheless being made in the limbic system and other regions of the brain where emotions are represented—and these emotional memories may determine one's behavior for a lifetime. And a recent paper by Oliver Turnbull et al. has shown that patients with amnesia can form emotional transferences to an analyst, even though they retain no explicit memory of the analyst or their previous meetings. Nevertheless, a strong emotional bond begins to develop. Clive and Deborah were newly married at the time of his encephalitis, and deeply in love for a few years before that. His passionate relationship with Deborah, a relationship that began before his encephalitis, and one that centers in part on their shared love for music, has engraved itself in him—in areas of his brain unaffected by the encephalitis—so deeply that his amnesia, the most severe amnesia ever recorded, cannot eradicate it.

Nonetheless, for many years he failed to recognize Deborah if she chanced to walk past and even now, he cannot say what she looks like unless he is actually looking at her. Her appearance, her voice, her scent, the way they behave with each other, and the intensity of their emotions and interactions—all this confirms her identity, and his own.

The other miracle was the discovery Deborah made early on, while Clive was still in the hospital, desperately confused and disoriented: that his musical powers were totally intact. "I picked up some music," Deborah wrote,

> and held it open for Clive to see. I started to sing one of the lines. He picked up the tenor lines and sang with me. A bar or so in, I suddenly realized what was happening. He could still read music. He was singing. His talk might be a jumble no one could understand but his brain was still capable of music. . . . I could hardly wait to get back to the ward and share this news. When he got to the end of the line I hugged him and kissed him all over his face. . . .

Clive could sit down at the organ and play with both hands on the keyboard, changing stops, and with his feet on the pedals, as if this were easier than riding a bicycle. Suddenly we had a place to be together, where we could create our own world away from the ward. Our friends came in to sing. I left a pile of music by the bed and visitors brought other pieces.

Miller's film showed dramatically the virtually perfect preservation of Clive's musical powers and memory. In these scenes from only a year or so after his illness, his face often appeared tight with torment and bewilderment. But when he was conducting his old choir, he did this with great sensitivity and grace, mouthing the melodies, turning to different singers and sections of the choir, cuing them, encouraging them, to bring out their special parts. It is obvious that Clive not only knew the piece perfectly, how all the parts contributed to the unfolding of the musical thought, but also retained all the special skills of conducting, his professional persona, and his own unique style.

Clive cannot retain any memory of passing events and experience and, in addition, has lost most of the memories of events and experiences *preceding* his encephalitis—how, then, does he retain his remarkable knowledge of music, his ability to sight-read, to play the piano and organ, sing, conduct a choir, in the masterly way he did before he became ill?

H.M., a famous and unfortunate patient described by Scoville and Milner in 1957, was rendered amnesic by the surgical removal of both hippocampi along with adjacent structures of the medial temporal lobes. (This was a desperate attempt at treating his intractable seizures; it was not yet realized that autobiographic memory and the ability to form new memories of events depended on these structures.) Yet H.M., though he lost many memories of his former life, had not lost any of the skills he had acquired, and indeed he could learn and perfect *new* skills with training and practice, even though he would retain no memory of the practice sessions.

Larry Squire, a neuroscientist who has spent a lifetime exploring mechanisms of memory and amnesia, emphasizes that no two cases of amnesia are the same. He wrote to me,

> If the damage is limited to the medial temporal lobe, then one expects an impairment such as H.M. had. With somewhat more extensive medial temporal lobe damage, one can expect something more severe, as in E.P. [this is a patient whom Squire and his colleagues have investigated intensively]. With the addition of frontal damage, perhaps one begins to understand Clive's impairment. Or perhaps one needs lateral temporal damage as well, or basal forebrain damage. Clive's case is unique, and not like H.M. or like Claparède's patient, because a particular pattern of anatomical damage occurred. We cannot write about amnesia as if it were a single entity like mumps or measles.

Yet H.M.'s case made it clear that two very different sorts of memory could exist: a conscious memory of events (episodic memory) and an unconscious memory for procedures—and that such procedural memory is unimpaired in amnesia.

This is dramatically clear with Clive, too, for he can shave, shower, look after his grooming, and dress elegantly, with taste and style; he moves confidently and is fond of dancing. He talks fluently and abundantly, using a large vocabulary; he can read and write in several languages. He is good at calculation. He can make phone calls, and he can find the coffee things and find his way about the home. If he is asked how to do these things, he cannot say, but he does them. Whatever involves a sequence or pattern of action, he does fluently, unhesitatingly.[7]

But can Clive's beautiful playing and singing, his masterly conducting, his powers of improvisation be adequately characterized as "skills" or "procedure"? For his playing is infused

---

7. An extraordinary but not uncommon condition, first recognized in the 1960s, is transient global amnesia, or TGA—an amnesia that lasts only a few hours but may be very severe. It has never been clear what causes TGAs, but they are more common in middle-aged and elderly patients and sometimes occur in the course of a migraine; there is often only a single attack in a lifetime. Such a transient amnesia may come on at any time, with effects that can be comic or alarming. My niece Caroline Bearsted, a physician in England, told me of a patient of hers, an ardent fisherman, who had longed for years to catch a giant trout in a nearby stream. By a bizarre coincidence, he had an attack of TGA while he was fishing one day. It did not impair his skills in the least, and he caught the trout—but catching it, the absolute peak of his fishing life, left no trace in his mind, and no memory of it was ever retrieved. When shown photographs of himself cradling the prize fish in his arms, he did not know whether to laugh or cry.

A more alarming story was related to me by the neurologist Harold Klawans, about a colleague of his, a general surgeon, who became amnesic towards the end of a gallbladder operation. He became uncertain, confused, repetitive: "Did I remove the gallbladder?" he asked repeatedly. "What am I doing? Where am I?" The nurse who was assisting him wondered if he had had a stroke but, seeing that his surgical skill was unimpaired despite a profound memory impairment, kept him going by handing him the sutures one by one—and so, with her help, he closed the abdomen successfully. While he was himself again in a few hours, he never recovered any memory of the operation he had performed. Klawans subsequently published a description of this incident, and of his own careful examination of the surgeon while still amnesic.

The commonest cause of a brief global amnesia is a "blackout," as may occur if one has drunk too heavily. It is typical here, as in attacks of TGA, that one may—like the fisherman or the surgeon—function at quite a high level; event memory may be knocked out, but procedural memory can carry one along. A correspondent, Matthew H., related the following story:

> I used to play keyboards in a rock band for many years, and for my twenty-second birthday we were playing in a small town at a small bar (luckily with not too many patrons). Being young and irresponsible, I drank a few too many alcoholic beverages in between sets. Then I seem to have blacked out, and "came to" on stage while playing a Rolling Stones song. I was so inebriated that I remember being amazed that my fingers could play the song, and I was completely disassociated from it, just watching them move and play the right notes and chords with the rest of the band. When I tried to interject and "play along" with the music, I literally could not remember how to play a single thing, and I completely interrupted the flow of my playing. Luckily I seem to have blacked out again after that, because that was all I remembered. Oddly enough, when I quizzed my band mates the next day, they said that I played along with every song just fine (aside from the brief interlude during the Stones song), and they had not known I was so drunk.

with intelligence and feeling, with a sensitive attunement to the musical structure, the composer's style and mind. Can any artistic or creative performance of this caliber be adequately explained by "procedural memory"? Episodic or explicit memory, we know, develops relatively late in childhood and is dependent on a complex brain system involving the hippocampi and temporal lobe structures, the system that is compromised in severe amnesiacs and all but obliterated in Clive. The basis of procedural or implicit memory is less easy to define, but it certainly involves larger and more primitive parts of the brain—subcortical structures like the basal ganglia and cerebellum and their many connections to each other and to the cerebral cortex. The size and variety of these systems guarantees the robustness of procedural memory and the fact that, unlike episodic memory, procedural memory can remain largely intact even in the face of extensive damage to the hippocampi and medial temporal lobe structures.

Episodic memory depends on the perception of particular and often unique events, and one's memories of such events, like one's original perception of them, are not only highly individual (colored by one's interests, concerns, and values), but prone to be revised or recategorized every time they are recalled. This is in fundamental contrast to procedural memory, where it is all-important that the remembering be literal, exact, and reproducible. Repetition and rehearsal, timing and sequence are of the essence here. Rodolfo Llinás, the neurophysiologist, uses the term "fixed action patterns" (FAPs) for such procedural memories. Some of these may be present even before birth (fetal horses, for example, may gallop in the womb). Much of the early motor development of the child depends on learning and refining such procedures, through play, imitation, trial and error, and incessant rehearsal. All of these start to develop long before the child can call on any explicit or episodic memories.

Is the concept of fixed action patterns any more illuminating than that of procedural memories in relation to the enormously complex, creative performances of a professional musician? In his book *I of the Vortex*, Llinás writes:

> When a soloist such as [Jascha] Heifetz plays with a symphony orchestra accompanying him, by convention the concerto is played purely from memory. Such playing implies that this highly specific motor pattern is stored somewhere and subsequently released at the time the curtain goes up.

But for a performer, Llinás writes, it is not sufficient to have implicit memory only; one must have explicit memory as well:[8]

> Without intact explicit memory, Jascha Heifetz would not remember from day to day which piece he had chosen to work on previously, or that he had ever worked on that piece before. Nor would he recall what he had accomplished the day before or by analysis of past experience what particular problems in execution should be a focus of today's practice session. In fact, it would not occur to him to have a practice session at all; without close direction from someone else he would be effectively incapable of undertaking the process of learning any new piece, irrespective of his considerable technical skills.

---

8. There is no one way to memorize a piece of music—different musicians use different ways, or combinations of ways: auditory, kinesthetic, visual, along with higher-order perceptions of the music's rules, grammar, feeling, and intentionality. We know this not only from personal accounts of musical memory and experimental studies of it, but from the many brain regions which (with fMRI) are visibly activated in the learning of a new piece.

But once a piece *is* learned, analyzed, studied, pondered, practiced, and incorporated into one's repertoire—one's procedural memory—then it can be played or will "play itself" automatically, without effort of deliberation or conscious thought.

This, too, is very much the case with Clive, who, for all his musical powers, needs "close direction" from others. He needs someone to put the music before him, to get him into action, and to make sure that he learns and practices new pieces.

What is the relationship of action patterns and procedural memories, which are associated with relatively primitive portions of the nervous system, to consciousness and sensibility, which depend on the cerebral cortex? Practice involves conscious application, monitoring what one is doing, bringing all one's intelligence and sensibility and values to bear—even though what is so painfully and consciously acquired may then become automatic, coded in motor patterns at a subcortical level. Each time Clive sings or plays the piano or conducts a choir, automatism comes to his aid. But what comes out in an artistic or creative performance, though it depends on automatisms, is anything but automatic. The actual performance reanimates him, engages him as a creative person; it becomes fresh and alive, and perhaps contains new improvisations or innovations.[9] Once Clive starts playing, his "momentum," as Deborah writes, will keep him, and keep the piece, going. Deborah, herself a musician, expresses this very precisely:

> The momentum of the music carried Clive from bar to bar. Within the structure of the piece, he was held, as if the

---

9. The ability to retain and enlarge artistic repertoire, even in the presence of amnesia, was also startlingly evident in an eminent actor who developed amnesia after open-heart surgery. Despite the loss of event memory, his enormous repertoire, from Marlowe to Beckett, and his superb acting skills were never affected, and he remains able to perform at the highest professional level. His ability to learn new parts is also quite intact—for learning a part, entering into it, taking it into oneself, is very different from acquiring new "information" and is essentially procedural in character. Lacking any explicit memory of his past performances, he feels, may even be an advantage, for it enables him to confront every night on stage as something new and unique, to which he will respond in rich and unexpected ways.

staves were tramlines and there was only one way to go. He knew exactly where he was because in every phrase there is context implied, by rhythm, key, melody. It was marvellous to be free. When the music stopped Clive fell through to the lost place. But for those moments he was playing he seemed normal.

Clive's performance self seems, to those who know him, just as vivid and complete as it was before his illness. This mode of being, this self, is seemingly untouched by his amnesia, even though his autobiographical self, the self that depends on explicit, episodic memories, is virtually lost. The rope that is let down from heaven for Clive comes not with recalling the past, as for Proust, but with performance—and it holds only as long as the performance lasts. Without performance, the thread is broken, and he is thrown back once again into the abyss.[10]

---

10. It was very similar for the amnesic narrator in Umberto Eco's novel *The Mysterious Flame of Queen Loana:*

> I started humming a tune to myself. It was automatic, like brushing my teeth . . . but once I began thinking about it, the song no longer came of its own accord, and I stopped on a single note. I held it a long time, at least five seconds, as if it were an alarm or dirge. I no longer knew how to go forward, and I didn't know how to go forward because I had lost what came before. . . . While I was singing without thinking I was actually myself for the duration of my memory, which in that case was what you might call throat memory, with the befores and afters linked together, and I was the complete song, and every time I began it my vocal cords were already preparing to vibrate the sounds to come. I think a pianist works that way, too: even as he plays one note he's readying his fingers to strike the keys that come next. Without the first notes, we won't make it to the last ones, we'll come untuned, and we'll succeed in getting from start to finish only if we somehow contain the entire song within us. I don't know the whole song anymore. I'm like . . . a burning log. The log burns, but it has no awareness of having once been part of a whole trunk nor any way to find out that it has been, or to know when it caught fire. So it burns up and that's all. I'm living in pure loss.

Eco's narrator may call it "pure loss," but the wonder of it, in fact, is that it is pure *gain*. One can gain the whole song without any explicit memory, any memory in the usual sense. The song almost miraculously seems to create itself, note by note, coming from nowhere—and yet, "somehow," as Eco puts it, we contain the entire song.

Deborah speaks of the "momentum" of the music in its very structure. A piece of music is not a mere sequence of notes, but a tightly organized organic whole. Every bar, every phrase, arises organically from what preceded it and points to what will follow. Dynamism is built into the nature of melody. And over and above this, there is the intentionality of the composer, the style, the order, and the logic which he has created to express his musical ideas and feelings. These, too, are present in every bar and phrase.[11] Marvin Minsky compares a sonata to a teacher or a lesson:

> No one remembers, word for word, all that was said in any lecture, or played in any piece. But if you understood it once, you now own new networks of knowledge, about each theme, and how it changes and relates to others. Thus, no one could remember Beethoven's Fifth Symphony entire, from a single hearing. But neither could one ever hear again those first four notes as just four notes! Once but a tiny scrap of sound, it is now a Known Thing—a locus in the web of all the other things we know, whose meanings and significances depend on each other.

A piece of music will draw one in, teach one about its structure and secrets, whether one is listening consciously or not. This is so even if one has never heard a piece of music before. Listening to music is not a passive process but intensely active, involving a stream of inferences, hypotheses, expectations, and anticipations (as David Huron and others have explored). We can grasp a new piece—how it is constructed, where it is going, what

---

11. Schopenhauer wrote of melody as having "significant and intentional connection from beginning to end" and as "one thought from beginning to end."

will come next—with such accuracy that even after a few bars we may be able to hum or sing along with it.[12]

When we "remember" a melody, it plays in our mind; it becomes newly alive.[13] There is not a process of recalling, imagining, assembling, recategorizing, re-creating, as when one attempts to reconstruct or remember an event or a scene from the past. We recall one tone at a time and each tone entirely fills our consciousness, yet simultaneously it relates to the whole. It is similar when we walk or run or swim—we do so one step, one stroke at a time, yet each step or stroke is an integral part of the whole, the kinetic melody of running or swimming. Indeed, if we think of each note or step too consciously, we may lose the thread, the motor melody.

---

12. Such anticipation, such singing along, is possible because one has knowledge, largely implicit, of musical "rules" (how a cadence must resolve, for instance) and a familiarity with particular musical conventions (the form of a sonata, or the repetition of a theme). But anticipation is not possible with music from a very different culture or tradition—or if musical conventions are deliberately shattered. Jonah Lehrer, in his book *Proust Was a Neuroscientist*, discusses how Stravinsky did this, famously, with his *Rite of Spring*, whose first performance in 1913 caused a riot that required the Paris police to intervene. The audience, which had expected a traditional, classical ballet, was enraged by Stravinsky's violation of the rules. But with time and repetition, the strange became familiar, and *The Rite of Spring* is now a beloved concert piece, as "tame" as a Beethoven minuet (though Beethoven, too, was hissed in his time, and some of his music regarded at first as unintelligible, mere noise).

13. Thus we can listen again and again to a recording of a piece of music, a piece we know well, and yet it can seem as fresh, as new, as the first time we heard it. Zuckerkandl addresses this paradox in *Sound and Symbol:*

> Time is always new; cannot possibly be anything but new. Heard as a succession of acoustical events, music will soon become boring; heard as the manifestation of time eventuating, it can never bore. The paradox appears at its most acute in the achievement of a performing musician, who attains the heights if he succeeds in performing a work with which he is thoroughly familiar, as if it were the creation of the present moment.

Pablo Casals, the consummate cellist, was also an excellent pianist, and once when he was in his nineties, he commented to an interviewer that he had played one of Bach's *Forty-Eight Preludes and Fugues* every morning for the past eighty-five years. Did he not get tired of this? the interviewer asked. Was it not boring? No, replied Casals, each playing for him was a new experience, an act of discovery.

It may be that Clive, incapable of remembering or anticipating events because of his amnesia, is able to sing and play and conduct music because remembering music is not, in the usual sense, remembering at all. Remembering music, listening to it, or playing it, is entirely in the present.

Victor Zuckerkandl, a philosopher of music, explores this paradox beautifully in his book *Sound and Symbol:*

> The hearing of a melody is a hearing *with* the melody. . . . It is even a condition of hearing melody that the tone present at the moment should fill consciousness *entirely*, that *nothing* should be remembered, nothing except it or beside it be present in consciousness. . . . Hearing a melody is hearing, having heard, and being about to hear, all at once. Every melody declares to us that the past can be there without being remembered, the future without being foreknown.

It has been twenty years since Clive's illness and, for him, nothing has moved on. One might say he is still in 1985 or, given his retrograde amnesia, in 1965. In some ways, he is not anywhere at all; he has dropped out of space and time altogether. He no longer has any inner narrative; he is not leading a life in the sense that the rest of us do. And yet one has only to see him at the keyboard or with Deborah to feel that, at such times, he is himself again and wholly alive. It is not the remembrance of things past, the "once" that Clive yearns for, or can ever achieve. It is the claiming, the filling, of the present, the now, and this is only possible when he is totally immersed in the successive moments of an act. It is the "now" that bridges the abyss.

As Deborah recently wrote to me, "Clive's at-homeness in music and in his love for me are where he transcends amnesia and finds continuum—not the linear fusion of moment after moment, nor based on any framework of autobiographical information, but where Clive, and any of us, *are* finally, where we are who we are."

Postscript

In the spring of 2008, Deborah sent me an update. More than twenty years after his initial illness, she wrote,

> Clive continues to surprise us. Recently he looked at my mobile phone and asked, "Does it take pictures?" (it doesn't), showing new semantic memory. Earlier this month I'd been with Clive, then went outside for about ten minutes. I rang the doorbell to get back in and Clive opened the door with the care assistant who had been with him the whole time. Clive said, "Welcome back!," perfectly aware that I'd been there previously. His care assistant commented on this change. The staff also told me how one day a care assistant had lost her lighter. Ten or fifteen minutes after hearing this, Clive came up to the same lady and gave her the lost lighter, saying, "Is this your lighter?" The staff could find no explanation for his remembering who had lost the lighter or that she had lost the lighter. . . .
>
> We are going to attend a rehearsal of Monteverdi Vespers the weekend after next. Whenever his care assistants mention this, Clive is clearly delighted, saying it is one of his favourite works. If he hears a piece he knew well in the past he can, when appropriate, sing along with it.
>
> Clive does not "think about" a piece of music in the sense that professional musicians might muse about how to perform it. An encounter with any piece of music will be as

"sight-reading." However, Clive shows when he does or doesn't remember the piece—for example, if I am slow to turn over the page, he will either pause because he doesn't know what comes next or he may start playing the next page of music before seeing it.

I would agree with your impression that Clive's instrumental performances are not fixed in tempo, phrasing, etc. But because Clive is a good musician, he consistently follows the dynamics and tempos—even metronome marks (without recourse to a metronome)—from the page. Where there is no metronome mark, his tempo will still usually be the tempo he would have set before his illness—and probably informed by long-term memory of a piece or of performance practice for the style/era of music.

Are Clive's performances mechanical? No, they are reflective of his sense of performance style, humour and a general exuberant joie de vivre. But because Clive is the same person, he may well respond to a piece of music consistently. Any musician will have his or her own interpretation of the phrasing or 'colour' of a piece (where not prescribed by the composer). However, where Clive's amnesia shows through is in repetition of similar music "jokes" at similar places—improvisatory witticisms. Any musician improvising on the hop may draw from a repertoire of possible formulae and may be likely to come up with similar ideas. Clive does have some fixed reactions to the same pieces of music— at a cadenza full of semi-quavers in the Bach Prelude he played for you, you may remember he "approximated" the scale very roughly, playing some fistfuls of notes. He always does this and always for the same reason, consistent with his priorities in performing: realising he would be unable to execute the scale at the very quick speed required, he sacrifices accuracy in a mad flurry in order not to lose the tempo. For a conductor, tempo is everything. He also exaggerates the wrong notes flurry, so even if it can't be accurate, he will at least make it amusing.

The context of all this is that Clive's performances are in any case not anything like the standard of performance from before he was ill. Principally a conductor, he was never a performing pianist—his keyboard skills were more workaday for the purpose of accompanying singers or score-reading, trying out a piece written for larger forces. There was a period when [there was a staff worker at the home who was] a very accomplished musician and practised with Clive almost daily. At that time, Clive's standard of performance was raised considerably. . . . How interesting that practising in a disciplined way, interacting with another musician, caused him to "learn" a piece even if he had no knowledge of playing it before. Likewise, being left to his own devices, never having another person to slow down a piece in order to learn to play it, means Clive's standard of performance, not surprisingly, doesn't get better.

What I've noticed lately is that when I sing with Clive he corrects me, pointing out when I am not pronouncing all the consonants with clarity, stopping me and saying, "No, no, it's a B flat there—take it from bar 11," with a new authority I haven't seen since before he was ill.

16

Speech and Song:
Aphasia and Music Therapy

Samuel S. developed severe expressive aphasia following a stroke in his late sixties, and he remained totally speechless, unable to retrieve a single word, despite intensive speech therapy, two years later. The break for him came when Connie Tomaino, the music therapist at our hospital, heard him singing one day outside her clinic—he was singing "Ol' Man River" very tunefully and with great feeling, but only getting two or three words of the song. Even though speech therapy had been given up with Samuel, who was by then regarded as "hopeless," Connie felt that music therapy might be helpful. She started to meet with him three times a week for half-hour sessions in which she would sing with him or accompany him on the accordion. Mr. S. was soon able, singing along with Connie, to get all the words of "Ol' Man River," and then of many other ballads and songs he had learned growing up in the 1940s—and as he did this, he started to show the beginnings of speech. Within two months, he was making short but appropriate responses to questions. For instance, if one of us asked Mr. S. about his weekends at home, he could reply, "Had a great time," or "Saw the kids."

Neurologists often refer to a "speech area" in the premotor zone of the brain's dominant (usually left) frontal lobe. Damage to a particular part of this—an area first identified by the French neurologist Paul Broca in 1862—whether from a degenerative disease, a stroke, or a brain injury, may produce expressive aphasia, a loss of spoken language. In 1873 Carl Wernicke had described a different speech area in the left temporal lobe— damage to this area was apt to produce difficulty understanding speech, a "receptive" aphasia. It was also recognized, at much the same time, that brain damage could produce disturbances of musical expression or appreciation—amusias—and that while some patients might suffer from both an aphasia and an amusia, others could have aphasia without amusia.[1]

We are a linguistic species—we turn to language to express whatever we are thinking, and it is usually there for us instantly. But for those with aphasia, the inability to communicate verbally may be almost unbearably frustrating and isolating; to make matters worse, they are often treated by others as idiots, almost as nonpersons, because they cannot speak. Much of this can change with the discovery that such patients can *sing*—sing not only tunes, but the words of operas, hymns, or songs. Suddenly their disability, their cut-offness, seems much less—and though singing is not propositional communication, it is a very

---

1. John C. Brust, in his extensive review of the literature on music and the brain, points out that such a case was recorded as early as 1745—this patient had severe expressive aphasia, and his speech was limited to the word "yes." But he could nonetheless sing hymns, if someone else sang along.

Similarly, the Russian composer Vissarion Shebalin suffered a series of strokes which produced a profound receptive aphasia. But, as Luria et al. described, he was able to continue composing at his previous level. (Shostakovich called Shebalin's Fifth Symphony, composed after his stroke, a "brilliant creative work, filled with highest emotion [and] optimism and full of life.")

basic existential communication. It not only says, "I am alive, I am here," but may express thoughts and feelings that cannot be expressed, at this point, by speech. Being able to sing words can be a great reassurance to such patients, showing them that their language capacities are not irretrievably lost, that the words are still "in" them, somewhere, even though it may take music to bring them out. Whenever I see patients with expressive aphasia, I sing "Happy Birthday" to them. Virtually all of them (often to their own astonishment) start to join in, singing the tune; about half of them will get the words, too.[2]

Speech itself is not just a succession of words in the proper order—it has inflections, intonations, tempo, rhythm, and "melody." Language and music both depend on phonatory and articulatory mechanisms that are rudimentary in other primates, and both depend, for their appreciation, on distinctly human

---

2. Autistic children may have specific difficulties both in speaking and in recognizing the spoken word (Isabelle Rapin has referred to this as verbal auditory agnosia)—but they may be able to sing or to understand speech if it is set to music. I have received many letters about this from their parents. Arlyn Kantz, a musician, wrote:

When my son was diagnosed with autism, one of the first things I noticed when he was a preschooler was that he could sing entire theme songs but could not respond to simple social questions like "What is your name?" He would echo the question or simply ignore us. When I set this speech lesson to music, leaving gaps for him to fill in, he quickly began to respond correctly. When I faded out the music, his correct responses continued. This led to setting more and more of his speech development drills to music, with the same successful results.

Kantz went on to form a singing-based curriculum for language-impaired children, which is now used in a number of institutions.

Similarly, Melanie Mirvis, a British speech and language therapist, wrote:

I was working with a very musical boy with autism, who had the typical difficulties with language; specifically he took a long time to "process" language and then questions would often have to be repeated several times before he produced a verbal response. I did, however, notice that when I sung him a question, he could sing me an answer immediately.

Another parent, Tracy King, wrote about her son, Sean (now twenty-one), who has Asperger's syndrome: "The most profoundly helpful 'therapy' in his life has been music. It has filled him with purpose and has often bridged the social gaps that have been so difficult for him to navigate. He uses his guitar and singing as a way to connect with others."

brain mechanisms dedicated to the analysis of complex, seg-mented, rapidly changing streams of sound. And yet there are major differences (and some overlaps) in the representation of speech and song in the brain.[3]

Patients with so-called nonfluent aphasia not only have an impairment of vocabulary and grammar, but have "forgotten" or lost the feeling of the rhythms and inflections of speech; hence the broken, unmusical, telegraphic style of their speech, to the extent that they still have any words available. It is such patients who, as a rule, do best with music therapy, and who feel most excited when they are able to sing lyrics—for in doing so, they discover not only that words are still available to them, but that the flow of speech is also accessible (though bound, apparently, to the flow of song).[4]

This may also be the case with a different form of aphasia, so-called dynamic aphasia, where it is not the structure of sentences

---

3. One might expect some coupling or correlation of musical and linguistic abilities, especially in regard to learning the accents, inflections, and prosody of a new language. This is often, but not necessarily, the case. Thus Steve Salemson, a former French horn player, wrote to me contrasting his superb ability to recognize linguistic accents with his "mediocre" musical skills and lack of absolute pitch:

> I can readily distinguish a major scale from a minor scale, but have no sense of any particular key without some point of reference. I know the keys of most sym-phonic works, but if you were to play me a recording of Brahms' Second Symphony (the "blue one" in D major) that had been transposed into E-flat or C-sharp major, I doubt whether I'd be likely to notice. I've tried to will myself to hear a difference in keys, but—alas!—to no avail. [But] I am an accomplished linguist, being totally bilingual in French and English, and also speaking excellent Hebrew, along with German and Macedonian (I'm a long-time Balkan folk dancer and fan of irregular Balkan meters). I've always had an outstanding ear for accents, so can only assume that this ability resides elsewhere in the brain than does that of pitch recognition.

But there *are* overlaps and, indeed, deep similarities between the brain's processing of language and of music (including their grammar), and these are especially the subject of Aniruddh D. Patel's book *Music, Language, and the Brain.*

4. The most common speech disorder is stuttering, and here—as the Greeks and Romans knew very well—even those who stutter so badly as to be almost incomprehensible can nearly always sing fluently and freely and, through singing or adopting a singsong manner of speech, can often overcome or bypass their stuttering.

that is affected but the initiation of speech. Patients with dynamic aphasia may speak very sparingly, yet produce syntactically correct sentences on the rare occasions when they do speak. Jason Warren et al. described how an elderly man with mild frontal lobe degeneration and extreme dynamic aphasia was nonetheless unimpaired in musical initiative. He played the piano, could read and write music, and took part in a weekly singing group. He was also able to recite, as Warren et al. noted: "He was able to read a passage chosen at random from the Torah using the heightened intonation (distinct from both singing and ordinary reading) reserved for reading aloud."

Many aphasic patients can get not only the words of songs, but can learn to repeat sequences or series—days of the week, months of the year, numerals, etc. They may be able to do this *as* a series, but not to disembed a particular item from the series. So one of my patients, for instance, can recite all the months of the year in order (January, February, March, April, May . . .); he knows what the current month is, but when I ask him, he cannot respond, simply, "April." Indeed, aphasics may be able to reproduce much more elaborate familiar sequences—a prayer, or lines from Shakespeare, or an entire poem—but only as automated sequences.[5] Such sequences unfold, once they are started, in much the same way as music does.

Hughlings Jackson long ago distinguished "propositional" speech from what he called, variously, "emotional," "ejaculate,"

---

5. In *Brave New World,* Aldous Huxley describes how sleep-teaching, hypnopedia, is used to feed information to the brains of sleeping children. Its powers are remarkable, but so are its limitations. Thus one child is able to give, in a single unbroken recitation, the names of all the longest rivers in the world and their lengths—but when he is asked, "What is the length of the Amazon?" he cannot bring this fact to explicit, conscious knowledge, cannot disembed it from the automated sequence.

One often has similar experiences in restaurants. Once, after a waiter reeled off a list of specials, I asked him to repeat what came after the tuna. He was unable to extract this one item from the sequence he held in memory, and had to reel off the entire list again.

or "automatic" speech, stressing that the latter could be preserved in aphasia, sometimes to a startling extent, even when the
former was grossly impaired. Cursing is often cited as a dramatic
form of automatic speech, but singing familiar lyrics can be seen
as equally automatic; a person with aphasia may be able to sing
or curse or recite a poem but not to utter a propositional phrase.

The question of whether singing has any use in the recovery
of speech, then, can be formulated another way: can language
embedded in unconscious automatism be "released" for conscious, propositional use?

During the Second World War, A. R. Luria began to investigate the neural basis of speech and language, of different forms
of aphasia, and of methods for restoring speech. (His work
was published in Russian in a massive monograph, *Traumatic
Aphasia*, in 1947, and in a small, startling book, *Restoration of
Function After Brain Injury*, in 1948—though neither was translated or known in the West until several decades later.) Given an
acute injury to the brain such as he saw in the stroke patients
or injured soldiers he studied, Luria emphasized, there would
always be two levels of disturbance. First, there was a "core" of
tissue destruction, which was irreversible; and second, a larger,
surrounding area, or "penumbra," of depressed or inhibited function, which under certain conditions, he felt, might be reversible.

When one first meets a patient immediately after a stroke or
head injury, one sees only the total effects of injury: paralysis, aphasia, or other disabilities. It is difficult to distinguish disabilities produced by anatomical damage from those produced by inhibition of
the surrounding neural tissue. Time will show the difference in
most patients, for inhibition tends to lift spontaneously, usually in
a matter of weeks. But in some patients, for reasons that are still
unclear, it does not. At this point (if not before), it is crucial to start
therapy, to promote what Luria called "de-inhibition."

Speech therapy may lead to de-inhibition, but it may sometimes fail; if it fails, one may wrongly assume that the patient's aphasia is due to permanent anatomical damage and is thus irreversible. But music therapy, for some patients, can succeed where conventional speech therapy has failed, as in the case of Samuel S. It may be that cortical areas previously inhibited but not destroyed can be de-inhibited, kick-started into action, by reexperiencing language, even if it is of a wholly automatic sort, language embedded in music.

A VERY CRUCIAL ASPECT of speech or music therapy for the aphasic patient is the relationship between therapist and patient. Luria emphasized that the origin of speech was social no less than neurological—it required the interaction of mother and child. It is likely that the same is true of song, and in this sense, music therapy for patients with aphasia is profoundly different from music therapy for a movement disorder like parkinsonism. In parkinsonism, it is the motor system which is being activated, almost automatically, by music—and a tape or CD, in this limited sense, can do as much as a therapist. But with speech disorders like aphasia, the therapist and her relationship with the patient—a relationship which involves not only musical and vocal interaction but physical contact, gesture, imitation of movement, and prosody—is an essential part of the therapy. This intimate working together, this working in tandem, depends on mirror neurons throughout the brain, which enable the patient not only to imitate but to incorporate the actions or abilities of others, as Rizzolatti et al. have explored.

The therapist not only provides support and an encouraging presence, but literally leads the patient into more and more complex forms of speech. With Samuel S., this involved drawing language out until he could sing all the words of "Ol' Man River," then leading him on to sing a whole range of old songs, then, by the right sort of questions, drawing him into short responsive phrases. Whether there is a chance of going beyond this, of restoring fluent narrative or propositional speech to patients with long-standing aphasia, remains an open question. Saying "Had a great time" or "Saw the kids" may be as far as Samuel S. can go. It might be said that such verbal responses are modest, limited, and formulaic—but they do represent a radical advance from purely automatic speech, and they can have an enormous effect on the daily reality of an aphasic person's life, allowing a formerly mute and isolated person to reenter a verbal world, a world he had seemingly lost forever.

In 1973 Martin Albert and his colleagues in Boston described a form of music therapy they called "melodic intonation therapy." Patients were taught to sing or intone short phrases—for example, "How are you today?" Then the musical elements of this were removed slowly until (in some cases) the patient regained the power to speak a little without the aid of intonation. One sixty-seven-year-old man, aphasic for eighteen months—he could only produce meaningless grunts, and had received three months of speech therapy without effect—started to produce words two days after beginning melodic intonation therapy; in two weeks, he had an effective vocabulary of a hundred words, and at six weeks, he could carry on "short, meaningful conversations."

What is happening in the brain when melodic intonation, or any type of music therapy, "works"? Albert et al. originally thought that it served to activate areas in the right hemisphere, areas homologous to Broca's area. Albert's close colleague, Norman Geschwind, had been fascinated by the way in which children could recover speech and language even after the removal of the entire left hemisphere of the brain (this was sometimes done in children with uncontrollable seizures). Such a recovery or reacquisition of language suggested to Geschwind that, though linguistic ability was generally associated with the left hemisphere, the right hemisphere also had linguistic potential and could take over language functions almost completely, at least in children. Albert and his colleagues thus felt, without clear evidence, that this might be the case, at least to some degree, even in aphasic adults, and that melodic intonation therapy, calling as it did upon right-hemisphere musical skills, could help to develop this potential.

Detailed imaging of patients undergoing MIT was not possible during the 1970s, and a 1996 PET scan study by Pascal Belin et al. seemed to show that there was no activation in the right hemisphere of such patients. They reported, moreover, that there was not only an inhibition of Broca's area in aphasic patients, but hyperactivity of a homologous area in the right hemisphere (we may call it, for convenience, the "right Broca's area"). This sustained hyperactivity on the right side exerts an active inhibiting action on the "good" Broca's area, which, in its weakened state, is powerless to resist. The challenge, then, is not only to stimulate the normal, left Broca's area, but to find a way to damp down the "right Broca's area," with its malignant hyperactivity. Singing and melodic intonation seem to do exactly this: by engaging the right-hemisphere circuits in normal activity, they disengage them from pathological activity. This process has a certain self-sustaining momentum of its own, for as the left Broca's area is released from inhibition, it can exert a suppressant action on the "right Broca's area." A vicious circle, in short, is replaced by a therapeutic one.[6]

---

6. There is some preliminary evidence that the same effect may be accomplished by using repetitive bursts of transcranial magnetic stimulation applied to the "right Broca's area" to suppress its hyperactivity. Paula Martin and her colleagues have recently tried this

For various reasons, little research attention was paid during the 1980s and 1990s to melodic intonation therapy for people with severe, nonfluent Broca's aphasia—or to the mechanisms by which it might work. Nonetheless, music therapists continued to observe that, in many cases, such therapy could allow very significant improvement.

Recent work by Gottfried Schlaug and his colleagues carefully documents the brain activity of eight patients undergoing melodic intonation therapy (this involves seventy-five sessions of intensive therapy). All of these patients, Schlaug et al. report, "showed significant changes in speech output measures and in a right-hemispheric fronto-temporal network while repeating simple words/phrases in the MRI scanner." Schlaug showed me a number of videos of such patients, and the change in their ability to speak was indeed striking. Initially many were incapable even of responding clearly to the question, "What is your address?" Following MIT, they were able to reply much more easily to such questions, even offering additional details beyond those asked for. They had clearly achieved at least a measure of propositional speech. These changes, both behavioral and anatomical, were retained even several months after the course of treatment had ended.

As Schlaug points out, "the neural processes that underlie post-stroke language recovery remain largely unknown and thus, have not been specifically targeted by most aphasia therapies." But MIT, at least, has been shown to be "ideally suited for facilitating language recovery in non-fluent aphasic patients, particularly in those with large left hemisphere lesions for whom the

---

technique in four patients who have been intractably aphasic for more than five years. Though they need confirmation, Martin et al.'s results are promising, and may lead, they propose, to "a novel, complementary treatment for aphasia."

only route to recovery may be the engagement of right hemi-spheric language regions."

We have become accustomed, in the last twenty years or so, to dramatic revelations of cortical plasticity. Auditory cortex, it has been shown, can be reallocated for visual processing in congeni-tally deaf people, and the visual cortex in blind people may be recruited for auditory and tactile functions. But perhaps even more remarkable is the notion that the right hemisphere, which in normal circumstances has only the most rudimentary linguis-tic capacities, can be turned into a reasonably efficient linguistic organ with less than three months of training—and that music is the key to this transformation.

17

Accidental Davening:
Dyskinesia and Cantillation

Solomon R. was an intelligent middle-aged man with a dyskinesia, an unusual movement disorder which, in him, took the form of rhythmic pulsions of various sorts: forcible expulsions of breath, accompanied by loud phonations ("eughh, eughhh . . ."), and a synchronous contraction of abdominal and trunk muscles, causing his body to bow or rock with each expiration.

Over the weeks that I saw him, there was a strange elaboration of this picture. The expiratory-phonatory "beat" began to acquire a sort of melody, a repetitive singsong to accompany it, and to this, in turn, was added a half-articulate, murmuring quality, like the prosody of a soft, unintelligible language. With this, and his now-increasing bowing movement, Mr. R. seemed to be cantillating, praying—"davening," as such murmuring, rhythmically motoric prayer is called by religious Jews. Indeed, a couple of weeks later, I was able to catch a number of Hebrew words, which seemed to confirm my impression. But when I asked Mr. R., he told me that though they were indeed Hebrew words, they made no sense—they were "plucked out of the air," he said, as if to fill the prosodic and melodic demand of his dyskinesia. Random though the words were, this strange activity gave Mr. R. a deep satisfaction and allowed him to feel he was "doing something," and not just the victim of a physical automatism.

Wanting to document this extraordinary scene, I went one day to the hospital with my tape recorder. As soon as I entered, I could hear Mr. R. down the hall. Or so I thought, but when I entered the room I found a Sabbath service in progress. The cantillation was coming not from my patient, but from the davening rabbi himself.

With the rabbi, presumably, the rhythmic emphases of prayer had led to a sympathetic rhythmic movement of the body—but with Mr. R., it had happened the other way round. Not originally a man attracted to cantillation or prayer, he had now been drawn to this through the physiological accident of dyskinesia.

Postscript

An automatism such as Mr. R.'s which engrosses a person can sometimes, however, be combined with or used for communication, as Ken Kessel, a clinical social worker, described to me. He was working in a nursing home with an elderly demented man named David:

> David . . . had been a strict Orthodox Jew. He spent his days davening and chanting, but rather than repeating Hebrew prayers, he constantly rocked and chanted, "Oy, vey. Oy vey vey. Vey ist mir, mir ist vey, oy ist vey, vey ist mir. Oy vey. Oy vey vey. . . ." This he repeated incessantly throughout

the day. The tune is etched in my memory; should we ever meet, I will be happy to sing it for you.

My assignment was to bring him breakfast. I felt it proper to ask what he wanted, but any attempt at questioning was met only with "Oy, vey. Oy vey vey. . . ." I felt uneasy, because I wanted to bring him what he wanted but seemingly had no way to discover what that was. . . .

I sat down next to David and began to rock, not exactly sure what I was doing or what would come next. The following conversation ensued, all in the tone and rhythm of his chanting, so it looks unremarkable in text, but it was operatic in its execution. Please interpolate a melody of your choosing:

Me: "David, what do you want for breakfast?"

David: "I don't know. What do you have?"

Me: "We have eggs and pancakes, toast and potatoes, oatmeal and cream of wheat."

David: "I'll have the eggs."

Me: "How do you want them?"

David: "What do you got?"

Me: "Scrambled or fried."

David: "I'll have the scrambled."

Me: "Do you want some toast?"

David: "Yes."

Me: "What kind?"

David: "What do you got?"

Me: "White or rye."

David: "I'll have the white."

Me: "Coffee or tea?"

David: "I'll have the coffee."

Me: "Black or cream?"

David: "Black."

Me: "Sugar or not?"

David: "No sugar."

Me: "Okay, thanks, I'll be back soon."

And off I went to get his breakfast, thinking to myself, "David is cured!" I returned triumphantly with his meal, announcing to him, "David, here's your breakfast."

To which he responded, "Oy, vey. Oy vey vey. . . ."

18

Come Together:
Music and Tourette's Syndrome

John S., a young man with Tourette's syndrome, recently wrote to me, describing the effect of music on his tics:

> Music is a huge part of my life. It can be both a blessing and a curse when it comes to ticcing. It can send me into a state where I forget all about Tourette's, or it can bring on a surge of tics that is difficult to control or bear.

He added that his tics were especially brought on by "certain kinds of music heavy with rhythm" and that their frequency and intensity might be determined by music, accelerating or slowing along with the music's tempo.

Reactions like this are very similar to those of parkinsonian patients, who may find themselves forgetting their parkinsonism, enjoying a delicious motor freedom, with some kinds of music, but being driven or entrained by others. But while

Tourette's may be considered, like parkinsonism, a movement disorder (albeit of an explosive rather than an obstructive kind), it is much more. It has a mind of its own. Tourette's is impulsive, productive, where parkinsonism is not. Sometimes this productivity is more or less confined to the production of simple tics or repetitive, fixed movements, and this seems to be the case with John S. But for some people, it may assume an elaborate, phantasmagoric form remarkable for its mimicry, antics, playfulness, inventions, and unexpected and sometimes surreal associations. People with this rarer, phantasmagoric form of Tourette's may show much more complex reactions to music.[1]

One such man, Sydney A., could have very extravagant reactions to music, as he did one day to a piece of Western music on the radio. He lurched, jerked, lunged, yelped, made faces, and gesticulated exuberantly—and, above all, he mimed and mimicked. The music seemed to trigger a cascade of wild mimetic representations of the tone, the tenor, the landscape of the music, and all the images and emotional reactions these provoked in him as he listened. This was not just an exacerbation of ticcing, but an extraordinary Tourettic representation of the music, a very personal expression of his sensibility and imagination, though dominated by Tourettic exaggeration, parody, and impulsiveness. I was reminded of a description by Henri Meige and E. Feindel in their 1902 book *Tics and Their Treatment*, of a man with Tourette's who showed on occasion "a veritable debauch of absurd gesticulations, a wild muscular carnival." I thought of Sydney sometimes as a mimetic virtuoso, but this was not a

---

1. People with phantasmagoric Tourette's may also have, if they can control and harness it, an exuberant and almost irrepressible creativity. Benjamin Simkin and others have wondered whether Mozart, famous for his impulsiveness, jokes, and salacities, might have had Tourette's—but the evidence is not too strong, as I wrote in a 1992 article in the *British Medical Journal*.

mimesis under his control, and for all its brilliance, it always had a certain flavor of the convulsive and the excessive.

And yet on another occasion, when Sydney took up his guitar and sang an old ballad, there was no ticcing at all, but a total immersion in or identification with the song and its mood.

Extraordinary, creative interactions can occur when someone with Tourette's performs as a musician. Ray G. was a man strongly drawn to jazz who played drums in a band on the weekends. He was noted for his sudden and wild solos, which would often arise from a convulsive drum-hitting tic—but the tic could initiate a cascade of percussive speed and invention and elaboration.[2]

Jazz or rock, with its heavy beat and its freedom to improvise, may be especially attractive to a musical person with Tourette's, and I have known a number of brilliant Tourettic musicians who are jazz artists (though I also know other musicians with Tourette's who are more drawn to the structure and rigor of classical music). David Aldridge, a professional jazz drummer, explored these themes in a memoir entitled "Rhythm Man":

> I've been banging on car dashboards since I was six years old, following and flowing with the rhythm until it poured out of my ears. . . . Rhythm and Tourette syndrome have been intertwined from the first day I found that drumming on a table could mask my jerky hand, leg and neck move-ments. . . . This newly found masking actually harnessed my unbounded energy, directing it into an orderly flow. . . . This "permission to explode" let me tap into vast reservoirs of sounds, and physical sensations, and I realized that my des-tiny lay clearly before me. I was to become a rhythm man.

---

2. Ray is more fully described in "Witty Ticcy Ray," a chapter in *The Man Who Mistook His Wife for a Hat.*

Aldridge relied on music frequently, both to mask his tics and to channel their explosive energy: "I would learn to harness the enormous energy of Tourette syndrome and control it like a high-pressure fire hose." Harnessing his Tourette's and expressing himself in creative, unpredictable musical improvisations seemed to be deeply intertwined: "The urge to play and the desire to release the endless tension of Tourette syndrome fed on each other like fuel on fire." For Aldridge, and perhaps for many with Tourette's, music was inseparably linked to movement and to sensation of all sorts.

The attractions, the joys, and the therapeutic powers of drumming and drum circles are widely known in the Tourette's community. In New York City recently, I took part in a drum circle organized by Matt Giordano, a gifted drummer with severe Tourette's. When he is not focused or engaged, Matt is in constant Tourettic motion—and, indeed, everyone in the room that day seemed to be ticcing, ticcing in their own time. I could see eruptions of tics, contagions of tics, rippling around the thirty-odd Touretters there—but once the drum circle started, with Matt leading them, all the ticcing disappeared within seconds. Suddenly there was synchronization, and they came together as a group, performing "in the moment with the rhythm," as Matt puts it—their Tourettic energy, motor exuberance, playfulness, and inventiveness all drawn upon creatively and given expression in the music. Music here had a double power: first, to reconfigure brain activity, and bring calm and focus to people who were sometimes distracted or preoccupied by incessant tics and impulses; and second, to promote a musical and social bonding with others, so that what began as a miscellany of isolated, often distressed or self-conscious individuals almost instantly became a cohesive group with a single aim—a veritable drum orchestra under Matt's baton.

. . .

NICK VAN BLOSS, a young English musician, has Tourette's of considerable severity—he reckons that he has nearly forty thousand tics a day, including his obsessions, imitations, counting compulsions, compulsive touchings, and so on. But when he plays the piano, he shows scarcely a hint of this. I asked him to play some Bach for me (Bach is his favorite composer, and Glenn Gould is his hero), and he did so without interruption. The only tics he displayed, a mild facial grimacing, were far less disturbing, I thought, than Gould's famous humming. Van Bloss developed his first, rather explosive symptoms when he was seven, attracting savage ridicule and bullying from his school-mates. There was no intermission in his ticcing until his family got a piano, and this was to transform his life. "Suddenly I had a piano," he writes in his memoir, *Busy Body*, "and, as if handed to me on a plate, I found my love. . . . When I played, my tics almost seemed to disappear. It was like a miracle. I would tic, gyrate, and verbally explode all day at school, get home exhausted from it all and run to the piano and play for as long as I could, not only because I loved the sounds I was making, but primarily because when I played I didn't tic. I got time off from the ticcy normality that had become me."

When I discussed this with van Bloss, he spoke of it partly in terms of "energy"—it was not, he felt, that his Tourette's had disappeared, but that it was now being "harnessed and focused" and, specifically, that his compulsions to touch could now be consummated by touching the keys of the piano. "I was simulta-neously feeding and fuelling my Tourette's by giving it a thing it so craved: touch," he writes. "The piano appealed to my fingers . . . provided touch heaven for me—eighty-eight keys all sitting and waiting for my needy little fingers."

Van Bloss feels that his repertoire of tics was fully developed by the age of sixteen and has changed little in the years since, but he is now far more accepting of them, for he recognizes that his Tourette's, in a paradoxical way, plays an essential role in his piano playing.

I found it especially fascinating to listen to a conversation between Nick van Bloss and Tobias Picker, the distinguished composer, who also has Tourette's—to listen to them compare notes on the role that Tourette's has played in their music making. Picker also has many tics, but when he is composing or playing the piano or conducting, his tics disappear. I have watched him as he sits almost motionless for hours, orchestrating one of his études for piano at his computer. The tics may have vanished, but this does not mean that the Tourette's itself has gone. Picker feels, on the contrary, that his Tourette's enters into his creative imagination, contributing to his music but also being shaped and modulated by it. "I live my life controlled by Tourette's," he said to me, "but I use music to control it. I have harnessed its energy— I play with it, manipulate it, trick it, mimic it, taunt it, explore it, exploit it, in every possible way." His newest piano concerto, in some sections, is full of turbulent, agitated whirls and twirls. But Picker writes in every mode—the dreamy and tranquil no less than the violent and stormy—and moves from one mood to another with consummate ease.

Tourette's brings out in stark form questions of will and determination: who orders what, who pushes whom around. To what extent are people with Tourette's controlled by a sovereign "I," a complex, self-aware, intentional self, or by impulses and feelings at lower levels in the brain-mind? Similar questions are brought up by musical hallucinations, and brainworms, and varied forms of quasi-automatic echoing and imitation. Normally we are not aware of what goes on in our brains, of the innumerable agencies

and forces inside us that lie outside or below the level of conscious experience—and perhaps this is just as well. Life becomes
more complicated, sometimes unbearably so, for people with
eruptive tics or obsessions or hallucinations, forced into daily,
incessant contact with rebellious and autonomous mechanisms
in their own brains. They face a special challenge; but they may
also, if the tics or hallucinations are not too overwhelming,
achieve a sort of self-knowledge or reconciliation that may significantly enrich them, in their strange fight, the double lives
they lead.

19

Keeping Time:
Rhythm and Movement

Nineteen seventy-four was an eventful year for me, in several respects, for it was a year in which I had musical hallucinations, twice; attacks of amusia, twice; and the complex musico-motor events I would later describe in *A Leg to Stand On*. I had had a bad climbing accident on a mountain in Norway, tearing off the quadriceps tendon of my left leg, as well as doing some nerve damage to it. The leg was useless, and I had to find a way to get down the mountain before nightfall. I soon discovered that the best strategy was to "row" myself down, somewhat as paraplegics do in their wheelchairs. At first I found this difficult and awkward, but soon I fell into a rhythm, accompanied by a sort of marching or rowing song (sometimes "The Volga Boatmen's Song"), with a strong heave on each beat. Before this I had muscled myself along; now, with the beat, I was musicked along. Without this synchronization of music and movement, the auditory with the motor, I could never have made my way down the mountain. And somehow, with this internal rhythm and music, it felt much less like a grim, anxious struggle.

I was rescued halfway down the mountain and taken to a hospital, where my leg was examined, X-rayed, and put into a cast, and then I was flown to England, where, forty-eight hours after the injury, I had surgery to repair the tendon. Nerve and other tissue damage had to await a natural healing, of course, and there was a fourteen-day period, therefore, in which I could not use the leg. Indeed, it seemed to be both numb and paralyzed, and not really even a part of me. On the fifteenth day, when it was judged safe for me to put weight on the leg, I found that I had, strangely, "forgotten" how to walk. There was only a sort of pseudowalking—conscious, cautious, unreal, step-by-step. I would make steps that were too large or too small, and on a couple of occasions managed to cross the left leg in front of the right one, almost tripping on it. The natural, unthinking spontaneity, the automaticity of walking completely evaded me until again, suddenly, music came to my aid.

I had been given a cassette of Mendelssohn's Violin Concerto in E minor—this was the only music I had, and I had been playing it for two weeks almost nonstop. Now suddenly, as I was standing, the concerto started to play itself with intense vividness in my mind. In this moment, the natural rhythm and melody of walking came back to me, and along with this, the feeling of my leg as alive, as part of me once again. I suddenly "remembered" how to walk.

The neural systems underlying the newly rediscovered skill of walking were still fragile and easily exhausted, and after half a minute or so of fluent walking, the inner music, the vividly imagined violin concerto, stopped suddenly, as if the needle had been lifted from a record—in that instant, walking stopped, too.

Then, after I had rested for a while, the music and motion came back to me, again in tandem.

After my accident, I wondered if this sort of experience occurred with others. And barely a month had gone by when I saw a patient at a nursing home—an old lady with an apparently paralyzed and useless left leg. She had suffered a complex hip fracture, followed by surgery and many weeks of immobility in a cast. Surgery had been successful, but her leg remained strangely inert and useless. Though there was no clear anatomical or neurological reason for this, she told me she could not imagine how to move the leg. Had the leg *ever* been able to move since the injury? I asked her. She thought for a moment and said yes, it had—once: it had kept time at a Christmas concert, "by itself," when an Irish jig was being played. This was enough; it indicated that whatever was going on, or not going on, in her nervous system, music could act as an activator, a de-inhibitor. We bombarde d her with dance tunes, especially Irish jigs, and saw for ourselves how her leg responded. It took several months, for the leg had become very atrophied; nevertheless, with music, she was not only able to delight in her own quasi-automatic motor responses—which soon included walking—but to extract from them an ability to make whatever discrete, voluntary movements she desired. She had reclaimed her leg, and her sensorimotor system, in full.

HIPPOCRATES, more than two thousand years ago, wrote of people who fell and broke their hips, which in those presurgical days demanded months of bandaging and immobility to let the bones knit. In such cases, he wrote, "the imagination is subdued, and the patient cannot remember how to stand or walk." With the advent of functional brain imaging, the neural basis of such "subduing" has been clarified.[1] There may be inhibition or deactivation not only peripherally, in the nerve elements of the damaged tendons and muscles and perhaps in the spinal cord, but also centrally, in the "body image," the mapping or representation of the body in the brain. A. R. Luria, in a letter to me, once referred to this as "the central resonances of a peripheral injury." The affected limb may lose its place in the body image, while the rest of the body's representation then expands to fill the vacancy. If this happens, the limb is not only rendered functionless, it no longer seems to belong to one at all—moving such a limb feels like moving an inanimate object. Another system must be brought in, and it is clear that music, above all else, can kick-start a damaged or inhibited motor system into action again.

Whether it was the singing of a simple rowing song on the mountain or the vivid imagining of the Mendelssohn Violin Concerto when I stood up in the hospital, the rhythm or beat of the music was crucial for me, as it was for my patient with the fractured hip. Was it just the rhythm or beat of the music, or was the melody, with *its* movement, its momentum, also important?

Beyond the repetitive motions of walking and dancing, music may allow an ability to organize, to follow intricate sequences, or to hold great volumes of information in mind—this is the narrative or mnemonic power of music. It was very clear with my patient Dr. P., who had lost the ability to recognize or identify even common objects, though he could see perfectly well. (He may have suffered from an early, and primarily visual, form of Alzheimer's.) He was unable to recognize a glove or a flower when I handed it to him, and he once mistook his own wife for a hat. His condition was almost totally disabling—but he discovered

---

1. In her book *Beyond Pain*, Angela Mailis-Gagnon, an expert on pain, discusses how fMRIs can be used to show the functional neurological effects of trauma.

that he could perform the needs and tasks of the day if they were organized in song. His wife explained to me:

> I put all his usual clothes out, in all the usual places, and he dresses without difficulty, singing to himself. He does every-thing singing to himself. But if he is interrupted and loses the thread, he comes to a complete stop, doesn't know his clothes—or his own body. He sings all the time—eating songs, dressing songs, bathing songs, everything. He can't do anything unless he makes it a song.

Patients with frontal lobe damage may also lose the ability to carry out a complex chain of actions—to dress, for example. Here, music can be very useful as a mnemonic or a narrative—in effect, a series of commands or promptings in the form of rhyme or a song, as in the childhood song "This Old Man." It is similar with some autistic people and with severely retarded people, who may be unable to perform fairly simple sequences involving perhaps four or five movements or procedures—but who can often do these tasks perfectly well if they set them to music. Music has the power to embed sequences and to do this when other forms of organization (including verbal forms) fail.

Every culture has songs and rhymes to help children learn the alphabet, numbers, and other lists. Even as adults, we are limited in our ability to memorize series or to hold them in mind unless we use mnemonic devices or patterns—and the most powerful of these devices are rhyme, meter, and song. We may have to sing the "ABC" song internally to remember the alphabet, or imagine Tom Lehrer's song to remember all the chemical elements. For someone who is gifted musically, a huge amount of information can be retained in this way, consciously or unconsciously. The composer Ernst Toch (his grandson Lawrence Weschler tells me) could readily hold in his mind a very long string of numbers after a single hearing, and he did this by converting the string of numbers into a tune (a melody he shaped "corresponding" to the numbers).

A neurobiology professor recounted to me the story of an extraordinary student, J., whose answers on one exam sounded suspiciously familiar. The professor wrote:

> A few sentences later, I thought, "No wonder I like her answers. She's quoting my lectures word for word!" There was also a question on the exam that she answered with a direct quote from the textbook. The next day, I called J. into my office to have a talk with her about cheating and plagiarism, but something did not add up. J. did not seem like a cheater; she seemed totally lacking in guile. So as she walked into my office, what came into my head and out of my mouth was the question, "J., do you have a photographic memory?" She answered very excitedly, "Yes, sort of like that. I can remember anything as long as I put it to music." She then sang back to me from memory whole portions of my lectures (and very prettily too). I was flabbergasted.

While this student is, like Toch, extraordinarily gifted, all of us use the power of music in this way, and setting words to music, especially in preliterate cultures, has played a huge role in relation to the oral traditions of poetry, storytelling, liturgy, and prayer. Entire books can be held in memory—*The Iliad* and *The Odyssey*, famously, could be recited at length because, like ballads, they had rhythm and rhyme. How much such recitation depends on musical rhythm and how much purely on linguistic rhyming is difficult to tell, but these are surely related—both "rhyme" and "rhythm" derive from the Greek, carrying the conjoined meanings of measure, motion, and stream. An articulate stream, a melody or prosody, is necessary to carry one along, and this is something that unites language and music, and may underlie their perhaps common origins.

The powers of reproduction and recitation may be achieved with very little idea of meaning. One has to wonder how much Martin, my retarded savant patient, understood of the two thousand cantatas and operas he knew by heart or how much Gloria Lenhoff, a woman with Williams syndrome and an IQ under 60, actually comprehends the thousands of arias in thirty-five languages which she can sing from memory.

The embedding of words, skills, or sequences in melody and meter is uniquely human. The usefulness of such an ability to recall large amounts of information, especially in a preliterate culture, is surely one reason why musical abilities have flourished in our species.

THE RELATIONSHIP BETWEEN motor and auditory systems has been investigated by asking people to tap to a beat or, where commands cannot be given verbally (as with infants or animals), by observing whether there is any spontaneous synchronization of movement with an external musical beat. Aniruddh Patel at the Neurosciences Institute has recently pointed out that "in every culture there is some form of music with a regular beat, a periodic pulse that affords temporal coordination between performers, and elicits synchronized motor response from listeners." This linking of auditory and motor systems seems universal in humans, and shows itself spontaneously, early in life.[2]

---

2. Humans, it seems, are the only primates with such a tight coupling of motor and auditory systems in the brain—apes do not dance, and though they sometimes drum, they do not anticipate a beat and synchronize to it in the same way that humans do.

The rather mechanical term "entrainment" is sometimes used in regard to the human tendency to keep time, to make motor responses to rhythm. But research has now shown that so-called responses to rhythm actually *precede* the external beat. We anticipate the beat, we get rhythmic patterns as soon as we hear them, and we establish internal models or templates of them. These internal templates are astonishingly precise and

---

The evidence for musical abilities in other species is mixed. In Thailand, some elephants have been trained to strike percussion instruments and "play together" on their own. Intrigued by accounts of this Thai Elephant Orchestra, Aniruddh Patel and John Iversen made careful measurements and video recordings of the elephants' performances. They found that an elephant could "play a percussion instrument [a large drum] with a highly stable tempo"—indeed, a tempo more stable than most humans could achieve. But the other elephants in the "orchestra" struck their instruments (cymbals, gongs, etc.) in seeming disregard of one another, without synchronizing to the auditory beat of the drum elephant.

But some bird species are known for their ability to sing duets or choruses, and some do keep time to human music. Patel, Iversen, and their colleagues have studied Snowball, a sulphur-crested Eleanora cockatoo who had achieved some reknown on YouTube for his dancing to the Backstreet Boys. Patel et al. found evidence of true synchronization to a musical beat by Snowball, who bobs his head and moves his feet in time with music. As they reported in a 2008 paper, "when the tempo of a song is increased or decreased over a limited range, Snowball adjusts his movements accordingly, and stays synchronized with the music."

Many animals, from the Lipizzaner horses of the Spanish Riding School of Vienna to circus elephants, dogs, and bears, have been trained to "dance" to music. It is not always clear whether such animals are responding to subtle visual or tactile cues from the humans around them, but it is hard to resist the impression that such animals are, on some level, enjoying the music and responding to it in a rhythmic way.

Many people report that their pets will respond or attend only to particular songs, or will "sing along" or "dance" to particular music. Such stories go back a long way, and a delightful 1814 book—titled *The Power of Music: In which is shown, by a variety of Pleasing and Instructive Anecdotes, the effects it has on Man and Animals*—includes accounts of snakes, lizards, spiders, mice, rabbits, bulls, and other animals responding to music in various ways. Ignacy Paderewski, the Polish pianist and composer, gives a very detailed account in his memoirs about a spider which could apparently distinguish thirds from sixths, and would come down from the ceiling to the piano whenever he played Chopin études in thirds, only to decamp ("sometimes, I used to think, quite angrily") when he switched to études in sixths.

As one correspondent wrote to me, "None of [this] rises to the level of scientific proof, of course, but having lived with animals for years . . . I firmly believe that we underestimate the emotional and the analytical capabilities of nonhuman vertebrates, especially mammals and birds." I replied that I agreed with him, and suspected that we underestimated the abilities of invertebrates, too.

stable; as Daniel Levitin and Perry Cook have shown, humans have very accurate memories for tempo and rhythm.[3]

Chen, Zatorre, and Penhune in Montreal have studied the ability of human beings to keep time, to follow a beat, and they have used functional brain imaging to visualize how this is reflected in the brain. Not surprisingly, they found activation of the motor cortex and of subcortical systems in the basal ganglia and cerebellum when subjects tapped or made other movements in response to music.

What is more remarkable is their finding that listening to music or imagining it, even without any overt movement or keeping time, activates motor cortex and subcortical motor systems, too. Thus the imagination of music, of rhythm, may be as potent, neurally, as actually listening to it.

Keeping time, physically and mentally, depends, as Chen and her colleagues have found, on interactions between the auditory and the dorsal premotor cortex—and it is only in the human brain that a functional connection between these two cortical areas exists. Crucially, these sensory and motor activations are precisely integrated with each other.

Rhythm in this sense, the integration of sound and move-ment, can play a great role in coordinating and invigorating basic locomotor movement. I found this when I was "rowing" myself down the mountain to "The Volga Boatmen's Song," and when the Mendelssohn enabled me to walk again. Musical rhythm can be valuable, similarly, to athletes, as the physi-cian Malonnie Kinnison, a competitive cyclist and triathlete, observed to me:

---

3. Galileo famously exemplified this in his experiments timing the descent of objects as they rolled down inclined planes. Having no accurate watches or clocks to go by, he timed each trial by humming tunes to himself, and this allowed him to get results with an accu-racy far beyond that of the timepieces of his era.

I have been a competitive cyclist for a number of years and have always been interested in the individual time trial, an event that pits the rider against the clock only. The effort required to excel at this event is painful. I often listen to music while I am training, and noticed fairly early that some pieces of music were particularly uplifting and inspired a high level of effort. One day, in the early stages of an important time trial event, a few bars of the overture to "Orpheus in the Underworld" by Offenbach started playing in my head. This was wonderful—it stimulated my performance, settled my cadence at just the right tempo, and synchronized my physical efforts with my breathing. Time collapsed. I was truly in the zone, and for the first time in my life, I was sorry to see the finish line. My time was a personal best.

Now all of Kinnison's competitive cycling is accompanied by bracing musical imagery (usually from operatic overtures). Many athletes have had similar experiences.

I have found it similar with swimming. In swimming freestyle, one usually kicks in groups of three, with a strong kick to every arm-stroke followed by two softer kicks. Sometimes I count these to myself as I swim—*one*, two, three, *one*, two, three—but then this conscious counting gives way to music with a similar beat. On long, leisurely swims, Strauss waltzes tend to play in my mind, synchronizing all my movements, providing an automatism and accuracy beyond anything I can achieve with conscious counting. Leibniz said of music that it is counting, but counting unconsciously, and this is precisely what swimming to Strauss is all about.

THE FACT THAT "rhythm"—in this special sense of combining movement and sound—appears spontaneously in human children, but not in any other primate, forces one to reflect on its phylogenetic origins. It has often been suggested that music did not evolve on its own but emerged as a by-product of other capacities with more obvious adaptive significance— such as speech. Did song, in fact, precede speech (as Darwin thought); did speech precede music (as his contemporary Herbert Spencer believed); or did both develop simultaneously (as Mithen proposes)? "How can this dispute be resolved?" Patel asks in his 2006 paper. "One approach is to determine whether there are fundamental aspects of music cognition which . . . cannot be explained as by-products or secondary uses of more clearly adaptive abilities." Musical rhythm, with its regular pulse, he points out, is very unlike the irregular stressed syllables of speech. The perception and synchronization of beat, Patel feels, "is an aspect of rhythm that appears to be unique to music . . . and cannot be explained as a by-product of linguistic rhythm." It seems probable, he concludes, that musical rhythm evolved independently of speech.

There is certainly a universal and unconscious propensity to impose a rhythm even when one hears a series of identical sounds at constant intervals. John Iversen, a neuroscientist and an avid drummer, has pointed this out. We tend to hear the sound of a digital clock, for example, as "tick-tock, tick-tock"— even though it is actually "tick, tick, tick, tick." Anyone who has been subjected to the monotonous volleys of noise from the oscillating magnetic fields that bombard one during an MRI has probably had a similar experience. Sometimes the deafening ticks of the machine seem to organize themselves in a waltzlike rhythm of threes, sometimes in groups of four or five.[4] It is as if

---

4. Iversen, Patel, and Ohgushi have found strong cultural differences in such rhythmic groupings. In one experiment, they exposed native American English speakers and native

the brain has to impose a pattern of its own, even if there is no objective pattern present. This can be true not only with patterns in time, but with tonal patterns, too. We tend to add a sort of melody to the sound of a train (there is a wonderful example of this, raised to the level of art, in Arthur Honegger's *Pacific 231*) or to hear melodies in other mechanical noises. One friend of mine feels that the hum of her refrigerator has a "Haydn-ish" quality. And for some people with musical hallucinations, these may first appear as an elaboration of a mechanical noise (as with Dwight Mamlok and Michael Sundue). Leo Rangell, another man with musical hallucinations, commented on how elementary rhythmic sounds, for him, became songs or jingles; and for Solomon R. (in chapter 17) rhythmic body movements gave rise to a singsong cantillation—their minds giving "meaning" to what would otherwise be a meaningless sound or movement.

Japanese speakers to tone sequences of alternating short and long duration. They found that while Japanese speakers preferred to group the tones in a long-short parsing, the English speakers preferred a short-long parsing. Iversen et al. propose that "experience with the native language creates rhythmic templates which influence the processing of nonlinguistic sound patterns." This raises the question as to whether there might be correspondences between the speech patterns and the instrumental music of particular cultures. There has long been an impression among musicologists that such correspondences exist, and this has now been formally, quantitatively studied by Patel, Iversen, and their colleagues at the Neurosciences Institute. "What makes the music of Sir Edward Elgar sound so distinctively English?" they ask. "What makes the music of Debussy sound so French?" Patel et al. compared rhythm and melody in British English speech and music to that of French speech and music, using the music of a dozen different composers. They found, by plotting rhythm and melody together, that "a striking pattern emerges, suggesting that a nation's language exerts a 'gravitational pull' on the structure of its music."

The Czech composer Leos Janáček, too, was greatly exercised by the resemblances between speech and music, and he spent more than thirty years sitting in cafes and other public places, notating the melodies and rhythms of people's speech, convinced that these unconsciously mirrored their emotional intent and states of mind. He attempted to incorporate these speech rhythms into his own music—or, rather, to find "equivalents" for them in the classical music grid of pitches and intervals. Many people, whether or not they speak Czech, have felt that there is an uncanny correspondence between Janáček's music and the sound patterns of Czech speech.

. . .

A NTHONY STORR, in his excellent book *Music and the
Mind*, stresses that in all societies, a primary function of
music is collective and communal, to bring and bind people
together. People sing together and dance together in every culture, and one can imagine them having done so around the first
fires, a hundred thousand years ago. This primal role of music
is to some extent lost today, when we have a special class of
composers and performers, with the rest of us often reduced to
passive listening. We have to go to a concert, or a church, or a
musical festival to reexperience music as a social activity, to
recapture the collective excitement and bonding of music. In
such a situation, music is a communal experience, and there
seems to be, in some sense, an actual binding or "marriage" of
nervous systems, a "neurogamy" (to use a word the early mes-
merists favored).

The binding is accomplished by rhythm—not only heard but
internalized, identically, in all who are present. Rhythm turns
listeners into participants, makes listening active and motoric,
and synchronizes the brains and minds (and, since emotion is
always intertwined with music, the "hearts") of all who participate. It is very difficult to remain detached, to resist being drawn
into the rhythm of chanting or dancing.

I observed this when I took my patient Greg F. to a Grateful
Dead concert at Madison Square Garden in 1991.[5] The music,
the rhythm, got everyone within seconds. I saw the whole vast
arena in motion with the music, eighteen thousand people dancing, transported, every nervous system there synchronized to the
music. Greg had had a massive tumor which had wiped out his

---

5. Greg's story is related in "The Last Hippie," in *An Anthropologist on Mars*.

memory and much of his spontaneity—he had been amnesic and inert, barely responsive except to music for many years. But he was taken over and animated by the thumping, pounding excitement of the crowd around him, the rhythmic clapping and chanting, and soon he, too, began shouting the name of one of his favorite songs, "'Tobacco Road,' 'Tobacco Road'!" I say I "observed" all this, but I found myself unable to remain a detached observer. I realized that I, too, was moving, stamping, clapping with the music, and soon lost all my usual diffidence and inhibition and joined the crowd in communal dancing.

Augustine, in his *Confessions*, described how, on one occasion, he went to a gladiatorial show with an aloof young man who professed disgust and contempt at the scenes before him. But when the crowd grew excited and began a rhythmic roaring and stamping, the young man could resist no longer, and joined in as orgiastically as everyone else. I have had similar experiences in religious contexts, even though I am largely lacking in religious faith or feeling. When I was a boy, I loved Simchas Torah, the Rejoicing of the Law, which was celebrated, even in our normally sober Orthodox congregation, with ecstatic chanting and dancing round and round the synagogue.

While in many cases religious practice now tends to be somewhat decorous and detached, there is evidence that religious practices began with communal chanting and dancing, often of an ecstatic kind and, not infrequently, culminating in states of trance.[6]

The almost irresistible power of rhythm is evident in many other contexts: in marching, it serves both to entrain and coordinate

---

6. Such practices are discussed in great depth and detail by the ethnomusicologist Gilbert Rouget in his book *Music and Trance;* more lyrically by Havelock Ellis in *The Dance of Life;* and with matchless personal insight by Mickey Hart, the drummer and ethnomusicologist, in his books *Planet Drum* and *Drumming at the Edge of Magic.*

movement and to whip up a collective and perhaps martial excitement. We see this not only with military music and war drums, but also with the slow, solemn rhythm of a funeral march. We see it with work songs of every sort—rhythmic songs that probably arose with the beginnings of agriculture, when tilling the soil, hoeing, and threshing all required the combined and synchronized efforts of a group of people. Rhythm and its entrainment of movement (and often emotion), its power to "move" people, in both senses of the word, may well have had a crucial cultural and economic function in human evolution, bringing people together, producing a sense of collectivity and community.

This, indeed, is central to the vision of cultural evolution presented by Merlin Donald in his astonishing 1991 book *Origins of the Modern Mind*, and in many subsequent papers. An essential feature of Donald's vision is his concept that human evolution moved from the "episodic" life of apes to a "mimetic" culture—and that this flourished and lasted for tens, perhaps hundreds of thousands of years before language and conceptual thinking evolved. Donald proposes that mimesis—the power to represent emotions, external events, or stories using only gesture and posture, movement and sound, but not language—is still the bedrock of human culture today. He sees rhythm as having a unique role in relation to mimesis:

> Rhythm is an integrative-mimetic skill, related to both vocal and visuomotor mimesis. . . . Rhythmic ability is supramodal; that is, once a rhythm is established, it may be played out with any motor modality, including the hands, feet, mouth, or the whole body. It is apparently self-reinforcing, in the way that perceptual exploration and motor play are self-reinforcing. Rhythm is, in a sense, the

quintessential mimetic skill. . . . Rhythmic games are widespread among human children, and there are few, if any,
human cultures that have not employed rhythm as an
expressive device.

Donald goes further, seeing rhythmic skill as a prerequisite
not only for all music, but for all sorts of nonverbal activities,
from the simple rhythmic patterns of agricultural life to the
most complex social and ritual behaviors.

Neuroscientists sometimes speak of "the binding problem,"
the process by which different perceptions or aspects of perception are bound together and unified. What enables us, for
example, to bind together the sight, sound, smell, and emotions
aroused by the sight of a jaguar? Such binding in the nervous
system is accomplished by rapid, synchronized firing of nerve
cells in different parts of the brain. Just as rapid neuronal oscillations bind together different functional parts within the brain
and nervous system, so rhythm binds together the individual
nervous systems of a human community.

20

Kinetic Melody:
Parkinson's Disease and Music Therapy

William Harvey, writing about animal movement in 1628, called it "the silent music of the body." Similar metaphors are often used by neurologists, who speak of normal movement as having a naturalness and fluency, a "kinetic melody." This smooth, graceful flow of movement is compromised in parkinsonism and some other disorders, and neurologists speak here of "kinetic stutter." When we walk, our steps emerge in a rhythmical stream, a flow that is automatic and self-organizing. In parkinsonism, this normal, happy automatism is gone.

Though I was born into a musical household and music has been important to me personally from my earliest years, I did not really encounter music in a clinical context until 1966, when I started work at Beth Abraham Hospital, a chronic care hospital for patients in the Bronx. Here, my attention was immediately drawn to a number of strangely immobile, some-

times entranced-looking patients, the post-encephalitic sur-
vivors I was later to write about in *Awakenings*. There were
nearly eighty of them at the time; I saw them in the lobby, in the
corridors, as well as on the wards, sometimes in strange postures,
absolutely motionless, frozen in a trancelike state. (A few of
these patients, rather than being frozen, were in the opposite
state—one of almost continuous driven activity, all their movements accelerated, excessive, and explosive.) All of them, I
discovered, were victims of encephalitis lethargica, the epidemic
sleeping sickness that swept the globe just after World War I, and
some had been in this frozen state since they had entered the
hospital forty or more years before.

In 1966, there was no medication of any use to these
patients—no medication, at least, for their frozenness, their
parkinsonian motionlessness. And yet it was common knowledge among the nurses and staff that these patients *could* move
on occasion, with an ease and grace that seemed to belie their
parkinsonism—and that the most potent occasioner of such
movement was, in fact, music.

Typically, these post-encephalitic patients, like people with
ordinary parkinsonism, could not easily initiate anything, and
yet often they were able to *respond*. Many could catch and return
a ball if it was thrown, and almost all of them tended to respond
in some way to music. Some of them could not initiate a single
step but could be drawn into dancing and could dance fluidly.
Some could scarcely utter a syllable; their voices, when they
could speak, lacked tone, lacked force, were almost spectral. But
these patients were able to sing on occasion, loudly and clearly,
with full vocal force and a normal range of expressiveness and tone.
Other patients could walk and talk but only in a jerky, broken
way, without a steady tempo, and sometimes with incontinent

accelerations—with such patients, music could modulate the stream of movement or speech, giving them the steadiness and control they so lacked.[1]

THOUGH "MUSIC THERAPY" was hardly a profession in the 1960s, Beth Abraham, most unusually, had its own music therapist, a dynamo called Kitty Stiles (it was only when she died in her late nineties that I realized she must already have been over eighty when I met her, but she had the vitality of a much younger person).

Kitty had a special feeling for our post-encephalitic patients, and in the decades before drugs such as L-dopa were available, it was only Kitty and her music which could bring them to life. Indeed, when we came to make a documentary film about these patients in 1973, the film's director, Duncan Dallas, immediately asked me, "Can I meet the music therapist? She seems to be the most important person around here." So she was, in the days before L-dopa, and so she continued to be when the effects of L-dopa became, in many patients, erratic and unstable.

While the power of music has been known for millennia, the idea of formal music therapy arose only in the late 1940s, especially in response to the large numbers of soldiers returning from the battlefields of the Second World War with head wounds and traumatic brain injuries or "battle fatigue" (or "shell shock," as

---

1. Somewhat similarly, music can temporarily restore some degree of motor control in those who have become uncoordinated from alcohol. A colleague, Dr. Richard Garrison, described to me a group of older people at a party:

> As they drank heavily, and the clock approached midnight, they became progressively more ataxic between tunes. As they would become drunker, and stagger between each [number], their dancing seemed unaffected. . . . One gentleman would spring out of his chair every time we started playing, then collapse after we quit. He seemed unable to walk onto the dance floor, but rather danced his way out.

it was called in the First World War, a condition we would now categorize as "post-traumatic stress disorder").[2] With many of these soldiers, it was found that their pain and misery and even, seemingly, some of their physiological responses (pulse rates, blood pressure, and so on) could be improved by music. Doctors and nurses in many veterans hospitals started to invite musicians to come and play for their patients, and musicians were only too happy to bring music to the dreadful wards of the wounded. But it was soon evident that enthusiasm and generosity were not enough—some professional training was needed as well.

The first formal music therapy program was set up in 1944 at Michigan State University, and the National Association for Music Therapy was formed in 1950. But music therapy remained, for the next quarter of a century, scarcely recognized. I do not know whether Kitty Stiles, our music therapist at Beth Abraham, had any formal training or was licensed as a music therapist, but she had an immense intuitive gift for divining what could get patients going, however regressed or disabled they might appear. Working with individual patients calls upon empathy and personal interaction as much as any formal therapy, and Kitty was very skilled at this. She was also an audacious improviser, and very playful—both on the keyboard and in life; without this, I suspect, many of her efforts would have been futile.[3]

---

2. The excellent and comprehensive 1948 volume *Music and Medicine*, edited by Dorothy M. Schullian and Max Schoen, discusses music as medicine in various historical and cultural contexts and contains important chapters on the uses of music both in military hospitals and more generally.

3. In 1979 Kitty retired, and in her place Beth Abraham hired a certified music therapist, Concetta Tomaino. (Tomaino would later become the president of the American Association for Music Therapy, founded in 1971, and go on to earn one of the first generation of doctoral degrees in music therapy.)

Connie, working full-time at the hospital, was able to formalize and extend a whole range of music therapy programs. In particular, she started programs for the hospital's

. . .

I ONCE INVITED the poet W. H. Auden to one of Kitty's sessions, and he was amazed by the instant transformations
which music could effect; they reminded him of an aphorism of
the German Romantic writer Novalis: "Every disease is a musical problem; every cure is a musical solution." This seemed
almost literally to be the case with these profoundly parkinsonian patients.

Parkinsonism is usually called a "movement disorder,"
though when it is severe it is not only movement that is affected,
but the flow of perception, thought, and feeling as well. The disorder of flow can take many forms; sometimes, as the term
"kinetic stutter" implies, there is not a smooth flow of movement but brokenness, jerkiness, starts and stops instead. Parkinsonian stutter (like verbal stuttering) can respond beautifully to
the rhythm and flow of music, as long as the music is of the
"right" kind—and the right kind is unique for every patient. For
one of my post-encephalitic patients, Frances D., music was as
powerful as any drug. One minute I would see her compressed,
clenched, and blocked, or else jerking, ticcing, and jabbering—
like a sort of human time bomb. The next minute, if we played
music for her, all of these explosive-obstructive phenomena

---

large population of patients with aphasia and other speech and language disorders. She
instituted programs, too, for patients with Alzheimer's and other forms of dementia. Connie and I, and many others, collaborated on these projects and continued the program for
parkinsonian patients that Kitty Stiles had started. We tried to introduce not only objective tests of motor, language, and cognitive function, but physiological tests, too—in particular EEGs taken before, during, and after music therapy sessions. In 1993, reaching out
to others in this growing field, Connie convened a conference on "Clinical Applications
of Music in Neurological Rehabilitation"; two years later, she helped to form the Institute
for Music and Neurologic Function at Beth Abraham, in the hope of increasing awareness
of the importance of music therapy not only in a clinical setting, but as a subject for laboratory research. Our efforts in the 1980s and 1990s were paralleled by a groundswell of
other similar efforts around the country and, increasingly, all over the world.

would disappear, replaced by a blissful ease and flow of movement, as Mrs. D., suddenly freed of her automatisms, would smilingly "conduct" the music, or rise and dance to it. But it was necessary—for her—that the music be legato; staccato, percussive music might have a bizarre countereffect, causing her to jump and jerk helplessly with the beat, like a mechanical doll or marionette. In general, the "right" music for parkinsonian patients is not only legato, but has a well-defined rhythm. If, on the other hand, the rhythm is too loud, dominating, or intrusive, patients may find themselves helplessly driven or entrained by it. The power of music in parkinsonism is not, however, dependent on familiarity, or even enjoyment, though in general music works best if it is both familiar and liked.

Another patient, Edith T., a former music teacher, spoke of her need for music. She said that she had become "graceless" with the onset of parkinsonism, that her movements had become "wooden, mechanical—like a robot or doll." She had lost her former naturalness and musicality of movement; in short, she said, she had been "unmusicked" by her parkinsonism. But when she found herself stuck or frozen, even the *imagining* of music might restore the power of action to her. Now, as she put it, she could "dance out of the frame," the flat, frozen landscape in which she was trapped, and move freely and gracefully: "It was like suddenly remembering myself, my own living tune." But then, just as suddenly, the inner music would cease, and she would fall once again into the abyss of parkinsonism. Equally dramatic, and perhaps in some way analogous, was Edith's ability to use, to share, other people's ambulatory abilities—she could easily and automatically walk with another person, falling into their rhythm, their tempo, sharing their kinetic melody, but the moment they stopped, she would stop, too.

The movements and perceptions of people with parkinsonism

are often too fast or too slow, though they may not be aware of this—they may be able to infer it only when they compare themselves to clocks, or to other people. The neurologist William Gooddy described this in his book *Time and the Nervous System:* "An observer may note how slowed a parkinsonian's movements are, but the patient will say, 'My own movements seem normal to me unless I see how long they take by looking at a clock. The clock on the wall of the ward seems to be going exceptionally fast.'" Gooddy wrote of the sometimes enormous disparities such patients can show between "personal time" and "clock time."[4]

But if music is present, its tempo and speed take precedence over the parkinsonism and allow parkinsonian patients to return, while the music lasts, to their own rate of moving, that which was natural for them before their illness.

Music, indeed, resists all attempts at hurrying or slowing, and imposes its own tempo.[5] I saw this recently at a recital by the eminent (and now parkinsonian) composer and conductor Lukas Foss. He rocketed almost uncontrollably to the piano, but once there, played a Chopin nocturne with exquisite control and timing and grace—only to festinate once again as soon as the music ended.

This power of music was invaluable with one extraordinary

---

4. I discussed this and other disorders of time in my 2004 essay "Speed."

5. Many musicians were upset when Beethoven's friend Johann Mälzel invented a portable metronome and Beethoven started using metronome indications on his piano sonatas. It was feared that this might lead to rigid, metronomic playing and make impossible the flexibility, the freedom, which creative piano playing demands.

Similarly, though the tick of a metronome can be used to "entrain" parkinsonian patients, allowing or driving them to walk step by step, this will produce locomotion that lacks the automaticity, the fluency, of true walking. It is not a series of discrete stimuli that the parkinsonian needs, but a continuous flow or stream of stimulation, with clear rhythmic organization. Michael Thaut and his colleagues at Colorado State University have been pioneers in the use of rhythmic auditory stimulation to facilitate walking in patients with parkinsonism (and also in patients who have become partly paralyzed, hemiparetic, on one side following a stroke).

post-encephalitic patient, Ed M., whose movements were too fast on the right side of his body and too slow on the left side. We could not find any good way to medicate him, for whatever improved one side would worsen the other. But he loved music, and he had a small organ in his room. With this—and this only—when he sat down and played, he could bring his two hands, his two sides, together in unison and synchrony.

A fundamental problem in parkinsonism is the inability to initiate movement spontaneously; parkinsonian patients are always getting "stuck" or "frozen." Normally there is a virtually instantaneous commensuration between our intentions and the subcortical machinery (the basal ganglia, especially) that allows their automatic enaction. (Gerald Edelman, in *The Remembered Present*, refers to the basal ganglia, along with the cerebellum and hippocampus, as the "organs of succession.") But it is the basal ganglia especially which are damaged in parkinsonism. If the damage is very severe, the parkinsonian may be reduced to virtual immobility and silence—not paralyzed but in a sense "locked in," unable by himself to initiate any movement, and yet perfectly able to respond to certain stimuli.[6] The parkinsonian is stuck, so to speak, in a subcortical box, and can only emerge from this (as Luria brings out) with the help of an outside stimulus.[7] Thus parkinsonian patients can be called into action,

---

6. I use "locked in" here metaphorically. Neurologists also use the term "locked-in syndrome" to denote a state in which a patient is deprived of speech and virtually all voluntary motion, save perhaps an ability to blink or move the eyes up and down. (This is usually the result of a deep midline stroke.) Such patients preserve normal consciousness and intentionality, and if some sort of communication code can be established (by blinking, for example), they can communicate their thoughts and words, albeit tantalizingly slowly. A most remarkable book, *The Diving Bell and the Butterfly*, was "dictated" in this way by the French journalist Jean-Dominique Bauby, who suffered from a locked-in syndrome.

7. The use of external cues and self-stimulation in parkinsonism was explored by A. R. Luria in the 1920s, and he described this in his 1932 book *The Nature of Human*

sometimes by something as simple as throwing them a ball (though once they catch the ball or throw it back, they will freeze again). To enjoy any real sense of freedom, a longer release, they need something which can last over time, and the most potent unlocker here is music.

This was very clear with Rosalie B., a post-encephalitic lady who tended to remain transfixed for hours each day, completely motionless, frozen—usually with one finger "stuck" to her spectacles. If one walked her down the hallway, she would walk in a passive, wooden way, with her finger still stuck to her spectacles. But she was very musical, and loved to play the piano. As soon as she sat down on the piano bench, her stuck hand came down to the keyboard, and she would play with ease and fluency, her face (usually frozen in an inexpressive parkinsonian "mask") full of expression and feeling. Music liberated her from her parkinsonism for a time—and not only playing music, but *imagining* it. Rosalie knew all of Chopin by heart, and we had only to say "Opus 49" to see her whole body, posture, and expression change, her parkinsonism vanishing as the F-minor *Fantasie* played itself in her mind. Her EEG, too, would become normal at such times.[8]

Conflicts. All the phenomena of parkinsonism, he felt, could be seen as "subcortical automatisms." But "the healthy cortex," he wrote, "enables [the parkinsonian] to use external stimuli and to construct a compensatory activity for the subcortical automatisms. . . . That which was impossible to accomplish by direct will-force becomes attainable when the action is included in another complex system."

8. If Rosalie could imagine music so effectively as to normalize her EEG, why did she not do this all the while? Why did she remain helpless and transfixed for most of the day? What she lacked, as all patients with parkinsonism lack to some extent, was not the power of imagination, but the power to *initiate* mental or physical action. Thus, by saying "Opus 49," we initiated matters, and all she had to do was respond. But without such a cue or stimulus, nothing would have happened.

Ivan Vaughan, a Cambridge psychologist who developed Parkinson's disease, wrote a memoir about living with the disease, and Jonathan Miller directed a 1984 BBC documentary (*Ivan,* broadcast as part of the Horizon series) based on this. In both the book and the film, Ivan describes a variety of ingenious, indirect stratagems for getting himself going,

When I came to Beth Abraham in 1966, music was chiefly provided by the indefatigable Kitty Stiles, who spent dozens of hours each week at the hospital. Sometimes there was music from a record player or radio, though Kitty herself seemed to have a stimulating power of her own. Recorded music was not portable at this time—battery-powered radios and tape recorders were still large and heavy. Now, of course, everything has changed, and we can have hundreds of tunes on an iPod the size and weight of a matchbook. While the extreme availability of music may have its own dangers (I wonder whether brainworms or musical hallucinations are more common now), this availability is an unmitigated boon for those with parkinsonism. Although most of the patients I see are the severely disabled residents of chronic care hospitals and nursing homes, I get letters from many parkinsonian people who are still relatively independent and living at home, perhaps with a little help. Recently Carolina Yahne, a psychologist in Albuquerque, wrote to tell me about her mother, who, because of Parkinson's disease, had had great difficulty walking. "I made up a goofy little song," the daughter wrote, "called 'Walkin' Mama' that included a finger-snapping beat. I have a rotten voice, but she liked hearing it. She would play it with the tape recorder hooked on her waistband, and earphones. It really seemed to help her navigate around the house."

WHILE MUSIC alone can unlock people with parkinsonism, and movement or exercise of any kind is also beneficial, an ideal combination of music *and* movement is provided by

---

which he could not do by sheer will. Thus, for example, he would allow his eyes to wander when he woke up, until he caught sight of a tree painted on the wall by his bed. This would act as a stimulus, in effect saying, "Climb me," and by imagining himself climbing, Ivan could climb out of bed—a simple act which he was unable to do directly.

dance (and dancing with a partner, or in a social setting, brings to bear other therapeutic dimensions). Madeleine Hackney and Gammon Earhart at the Washington University in St. Louis School of Medicine have published careful studies not only on the immediate effects of dancing, but on the improvements in functional mobility and confidence which follow a therapeutic regimen of dancing. The dance they employ is the Argentine tango, and they enumerate the advantages of this:

> Argentine tango is a dance done in an embrace or frame, unlike swing or salsa. This aspect is particularly useful to individuals who are challenged in terms of balance, because the partner may provide helpful sensory information and stabilizing support that leads to improved balance and gait. Argentine tango "steps" are themselves composed of balance exercises: steps in all directions, placing one foot in front of another in tandem, rolling through the foot from heel to toe, or toe to heel, leaning toward or away from a partner, and dynamic balances in single stance. The tango technique develops focus and attention to task while a dancer executes the movements, be it turning, stepping, balancing, or a combination of all three. . . . Argentine tango allows both participants an enormous amount of flexibility and choice in movement. Unlike waltz or foxtrot, no one step must follow another. The leader can choose to turn in place, to travel in any direction, or to remain stationary while enjoying the music. The interpretation of tempo and rhythm are also up to the whim of the leader, and beautifully matched by the follower because it is acceptable to move energetically or to pause for an extra beat. Free to constantly improvise, and create unique rhythms for every moment of the dance, a couple dances in sync to the meter of the

music. One can rarely be "wrong" while dancing Argentine tango. . . .

Since a dancer's attention must be divided between navigation and balance, Argentine tango helps develop cognitive skills like dual tasking. Exercises designed to improve balance engender functional mobility. These tasks may be walking on a straight line, practicing turns of various natures, placing the feet mindfully, and postural awareness during locomotion. . . . The touch of others, the rhythm of the music, and the novelty of the experience all contributed to the beneficial effects.

Dance is an essential part of the music therapy program at Beth Abraham Hospital, and I saw its effects strikingly in my post-encephalitic and parkinsonian patients there. Dance was effective for many of these patients not only before they received L-dopa (when, if not actually frozen, they had major difficulties with stepping, turning, and balance), but later, when some of them developed chorea—sudden, irregular, uncontrollable movements affecting trunk, limbs, and face—as a side effect of treatment with L-dopa. The power of dancing to control or facilitate movement for these patients was dramatically shown in a 1974 documentary (Discovery series, *Awakenings*, Yorkshire Television).

People with Huntington's disease, who sooner or later develop intellectual and behavioral problems in addition to chorea, may also benefit from dancing—and, indeed, from any activity or sport with a regular rhythm or "kinetic melody." One correspondent writes to me that his brother-in-law, who has Huntington's disease, "seems to get caught in repetitive behavioral loops, as if he cannot stop thinking a thought, and as a result he becomes rooted to the spot, unable to move, and repeats the same phrase over and over again." He is nevertheless able to play tennis, and this gives him a flow, a freedom from the "behavioral loops," for the duration of the game.

Patients with various other types of movement disorders may also be able to pick up the rhythmic movement or kinetic melody of an animal, so, for example, equestrian therapy may have startling effectiveness for people with parkinsonism, Tourette's syndrome, chorea, or dystonia.

N IETZSCHE WAS intensely interested, throughout his life, in the relationship of art, and especially music, to physiology. He spoke of its "tonic" effect—its power of arousing the nervous system in a general way, especially during states of physiological and psychological depression (he was himself often depressed, physiologically and psychologically, by severe migraines).

He also spoke of the "dynamic" or propulsive powers of music—its ability to elicit, to drive, and to regulate movement. Rhythm, he felt, could propel and articulate the stream of movement (and the stream of emotion and thought, which he saw as no less dynamic or motoric than the purely muscular). And rhythmic vitality and exuberance, he thought, expressed itself most naturally in the form of dance. He called his own philosophizing "dancing in chains" and thought the strongly rhythmic music of Bizet as ideally suited to this. He would often take his notebook to Bizet concerts; he wrote, "Bizet makes me a better philosopher."[9]

9. Nietzsche, in his essay "Nietzsche contra Wagner," speaks of Wagner's late music as exemplifying "the pathological in music," marked by a "degeneration of the sense of rhythm" and a tendency to "endless melody . . . the polypus in music." The lack of rhythmic organization in late Wagner makes it almost useless for parkinsonians; this is also true of plainsong and various forms of chant which, as Jackendorff and Lerdahl remark, "have pitch organization and grouping but no metrical organization of any consequence."

·I had read Nietzsche's notes on physiology and art as a student, many years before, but his concise and brilliant formulations in *The Will to Power* came alive for me only when I came to Beth Abraham and saw the extraordinary powers of music with our post-encephalitic patients—its power to "awaken" them at every level: to alertness when they were lethargic, to normal movements when they were frozen, and, most uncannily, to vivid emotions and memories, fantasies, whole identities which were, for the most part, unavailable to them. Music did everything that L-dopa, still in the future, was subsequently to do, and more—but only for the brief span while it lasted, and perhaps for a few minutes afterwards. Metaphorically, it was like auditory dopamine—a "prosthesis" for the damaged basal ganglia.

It is music that the parkinsonian needs, for only music, which is rigorous yet spacious, sinuous and alive, can evoke responses that are equally so. And he needs not only the metrical structure of rhythm and the free movement of melody—its contours and trajectories, its ups and downs, its tensions and relaxations—but the "will" and intentionality of music, to allow him to regain the freedom of his own kinetic melody.

21

Phantom Fingers:
The Case of the One-Armed Pianist

Some years ago I received a letter from Erna Otten, a piano student who had once studied with the Viennese pianist Paul Wittgenstein. Wittgenstein, she explained,

> had lost his right arm in World War I—I had many occasions to see how involved his right stump was whenever we went over the fingering for a new composition. He told me many times that I should trust his choice of fingering because he felt every finger of his right hand. At times I had to sit very quietly while he would close his eyes and his stump would move constantly in an agitated manner. This was many years after the loss of his arm.

As a postscript, she added, "His finger choice was always the best!"

The varied phenomena of phantom limbs were first explored in detail by the physician Silas Weir Mitchell during the Civil War, when great numbers of veterans came to the many hospitals established to treat their wounds, including what was known as the "stump" hospital in Philadelphia. Weir Mitchell, a novelist as well as a neurologist, was fascinated by the descriptions he received from these soldiers, and he was the first to take the phenomenon of phantom limbs seriously. (Prior to this, they had been regarded as purely "in the mind," apparitions conjured up by loss and grief, like the apparitions of recently deceased children or parents.) Weir Mitchell showed that the appearance of a phantom limb occurred in every patient who had an amputation, and he surmised that it was a sort of image or memory of the lost limb, a persistent neural representation of the limb in the brain. He first described the phenomenon in his 1866 short story "The Case of George Dedlow," published in the *Atlantic Monthly*. It was only some years later, in his 1872 book *Injuries of Nerves and Their Consequences*, that he addressed his fellow physicians on the subject:

> [The majority of amputees] are able to will a movement, and apparently to themselves execute it more or less effectively. . . . The certainty with which these patients describe their [phantom motions], and their confidence as to the place assumed by the parts moved, are truly remarkable . . . the effect is apt to excite twitching in the stump. . . . In some cases the muscles which act on the hand are absent altogether; yet in these cases there is fully as clear and definite a consciousness of the movement of the fingers and of their change of positions as in cases [where the muscles to the hand are partially preserved].

Such phantom memories and images occur to some extent in almost all amputees, and may last for decades. Although the phantoms may be intrusive or even painful (especially if the limb was painful immediately before amputation), they may also be of great service to the amputee, enabling him to learn how to move a prosthetic limb or, in the case of Wittgenstein, determine the fingering of a piano piece.

Before Weir Mitchell's account, phantom limbs were regarded as purely psychic hallucinations conjured up by bereavement, mourning, or yearning—comparable to the apparitions of loved ones that mourners may experience for some weeks after their loss. Weir Mitchell was the first to show that these phantom limbs were "real"—neurological constructs dependent on the integrity of the brain, the spinal cord, and the remaining, proximal portions of the sensory and motor nerves to the limb—and that their sensation and "motions" were accompanied by excitation in all of these. (That such an excitation in fact occurred during phantom motion was proved for him by its "overflow" into movements of the stump.)

Recent neurophysiology has confirmed Weir Mitchell's hypothesis that the entire sensory-ideational-motor unit is activated in phantom motions. Farsin Hamzei et al. in Germany described in 2001 how there can be striking functional reorganization in the cortex after the amputation of an arm—in particular, "cortical disinhibition and enlargement of the excitable area of the stump." We know that movement and sensation continue to be represented in the cortex when the limb is physically lost, and Hamzei et al.'s findings suggest that the missing limb's representation may be conserved and concentrated in the now-enlarged, hyperexcitable stump area of the cortex. This might explain why, as Otten noted, Wittgenstein's stump moved "in an agitated manner" when he "played" with his phantom arm.[1]

---

1. My colleague Jonathan Cole has described to me "phantom" sensations and movements in a musician paralyzed by ALS. (This musician, Michael, was filmed for *The*

The last few decades have seen great advances in neuroscience and biomechanical engineering, advances particularly pertinent to the Wittgenstein phenomenon; and engineers are developing highly sophisticated artificial limbs with delicate "muscles," amplification of nerve impulses, servomechanisms, and so on, that can be married to the still-intact portion of the limb and allow phantom motions to be turned into real ones. The presence of strong phantom sensations and of willed phantom movements is, indeed, essential to the success of such bionic limbs.

Thus it seems possible, in the not-so-far-off future, that a one-armed pianist may be fitted with such a limb, and with it be able to play the piano again. One wonders what Paul Wittgenstein or his brother would have thought of such a development.[2] Ludwig Wittgenstein's final book speaks of our first, grounding certainty as being the certainty of our bodies; indeed, his opening proposition is, "If you do know that here is one hand, we'll grant you all the rest." Although Wittgenstein's *On Certainty* is well known

---

Process of Portrayal, a Wellcome Trust Sciart project with Andrew Dawson, Chris Rawlence, and Lucia Walker.) At first Michael, unable to practice as he had for his entire life, could not bear to listen to music at all. But then, as Cole writes:

> Towards the end of his life he began to listen to music again, when paralysed. I asked him what he felt and how it was different now he could not move.... At first it had been unbearable, but now he had reached a peace, and could joke about the pleasures of no longer having to practice. But he also said that when he heard music he saw the music notation, as though hovering above his head. Listening to the cello, for example, he also felt his hands and fingers were moving. He was imagining the making of the music as well as seeing its notation while he was hearing it. We filmed him with a cello player as we moved his hand and arms crudely in an attempt to close the circle for him. It struck me that to be left with entirely normal sensation but unable to move might lead to awful sensations from the body, perhaps worse than sensory loss and paralysis. And to be deprived of movement as a musician must be a unique torture. His movement/musical brain seemed to want to keep playing in some way.

2. Ludwig Wittgenstein was also intensely musical and would amaze his friends by whistling entire symphonies or concertos from beginning to end.

to have been written in response to the ideas of the analytic philosopher G. E. Moore, one must wonder, too, whether the strange matter of his brother's hand—a phantom, indeed, but real, effectual, and certain—did not also play a part in inciting Wittgenstein's thinking.

22

Athletes of the Small Muscles:
Musician's Dystonia

In 1997 I received a letter from a young Italian violinist, who related to me how he had started playing the violin when he was six, had gone on to the conservatory, and then embarked on a career as a concert violinist. But then, at the age of twenty-three, he started to experience peculiar difficulties with his left hand—difficulties which, he wrote, "have cut short my career, and my life.

"Playing pieces of a certain degree of difficulty," he continued, "I found that the middle finger was not responding to my commands, and imperceptibly tended to shift from the position where I wanted to place it on the string, affecting the pitch."

He consulted a physician—one of many he was to consult in the years to come—and was told that the overwork of this hand had caused "an inflammation of the nerves." He was advised to rest and desist from playing for three months—but this, he found, had no effect. Indeed, when he resumed playing, the problem had become worse, and the strange difficulty in controlling finger movement had spread to the fourth and fifth fingers. Now only the index finger remained unaffected. It was only when he played the violin, he stressed, that his fingers "disobeyed" him; they functioned normally in all other activities.

He went on to describe an odyssey of eight years in which he had consulted physicians, physiotherapists, psychiatrists, therapists, and healers of every sort, all over Europe. He had been given many diagnoses: strained muscles, inflamed tendons, "trapped" nerves. He had undergone carpal tunnel surgery, faradization of nerves, myelograms, MRIs, and a great deal of intensive physical therapy and psychotherapy—all to no avail. Now, at thirty-one, he felt that he could no longer maintain any hope of resuming his career. He had a deep sense of bewilderment, too. He felt that his condition was organic, that in some way it came from his brain, and that if there were any peripheral factors, such as nerve injuries, these had at most played a subsidiary part.

He had heard, he wrote, of other performers with similar problems. With almost all of them a seemingly trivial problem had grown steadily more severe, resisted all attempts at treatment, and ended performance careers.

I HAD RECEIVED a number of similar letters over the years and had always referred my correspondents to a neurologist colleague, Frank Wilson, who had written an important early paper in 1989, "Acquisition and Loss of Skilled Movement in Musicians." As a result, Wilson and I had been corresponding about so-called focal dystonia in musicians for some time.

The problems my Italian correspondent described were not, indeed, anything new—such problems have been observed for centuries, not only in players of musical instruments, but in a variety of other activities that demanded continuous, rapid movements of the hands (or other parts of the body) over long periods. In 1833, Sir Charles Bell, the famous anatomist, gave a detailed description of the problems that could affect the hands of people who wrote incessantly, such as clerks in government offices. He later called this "scrivener's palsy," though it was already well recognized among such writers, who called it "writer's cramp." Gowers, in his 1888 *Manual* (of diseases of the nervous system), devoted twenty close-packed pages to discussing writer's cramp and other "occupation neuroses," the generic term he adopted for "a group of maladies in which certain symptoms are excited by the attempt to perform some oft-repeated muscular action, commonly one that is involved in the occupation of the sufferer."

"Among clarks who suffer" writer's cramp, Gowers said, "lawyers' clarks constitute an undue proportion. This is no doubt due to the cramped style in which they commonly write. On the other hand, writers' cramp is practically unknown among those who write more, and under higher pressure, than any other class, shorthand writers." Gowers attributed this freedom to their using "a very free style of writing, generally from the shoulder, which is also adopted by them in long hand writing."[1]

Gowers spoke of the susceptibility of pianists and violinists to their own "occupation neuroses"; other provocative occupations included "those of painters, harpists, artificial flower makers, turners, watchmakers, knitters, engravers ... masons ... compositors, enamellers, cigarette makers, shoemakers, milkers,

---

1. Gowers himself was an avid proponent of shorthand, and invented a system that vied with the Pitman one. He felt that all physicians should learn his method, because it would enable them to take down their patients' words verbatim and in full.

money counters . . . and zither players"—a veritable tally of Victorian occupations.

Gowers did not see these task-specific problems as benign: "The disease, when well developed, is one in which the prognosis is always uncertain, and often unfavourable." Interestingly, at a time when such symptoms were either ascribed to peripheral problems with muscles, tendons, or nerves or seen as hysterical or "mental," Gowers did not feel satisfied with either explanation (though he allowed that these factors could play a subsidiary role). He insisted, rather, that these occupational "neuroses" had an origin in the brain.

One reason for this thought was the fact that, though different parts of the body could be afflicted, all the provocative occupations involved rapid, repetitive movements of small muscles. Another was the conjunction of inhibitory features such as unresponsiveness or "paralysis" with excitatory ones—abnormal movements or spasms, which increased the more one fought against the inhibition. These considerations disposed Gowers to see "occupation neuroses" as disorders of motor control in the brain, disorders he thought might involve the motor cortex (the functions of the basal ganglia were unknown at this time).

Once "occupation neuroses" developed, there was little chance of continuing in the same occupation or profession. But despite the mysterious nature and crippling consequences of this condition, remarkably little attention was paid to it, medically, for almost a century.

Though it was well known in the world of performing musicians that this dread condition could lie in wait for anyone—perhaps one in a hundred musicians would be affected, at some point in their career—a natural reserve, even secrecy, prevailed. To acknowledge an occupation-related cramp was close to professional suicide—it would be understood that one would have to give up performing and become a teacher, a conductor, perhaps a composer, instead.[2]

Not until the 1980s was this veil of secrecy finally torn away, with great courage, by two virtuoso pianists, Gary Graffman and Leon Fleisher. Their stories were remarkably similar. Fleisher, like Graffman, had been a child prodigy and one of the preeminent pianists in the world from his teenage years. In 1963, at the age of thirty-six, he found the fourth and fifth fingers of his right hand starting to curl under his hand when he played. Fleisher fought against this and continued to play, but the more he fought, the worse the spasm became. A year later, he was forced to give up performing. In 1981, in an interview with Jennifer Dunning in the *New York Times*, Fleisher gave a precise and graphic description of the problems that had put a stop to his performance, including the years of misdiagnosis and sometimes mistreatment he had received. Not the least of his problems, when seeking treatment, was not being believed, for his symptoms came on only with piano playing, and very few doctors had a piano in their office.

Fleisher's public acknowledgment of his condition came soon after Graffman acknowledged his own problem in 1981, and this spurred other musicians to admit that they, too, had been having similar problems. It also stimulated the first medical and scientific attention to the problem in almost a century.

In 1982, David Marsden, a pioneer investigator of movement disorders, suggested that writer's cramp was an expression of disordered function in the basal ganglia—and that the disorder was akin to dystonia.[3] (The term "dystonia" had long been used for

---

2. Richard J. Lederman of the Cleveland Clinic has proposed that this may be what happened to Schumann, who developed a strange hand condition in his pianistic days, which, in desperation, he attempted to treat himself (and perhaps rendered irreparable) by the use of a finger-stretching device.

3. See Sheehy and Marsden, 1982.

certain twisting and posturing spasms of the muscles such as tor-
ticollis. It is typical of dystonias, as of parkinsonism, that the
reciprocal balance between agonist and antagonistic muscles is
lost, and instead of working together as they should—one set
relaxing as the others contract—they contract together, producing a clench or spasm.)

Marsden's suggestion was taken up by other researchers, most
notably Hunter Fry and Mark Hallett at the National Institutes of
Health, who launched an intensive investigation of task-specific
focal dystonias such as writer's cramp and musician's dystonia.
But rather than thinking of these in purely motor terms, they
wondered, too, whether rapid, repetitive movements might cause
a sensory overload which could then cascade into a dystonia.[4]

At the same time, Frank Wilson, who had long been fascinated
by the speed and skill of pianists' hands and the "dystonic"
mishaps that could befall them, found himself thinking in general terms of the sort of control systems which would have to
underlie the repeated, "automatic" performance of very fast,
intricate sequences of small, precise finger movements, with the
activity of agonist and antagonist muscles in perfect reciprocal
balance. Such a system, involving the coordination of many
brain structures (sensory and motor cortex, thalamic nuclei,
basal ganglia, cerebellum), would be operating, he argued, at or
close to its functional capacity. "The musician in full flight," he
wrote in 1988, "is an operational miracle, but a miracle with
peculiar and sometimes unpredictable vulnerabilities."

By the 1990s, the tools had become available for a minute
exploration of this question, and the first surprise, given that
focal dystonia seemed to be a motor problem, was to find that
cortical disturbances in the *sensory* system were, indeed, of

4. See Fry and Hallett, 1988; Hallett, 1998; and Garraux et al., 2004.

crucial importance. Hallett's group found that the mapping of dystonic hands in the sensory cortex was disorganized both functionally and anatomically. These changes in mapping were greatest for the fingers which were most affected. With the onset of dystonia, the sensory representations of the affected fingers started to enlarge excessively, and then to overlap and fuse, to "de-differentiate." This led to a deterioration in sensory discrimination and a potential loss of control—which the performer, usually, would fight against by practicing and concentrating more, or by playing with more force. A vicious cycle would develop, abnormal sensory input and abnormal motor output exacerbating each other.

Other researchers found changes in the basal ganglia (which, with the sensory and motor cortex, form an essential circuit for the control of movement). Were these changes caused by the dystonia or were they in fact primary, disposing certain susceptible individuals to the problem? The fact that the sensorimotor cortex in dystonic patients also showed changes on the "normal" side suggested that these changes were indeed primary, and that there was probably a genetic predisposition to dystonia, which might become apparent only after years of rapid, repetitive movements in adjacent muscle groups.

In addition to genetic vulnerabilities, there may be, as Wilson has pointed out, significant biomechanical considerations: the shape of a pianist's hands and the way he holds them, for example, might play a part in determining whether or not, after years of intensive practice and performance, he gets a dystonia.[5]

The fact that similar cortical abnormalities can be experimentally induced in monkeys has allowed Michael Merzenich and

---

5. Wilson's work, which he summarized in a paper in 2000, was done in conjunction with Christoph Wagner at the Musikphysiologische Institut in Hanover. See also Wagner's monograph, published in 2005.

his colleagues in San Francisco to explore an animal model of focal dystonia, and to demonstrate the abnormal feedbacks in the sensory loop and the motor misfirings that, once started, grow relentlessly worse.[6]

Could the cortical plasticity that allows focal dystonia to develop also be used to reverse it? Victor Candia and his colleagues in Germany have used sensory retraining to redifferentiate the degraded finger representations. Though the investment of time and effort is considerable and success is not certain, they have shown that, in some cases at least, this sensorimotor "retuning" can restore relative normality of finger movement and its representation in the cortex.

A sort of perverse learning is involved in the genesis of focal dystonia, and once the mappings in the sensory cortex have gone wrong, a massive act of unlearning is needed if a healthier relearning is to occur. And unlearning, as all teachers and trainers know, is very difficult, sometimes impossible.

A N ENTIRELY DIFFERENT approach was introduced in the late 1980s. One form of botulinum toxin, which in large doses causes paralysis, had been used in tiny doses to control various conditions in which muscles are so tense, or in such spasm, that they can hardly be moved. Mark Hallett and his group were pioneers in the experimental use of Botox to treat musician's dystonia, and they found that small, carefully placed injections might allow a level of muscular relaxation that did not trigger the chaotic feedback, the aberrant motor programs, of focal dystonia. Such injections—though not always effective—have enabled some musicians to resume playing their instruments.

---

6. See, for example, Blake, Byl, et al., 2002.

Botox does not remove the underlying neural and perhaps genetic disposition to dystonia, and it may be unwise or provocative to attempt a return to performance. This was the case, for example, with Glen Estrin, a gifted French horn player who developed an embouchure dystonia affecting the muscles of the lower face, jaw, and tongue. Though dystonias of the hand usually occur only in the particular act of making music (this is why it is called "task-specific"), dystonias in the lower face and jaw may be different. Steven Frucht and his colleagues, in a pioneer study of twenty-six professional brass and woodwind players affected with this type of dystonia, observed that in more than a quarter of them, the dystonia spread to other activities. This happened with Estrin, who developed disabling mouth movements not only when playing the horn, but when eating or speaking, severely disabling him in daily life.

Estrin has been treated with Botox but has stopped playing, given the danger of recurrence and the disabling nature of his symptoms. Instead, he has turned his attention to working with Musicians with Dystonia, a group that he and Frucht founded in 2000 to publicize the condition and help musicians who are struggling with it. A few years ago, musicians like Fleisher and Graffman, or the Italian violinist who wrote to me in 1997, might go for years without a proper diagnosis or treatment, but now the situation has been transformed. Neurologists are much more aware of musician's dystonia, as are musicians themselves.

R ECENTLY LEON FLEISHER came to visit me a few days before he was to give a performance at Carnegie Hall. He spoke of how his own dystonia had first hit him: "I remember the piece that brought it on," he began, and described how he had been practicing the Schubert *Wanderer* Fantasy for eight or nine hours a day. Then he had to take an enforced rest—he had a small accident to his right thumb and could not play for a few days. It was on his return to the keyboard after this that he noticed the fourth and fifth fingers of that hand starting to curl under. His reaction to this, he said, was to work through it, as athletes are often told to "work through" the pain. But "pianists," he said, "should not work through pain or other symptoms. I warn other musicians about this. I warn them to treat themselves as athletes of the small muscles. They make extraordinary demands on the small muscles of their hands and fingers."

In 1963, however, when the problem first arose, Fleisher had no one to advise him, no idea what was happening to his hand. He forced himself to work harder, and more and more effort was needed as other muscles were brought into play. But the more he exerted himself, the worse it became, until finally, after a year, he gave up the struggle. "When the gods go after you," he said, "they really know where to strike."

He had a period of deep depression and despair, feeling his career as a performer was over. But he had always loved teaching, and now he turned to conducting as well. In the 1970s, he made a discovery—in retrospect, he is surprised he did not make it earlier. Paul Wittgenstein, the dazzlingly gifted (and immensely wealthy) Viennese pianist who had lost his right arm in the Great War, had commissioned the great composers of the world—Prokofiev, Hindemith, Ravel, Strauss, Korngold, Britten, and others—to write piano solos and concertos for the left hand. And this was the treasure trove that Fleisher discovered, one that enabled him to resume his career as a performing artist—but now, like Wittgenstein and Graffman, as a one-handed pianist.

Playing only with the left hand at first seemed to Fleisher a great loss, a narrowing of possibilities, but gradually he came to feel that he had been "on automatic," following a brilliant but (in a sense) one-directional course. "You play your concerts, you play with orchestras, you make your records . . . that's it, until you have a heart attack on stage and die." But now he started to feel that his loss could be "a growth experience."

"Suddenly I realized that the most important thing in my life was not playing with two hands, it was *music*. . . . In order to be able to make it across these last thirty or forty years, I've had to somehow de-emphasize the number of hands or the number of fingers and go back to the concept of music as music. The instrumentation becomes unimportant, and it's the substance and content that take over."

And yet, throughout those decades, he never fully accepted that his one-handedness was irrevocable. "The way it came upon me," he thought, "might be the way it would leave me." Every morning for thirty-odd years, he tested his hand, always hoping.

Though Fleisher had met Mark Hallett and tried Botox treatments in the late 1980s, it seemed that he needed an additional mode of treatment, in the form of Rolfing to soften up the dystonic muscles in his arm and hand—a hand so clenched that he could not open it and an arm "as hard as petrified wood." The combination of Rolfing and Botox was a breakthrough for him, and he was able to give a two-hand performance with the Cleveland Orchestra in 1996 and a solo recital at Carnegie Hall in 2003. His first two-handed recording in forty years was entitled, simply, *Two Hands*.

Botox treatments do not always work; the dose must be minutely calibrated or it will weaken the muscles too much, and it must be repeated every few months. But Fleisher has been one of the lucky ones, and gently, humbly, gratefully, cautiously, he has returned to playing with two hands—though never forgetting for a moment that, as he puts it, "once a dystonic, always a dystonic."

Fleisher now performs once again around the world, and he speaks of this return as a rebirth, "a state of grace, of ecstasy." But the situation is a delicate one. He still has regular Rolfing therapy and takes care to stretch each finger before playing. He is careful to avoid provocative ("scaley") music, which may trigger his dystonia. Occasionally, too, he will "redistribute some of the material," as he puts it, modifying the fingering, shifting what might be too taxing for the right hand to the left hand.

At the end of our visit, Fleisher agreed to play something on my piano, a beautiful old 1894 Bechstein concert grand that I had grown up with, my father's piano. Fleisher sat at the piano and carefully, tenderly, stretched each finger in turn, and then, with arms and hands almost flat, he started to play. He played a piano transcription of Bach's "Sheep May Safely Graze," as arranged for piano by Egon Petri. Never in its 112 years, I thought, had this piano been played by such a master—I had the feeling that Fleisher had sized up the piano's character and perhaps its idiosyncrasies within seconds, that he had matched his playing to the instrument, to bring out its greatest potential, its particularity. Fleisher seemed to distill the beauty, drop by drop, like an alchemist, into flowing notes of an almost unbearable beauty—and, after this, there was nothing more to be said.

Part IV

Emotion, Identity, and Music

23

Awake and Asleep:
Musical Dreams

L
ike most people, I dream of music occasionally. Sometimes I have panicked dreams that I have to perform in
public music that I have never played before, but generally, in my dreams, I am listening to or playing music I know
well. And though I may be deeply affected by the music while I
am dreaming, when I awake I sometimes have only the recollection that I have dreamed of music or of the feelings that went
with it, without being able to say what the music actually was.

But on two occasions in 1974 it was different. I was severely
insomniac and had been taking chloral hydrate, an old-fashioned
hypnotic, in rather large doses. This disposed me to excessively
vivid dreams, which could sometimes continue as a sort of quasi-
hallucination even after waking. On one such occasion, I dreamed
of the Mozart horn quintet, and this continued, delightfully,
when I got up. I heard (as I never do with my normal musical
imagery) every instrument clearly. The piece unfolded, played

itself unhurriedly, at its proper tempo, in my mind. And then suddenly, as I was drinking a cup of tea, it stopped, vanished like the
bursting of a bubble.[1]

During the same period, I had another musical dream, and this
too continued into the waking state. Here, in contrast to the
Mozart, I found something deeply disturbing and unpleasant
about the music, and longed for it to stop. I had a shower, a cup of
coffee, went for a walk, shook my head, played a mazurka on the
piano—to no avail. The hateful hallucinatory music continued
unabated. Finally I phoned a friend, Orlan Fox, and said that I
was hearing songs that I could not stop, songs that seemed to me
full of melancholy and a sort of horror. The worst thing, I added,
was that the songs were in German, a language I did not know.[2]
Orlan asked me to sing or hum some of the songs. I did so, and
there was a long pause.

---

1. Many other drugs can tip one into strange oneiric states. Stan Gould, a correspondent,
wrote that when, around the age of forty, he was given gabapentin to treat severe
migraine, "It literally changed my life; the migraines disappeared almost completely, virtually overnight." But there was a strange side effect:

> It was after I started taking gabapentin that I began to experience intense, almost-
> difficult-to-awaken-from dreams associated with loud, highly dramatic sym-
> phonic music; I have even delayed awakening, just to "finish" these orchestral
> works. The music almost never interrupts my waking hours, but I find the night-
> time highly enjoyable because the music is extremely pleasing to me in an odd,
> relaxing sort of way, despite being highly complex and, often, quite loud. I have
> never "heard" this music "in public," and I know that it is "mine." I am the pro-
> ducer of this music—the music is in me.

2. One correspondent, Philip Kassen, wrote to me about his father, a psychoanalyst:

> My dad had an episode a year or so before he died when he heard someone singing
> songs in Spanish for a couple of weeks; no one else heard this. He did not speak
> Spanish. We live in a heavily Hispanic neighborhood and he spent hours looking
> out of his window for the person singing.

One does not need to know a language to remember, recite, sing, or hallucinate it. I
can recite much of the Hebrew liturgy for the Shabbos and the High Holy Days by heart (I
was brought up in an Orthodox household), but as I do not know Hebrew, I have no idea
what it means. Gloria Lenhoff (who is described in chapter 28) sings songs in dozens of
languages, without actually knowing the meaning of any of them.

"Have you abandoned some of your young patients?" he asked. "Or destroyed some of your literary children?"

"Both," I answered. "Yesterday. I resigned from the children's unit at the hospital where I have been working, and I burned a book of essays I had just written. . . . How did you guess?"

"Your mind is playing Mahler's *Kindertotenlieder*," he said, "his songs of mourning for the death of children." I was amazed by this, for I rather dislike Mahler's music and would normally find it quite difficult to remember in detail, let alone sing, any of his *Kindertotenlieder*. But here my dreaming mind, with infallible precision, had come up with an appropriate symbol of the previous day's events. And in the moment that Orlan interpreted the dream, the music disappeared; it has never recurred in the thirty years since.

In the curious intermediate states between waking and sleep—the "hypnagogic" state that may precede sleep or the "hypnopompic" state that may follow awakening—free-floating reverie and dreamlike or hallucinatory apparitions are particularly common. These tend to be highly visual, kaleidoscopic, elusive, and difficult to remember—but on occasion they may take the form of coherent musical hallucination. Later in 1974, I had an accident requiring surgery to one leg and was hospitalized for several weeks in a tiny windowless room that did not allow any radio reception. A friend brought me a tape recorder, along with a single cassette—of the Mendelssohn Violin Concerto.[3] I played this constantly, dozens of times a day, and one morning, in that delicious hypnopompic state that follows waking, I heard the Mendelssohn playing. I was not dreaming but fully aware that I was lying in a hospital bed, and that my tape recorder was by my side. One of the nurses, I thought, must have put it on, as a novel way of waking

---

3. See page 255; I have also described this in more detail in *A Leg to Stand On*.

me up. Gradually I surfaced, the music continuing all the while, until I was able to stretch out a sleepy hand to turn the recorder off. When I did this, I found that the machine *was* off. In the moment of realizing this, and being startled into full wakefulness, the hallucinatory Mendelssohn abruptly ceased.

I had never experienced coherent, continuous, perception-like music in hypnagogic or hypnopompic states before this, nor have I since. I suspect that it was a combination of events that tipped me into "hearing" music in this way: the almost nonstop exposure to Mendelssohn, which had supersaturated my brain, *plus* the hypnopompic state.

But after speaking to a number of professional musicians about this, I find that intensely vivid musical imagery or quasi-hallucination is not uncommon in such states. Melanie Challenger, a poet who writes libretti for operas, told me that when she wakes from her afternoon siesta and is in a "borderline" state, she may experience very loud, very vivid orchestral music—"it is like having an orchestra in the room." She is perfectly aware at such times that she is lying in bed in her own room and that there is no orchestra, but she can hear all the individual instruments and their combinations with a richness and a realness that she does not have with her ordinary musical imagery. She says that it is never a single piece that she hears, but a patchwork of musical fragments and musical devices "stitched together," a sort of kaleidoscopic playing with music. Nonetheless, some of these hypnopompic fragments may stick in her mind and play an important role in her subsequent compositions.[4]

---

4. There have been very few systematic studies of music in dreams, though one such, by Valeria Uga and her colleagues at the University of Florence in 2006, compared the dream logs of thirty-five professional musicians and thirty nonmusicians. The researchers concluded that "musicians dream of music more than twice as much as non-musicians [and]

With some musicians, however, especially if there has been long and intensive incubation of a new composition, such experiences may be coherent and full of meaning, even providing the long-sought-after parts of a major composition. Such an experience was described by Wagner, who wrote of how the orchestral introduction to *Das Rheingold* came to him, after long waiting, when he was in a strange, quasi-hallucinatory twilight state:

> After a night spent in fever and sleeplessness, I forced myself to take a long tramp the next day through the hilly country, which was covered with pinewoods. It all looked dreary and desolate, and I could not think what I should do there. Returning in the afternoon, I stretched myself, dead tired, on a hard couch, awaiting the long-desired hour of sleep. It did not come; but I fell into a kind of somnolent state, in which I suddenly felt as though I were sinking in swiftly flowing water. The rushing sound formed itself in my brain into a musical sound, the chord of E-flat major, which continued re-echoed in broken forms; these broken forms seemed to be melodic passages of increasing motion, yet the pure triad of E-flat major never changed, but seemed by its continuance to impart infinite significance to the element in which I was sinking. I awoke in sudden terror from my doze, feeling as though the waves were rushing high above my head. I at once recognized that the orchestral overture to the Rheingold, which must have long lain latent within me, though it had been unable to find definite form, had at last been

---

musical dream frequency is related to the age of commencement of musical instruction, but not to the daily load of musical activity. Nearly half of the recalled music was non-standard, suggesting that original music can be created in dreams." While there have been many anecdotal stories of composers creating original compositions in dreams, this is the first systematic study to lend support to the idea.

revealed to me. I then quickly realized my own nature; the stream of life was not to flow to me from without, but from within.

Ravel noted that the most delightful melodies came to him in dreams, and Stravinsky said much the same. Indeed, many of the great classical composers spoke of musical dreams and often found inspiration in dreams—a short list would include Handel, Mozart, Chopin, and Brahms. And there is a famous story told by Paul McCartney (related in Barry Miles's book):

> I woke up with a lovely tune in my head. I thought, "That's great, I wonder what that is?" There was an upright piano next to me, to the right of the bed by the window. I got out of bed, sat at the piano, found G, found F sharp minor 7th—and that leads you through then to B to E minor, and finally back to E. It all leads forward logically. I liked the melody a lot, but because I'd dreamed it, I couldn't believe I'd written it. I thought, "No, I've never written anything like this before." But I had the tune, which was the most magic thing!

Perhaps the most poignant example, though, is the one Berlioz provided in his *Memoirs*:

> Two years ago, at a time when my wife's state of health was involving me in a lot of expense, but there was still some hope of its improving, I dreamed one night that I was composing a symphony, and heard it in my dream. On waking next morning I could recall nearly the whole of the first movement, which was an allegro in A minor in two-four time. . . . I was going to my desk to begin writing it down, when I suddenly thought: "If I do, I shall be led on to com-

pose the rest. My ideas always tend to expand nowadays, this symphony could well be on an enormous scale. I shall spend perhaps three or four months on the work (I took seven to write *Romeo and Juliet*), during which time I shall do no articles, or very few, and my income will diminish accordingly. When the symphony is written I shall be weak enough to let myself be persuaded by my copyist to have it copied, which will immediately put me a thousand or twelve hundred francs in debt. Once the parts exist, I shall be plagued by the temptation to have the work performed. I shall give a concert, the receipts of which will barely cover one half of the costs—that is inevitable these days. I shall lose what I haven't got and be short of money to provide for the poor invalid, and no longer able to meet my personal expenses or pay my son's board on the ship he will shortly be joining." These thoughts made me shudder, and I threw down my pen, thinking: "What of it? I shall have forgotten it by tomorrow!" That night the symphony again appeared and obstinately resounded in my head. I heard the allegro in A minor quite distinctly. More, I seemed to see it written. I woke in a state of feverish excitement. I sang the theme to myself; its form and character pleased me exceedingly. I was on the point of getting up. Then my previous thoughts recurred and held me fast. I lay still, steeling myself against temptation, clinging to the hope I would forget. At last I fell asleep; and when I next awoke all recollection of it had vanished for ever.

I RVING J. MASSEY points out that "music is the only faculty that is not altered by the dream environment, whereas action, character, visual elements and language may all be modified or distorted in dreams." More specifically, he writes, "music in dream does not become fragmented, chaotic or incoherent, neither does it decay as rapidly as do the other components of dreams on our awakening." Thus Berlioz, on awakening, could recall nearly the whole of the first movement of his dream symphony, and he found it as pleasing in form and character as he had in his dream.

There are many stories, some true, some apocryphal, of mathematical theories, scientific insights, designs for novels or paintings occurring in dreams and being remembered upon waking. "What distinguishes music in dreams from these other achievements," Massey stresses, "is that it is consistently normal, whereas normal or superior function in other areas is exceptional or, at least, intermittent." (Somewhat startled by this, and noting that many of the dreamers whom Massey refers to are professional musicians, I decided to make an informal sampling of an unselected population of Columbia University undergraduates, asking those who had musical dreams to describe them. Their replies seem to support Massey's contention that dream music, when it occurs, is accurately perceived or "played" by the dreaming mind and readily recalled upon waking.)

Massey concludes that "Music in dreams then is the same as music in our waking life. . . . One might say that music never sleeps. . . . It is as if it were an autonomous system, indifferent to our consciousness or lack of it." His conclusion also seems supported by the accuracy and seemingly indelible quality of musical memory as it is manifest in musical imagery, brainworms, and, most strikingly, in musical hallucinations—as well as the apparent imperviousness of music to the ravages of amnesia or dementia.

Massey wonders why musical dreams are immune to the distortions and (if Freud is right) the disguises which are characteristic of almost all other elements in dreams, and which make it so necessary (and often so tricky) to interpret them. Why is music different? Why are musical dreams so literal, so faithful to reality? Is it because music has "a formal contour and inner momentum—a purpose of its own"? Or is it that music has a special cerebral organization of its own, is "served by different . . . processes from those associated with image, a language and narrative, and so may not be subject to the same amnestic forces as these"? It is clear, as Massey points out, that "the musical dream is not merely a curiosity, but a potential source of valuable information" on some of the deepest questions about the nature of art and brain.

24

Seduction and Indifference

There is a tendency in philosophy to separate the mind, the intellectual operations, from the passions, the emotions. This tendency moves into psychology, and thence into neuroscience. The neuroscience of music, in particular, has concentrated almost exclusively on the neural mechanisms by which we perceive pitch, tonal intervals, melody, rhythm, and so on, and, until very recently, has paid little attention to the affective aspects of appreciating music. Yet music calls to both parts of our nature—it is essentially emotional, as it is essentially intellectual. Often when we listen to music, we are conscious of both: we may be moved to the depths even as we appreciate the formal structure of a composition.

We may, of course, lean to one side or the other, depending on the music, our mood, our circumstances. "Dido's Lament" from Purcell's *Dido and Aeneas* is heartbreaking, tender emotion incarnate; *The Art of Fugue*, on the other hand, demands extreme intellectual attention—its beauty is of a sterner, perhaps more impersonal kind. Professional musicians, or anyone practicing a piece of music, may sometimes have to listen with a detached, critical ear to ensure that all the minutiae of a performance are technically correct. But technical correctness alone is not enough; once this is achieved, emotion must return, or one may be left with nothing beyond an arid virtuosity. It is always a balance, a coming together, that is needed.

That we have separate and distinct mechanisms for appreciating the structural and the emotional aspects of music is brought home by the wide variety of responses (and even "dissociations") that people have to music.[1] There are many of us who lack some of the perceptual or cognitive abilities to appreciate music but nonetheless enjoy it hugely, and enthusiastically bawl out tunes, sometimes shockingly off-key, in a way that gives us great happiness (though it may make others squirm). There are others with an opposite balance: they may have a good ear, be finely sensitive to the formal nuances of music, but nevertheless do not care for it greatly or consider it a significant part of their lives. That one may be quite "musical" and yet almost indifferent to music, or almost tone-deaf yet passionately sensitive to music, is quite striking.

While musicality, in the sense of one's perceptual abilities, is probably hardwired to a considerable extent, emotional susceptibility to music is more complex, for it may be powerfully influenced

---

1. Anthony Storr gives a very nice example of such a dissociation in *Music and the Mind:*

> Many years ago, I acted as a "guinea-pig" for one of my colleagues who was investigating the effects of the drug mescaline. Whilst still under its influence, I listened to music on the radio. The effect was to enhance my emotional responses whilst concurrently abolishing my perception of form. Mescaline made a Mozart string quartet sound as romantic as Tchaikovsky. I was conscious of the throbbing, vibrant quality of the sounds which reached me; of the bite of bow upon string; of a direct appeal to my emotions. In contrast, appreciation of form was greatly impaired. Each time a theme was repeated, it came as a surprise. The themes might be individually entrancing, but their relation with one another had disappeared. All that was left was a series of tunes with no connecting links: a pleasurable experience, but one which also proved disappointing.
>
> My reaction to mescaline convinced me that, in my own case, the part of the brain concerned with emotional responses is different from the part which perceives structure. The evidence suggests that this is true of everyone.

by personal factors as well as neurological ones. When one is depressed, music may "go dead" on one—but this is usually part of an overall flattening or withdrawal of emotion. What is clear and dramatic, though fortunately rare, is the sudden and isolated loss of the ability to respond to music emotionally, while responding normally to everything else, including the formal structure of music.

Such a temporary extinction of emotional response to music can occur after a concussion. Lawrence R. Freedman, a physician, told me of how he was confused and disoriented for six days following a bicycle accident, and then experienced a specific indifference to music. In a subsequent article about this, he observed:

> There was one thing I noticed in the early days at home that disturbed me greatly. I was no longer interested in listening to music. I heard the music. I knew it was music, and I also knew how much I used to enjoy listening to music. It had always been the primary unfailing source that nourished my spirit. Now it just didn't *mean* anything. I was indifferent to it. I knew something was very wrong.

This loss of emotional reaction to music was very specific. Dr. Freedman noted that he felt no diminution of his passion for visual art after his concussion. He added that since writing about his experience, he had spoken to two other people, both musicians, who had had the same experience after a head injury.

Those who experience this peculiar indifference to music are not in a state of depression or fatigue. They do not have a generalized anhedonia. They respond normally to everything *except* music, and their musical sensibility usually returns in days or weeks. It is difficult to know exactly what is being affected in such postconcussion syndromes, for there may be widespread, if temporary, changes in brain function, affecting many different parts of the brain.

There have been a number of anecdotal reports of people who, following strokes, have lost interest in music, finding it emotionally flat, while apparently retaining all of their musical perceptions and skills. (It has been suggested that such losses or distortions of musical emotion are more common with damage to the right hemisphere of the brain.) Occasionally there is not so much a complete loss of musical emotion as a change in its valence or direction, so that music which previously delighted one may now arouse an unpleasant feeling, sometimes so intense as to produce anger, disgust, or simply aversion. One correspondent, Maria Ralescu, described this to me in a letter:

> My mother recovered from a six-day coma after a head injury to the right side of the brain and started the process of relearning with enthusiasm. . . . When she was moved from the ICU to a hospital room, I brought her a small radio, because she had always listened to music with a passion. . . . But after the accident, while in hospital, she adamantly refused to have any kind of music on. It seemed to annoy her. . . . It took a couple of months for her to finally appreciate and enjoy music again.

There have been very few detailed studies of such patients, but Timothy Griffiths, Jason Warren, et al., have described how one man, a fifty-two-year-old radio announcer who suffered a dominant-hemisphere stroke (with a transient aphasia and hemiplegia), was left with "a persistent alteration in auditory experience."

> He was in the habit of listening to classical music . . . and had derived particular pleasure from listening to Rachmaninov

preludes. He experienced an intense, altered state of "transformation" when he did this. . . . This emotional response to the
music was lost following the [stroke], and remained absent
during the period of testing between 12 and 18 months after
the stroke. During this period he was able to enjoy other
aspects of life, and reported no (biological) features of depression. He had noticed no change in his hearing and was still able
to identify speech, music and environmental sounds correctly.

Isabelle Peretz and her colleagues have been especially concerned with amusia—the loss (or congenital lack) of ability to
make structural judgments about music. They were astounded to
find, in the early 1990s, that some of their subjects rendered virtually amusic by brain injuries were nonetheless still able to enjoy
music and to make emotional judgments about it. One such
patient, listening to Albinoni's Adagio (from her own record col-
lection), first said that she had never heard the piece before, then
commented that "it makes me feel sad and the feeling makes me
think of Albinoni's Adagio." Another patient of Peretz's was I.R., a
forty-year-old woman who had "mirror" aneurysms of both
middle cerebral arteries; when these were clipped the surgery
caused extensive infarctions in both temporal lobes. After this, she
lost the ability to recognize previously familiar melodies, and even
to discriminate musical sequences. "Despite these gross deficits,"
Peretz and Gagnon wrote in 1999, "I.R. claimed that she could still
enjoy music." Detailed testing supported her claim.

Darwin might have been a good subject for such testing, too,
for as he wrote in his autobiography:

I acquired a strong taste for music, and used very often to
time my walks so as to hear on week days the anthem in

King's College Chapel. This gave me intense pleasure, so that my backbone would sometimes shiver. . . . Nevertheless I am so utterly destitute of an ear, that I cannot perceive a discord, or keep time and hum a tune correctly; and it is a mystery how I could possibly have derived pleasure from music.

My musical friends soon perceived my state, and sometimes amused themselves by making me pass an examination, which consisted in ascertaining how many tunes I could recognise, when they were played rather more quickly or slowly than usual. "God save the King," when thus played, was a sore puzzle.

Peretz thinks that there must be "a particular functional architecture underlying the emotional interpretation of music," an architecture which could be spared even if amusia was present. The details of this functional architecture are being slowly worked out, partly through the study of patients who have had strokes, brain injuries, or surgical removal of parts of the temporal lobes, and partly through functional brain imaging of subjects as they experience intense emotional arousal while listening to music—this has been a focus of work by Robert Zatorre and his lab (see, for example, Blood and Zatorre's 2001 paper). Both lines of research have implicated a very extensive network involving both cortical and subcortical regions as the basis for emotional responses to music. And the fact that one may have not only a selective loss of musical emotion but an equally selective sudden musicophilia (as described in chapters 1 and 27) implies that the emotional response to music may have a very specific physiological basis of its own, one which is distinct from that of emotional responsiveness in general.

. . .

INDIFFERENCE TO music's emotional power may occur in people with Asperger's syndrome. Temple Grandin, the brilliant autistic scientist I described in *An Anthropologist on Mars*, is fascinated by musical form and is particularly attracted to music by Bach. She told me once that she had been to a concert of Bach's *Two- and Three-Part Inventions*. I asked if she had enjoyed them. "They were very ingenious," she replied, adding that she wondered whether Bach would have been up to four- or five-part inventions. "But did you *enjoy* them?" I asked again, and she gave me the same answer, saying that she got intellectual pleasure from Bach, but nothing more. Music, she said, did not "move" her, move her to the depths, as it apparently could (she had observed) with other people. There is some evidence, indeed, that those medial parts of the brain involved with experiencing deep emotions—the amygdala, in particular—may be poorly developed in people with Asperger's. (It was not only music that failed to move Temple deeply; she seemed to experience a certain flattening of emotion generally. Once when we were driving together in the mountains and I remarked on them with awe and wonder, Temple said she did not know what I meant. "The mountains are pretty," she said, "but they don't give me a special feeling.")

And yet though Temple seemed indifferent to music, this is not true of all people with autism. Indeed, I formed an opposite impression during the 1970s, when I worked with a group of young people with severe autism. It was only through music that I could establish any contact with the most inaccessible among them, and I felt this so strongly that I brought my own piano (an old, secondhand upright at the time) into the hospital ward where I worked. It seemed to act as a sort of magnet for some of these nonverbal youngsters.[2]

W E M O V E O N T O more uncertain ground with regard to certain historical figures who have been, by their own and others' description, indifferent (or sometimes averse) to music. It is possible that they were profoundly amusic—we have no evidence to either support or refute this possibility. It is difficult, for example, to know what to make of the virtual omission of any reference to music in the work of the James brothers. There is only a single sentence devoted to music in the fourteen hundred pages of William James's *Principles of Psychology*, which treats virtually every other aspect of human perception and thought; and looking through biographies of him, I can find no reference to music. Ned Rorem, in his diary *Facing the Night*, observes something similar with Henry James—that there is almost no mention of music in his novels, or in biographies of him. Perhaps the brothers grew up in a musicless household. Could lack of exposure to music in one's earliest years cause a sort of emotional amusia, as lack of language in the critical period may undermine linguistic competence for the rest of one's life?

A different and rather sad phenomenon, a loss of feeling for music and much else, is expressed by Darwin in his autobiography:

---

2. In the early 1980s, I saw *The Music Child*, a remarkable BBC film made about the work of Paul Nordoff and Clive Robbins, pioneers in the use of music therapy with deeply autistic children (as well as children with other communicative disorders). Since Nordoff and Robbins's first pilot projects in the early 1960s, the use of music therapy in autism has developed greatly, and it is now widely used to reduce stress, agitation, and stereotyped movements (rocking, flapping, etc.), and to facilitate relationship with otherwise inaccessible autistic people.

In one respect my mind had changed during the last twenty or thirty years. . . . Formerly pictures gave me considerable, and music very intense delight. But now . . . I have almost lost my taste for pictures or music. . . . My mind seems to have become a sort of machine for grinding general laws out of large collections of fact. . . . The loss of these tastes, this curious and lamentable loss of the higher aesthetic tastes, is a loss of happiness, and may possibly be injurious to the intellect, and more probably to the moral character, by enfeebling the emotional part of our nature.[3]

And we are on much more complex ground when it comes to Freud, who (as far as one can judge from accounts) never listened to music voluntarily or for pleasure and never wrote about music, though he lived in intensely musical Vienna. He would rarely and reluctantly let himself be dragged to an opera (and

---

3. This paragraph, Janet Browne writes in her biography of Darwin,

> bothered the rest of the family. It was as if Darwin was denying his sensitivity to nature, almost turning his back on his special gifts. One by one, after his death, members of the next generation pointed out counter-examples, where Darwin had enjoyed a scenic view or an evening of music. . . . Unanimously, the children rejected their father's own view of himself as a deadened, anaesthetic man.

Darwin's son Francis, in *The Autobiography of Charles Darwin*, describes how

> in the evening—that is, after he had read as much as his strength would allow, and before the reading aloud began—he would often lie on the sofa and listen to my mother playing the piano. [Eric Korn, an expert on Darwin, tells me that Emma Darwin was trained by no less than Moscheles and Chopin.] He had not a good ear, yet in spite of this he had a true love of fine music. He used to lament that his enjoyment of music had become dulled with old age, yet within my recollection his love of a good tune was strong. . . . From his want of ear he was unable to recognise a tune when he heard it again, but he remained constant to what he liked, and would often say, when an old favourite was played, "That's a fine thing; what is it?" He liked especially parts of Beethoven's symphonies and bits of Handel. He was sensitive to differences in style. . . . He enjoyed good singing and was moved almost to tears by grand or pathetic songs. . . . He was humble in the extreme about his own taste, and correspondingly pleased when he found that others agreed with him.

then only a Mozart one), and when he did, would use such occasions to think about his patients or his theories. Freud's nephew Harry (in a not-entirely-reliable memoir, *My Uncle Sigmund*) wrote that Freud "despised" music and that the whole Freud family was "very unmusical"—but neither of these assertions seems to be true. A much more delicate and nuanced comment was made by Freud himself, on the only occasion on which he wrote about the subject, in the introduction of "The Moses of Michelangelo":

> I am no connoisseur in art . . . nevertheless, works of art do exercise a powerful effect on me, especially those of literature and sculpture, less often of painting. . . . [I] spend a long time before them trying to apprehend them in my own way, i.e. to explain to myself what their effect is due to. Wherever I cannot do this, as for instance with music, I am almost incapable of obtaining any pleasure. Some rationalistic, or perhaps analytic, turn of mind in me rebels against being moved by a thing without knowing why I am thus affected and what it is that affects me.

I find this comment at once puzzling and rather poignant. One wishes that Freud might have been able, on occasion, to abandon himself to something as mysterious, as delightful, and (one would think) as unthreatening as music. Did he enjoy and respond to music as a boy, when he was not committed to explaining and theorizing? We know only that he was denied the pleasure of music as an adult. Perhaps "indifference" is not quite the word here and the Freudian term "resistance" would be nearer the mark—resistance to the seductive and enigmatic power of music.

Theodor Reik, who knew Freud well, opens his book *The*

Haunting Melody with a discussion of Freud's seeming indifference to music. "It is certain," Reik writes, "that Freud heard very
little music in the first four years he spent in the little town of
Freiburg in Moravia [and] we know how important the impressions of those early years are for the development of musical sensitivity and interests." Yet, Reik continues, he had at least twice
seen Freud enjoy music, *seen* him affected by music.[4] So it was
not indifference, Reik felt, but

> turning-away . . . [an] act of will in the interest of self-
> defense . . . [and the] more energetic and violent, the more
> the emotional effects of music appeared undesirable to him.
> He became more and more convinced that he had to keep his
> reason unclouded and his emotions in abeyance. He devel-
> oped an increasing reluctance to surrendering to the dark
> power of music. Such an avoidance of the emotional effect of
> melodies can sometimes be seen in people who feel endan-
> gered by the intensity of their feelings.

For many of us, indeed, the emotions induced by music may be
overwhelming. A number of my friends who are intensely sensitive to music cannot have it on as background when they work;
they must attend to music completely or turn it off, for it is too
powerful to allow them to focus on other mental activities.
States of ecstasy and rapture may lie in wait for us if we give ourselves totally to music; a common scene during the 1950s was to
see entire audiences swooning in response to Frank Sinatra or
Elvis Presley—seized by an emotional and perhaps erotic excitement so intense as to induce fainting. Wagner, too, was a master

---

4. It also seems (so Danielle Ofri tells me), that Freud played piano duets with at least one
talented Viennese pianist, Anna Hillsberg.

of the musical manipulation of emotions, and this, perhaps, is a reason why his music is so intoxicating to some and so disturbing to others.[5]

Tolstoy was deeply ambivalent about music, because it had, he felt, a power to induce in him "fictitious" states of mind— emotions and images that were not his own and not under his control. He adored Tchaikovsky's music but often refused to listen to it, and in "The Kreutzer Sonata," he described the seduction of the narrator's wife by a violinist and his music—the two of them play Beethoven's *Kreutzer* Sonata together, and this music is so powerful, the narrator comes to think, that it can change a woman's heart and cause her to be unfaithful. The story ends with the outraged husband murdering his wife—though the real enemy, he feels, the enemy he cannot kill, is the music.

---

5. The theme of seductive but dangerous music has always exercised the imagination. In Greek mythology, it was the bewitching music of the Sirens which lured sailors to their destruction. In *The Coldest Winter*, David Halberstam gives a vivid description of the use of uncanny, ominous music during the Korean War:

> They heard musical instruments, like weird Asian bagpipes. Some of the officers thought for a moment that a British brigade was arriving to help them out. But it was not bagpipes; instead it was an eerie, very foreign sound, perhaps bugles and flutes, a sound many of them would remember for the rest of their lives. It was the sound they would come to recognize as the Chinese about to enter battle, signaling to one another by musical instrument what they were doing, and deliberately striking fear into their enemy as well.

And in an ironic 1933 story by E. B. White, "The Supremacy of Uruguay," the country secures world domination by flying pilotless planes equipped with loudspeakers which broadcast an endlessly repeating, hypnotic musical phrase. "This unendurable sound," he wrote, "[played] over foreign territories would immediately reduce the populace to insanity. Then Uruguay, at her leisure, could send in her armies, subdue the idiots, and annex the land."

Similar themes have been used in a number of films, including Tim Burton's parody *Mars Attacks!*, in which the invading Martians are finally defeated by a particularly insidious song, which causes their heads to explode. The "Indian Love Call" thus comes to the rescue of mankind, much as simple earthly bacteria do in *The War of the Worlds*.

25

Lamentations:
Music, Madness, and Melancholia

Robert Burton, in *The Anatomy of Melancholy*, wrote at length of music's power, and John Stuart Mill found that when he fell into a state of melancholia or anhedonia as a young man, music and nothing else had the power to pierce through this, to give him, at least for a while, a feeling of pleasure and being alive. Mill's depression, it is thought, stemmed from the ruthless regime imposed by his father, who demanded incessant intellectual work and achievement from the time John Stuart was three, while doing little to nurture or even recognize his son's emotional needs. Not surprisingly, the young prodigy had a crisis when he reached adulthood and entered a state in which nothing could move him except music. Mill was not choosy about the music; Mozart, Haydn, and Rossini were equally to his taste. His only fear was that he might exhaust the musical repertoire and have nothing left to turn to.

The continuing and general need for music which Mill described is distinct from the crucial effect that particular pieces of music may have at particular times. William Styron, in his memoir *Darkness Visible*, described such an experience, when he was very close to suicide:

> My wife had gone to bed, and I had forced myself to watch the tape of a movie. . . . At one point in the film, which was set in late-nineteenth-century Boston, the characters moved down the hallway of a music conservatory, beyond the walls of which, from unseen musicians, came a contralto voice, a sudden soaring passage from the Brahms Alto Rhapsody.
>
>   This sound, which like all music—indeed, like all pleasure—I had been numbly unresponsive to for months, pierced my heart like a dagger, and in a flood of swift recollection I thought of all the joys the house had known: the children who had rushed through its rooms, the festivals, the love and work . . .

I have had a few similar experiences myself, in which music has "pierced my heart," in Styron's words, when nothing else could.

I was passionately fond of my mother's sister, my Auntie Len; I often felt she had saved my sanity, if not my life, when I was sent away from home as a child, evacuated from London during the war. Her death left a sudden huge hole in my life, but, for some reason, I had difficulty mourning. I went about my work, my daily life, functioning in a mechanical way, but inside I was in a state of anhedonia, numbly unresponsive to all pleasure—and, equally, sadness. One evening I went to a concert, hoping against hope that the music might revive me, but it did not work; the whole concert bored me—until the last piece was played. It was a piece I had never heard before, by a composer I had never heard of, *The Lamentations of Jeremiah* by Jan Dismus Zelenka (an obscure Czech contemporary of Bach's, I later learned). Suddenly, as I listened, I found my eyes wet with tears. My emotions, frozen for weeks, were flowing once again. Zelenka's *Lamentations* had broken the dam, letting feeling flow where it had been obstructed, immobilized inside me.

A similar reaction to music was described by Wendy Lesser in her book *Room for Doubt*. She, too, lost a Lenny, in her case a beloved friend rather than a beloved aunt. Where for me the releaser of emotion, the cathartic, was Zelenka's *Lamentations*, for Lesser it was Brahms's *Requiem:*

> That performance of the Brahms Requiem had a powerful effect on me. I went to Berlin thinking I would write about David Hume there . . . but . . . as the waves of music poured over me—listening with my whole body, it seemed, and not just my ears—I realized I was going to have to write about Lenny instead.
>
> I had been carrying Lenny's death in a locked package up till then, a locked frozen package that I couldn't get at but couldn't throw away either. . . . It wasn't just Lenny that had been frozen; I had, too. But as I sat in the Berlin Philharmonic Hall, and listened to the choral voices singing their incomprehensible words, something warmed and softened in me. I became, for the first time in months, able to feel again.

WHEN I GOT the news of my mother's death, I flew at once to London, to the parental house, where, for a week, we sat shivah for her. My father, my three brothers, and I, along with my mother's surviving brothers and sisters, all sat on low chairs, nourished emotionally and physically by the continual succession of relatives and friends who brought food and memories. Very movingly, many of my mother's patients and students came to pay their respects. Everywhere there was warmth, care, love, support, a flowing and sharing of feelings. But when I returned after this week to my empty and frigid apartment in New York, my feelings "froze" and I fell into what is inadequately called a depression.

For weeks I would get up, dress, drive to work, see my patients, try to present a normal appearance. But inside I was dead, as lifeless as a zombie. Then one day as I was walking down Bronx Park East, I felt a sudden lightening, a quickening of mood, a sudden whisper or intimation of life, of joy. Only then did I realize that I was hearing music, though so faintly it might have been no more than an image or a memory. As I continued to walk, the music grew louder, until finally I came to its source, a radio pouring Schubert out of an open basement window. The music pierced me, releasing a cascade of images and feelings—memories of childhood, of summer holidays together, and of my mother's fondness for Schubert (she would often sing his *Nachtgesang* in a slightly off-key voice). I found myself not only smiling for the first time in weeks, but laughing aloud—and alive once again.

I wanted to linger by the basement window—Schubert and only Schubert, I felt, was life. Only his music had the secret of keeping me alive. But I had a train to catch and kept walking. And I fell into my depression again.

A few days later, by chance, I heard that the great baritone Dietrich Fischer-Dieskau would be performing Schubert's *Winterreise* at Carnegie Hall. The performance was sold out, but I joined a crowd of people outside hoping to get in, and managed to buy a ticket for a hundred dollars. This was a huge amount in 1973, and my earnings then were modest, but it seemed a small price to pay (as I put it to myself) for my life. But when Fischer-Dieskau opened his mouth to sing the first notes, I realized that something was terribly wrong. He was, as always, technically flawless, but his singing for some reason seemed utterly flat, horribly and completely devoid of life. All around me people seemed to be in a raptus of attention, listening with profound and unfathomable expressions. They were simulating these, I decided—politely pretending to be moved, when they knew as well as I that Fischer-Dieskau had lost the wonderful warmth and sensibility that used to pervade his voice. I was, of course, totally mistaken, as I came to realize afterwards. The reviewers the next day agreed that Fischer-Dieskau had never been better. It was I who had become lifeless again, cocooned and frozen—so frozen this time that not even Schubert could get to me.

Perhaps I was defending myself, walling myself up, against feelings that threatened to be overwhelming; perhaps, more simply, I was demanding that the music work, where experience had shown me that demanding never succeeds. The power of music, whether joyous or cathartic, must steal on one unawares, come spontaneously as a blessing or a grace—as it did when the music stole from the basement window, or when I was prized open, helplessly, by the brokenhearted eloquence of Zelenka's *Lamentations*. ("The Arts are not drugs," E. M. Forster once wrote. "They are not guaranteed to act when taken. Something as mysterious and capricious as the creative impulse has to be released before they can act.")

John Stuart Mill wanted cheerful music, and it seemed to act as a tonic for him, but Lesser and I, both dealing with the loss of a beloved figure, had very different needs and a very different experience with music. It is not coincidental that the music which released our grief and allowed emotion to flow again was a requiem, in Lesser's case, and a lamentation, in my own. This was music designed for occasions of loss and death. And, indeed, music may have a unique power to speak to our condition when we ourselves are facing death.

The psychiatrist Alexander Stein has described his experience of 9/11: he lived opposite the World Trade Center and he saw it hit, watched it crumple, and was caught up in the terrified crowds fleeing down the street, not knowing whether his wife was alive or dead. He and his wife were homeless refugees for the next three months. During this time, he writes,

> My internal world was dominated by a dense and silent pall, as if an entire mode of existence were in an airless vacuum. Music, even the usual internal listening of especially beloved works, had been muted. Paradoxically, life in the auditory sphere was in other respects heightened immeasurably, but calibrated, so it seemed, to a narrow spectrum of sounds: my ears now were attuned more to the roar of fighter jets and the wail of sirens, to my patients, to my wife's breathing at night.

It was only after several months, he writes, that "music finally returned as a part of life for and in me," and the piece he first heard internally was Bach's Goldberg Variations.

On the recent fifth anniversary of September 11, on my morning bike ride to Battery Park, I heard music as I approached the tip of Manhattan, and then saw and joined a silent crowd who sat gazing out to sea and listening to a young man playing Bach's Chaconne in D on his violin. When the music ended and the crowd quietly dispersed, it was clear that the music had brought them some profound consolation, in a way that no words could ever have done.

Music, uniquely among the arts, is both completely abstract and profoundly emotional. It has no power to represent anything particular or external, but it has a unique power to express inner states or feelings. Music can pierce the heart directly; it needs no mediation. One does not have to know anything about Dido and

Aeneas to be moved by her lament for him; anyone who has ever lost someone knows what Dido is expressing. And there is, finally, a deep and mysterious paradox here, for while such music makes one experience pain and grief more intensely, it brings solace and consolation at the same time.[1]

R ECENTLY I RECEIVED a letter from a young man in his early thirties, saying that he had bipolar disorder, which had been diagnosed when he was nineteen. His episodes were clearly severe—there would be months in which he would scarcely go out or speak to anyone, and manic episodes manifest in his "spending outrageous amounts of money, staying awake at night working out math problems or writing music, and socializing non-stop." He wrote to me because he had discovered, when he was in his twenties, that piano playing could have a striking effect on his state of mind:

> If I sat at a piano, I could start to play, to improvise, and to tune into my mood. If my mood was elevated, I could match that elevated mood with the music, and after a period of playing, in almost a trance-like state, I could bring my mood down to a more normal level. Likewise, if my mood was depressed, I was able to bring my mood up. It is as if I am

---

1. Usually—but not always. One correspondent, in a state of deep distress, felt this was exacerbated by music:

> I found myself to be unable to listen to the classical music I had always loved. . . . It didn't seem to matter much what the music was—it became impossible to listen to. . . . Music induced feelings of being overwhelmed both by terror and sadness, so much so that I had to turn the music off, crying, and continue to cry for quite a while.

It was only after a year of mourning and psychotherapy that she was able to enjoy music once again.

able to use music in the same way that some people use therapy or medications to stabilize their moods. . . . Listening to music doesn't do the same thing for me by any means—it has to do with the output, and the way that I am able to control every aspect of the music—style, texture, tempo and dynamics.

In many years of working in state mental hospitals, I have seen again and again how deeply regressed schizophrenic patients who have spent most of their adult lives in the back wards of mental institutions may show "normal" responses to music—often to the astonishment of the staff, and sometimes to their own, too.[2] Psychiatrists speak of schizophrenic people as having "negative" symptoms (difficulties making contact with others, lack of motivation, and, above all, flat affect) as well as "positive" ones (hallucinations, delusions). While medication can damp down the positive symptoms, it rarely has any effect on the negative ones, which are often more disabling—and it is here (as Ulrich et al. have shown) that music therapy can be particularly useful and may help open up isolated, asocial people in a humane and uncoercive way.

Music can sometimes counter the positive symptoms, too. Thus in his *Memoirs of My Nervous Illness*, Daniel Paul Schreber, an eminent German jurist who was immersed in a deep schizophrenic psychosis for many years, wrote, "During piano playing the nonsensical twaddle of the voices which talk to me is

---

2. An account of this is even to be found in the notes of June 1, 1828, in the "Register of Lunatics" from the Sunnyside Royal Hospital in Scotland, describing one inmate, Martha Wallace: though "far advanced in years . . . and forty-four years in the Asylum, without any variation in the state of her mind during the whole of that time . . . [yet] her susceptibility to music was evinced when on Saturday . . . rising from her seat, and with a cheerful countenance, she hobbled and danced to the utmost of her strength to the sprightly tune called Neil Gow by a fiddler."

drowned. . . . Every attempt at 'representing' me by the 'creation of a false feeling' and suchlike is doomed to end in failure because of the real feeling one can put into piano playing."

There are professional musicians who are deeply schizophrenic but can nonetheless perform at the highest professional level, and their performances bear no trace of their disturbed mental states. Tom Harrell, an acclaimed jazz trumpeter and composer, is considered one of the foremost horn players of his generation, and he has maintained his artistry for decades, despite having lived with schizophrenia and virtually constant hallucinations since adolescence. Almost the only time he is not psychotic is when he is playing, or, as he puts it, "the music is playing me."

And there is the gifted classical violinist Nathaniel Ayers, who, after a brilliant start as a student at Juilliard, fell into a deep schizophrenia and ultimately lived as a homeless man on the streets of downtown Los Angeles, where occasionally he would play, ravishingly, on a battered violin with two missing strings. A very moving account of Ayers and the "redemptive power" of music for him is given by Steve Lopez in his book *The Soloist*.

As music seems to resist or survive the distortion of dreams or of parkinsonism, or the losses of amnesia or Alzheimer's, so it may resist the distortions of psychosis and be able to penetrate the deepest states of melancholia or madness, sometimes when nothing else can.

26

The Case of Harry S.:
Music and Emotion

Perhaps one should not have favorite patients, or patients who break one's heart—but I do, and among them was Harry S. He was the first patient I saw when I came to Beth Abraham Hospital in 1966, and I saw him frequently until his death thirty years later.

When I met him, Harry was in his late thirties, a brilliant mechanical engineer—he had studied at MIT—who had had a sudden rupture of a brain aneurysm while cycling up a hill. He had bled extensively into both frontal lobes, and the right was severely damaged, the left less so. He was in a coma for several weeks and remained irreparably damaged, so it seemed, for months afterwards—months in which his wife, despairing, divorced him. When he finally left the neurosurgical unit and came to Beth Abraham, a hospital for the chronically ill, he had lost his work, his wife, the use of his legs, and a large chunk of his mind and personality. And though he began slowly to regain most of his former intellectual powers, he remained severely impaired emotionally—inert, flat, and indifferent. He would do very little by himself, or for himself, but depended on others for incentive and "go."

He still subscribed, out of habit, to *Scientific American* and would read every issue from cover to cover, as he had before his accident. But while he understood everything he read, none of the articles, he admitted, excited his interest, his wonder, anymore— and "wonder," he said, had been at the core of his previous life.

He would read the daily papers conscientiously, taking in everything, but with an uncaring, indifferent eye. Surrounded by all the emotions, the drama, of others in the hospital—people agitated, distressed, in pain, or (more rarely) laughing and joyful—surrounded by their wishes, fears, hopes, aspirations, accidents, tragedies, and occasional jubilations, he himself remained entirely unmoved, seemingly incapable of feeling. He retained the forms of his previous civility, his courtesy, but we had the sense that these were no longer animated by any real feeling.

But all this would change, suddenly, when Harry sang. He had a fine tenor voice and loved Irish songs. When he sang, he showed every emotion appropriate to the music—the jovial, the wistful, the tragic, the sublime. And this was astounding, be- cause one saw no hint of this at any other time and might have thought his emotional capacity was entirely destroyed.

It was as if music, its intentionality and feeling, could "unlock" him or serve as a sort of substitute or prosthesis for his frontal lobes and provide the emotional mechanisms he seem- ingly lacked. He seemed to be transformed while he sang, but when the song was over he would relapse within seconds, becoming vacant, indifferent, and inert once again.

Or so it seemed to most of us at the hospital; others had

doubts. My colleague Elkhonon Goldberg, a neuropsychologist especially interested in frontal lobe syndromes, was not convinced. Goldberg stressed that such patients may involuntarily echo another's gestures or actions or speech, and tend to a sort of involuntary simulation or mimicry.

Was Harry's singing, then, nothing more than an elaborate, automatic sort of mimicry, or did the music somehow allow him to feel emotions to which he normally had no access? Goldberg was uncertain about this. For myself, and many others at the hospital, it was hard to believe that these emotions we saw in Harry were simulated—but perhaps that speaks to the power of music for the listener.

In 1996, the last time I saw Harry, thirty years after his accident, he had developed hydrocephalus and large cysts in his frontal lobes; he was too ill and fragile for any surgical intervention. But, though so weak, he gathered his last bit of animation and sang for me—"Down in the Valley" and "Goodnight, Irene"—with all the delicacy and tenderness of his earlier days. It was his swan song; a week later he was dead.

ONE OF MY post-encephalitic patients, Hester, after being "awakened" by L-dopa and restored for a while to normal movement and feeling, wrote in her diary, "I would like to express my feelings fully. It is so long since I *had* any feelings." Magda, another post-encephalitic patient, wrote about the apathy and indifference she had experienced during the decades when she had been virtually motionless: "I ceased to have any moods. I ceased to care about anything. Nothing *moved* me—not even the death of my parents. I forgot what it felt like to be happy or unhappy. Was it good or bad? It was neither. It was nothing."

Such an incapacity for emotion—apathy in its strictest sense—occurs only if there is severe compromise of the frontal lobe systems (as in Harry) or the subcortical systems (as in Hester and Magda) that subserve emotion.

But short of such complete apathy, there are other neurological conditions in which the capacity for genuine emotion is compromised. One sees this in some forms of autism, in the "flat affect" of some schizophrenics, and in the "coldness" or "callousness" often shown by psychopaths (or, to use the term favored now, sociopaths). But here, as with Harry, music can often break through, if only in a limited way or for a brief time, and release seemingly normal emotions.

In 1995 a therapist wrote to me about a patient of hers, a "psychopath" she had observed closely for five years, and his relationship to music:

> As you know, [psychopaths] are charming con men whose most salient characteristic is lack of emotion. They study normal people and are able to give an exact simulation of emotion in order to survive among us, but the feeling just isn't there. No loyalty, no love, no empathy, no fear . . . none of those intangibles which make up our inner world. . . .
>
> My psychopath was also a very gifted composer and musician. He had no formal training, yet he could pick up any instrument and play it, master it in a year or two. I gave him an electronic music studio so he could compose. He quickly learned the equipment and began producing tapes of his own compositions. . . . The music seemed to pour from him whole. . . . After hearing his first tape, I wrote: "Fresh and alive, bursting with raw energy; sweet and powerful and passionate; intellectual yet mystical; full of surprises." . . .
> After I sent him away, it crossed my mind to wonder if he

had simulated the emotions in his music . . . though I had a deep intuitive sense that the feeling in the music was genuine . . . that music was the only way he had of expressing emotion, and that his music contained all the purity and depth of emotion so utterly devoid in the rest of him. . . .

He bought a saxophone [and] within a year he was playing professionally at popular clubs here, then left and went busking for spare change in his beloved Europe as he works his schemes for defrauding innocent, trusting people. Somewhere, on some dark street corner in Prague, Zurich, Athens or Amsterdam, crowds pass by a lone saxophone player playing his heart out, and never suspect he's the one I call "America's Greatest Living Composer," nor that he is a dangerous psychopath.

One wonders whether, in such cases, the music allows access to emotions which, for most of the time, are blocked or cut off from consciousness or expression—or whether we are observing a sort of impersonation, a brilliant but in some sense superficial or artificial performance. I had similar uncertainties when I saw Stephen Wiltshire, the autistic savant I have written about in *An Anthropologist on Mars*. Stephen barely spoke and normally showed very little emotion, even while he was producing his extraordinary drawings. But he could sometimes (so it seemed to me) be transformed by music. Once, when we were in Russia together, we listened to the choir in the Alexander Nevsky Monastery, and Stephen seemed profoundly moved (so I thought, though Margaret Hewson, who had known him well for many years, felt that at a deeper level he was indifferent to the singing).

Three years later, as a teenager, Stephen started singing himself. He sang the Tom Jones song "It's Not Unusual" with great enthusiasm, swinging his hips, dancing, gesticulating. He seemed possessed by the music, and there was none of the stilt-edness, the ticcing, the aversion of gaze that he normally evinced. I was very startled at this transformation, and wrote "AUTISM DISAPPEARS" in my notebook. But as soon as the music ended, Stephen looked autistic once again.

27

Irrepressible: Music and the
Temporal Lobes

In 1984 I met Vera B., an elderly woman who had just been admitted to a nursing home because of medical problems (including severe arthritis and breathlessness) that made independent life increasingly difficult for her. I found no neurological problems, but I was struck by the fact that Vera was so high-spirited—talkative, jokey, and a trifle flirtatious. I did not think this was of any neurological import at the time, but just an expression of character.

When I saw her again four years later, I observed in my notes, "She shows impulses to sing old Yiddish songs, and at times, a near-irrepressible chutzpah. It seems to me now that she is losing her inhibitions."

By 1992, this picture of disinhibition had become florid. Sitting outside the clinic, awaiting me, Vera was singing "A Bicycle Built for Two" in a loud voice, interlarding the lyrics with words of her own invention. In my office, she continued to sing: songs in English, Yiddish, Spanish, Italian, and a polyglot mixture that contained, I suspected, all of these, plus some of her native Latvian. When I phoned Connie Tomaino, our music therapist, she told me that Vera now tended to sing nonstop the entire day. Previously, she had not been terribly musical, Connie said, but "she's musical *now*."

It was not easy to have a conversation with Vera. She was impatient with questions and often broke off in mid-answer to sing. I did what mental testing I could, and it was obvious that Vera was basically alert and oriented to her surroundings. She knew that she was an old lady in a hospital; she knew Connie ("a young maideleh—I forget her name"); she was able to write and draw a clock.

I was not sure what to make of all this. "A peculiar form of dementia," I wrote in my notes. "Cerebral disinhibition has proceeded apace. This may be due to an Alzheimer-like process (though surely with Alzheimer's she would be more impaired and confused). But I cannot help wondering about other, rarer entities." In particular I wondered whether she had damage to the frontal lobes of the brain. Damage to the lateral portions of the frontal lobes can lead to inertia and indifference, as with Harry S. But damage to the medial or orbitofrontal areas has a very different effect, depriving one of judgment and restraint and opening the way to a nonstop stream of impulses and associations. People with this type of frontal lobe syndrome may be jokey and impulsive, like Vera—but I had never heard of excessive musicality as one of its symptoms.

When Vera died a few months later, from a massive heart attack, I tried to get an autopsy, wondering what the brain would show. But autopsies had become rare and difficult to obtain, and I was not successful.

I was soon distracted by other matters and did not think about the puzzling case of Vera, with her strange and in a way creative disinhibition, the wild singing and wordplay that had characterized her final years. It was only in 1998, when I read a paper by Bruce Miller and his colleagues in San Francisco on the "Emergence of Artistic Talent in Frontotemporal Dementia," that I suddenly thought of Vera again, and realized that it was probably just such a dementia that she had had—although the "emergence" with her had been musical rather than visual. But if there could be emergence of visual, artistic talents, why not musical ones? Indeed, in 2000, Miller et al. published a short paper on the emergence of unprecedented musical tastes in some of their patients in the dementia unit at the University of California–San Francisco and a longer, comprehensive paper, with vivid case histories, on "Functional Correlates of Musical and Visual Ability in Frontotemporal Dementia."

Miller et al. described a number of patients who showed heightenings of musical talents or, in some cases, the startling appearance of musical inclination and talents in previously "unmusical" people. Such patients had been described before in an anecdotal way, but no one before had seen and followed so many patients or explored their experiences in such depth and detail. I wanted to meet Dr. Miller and, if possible, some of his patients.

When we met, Miller first talked in general terms about frontotemporal dementia, how its symptoms and the underlying brain changes that caused them had been described in 1892 by Arnold Pick, even before Alois Alzheimer had described the better-known syndrome that now carries his name. For a time, "Pick's disease" was considered relatively rare, but it is now becoming clear, Miller pointed out, that it is far from uncommon. Indeed, only about two-thirds of the patients Miller sees in his dementia clinic have Alzheimer's disease; the remaining third have several other conditions, of which frontotemporal dementia is perhaps the most common.[1]

Unlike Alzheimer's disease, which usually manifests itself with memory or cognitive losses, frontotemporal dementia often starts with behavioral changes—disinhibitions of one sort or another. This is perhaps a reason why relatives and physicians alike may be slow to recognize its onset. And, confusingly, there is no constant clinical picture but a variety of symptoms, depending on which side of the brain is chiefly affected and whether the damage is mainly in the frontal or the temporal lobes. The artistic and musical emergences that Miller and others have observed occur only in patients with damage chiefly in the left temporal lobe.

Miller had arranged for me to meet one of his patients, Louis F., whose story bore a striking resemblance to Vera B.'s. Even before I saw him, I heard Louis singing in the corridor, as, years before, I had heard Vera singing outside my clinic. When he entered the consulting room with his wife, there was barely a chance for hellos or handshakes, for he instantly burst into speech. "Near my house are seven churches," he started. "I go to three churches on Sunday." Then, presumably moved by the association of "church," he burst into "We wish you a merry

---

1. Alois Alzheimer (who was much more of a neuropathologist than Pick) showed that several of Pick's patients, at autopsy, showed peculiar microscopic structures in their brains, and these came to be called Pick bodies, as the disease itself came to be called Pick's disease. Sometimes the term "Pick's disease" is restricted to those patients who have Pick bodies in their brains, but, as Andrew Kertesz has pointed out, this differentiation does not have much value: there may be an essentially similar frontotemporal degeneration whether or not Pick bodies are present.

Kertesz has also described large families in which there is a high incidence not only of frontotemporal dementia but of other neurodegenerative conditions such as cortico-basal degeneration, progressive supranuclear palsy, and perhaps some forms of parkinsonism or ALS with dementia. All of these conditions, he feels, may be related; he suggests, therefore, that they be subsumed under the term "Pick complex."

Christmas, we wish you a merry Christmas . . ." Seeing me sip a cup of coffee, he said, "Go on—when you're old you can't drink coffee," and this then led to a little singsong: "A cup of coffee, coffee for me; a cup of coffee, coffee for me." (I did not know if this was a "real" song or just the immediate thought of coffee transformed into a repetitive jingle.)

A plate of cookies attracted his attention; he took one and ate it voraciously, then another and another. "If you don't take the plate away," his wife said, "he'll eat them all. He'll *say* he's full, but he'll go on eating. . . . He's put on twenty pounds." He sometimes put nonfood items into his mouth, she added: "we had some bath salts shaped like candies, and he grabbed one, but had to spit it out."

It was not so easy, however, to take the food away. I moved the plate, kept moving it into more and more inaccessible places, but Louis, without seeming to pay any attention to this, observed all my movements and would infallibly home in on the plate— under the desk, by my feet, in a drawer. (His ability to spot things was very acute, his wife told me; he would see coins or glittering objects in the street and pick up tiny crumbs from the floor.) Between eating and finding the cookie plate, Louis moved about restlessly and talked or sang nonstop. It was almost impossible to interrupt his speaking to have a conversation, or to get him to concentrate on any cognitive task—though he did, at one point, copy a complex geometrical figure and do an arithmetical calculation of a sort that would have been impossible for someone with advanced Alzheimer's.

Louis works twice a week at a senior center, leading others in singing sessions. He loves this; his wife feels it may be the only thing that gives him any true pleasure now. He is only in his sixties, and he is not unconscious of what he has lost. "I don't remember that stuff anymore, I don't work anymore, I don't do anything anymore—that's why I help all the seniors," he commented, but he said this with little emotional expression in his face or voice.

For the most part, left to his own devices, he will sing upbeat songs with great gusto. I thought that he sang a variety of such songs with sense and sensibility, but Miller cautioned me about assuming too much. For while Louis sang "My Bonnie Lies over the Ocean" with great conviction, he could not say, when asked, what an "ocean" was. Indre Viskontas, a cognitive neuroscientist working with Miller, demonstrated Louis's indifference to the meaning of words by giving him a nonsensical but phonemically and rhythmically similar version to sing:

> *My bonnie lies over the ocean,*
> *My bonnie lies under the tree,*
> *My bonnie lies table and then some,*
> *Oh, bring tact my bonnie to he.*

Louis sang this with the same animation, the same emotion and conviction, as he had sung the original.

This loss of knowledge, of categories, is characteristic of the "semantic" dementia which such patients develop. When I started him singing "Rudolph, the Red-Nosed Reindeer," he continued it perfectly. But he was not able to say what a reindeer was or to recognize a drawing of one—so it was not just the verbal or visual representation of reindeers that was impaired, but the *idea* of a reindeer. He could not say, when I asked him, what "Christmas" was, but instantly reverted to singing, "We wish you a merry Christmas."

In some sense, then, it seemed to me that Louis existed only in the present, in the act of singing or speaking or performing. And, perhaps because of this abyss of nonbeing which yawned beneath him, he talked, he sang, he moved ceaselessly.

Patients like Louis often seem quite bright and intellectually intact, unlike patients with comparably advanced Alzheimer's disease. On formal mental testing, they may, indeed, achieve normal or superior scores, at least in the earlier stages of their illness. So it is not really a dementia that such patients have but an amnesia, a loss of factual knowledge, such as the knowledge of what a reindeer is, or Christmas, or an ocean. This forgetting of facts—a "semantic" amnesia—is in striking contrast to their vivid memories for events and experiences in their own lives, as Andrew Kertesz has commented. It is the reverse, in a way, of what one sees in most patients with amnesia, who retain factual knowledge but lose autobiographical memories.

Miller has written about "empty speech" with regard to patients with frontotemporal dementia, and most of what Louis said was repetitive, fragmentary, and stereotyped. "Every utterance, I've heard before," his wife remarked. And yet there were islands of meaning, moments of lucidity, as when he had spoken of not working, not remembering, not doing anything—which were surely real, and heartbreaking, even though they lasted only a second or two before they were forgotten, swept away in the torrent of his distraction.

Louis's wife, who has seen this deterioration descend on her husband over the last year, looked frail and exhausted. "I wake at night," she said, "and see him there, but he is not really there, not really present. . . . When he dies, I will miss him very much, but in some sense, he is already no longer here—he is not the same vibrant person I knew. It is a slow grieving, all the way through." She fears, too, that with his impulsive, restless behavior, he will sooner or later have an accident. What Louis himself feels at this stage, it is difficult to know.

Louis has never had any formal musical education or vocal training, though he had occasionally sung in choruses. But now music and singing dominate his life. He sings with great energy and gusto, it obviously gives him pleasure, and, between songs, he likes to invent little jingles, like the "coffee" song. When his mouth is occupied in eating, his fingers will find rhythms, improvise, tap. It is not just the feeling, the emotion of songs—which I am sure he "gets," despite his dementia—but musical patterns that excite and enchant him and, perhaps, hold him together. When they play cards in the evening, Mrs. F. said, "he loves to listen to music, taps his fingers or foot or sings while he plans his next move. . . . He likes country music or golden oldies."

Bruce Miller had perhaps chosen Louis F. for me to see because I had spoken of Vera, her disinhibition, her incessant babbling and singing. But there were many other ways, Miller said, that musicality could emerge and come to take over a person's life in the course of a frontotemporal dementia. He had written about several such patients.

Miller has described one man who developed frontotemporal dementia in his early forties (the onset of frontotemporal dementia is often considerably earlier than that of Alzheimer's) and who constantly whistled. He became known as "the Whistler" at work, mastering a great range of classical and popular pieces and inventing and singing songs about his bird.[2]

Musical tastes, too, may be affected. C. Geroldi et al. described two patients whose lifelong musical tastes changed with the

---

2. In 1995, I received a letter from Gaylord Ellison of UCLA, who wrote:

My sister is sixty years old . . . and was diagnosed with Pick's disease a few years ago. Things are taking their expected course, and her speech is now largely one- or two-word utterances. She and I recently attended our mother's funeral, and afterwards . . . I started playing the piano, and Annette began whistling along to what I was playing. She had never heard the song before, but she was absolutely extraordinary in her talent. She trills like a bird and follows melodies and shifts chords easily. I mentioned this to her husband, and he said yes, she had never been able to whistle like that until about two years ago.

onset of frontotemporal dementia. One of them, an elderly lawyer with a strong preference for classical music and an antipathy to pop music (which he regarded as "mere noise"), developed a passion for what he previously hated and would listen to Italian pop music at full volume for many hours each day. B. F. Boeve and Y. E. Geda described another patient with frontotemporal dementia who developed a consuming passion for polka music.[3]

At a much deeper level, a level beyond action, improvisation, and performance, Miller and his colleagues described (in a 2000 paper in the *British Journal of Psychiatry*) an elderly man with very little musical training or background who at sixty-eight began composing classical music. Miller emphasized that what occurred, suddenly and spontaneously, to this man were not musical ideas but musical patterns—and it was from these, by elaboration and permutation, that he built up his compositions.[4] His mind, Miller wrote, was "taken over" during composition, and his

---

3. Since the original publication of *Musicophilia*, I have received a number of letters concerning similar changes in musical taste, although it is not always clear whether the underlying problem is frontotemporal dementia or something else. One woman, a classically trained pianist, wrote about her eighty-six-year-old mother, who had Parkinson's, epilepsy, and some dementia:

> My mother used to love classical music, but something has happened to her in the past few months: she loves jazz, and seems to need this playing full blast all day, along with 24-hour cable news. . . . The importance of jazz in her life now seems very odd and even a little comical, because when she was "normal" she hated it.

4. Allan Snyder has proposed that a similar "bottom-up" process, rather than any overall or organizing schema, is typical of autistic creativity, where, as with frontotemporal dementia, there may be an extraordinary facility with visual or musical patterns but poor development of verbal and abstract thinking. There may be a continuum between obvious pathology, such as autism or frontotemporal dementia, and the expression of normal "style." With a composer like Tchaikovsky, for example, composition emerged from tunes—there was an endless number of these constantly running in his head; this seems very different from the grand musical ideas, the architectonic structures typical of Beethoven's compositions.

"I never work in the abstract," Tchaikovsky wrote, "the musical thought never appears otherwise than in a suitable external form." The result, noted Robert Jourdain, was "music with splendid surface texture but shallow structure."

compositions were of real quality (several were publicly performed). He continued composing even when his loss of language and other cognitive skills became severe. (Such creative concentration would not be possible for Vera or Louis, because they had severe frontal lobe damage early in their illnesses, and thus were deprived of the integrative and executive powers needed to reflect on the musical patterns rushing through their heads.)

Maurice Ravel, the composer, suffered in the last years of his life from a condition that was sometimes called Pick's disease and would probably now be diagnosed as a form of frontotemporal dementia. He developed a semantic aphasia, an inability to deal with representations and symbols, abstract concepts, or categories. His creative mind, though, remained teeming with musical patterns and tunes—patterns and tunes which he could no longer notate or put on paper. Théophile Alajouanine, Ravel's physician, was quick to realize that his illustrious patient had lost musical language but not his musical inventiveness. One wonders, indeed, whether Ravel was on the cusp of a dementia when he wrote his *Boléro,* a work characterized by the relentless repetition of a single musical phrase dozens of times, waxing in loudness and orchestration but with no development. While such repetition was always part of Ravel's style, in his earlier works it formed a more integral part of much larger musical structures, whereas in *Boléro,* it could be said, there is the reiterative pattern and nothing else.

FOR HUGHLINGS JACKSON, a hundred and fifty years ago, the brain was not a static mosaic of fixed representations or points, but incessantly active and dynamic, with certain potentials being actively suppressed or inhibited—potentials that could be "released" if this inhibition was lifted. That musicality might be not only spared but heightened with damage to the language functions of the left hemisphere was suggested by Jackson as early as 1871, when he wrote of singing in aphasic children. For him, this was an example—one of many—of normally suppressed brain functions being released by damage to others. (Such dynamic explanations also seem very plausible in relation to other strange emergences and excesses: the musical hallucinations sometimes "released" by deafness, the synesthesia sometimes "released" by blindness, and the savant functions sometimes "released" by damage to the left hemisphere.)

Normally there is a balance in each individual, an equilibrium between excitatory and inhibitory forces. But if there is damage to the (more recently evolved) anterior temporal lobe of the dominant hemisphere, then this equilibrium may be upset, and there may be a disinhibition or release of the perceptual powers associated with the posterior parietal and temporal areas of the nondominant hemisphere.[5] This, at least, is the hypothesis which Miller and others entertain, a hypothesis which is now gaining support from physiological and anatomical studies. Miller's group has recently described a patient who developed a progressive aphasia and showed a simultaneous heightening of visual creativity (see Seeley et al.). This involved not only functional facilitation of posterior areas in the right hemisphere, but actual anatomical changes, with increased volumes of gray matter in parietal, temporal, and occipital cortices. The authors speak of her right parietal cortex as being "supranormal" during the peak of her creativity.

This hypothesis gains support clinically, too, from cases in which there is an emergence of musical or artistic talent following

---

5. This "paradoxical functional facilitation" was a notion first proposed by Narinder Kapur in 1996, in a more general context.

strokes or other forms of damage to the left hemisphere. This seemed to have been the case with a patient described by Daniel E. Jacome in 1984. Jacome's patient had a postsurgical stroke causing extensive damage in the dominant left hemisphere—especially the anterior frontotemporal areas—which produced not only severe difficulties with expressive language (aphasia) but a strange access of musicality, with incessant whistling and singing and a passionate interest in music, a profound change in a man whom Jacome described as "musically naïve" before his stroke.

But the strange change did not last; it diminished, Jacome wrote, "in parallel with very good recovery of verbal skills." These findings, he felt, "seem to support the greater role of the non-dominant hemisphere in music, somehow normally dormant and 'released' by dominant hemisphere damage."

One correspondent, Rolf Silber, described his own experiences after having a cerebral hemorrhage which caused damage to his dominant (left) hemisphere. Recovering consciousness, he found himself paralyzed on the right side and unable to speak or understand words. As he was recuperating, he later wrote:

> my wife brought my then newest gadget, a little CD player, to the hospital and I listened to music as if my life depended on it (my musical taste is very, very eclectic . . .). Still strongly handicapped on my right side and just hardly able to form an intelligible sentence, I went through a phase where my ability to "process" or analyze or—even more basically—understand music was for a few weeks greatly enhanced. . . . This not only in technical terms of "high fidelity," but much more in a . . . sense of having—for a short time—the ability to distinguish the different groups of instruments or solo instruments and being able to discern exactly what all of them do at the same time. This was the

case with both classical and ethno/pop music. For two to four weeks, I felt I had the ability to hear music as I had always suspected a musician does. And as I had always envied them for.

This remarkable musical ability, he continued, disappeared when his powers of language returned. This left him "grinding his teeth a little," but, realizing that the enhancement or release of musical powers may have been dependent on his loss of language, he accepted the dynamic balance, the give-and-take of the brain, and was more than happy to have come out of his experience with his original faculties unscathed.

There have been many other stories, both in the medical literature and in the popular press, of people who have developed artistic talent following left-hemisphere strokes, or whose art has changed in character following such strokes—often becoming less constrained formally and freer emotionally. Such emergences or changes are often rather sudden.

The musical or artistic powers that may be released in frontotemporal dementia or other forms of brain damage do not come out of the blue; they are, one must presume, potentials or propensities that are already present but inhibited—and undeveloped. Once released by damage to these inhibitory factors, musical or artistic powers can potentially be developed, nurtured, and exploited to produce a work of real artistic value—at least as long as frontal lobe function, with its executive and planning powers, is intact. In the case of frontotemporal dementia, this may provide a brief, brilliant interlude as the disease advances. The degenerative process in frontotemporal dementia, unfortunately, does not come to a halt, and sooner or later, all is lost—but for a brief time, for some, there can at least be music or art, with some of the fulfillment, the pleasure, and joy it can so uniquely provide.

One must wonder, finally, about the "Grandma Moses" phenomenon—the unexpected and sometimes sudden appearance of new artistic or mental powers in the absence of any clear pathology. Perhaps one should speak of "health" rather than "pathology" here, since there may be, even at an advanced age, a relaxing or release of lifelong inhibitions. Whether this release is primarily psychological, social, or neurological, it can unleash a torrent of creativity as surprising to oneself as it is to others.

28

A Hypermusical Species:
Williams Syndrome

In 1995 I visited a special summer camp in Lenox, Massachu-setts, to spend a few days with a unique group of people, all of whom had a congenital disorder called Williams syndrome, which results in a strange mixture of intellectual strengths and deficits (most have an IQ of less than 60). They all seemed extraordinarily sociable and inquisitive, and though I had met none of these campers before, they instantly greeted me in the most friendly and familiar way—I could have been an old friend or an uncle, rather than a stranger. They were effusive and chatty, asking about my journey there, whether I had family, what colors and music I liked best. None of them was reticent— even the younger ones, at an age when most children are shy or wary of strangers, felt free to come up, take me by the hand, look deep into my eyes, and converse with me with an adeptness that belied their years.

Most were in their teens or twenties, though there were a few younger children, as well as a woman of forty-six. But age and sex made relatively little difference in their appearance—all of them had wide mouths and upturned noses, small chins, and round, curious, starry eyes. Despite their individuality, they seemed like members of a single tribe marked by an extraordinary loquacity, effervescence, fondness for telling stories, reaching out to others, fearlessness of strangers, and, above all, a love of music.

Soon after I arrived, the campers trooped to a big tent, pulling me along with them, excited at the thought of a Saturday evening dance. Almost all of them would be performing and dancing. Steven, a stocky fifteen-year-old, was practicing on his trombone—the pure, assertive, brassy sounds of this, it was clear, satisfied him deeply. Meghan, a romantic and outgoing soul, was strumming her guitar and singing soft ballads. Christian, a tall, gangly youth wearing a beret, had a very good ear and was able to pick out and reproduce on the piano songs he had never heard before. (It was not just music that the campers were so sensitive, so attuned to; there seemed to be an extraordinary sensitivity to sounds generally—or, at least, attention to them. Tiny background sounds the rest of us did not hear or were not conscious of were immediately picked up and often imitated by them. One boy could identify the make of a car by the sound of its engine as it approached. As I walked in the woods with another boy the next day, we chanced on a beehive, and he was enchanted by this and started his own humming, which lasted the rest of the day. The sensitivity to sounds is highly individual and can vary moment by moment. One child at the camp might be enthralled by the noise of a particular vacuum cleaner, while another would be unable to stand it.)

Anne, the eldest at forty-six, had undergone many surgeries to treat the physical problems that can come with Williams syndrome. She looked much older than her age, but she also conveyed a sense of wisdom and insight, and often seemed to be regarded by the others as a sort of adviser and honored elder. She favored Bach, and played some of the *Forty-eight Preludes and Fugues* for me on the piano. Anne lived quasi-independently, with some help; she had her own apartment and her own phone—though with her Williams loquacity, she said, she would often run up huge phone bills. Very important to Anne was her close relationship with her music teacher, who seemed to have a most sensitive ability to help her find musical expression for her feelings—as well as helping with the technical challenges of piano playing, which were exacerbated by Anne's medical problems.

Even as toddlers, children with Williams syndrome are extraordinarily responsive to music, as I later saw at a Williams syndrome clinic at the Children's Hospital at Montefiore in the Bronx. Here people of all ages go for periodic medical evaluation, but also to see one another and to make music with a gifted music therapist, Charlotte Pharr, whom they seem to adore. Majestic, a small three-year-old, was withdrawn and unresponsive to everyone and everything in his environment. He was making odd noises of every sort, but Charlotte began to imitate his noises, immediately catching his attention. The two of them began to exchange a volley of noises, which soon became rhythmic patterns, then musical tones and short improvised melodies. With this, Majestic was transformed in a remarkable way—he became fully engaged and even grabbed Charlotte's guitar (it was bigger than he was) and plucked its strings one by one for himself. His eyes were constantly fixed on Charlotte's face, drawing encouragement, support, and orientation from her. But when the session was over and Charlotte left, he soon reverted to the unresponsive state he had been in before.

Deborah, an engaging seven-year-old, was diagnosed with Williams syndrome before she was a year old. Storytelling and playacting were as important for Debbie as music—she always wanted a dramatic accompaniment of words and actions, rather than "pure" music. She knew by heart all the songs from her synagogue, but when her mother began to demonstrate this, she inadvertently sang a melody from her own childhood. "No!" said Debbie. "I want to do the song from *my* synagogue!" And she proceeded to sing it. (The songs from the synagogue are, of course, charged with meaning and narrative, the drama of ritual and liturgy—it is not coincidental that some cantors, like Richard Tucker, have become opera singers, going from the drama of the synagogue to that of the stage.)

Tomer, at six, was a strong, energetic boy, with a tough, outgoing personality to match. He adored drumming and seemed intoxicated by rhythms. When Charlotte demonstrated various complex rhythms, he got these instantly—indeed, he could simultaneously drum different rhythms with each hand. He anticipated rhythmic phrases and could improvise easily. At one point, the exuberance of drumming so overcame him that he flung the drumsticks down and started dancing instead. When I asked him about the names of different types of drums, he rapidly reeled off twenty different kinds from around the world. With training, Charlotte thought, he could certainly become a professional drummer when he grew up.

Pamela, at forty-eight, was, like Anne at the camp, the eldest, and she was highly, at times heartbreakingly, articulate. She became tearful at one point, speaking of the group home where she lived with other "disabled" people. "They call me all kinds of hurtful things," she said. They did not understand her, could not comprehend, she said, how she could be so articulate and yet so disabled in other ways. She longed for a friend, for someone else with Williams syndrome with whom she could feel at ease, talk, and make music. "But there are not enough of us," she said, "so I'm the only Williams in the place." I had the feeling, as I had

had with Anne, that Pamela had acquired a painful wisdom, a larger perspective, with age.

Pamela's mother mentioned that she liked the Beatles, so I started singing "Yellow Submarine," and Pamela joined in, bursting into a loud, joyful rendition and smiling broadly. "She comes alive with music," her mother said. She had a huge repertoire, from Yiddish folk songs to Christmas hymns, and once she had started, there was no stopping her. She sang sensitively, always getting the emotion, and yet—I was surprised by this—she was often off-key, sometimes without any clear tonal center whatever. Charlotte, too, had observed this and had difficulty accompanying Pamela with her guitar. "People with Williams all love music," she said, "they are all deeply moved by it, but not all of them are geniuses, not all of them are musically talented."

WILLIAMS SYNDROME IS very rare, affecting perhaps one child in ten thousand, and it was not formally described in the medical literature until 1961, when J. C. P. Williams, a New Zealand cardiologist, published a paper on it; the following year, it was independently described by Alois J. Beuren and his colleagues in Europe. (In Europe, therefore, people tend to refer to Williams-Beuren syndrome, but in the United States it is usually known as Williams syndrome.) They each described a syndrome characterized by defects of the heart and great vessels, unusual facial conformations, and retardation.

The term "retardation" suggests an overall or global intellectual defect, one that impairs language ability along with all other cognitive powers. But in 1964, G. von Arnim and P. Engel, who noted the elevated calcium levels that seemed to go along with Williams syndrome, also observed a curiously uneven profile of abilities and disabilities. They spoke of the children's "friendly and loquacious personalities" and "their unusual command of language"—the last thing one would expect to find in a "retarded" child. (They noted, too, though only in passing, that these children seemed to have a strong attachment to music.)

Individual parents of these children, similarly, were often struck by the unusual constellation of strengths and intellectual disabilities their children displayed and found it very difficult to find appropriate environments or schooling for them, as they were not "retarded" in the usual sense. In the early 1980s, a group of such parents in California discovered one another and came together to form the nucleus of what would become the Williams Syndrome Association.[1]

At much the same point, Ursula Bellugi, a cognitive neuroscientist who had pioneered research on deafness and sign language, became fascinated by Williams syndrome. She had met Crystal, a fourteen-year-old girl with Williams syndrome, in 1983 and was intrigued and charmed by her, not least by her ready improvisations of songs and lyrics. Bellugi arranged to see Crystal every week for a year, and this was the start of an enormous enterprise.

Bellugi is a linguist, albeit one as much attuned to the emotional powers of speech, and all the poetic uses of language, as to its formal linguistic character. She was fascinated by the large vocabularies and unusual words that youngsters with Williams syndrome would use, despite their low IQs—words like "canine," "abort," "abrasive," "evacuate," and "solemn." When asked to name as many animals as she could, one child's first

---

1. There are striking analogies here to the situation with other disorders. In 1971 half a dozen families whose children had Tourette's syndrome came together in an informal support group, which soon evolved into a nationwide and then worldwide Tourette Syndrome Association. It was similar with autism and many other disorders. Such groups have been crucial not only in providing support for families, but in raising public and professional awareness, funding research, and fostering new legislation and educational policies.

responses were "newt, saber-tooth tiger, ibex, antelope."[2] And it was not only a large and unusual vocabulary, but all communicative powers that seemed highly developed in these children, especially in contrast to IQ-matched youngsters with Down's syndrome. Those with Williams particularly showed a special feeling for narrative. They would use vivid sound effects and other devices to convey feeling and heighten the impact of what they said; Bellugi called these "audience-hookers"—locutions like "All of a sudden," "Lo and behold!," and "Guess what happened next?" It became increasingly clear to Bellugi that this narrative skill went with their hypersociability—their longing to connect and bond with others. They were minutely aware of personal details, they seemed to study people's faces with extraordinary attention, and they showed great sensitivity in reading others' emotions and moods.

They seemed strangely indifferent, though, to the nonhuman in their environments. Indifferent and inept—in some cases, children with Williams syndrome were unable to tie their shoes, to judge obstacles and steps, to "get" how things were arranged in the house. (This was in striking contrast to autistic children, who might fixate on inanimate objects and seemed indifferent to the emotions of others. In some ways, Williams seemed to be the exact opposite of severe autism.) Some children with Williams syndrome were utterly unable to put simple Lego blocks together—toys that IQ-matched children with Down's syndrome could easily assemble. And many children with Williams syndrome were unable to draw even a simple geometric shape.

Bellugi showed me how Crystal, despite her IQ of 49, had given a vivid, quirky description of an elephant, but the drawing of an

---

2. Doris Allen and Isabelle Rapin have observed a similar style of speech, with large vocabularies and a "pseudosocial" manner, in some children with Asperger's syndrome.

elephant she had done a few minutes earlier bore little resemblance to an elephant; none of the features she had painstakingly
described had actually made their way into the drawing.[3]

OBSERVANT and often puzzled parents, while noting the
problems and difficulties of their children, also noted their
unusual social attention and friendliness, their reaching out to
others. Many were struck by how, even as infants, their children
listened with great attention to music and began to reproduce
melodies accurately by singing or humming, even before they
could speak. Some parents observed that their children would be
so completely absorbed in music that they were unable to attend
to anything else; other children were extremely sensitive to the
emotions expressed in music and might burst into tears at a sad
song. Others would play their instruments for hours each day, or
might learn songs in three or four other languages, if they liked
the melody and beat.

This was very much the case with Gloria Lenhoff, a young
woman with Williams syndrome who learned to sing operatic

---

3. "What an elephant is, it is one of the animals. And what an elephant does, it lives in
the jungle. It can also live in the zoo. And what it has, it has long, gray ears, fan ears, ears
that can blow in the wind. It has a long trunk that can pick up grass or pick up hay. If
they're in a bad mood, it can be terrible. If the elephant gets mad, it could stomp; it could
charge. Sometimes elephants can charge. They have big long tusks. They can damage a
car. It could be dangerous. When they're in a pinch, when they're in a bad mood, it can be
terrible. You don't want an elephant as a pet. You want a cat or a dog or a bird."

*Illustration copyright Ursula Bellugi, The Salk Institute for Biological
Studies, reprinted by permission.*

arias in more than thirty languages. In 1988, *Bravo, Gloria,* a documentary about Gloria's remarkable musical abilities, was aired on public television. Soon after, her parents, Howard and Sylvia Lenhoff, were surprised to get a phone call from someone who had seen the documentary, saying, in effect, "That was a wonderful film—but why did you not mention that Gloria has Williams syndrome?" The viewer, a parent, had identified Gloria right away from the characteristic facial features and behaviors of Williams syndrome. This was the first the Lenhoffs had heard of the syndrome; their daughter was thirty-three.

Since then, Howard and Sylvia Lenhoff have been instrumental in bringing awareness to the condition. In 2006, they collaborated with the writer Teri Sforza on *The Strangest Song,* a book about Gloria's remarkable life. In this, Howard described Gloria's musical precocity. At the age of one, he said, "Gloria could listen to 'The Owl and the Pussycat' and 'Baa Baa Black Sheep' over and over again—rhythm and rhyme delighted her." In her second year, she became able to respond to rhythm.

"When Howard and Sylvia played their records," Sforza wrote, "Gloria grew excited and focused all at once, pulling herself up in the crib, holding onto the railings, and bouncing up and down . . . keeping time to the beat." Howard and Sylvia encouraged Gloria's passion for rhythm by giving her tambourines, drums, and a xylophone, which she played with to the exclusion of all other toys. By her third year, Gloria could carry and sing a tune, and by her fourth year, Sforza noted, she was "ravenous for language . . . greedily picked up bits of Yiddish, Polish, Italian, whatever she heard . . . absorbed them like a sponge, and started to sing little songs in other languages." She did not know these languages, but she had learned their prosody, their intonations and stresses, by listening to records, and could reproduce them fluently. Already then, at four, there was something extraordinary about Gloria, prefiguring the opera singer she was to become. In 1992, when Gloria was thirty-eight, Howard wrote to me:

> My daughter Gloria has a rich soprano voice and can play on the full-sized piano accordion almost any song she hears. She has a repertoire of about 2,000 songs. . . . Yet, like most individuals with Williams syndrome, she cannot add five plus three, nor can she get along independently.

Early in 1993, I met Gloria and accompanied her on the piano while she sang a few numbers from *Turandot*, which she performed, as always, with brilliance and an impeccable ear. Gloria, despite her deficits, is a dedicated professional who spends most of her time perfecting and expanding her repertoire. "We know she is 'retarded,'" her father says, "but in comparison to her and others with Williams syndrome, are not most of us 'retarded' when it comes to learning and retaining complex music?"

Gloria's talents are extraordinary, but not unique. At much the same time as her talents were emerging, another unusual youngster, Tim Baley, was showing a similar picture of striking musical abilities and fluent speech, along with severe intellectual impairments in many other respects. His musicality, and the support of his parents and teachers, allowed him, like Gloria, to become a performing musician (in his case, a pianist), and in 1994 Gloria and Tim joined three other musically talented people with Williams syndrome to form the Williams Five. They had their debut in Los Angeles, an event that led to features in the *Los Angeles Times* and on NPR's *All Things Considered*.

While all this delighted Howard Lenhoff, it left him dissatisfied. He was a biochemist, a scientist—and what had science to say about the musical gifts of his daughter and others like her?

There had been no scientific attention to the musical passions and talents of people with Williams syndrome. Ursula Bellugi was primarily a linguist, and though she had been struck by the musicality of people with Williams syndrome, she had not made a systematic study of it. Lenhoff pressed her and other researchers to investigate this.

Not all people with Williams syndrome are as musically talented as Gloria—few "normal" people are. But virtually all share her passion for music and are extraordinarily responsive to music on an emotional level. Lenhoff felt, therefore, that there needed to be a proper arena, a musical arena, where people with Williams could meet and interact. He played a crucial role in setting up, in 1994, the camp in Massachusetts, where people with Williams could socialize and make music together, and receive formal training in music. In 1995, Ursula Bellugi went to the camp for a week; she returned the next year, accompanied by Daniel Levitin, a neuroscientist and professional musician. Bellugi and Levitin were thus able to put together and publish the first survey of rhythm in such a musical community, in which they wrote:

> People with Williams syndrome . . . had a good, if implicit, understanding of rhythm and its role in musical grammar and form. It was not only rhythm but all aspects of musical intelligence that seemed to be highly and often precociously developed in people with Williams syndrome.
>
> . . . We heard many stories about infants (12 months) who could match pitch with a parent playing the piano, or toddlers (24 months) who could sit down at the piano and play back their older siblings' piano lessons—such anecdotal accounts demand controlled experimental verification, but

the similarities among them—and the sheer number of them—lead us to believe that Williams syndrome individuals do have a much higher degree of musical involvement and "musicality" than normals.

That the whole panoply of musical talents could be so strikingly developed in people who were deficient (sometimes severely so) in general intelligence showed, like the isolated powers of musical savants, that one could indeed speak of a specific "musical intelligence," as Howard Gardner had postulated in his theory of multiple intelligences.

The musical talents of people with Williams syndrome differ from those of musical savants, however, for savant talents often seem to emerge full-blown, to have something of a mechanical quality, to require little reinforcement by learning or practice, and to be largely independent of influence by others. In children with Williams syndrome, by contrast, there is always a strong desire to play music with and for others. This was very clear with several young people I observed, including Meghan, whom I watched during one of her music lessons. She was clearly much attached to her teacher, listened to him carefully, and worked assiduously on suggestions he made.

Such engagement manifests itself in many ways, as Bellugi and Levitin found when they visited the music camp:

> Williams syndrome individuals had an unusually high degree of engagement with music. Music seemed to be not just a very deep and rich part of their lives, but one that was omnipresent; most of them spent a great proportion of the day singing to themselves or playing instruments, even while walking to the mess hall. . . . When one

> camper encountered another camper or group of campers
> involved in a musical activity . . . the newcomer would
> either join in immediately or begin swaying appreciatively
> to the music. . . . This consuming involvement with music
> is unusual in normal populations. . . . [We have] rarely
> encountered this type of total immersion even among pro-
> fessional musicians.

The three dispositions which are so heightened in people
with Williams syndrome—the musical, the narrative, and the
social—seem to go together, distinct yet intimately associated
elements of the ardent expressive and communicative drive that
is absolutely central in Williams syndrome.

GIVEN SO EXTRAORDINARY a constellation of cognitive
talents and deficits, Bellugi and others started to explore
what their cerebral basis might be. Brain imaging, along with,
more rarely, autopsy reports, revealed remarkable divergences
from the normal. The brains of people with Williams syndrome
were, on average, twenty percent smaller than normal brains,
and their shape was quite unusual, for the decrease in size and
weight seemed to be exclusively at the back of the brain, in
the occipital and parietal lobes, whereas the temporal lobes were
of normal and sometimes supernormal size. This corresponded
with what had been so clear in the uneven cognitive abilities
of those with Williams—the devastating impairments of visuospatial sense could be attributed to the underdevelopment of
parietal and occipital areas, while the strong auditory, verbal, and
musical abilities could, in general terms, be attributed to the
large size and rich neuronal networks of the temporal lobes. The

primary auditory cortex was larger in people with Williams syndrome, and there seemed to be significant changes in the planum temporale—a structure known to be crucial for the perception of both speech and music, as well as for absolute pitch.[4]

Finally, Levitin, Bellugi, and others turned to investigating the functional correlates of musicality in Williams syndrome. Were the musicality and the emotional response to music in those with Williams syndrome, they wondered, subserved by the same sort of neurofunctional architecture as that in normal subjects or in professional musicians? They played a variety of music, from Bach cantatas to Strauss waltzes, to all three groups, and it was evident from brain imaging that people with Williams syndrome processed the music very differently from the others. They employed a much wider set of neural structures to perceive and respond to music, including regions of the cerebellum, brain stem, and amygdala which are scarcely activated at all in normal subjects. This very extensive brain activation, particularly of the amygdala, seemed to go with their almost helpless attraction to music and their sometimes overwhelming emotional reactions to it.

All of these studies, Bellugi feels, suggest that "the brains of Williams syndrome individuals are organized differently from normals, at both a macro and a micro level." The very distinctive mental and emotional characteristics of people with Williams syndrome are reflected, very precisely and beautifully, in the peculiarities of their brains. Though this study of the neural basis of Williams syndrome is far from complete, it has nonethe-

---

4. When I visited the music camp in 1995, I was struck by the fact that many of the children had absolute pitch; earlier that year, I had read a paper by Gottfried Schlaug et al. reporting that professional musicians showed an enlargement of the planum temporale on the left side, especially if they had absolute pitch. So I suggested to Bellugi that this area of the brain be examined in individuals with Williams, and these too showed similar enlargement. (Subsequent studies have indicated more complex and variable changes in these structures.)

less already made possible the most extensive correlation ever made between a multitude of mental and behavioral characteristics and their cerebral basis.

In people with Williams syndrome, it is now known, there is a "microdeletion" of fifteen to twenty-five genes on one chromosome. The deletion of this tiny gene cluster (less than a thousandth part of the twenty-five thousand or so genes in the human genome) is responsible for all of the features of Williams syndrome: the abnormalities of the heart and blood vessels (which have insufficient elastin); the unusual facial and bony features; and, not least, the unusual development of the brain—so well developed in some ways, so underdeveloped in others—which underlies the unique cognitive and personality profile of those with Williams.

More recent research has suggested differentiation within this gene cluster, but the most tantalizing part of the puzzle still eludes us. We think we know which genes are responsible for some of the cognitive deficits of Williams syndrome (such as the lack of visuospatial sense), but we do not know how such a deletion of genes can give rise to the special gifts of people with Williams syndrome. It is not even certain that these have a direct genetic basis; it is possible, for example, that some of these skills are simply spared by the vicissitudes of brain development in Williams syndrome, or that they may arise as a sort of compensation for the relative lack of other functions.

Freud once wrote, "Anatomy is destiny." Now we tend to think that destiny is written in our genes. Certainly Williams syndrome affords an extraordinarily rich and precise view of how a particular genetic endowment can shape the anatomy of a brain and how this, in turn, will shape particular cognitive strengths and weaknesses, personality traits, and perhaps even creativity. And yet, beneath the superficial similarities among people with

Williams syndrome, there is an individuality that, as with us all, is largely determined by experience.

I N 1994, I visited Heidi Comfort, a young girl with Williams syndrome, at her home in southern California. A very self-possessed eight-year-old, she immediately detected my own diffidence and said, encouragingly, "Don't be shy, Mr. Sacks." As soon as I arrived, she offered me some just-baked muffins. At one point, I covered the tray of muffins and asked her to tell me how many there were. She guessed three. I uncovered the tray and invited her to count them. She pointed to them, one by one, and came up with a total of eight; there were, in fact, thirteen. She showed me her room and her favorite things, as any eight-year-old might.

A few months later, we met again in Ursula Bellugi's lab, then went out for a walk. We watched the kites and hang gliders sailing above the La Jolla cliffs; in town we gazed into the windows of a pastry shop and then stopped for lunch at a sandwich shop, where Heidi instantly befriended the half dozen workers behind the counter, learning all their names. At one point, she leaned so far over the counter, fascinated by the sandwich-making, that she nearly fell into the tuna fish. Her mother, Carol Zitzer-Comfort, told me that she had once warned her child not to speak to strangers and Heidi had replied, "There are no strangers, there are only friends."

Heidi could be eloquent and funny, and she loved to spend hours listening to music and playing the piano; she was already composing little songs at eight. She had all the energy, impulsiveness, verbosity, and charm of Williams syndrome, and many of the problems. She could not form a simple geometric shape with some wooden blocks, as most children can do by nursery school. She had great difficulty placing a set of nesting cups into the right order. We went to the aquarium, where we saw a giant octopus, and I asked her how much it might weigh. "Thirty-two hundred pounds," she replied. Later that day, she estimated that the creature had been "as big as a building." Her cognitive impairments might be, I thought, quite disabling—both in school and in the world. And I could not avoid the feeling that there might be a sort of formulaic quality to her sociability, an automaticity. It was difficult for me to see her, at eight, as an individual separate from the superficial qualities of her Williams syndrome.

But ten years later, I received a letter from her mother. "Heidi has just had her eighteenth birthday," Carol wrote. "I'm attaching a picture of her with her boyfriend at their homecoming dance. She is in her senior year at high school and has definitely come into her own as a young woman. Dr. Sacks, you were right when you predicted that the 'who' would emerge through the 'what' of Williams syndrome."[5]

Heidi was nineteen now, and despite several brain surgeries to treat increased pressure (such procedures are occasionally necessary in some people with Williams syndrome), she was planning to leave home soon, to attend a residential college program where she would take academic courses, receive job coaching, and prepare to live independently. She planned to learn how to be a professional baker—she loved watching people decorate cakes and make desserts.

But a few months ago, I received another letter from her

---

5. Dr. Carol Zitzer-Comfort, who wrote her dissertation on Williams syndrome, is writing (with help from Heidi) a book about it, exploring the unique strengths and weaknesses of Williams and how these are played out at home and at school. Zitzer-Comfort has also coauthored, with Bellugi and others, a study of how cultural differences in Japan and the United States influence the hypersociability of people with Williams syndrome.

mother, telling me that Heidi had started a new job—and it sounds as though she may have found another calling:

> She is working at a convalescent home and just loves it. The patients say that Heidi's bright smile cheers them up and helps them feel better. Heidi enjoys the socializing so much that she has asked if she can visit the patients on the weekends. She plays bingo, paints their fingernails, gets them coffee, and, of course, talks and listens. This job is a perfect fit for her.

29

Music and Identity:
Dementia and Music Therapy

O f the five hundred or so neurological patients at my hospital, about half have dementia of various sorts—from multiple strokes, from cerebral hypoxia, from toxic or metabolic abnormalities, from brain injuries or infections, from frontotemporal degeneration, or, most commonly, from Alzheimer's disease.

Some years ago, Donna Cohen, a colleague of mine, after studying our large population of patients with Alzheimer's, coauthored a book called *The Loss of Self.* For various reasons, I deplored the title (though it is a very good book as a resource for families and caregivers) and set myself to contradicting it, lecturing here and there on "Alzheimer's Disease and the Preservation of Self." And yet, I am not sure that we were in real disagreement.

Certainly someone with Alzheimer's loses many of his powers or faculties as the disease advances (though this process may take many years). The loss of certain forms of memory is often an early indicator of Alzheimer's, and this may progress to a profound amnesia. Later there may be impairment of language and, with the involvement of the frontal lobes, loss of subtler and deeper powers, like judgment, foresight, and the ability to plan. Eventually a person with Alzheimer's may lose some fundamental aspects of self-awareness, in particular the awareness of their own incapacities. But does the loss of one's self-awareness, or some aspects of mind, constitute loss of *self?*

Shakespeare's Jaques, in *As You Like It,* considering the seven ages of man, sees the final one as "sans everything." Yet though one may be profoundly reduced and impaired, one is never sans everything, never a tabula rasa. Someone with Alzheimer's may undergo a regression to a "second childhood," but aspects of one's essential character, of personality and personhood, of self, survive—along with certain, almost indestructible forms of memory—even in very advanced dementia. It is as if identity has such a robust, widespread neural basis, as if personal style is so deeply ingrained in the nervous system, that it is never wholly lost, at least while there is still any mental life present at all. (This, indeed, is what one might expect if perceptions and actions, feelings and thoughts, have molded the structure of one's brain from the start.) This is poignantly clear in such memoirs as John Bayley's *Elegy for Iris.*

In particular, the response to music is preserved, even when dementia is very advanced. But the therapeutic role of music in dementia is quite different from what it is in patients with motor or speech disorders. Music that helps patients with parkinsonism, for example, must have a firm rhythmic character, but it need not be familiar or evocative. With aphasics it is crucial to have songs with lyrics or intoned phrases, and interaction with a therapist. The aim of music therapy in people with dementia is far broader than this— it seeks to address the emotions, cognitive powers, thoughts, and memories, the surviving "self" of the patient, to stimulate these and bring them to the fore. It aims to enrich and enlarge existence, to give freedom, stability, organization, and focus.

This might seem a very tall order—nearly impossible, one would think, seeing patients with advanced dementia, who may sit in a seemingly mindless, vacant torpor or scream agitatedly in incommunicable distress. But music therapy with such patients is possible because musical perception, musical sensibility, musical emotion, and musical memory can survive long after other forms of memory have disappeared.[1] Music of the right kind can serve to orient and anchor a patient when almost nothing else can.

I see this continually with my patients, and I hear of it constantly in the letters I receive. One man wrote to me about his wife:

> Although my wife has Alzheimer's—diagnosed at least seven years ago—the essential person miraculously remains. . . . She plays piano several hours daily, very well. Her present ambition is to memorize the Schumann A-minor Piano Concerto.

And yet this is a woman who is, in most other spheres, grossly forgetful and disabled. (Nietzsche, too, continued to improvise at

---

1. Elliott Ross and his colleagues in Oklahoma published a case study of their patient S.L. (see Cowles et al., 2003). Although he was demented, probably from Alzheimer's disease, S.L. could still remember and skillfully play a large musical repertoire from the past, even though he had "profound disturbance in both recall and recognition on other anterograde memory tests," such as word lists or the sounds of musical instruments. He also showed "marked impairment on measures of remote memory (famous faces, autobiographical memory)." Even more remarkably, this amnesic and demented man was able to learn a new song on his violin, despite having virtually no episodic memory—a situation reminiscent of that of Clive Wearing (in chapter 15).

There have been formal studies of the persistence of musical powers in advanced dementia, including those of Cuddy and Duffin, 2005; Fornazzari, Castle, et al., 2006; and Crystal, Grober, and Masur, 1989.

the piano long after he had been rendered mute, demented, and partially paralyzed by neurosyphilis.)

The extraordinary neural robustness of music is also brought out in the following letter I was sent, about a well-known pianist:

> [He] is 88 now and has lost language . . . but he plays every day. When we read through Mozart, he points back and ahead well in advance of the repeats. Two years ago we recorded the complete four-hand repertoire of Mozart that he had recorded . . . in the 1950s. While his language has begun to fail him, I love his recent playing and conception even more than the earlier recording.

Especially moving here is not merely the preservation but the apparent heightening of musical powers and sensitivity, as other powers wane. My correspondent concluded: "The extremes of musical accomplishment and illness are so plainly evident in his case; a visit becomes miraculous as he transcends the disease with music."

MARY ELLEN GEIST, a writer, contacted me a few months ago about her father, Woody, who began to show signs of Alzheimer's thirteen years ago, at the age of sixty-seven. Now, she said,

> The plaque has apparently invaded a large amount of his brain, and he can't remember much of anything about his life. However, he remembers the baritone part to almost every song he has ever sung. He has performed with a twelve-man a capella singing group for almost forty years. . . . Music

is one of the only things that keep him grounded in this world.

He has no idea what he did for a living, where he is living now, or what he did ten minutes ago. Almost every memory is gone. Except for the music. In fact, he opened for the Radio City Music Hall Rockettes in Detroit this past November. . . . The evening he performed, he had no idea how to tie a tie . . . he got lost on the way to the stage—but the performance? Perfect. . . . He performed beautifully and remembered all the parts and words.[2]

A few weeks later, I had the pleasure of meeting Mr. Geist, his daughter, and his wife, Rosemary. Mr. Geist was, in fact, carrying a newspaper, a neatly furled *New York Times*—though he did not know it was the *New York Times*, nor (apparently) what a "newspaper" was.[3] He was well-groomed and neatly dressed, though this, his daughter later told me, had needed supervision, for left alone he might put on his pants backwards, not recognize his shoes, shave with toothpaste, and so on. When I asked Mr. Geist how he was, he replied, pleasantly, "I think I am in good health." This reminded me of how Ralph Waldo Emerson, after he became severely demented, would answer such questions by saying,

---

2. It was similar, Gena Raps tells me, with the great pianist Artur Balsam, who became so amnesic from Alzheimer's disease that he lost all memory of the major events of his life and was confused about the identity of friends he had known for decades. At his final concert at Carnegie Hall, it was not clear that he even knew he was there to perform, and there was another pianist backstage prepared to take his place. But he performed magnificently, as always, and received tremendous reviews.

3. Besides singing, Woody retains certain other types of procedural memory. If one shows him a tennis racket, he may fail to recognize it, even though he was once a good amateur player. But put the racket in his hand, on a tennis court, and he knows how to use it—indeed, he can still play a mean game of tennis. He does not know what the racket *is*, but he knows how to use it.

"Quite well; I have lost my mental faculties but am perfectly well."[4]

Indeed, there was an Emersonian sweetness and reasonableness and serenity in Woody (as he immediately introduced himself)—he was profoundly demented, without doubt, but he had preserved his character, his courtesy, his thoughtfulness. Despite the manifest ravages of Alzheimer's—his loss of event memory and of general knowledge, his disorientation, his cognitive defects—the behaviors of civility, it seemed, were ingrained, perhaps at a much deeper and older level. I wondered whether these were merely habits, mimicries, residues of once-meaningful behavior, now empty of feeling and meaning. But Mary Ellen had never thought this—she felt her father's civility and courtesy, his sensitive and thoughtful behavior, to be "almost telepathic."

"The way he reads my mother's face to find out how she is doing," she wrote, "the way he reads her mood, the way he reads people in social situations and acts accordingly . . . is beyond mimicking."

Woody seemed to be tiring of questions to which he could not supply an answer (such as "Can you read this?" or "Where were you born?"), so I asked him to sing. Mary Ellen had told me how, since she could first remember, the whole family—Woody, Rosemary, and the three daughters—had sung together, and how singing had always been a central part of family life. Woody had been whistling when he came in, whistling "Somewhere over the Rainbow," so I asked him to sing it. Rosemary and Mary Ellen joined in, and the three of them sang beautifully, each harmonizing in different ways. When Woody sang, he showed all the expres-

---

4. Emerson developed a dementia, probably Alzheimer's, in his early sixties, and this gradually grew more severe over the years, though he retained his sense of humor and ironical insight almost to the end. The trajectory of Emerson's illness is portrayed with great sensitivity by David Shenk in his remarkable book, *The Forgetting: Alzheimer's: Portrait of an Epidemic.*

sions, emotions, and postures appropriate to the song, and to singing in a group—turning to the others, awaiting their cues, and so on. This was so with all the songs they sang—whether they were exuberant, jazzy, lyrical and romantic, funny, or sad.

Mary Ellen had brought along a CD Woody had recorded years before with his a cappella group, the Grunyons, and when we played this, Woody sang along beautifully. His musicality, at least his performing musicality, like his civility and equanimity, was completely intact—but again, I wondered if it could be just a mimesis, just a performance, representing feelings and meanings he no longer had. Certainly Woody *looked* more "present" when singing than at any other time. I asked Rosemary whether she felt that he, the man she had known and loved for fifty-five years, was totally present in his singing. She said, "I think he probably is." Rosemary looked tired, exhausted, from her almost nonstop caring for her husband, and the inch-by-inch way in which she was being widowed, as he lost more and more of what used to constitute his self. But she was least sad, least widowed, when they all sang together. He seemed so present at such times that his absence a few minutes later, his forgetting that he had sung (or could sing), would always come as a shock.

Given her father's powerful musical memory, Mary Ellen asked, "Why can't we use this as an opening . . . embed shopping lists, information about himself, in his songs?" I said I feared this would not work.

Mary Ellen had, in fact, found this out already for herself. "Why couldn't we sing him his life story?" she had written in her journal in 2005. "Or the directions from one room to the next? I've tried—it doesn't work." I too had had this thought, in relation to Greg, an intelligent, very musical, very amnesic patient I had seen years before. Writing about him in the *New York Review of Books* in 1992, I observed:

It is easy to show that simple information can be embedded in songs; thus we can give Greg the date every day, in the form of a jingle, and he can readily isolate this, and say it when asked—give it, that is, without the jingle. But what does it mean to say, "This is December the 19th, 1991," when one is sunk in the profoundest amnesia, when one has lost one's sense of time and history, when one is existing from moment to moment in a sequenceless limbo? "Knowing the date" means nothing in these circumstances. Could one, however, through the evocativeness and power of music, perhaps using songs with specially written lyrics— songs which relate something valuable about himself or the current world—accomplish something more lasting, deeper? Give Greg not only "facts," but a sense of time and history, of the relatedness (and not merely the existence) of events, an entire (if synthetic) framework for thinking? This is something which Connie Tomaino and I are trying to do now. We hope to have an answer in a year.

But by 1995, when "The Last Hippie" was republished in book form (in *An Anthropologist on Mars*), we had got our answer, and it was resoundingly negative. There was not, and perhaps could never be, any carryover from performance and procedural memory to explicit memory or usable knowledge.

While, at least in someone as amnesic as Greg or Woody, singing cannot be used as a sort of back door to explicit memory, still the act of singing is important in itself. Finding, remembering anew that he *can* sing is profoundly reassuring to Woody, as the exercise of any skill or competence must be—and it can stimulate his feelings, his imagination, his sense of humor and creativity, and his sense of identity as nothing else can. It can enliven him, calm him, focus and engage him. It can give him back himself, and not least, it can charm others, arouse their amazement and admiration—reactions more and more necessary to someone who, in his lucid moments, is painfully aware of his tragic disease and sometimes says that he feels "broken inside."

The mood engendered by singing can last awhile, sometimes even outlasting the memory that he *has* sung, which may be lost within a couple of minutes. I could not help thinking of my patient Dr. P., the man who mistook his wife for a hat, and how vital singing was for him, and how my "prescription" for him was a life that consisted entirely of music and singing.

Perhaps Woody, though he could not have put it into words, knows that this is the case for him, for in the last year or so he has taken to whistling. He whistled "Somewhere over the Rainbow" softly to himself for the entire afternoon we spent together. Whenever he is not actively singing or otherwise engaged, Mary Ellen and Rosemary told me, he now whistles all the while. Not only through his waking hours; he whistles (and sometimes sings) in his sleep—so, at least in this sense, Woody is companioned by music, calls on it, around the clock.[5]

WOODY, OF COURSE, has been musically gifted from the start, and still has these gifts even though he is severely demented. Most patients with dementia are not specially gifted in this regard, and yet—remarkably, and almost without exception—they retain their musical powers and tastes even when most other mental powers have been severely compromised. They can recognize music and respond to it emotionally even when little else can get through. Hence the great importance of access to

---

5. Mary Ellen Geist has written very movingly of her father's dementia—both musically and otherwise—and of a family adapting to the challenges of dementia in her 2008 memoir, *Measure of the Heart: A Father's Alzheimer's, a Daughter's Return.*

music, whether through concerts, recorded music, or formal music therapy.

Sometimes music therapy is communal, sometimes individual. It is astonishing to see mute, isolated, confused individuals warm to music, recognize it as familiar, and start to sing, start to bond with a therapist. It is even more astonishing to see a dozen deeply demented people—all in worlds or nonworlds of their own, seemingly incapable of any coherent reactions, let alone interactions—and how they respond to the presence of a music therapist who begins to play music in front of them. There is a sudden attention: a dozen pairs of distracted eyes fasten on the player. Torpid patients become alert and aware; agitated ones grow calmer. That it may be possible to gain the attention of such patients and hold it for minutes at a time is itself remarkable. Beyond this, there is often a specific engagement with what is being played (it is usual, in such groups, to play old songs that everyone of a similar age and background will have known).

Familiar music acts as a sort of Proustian mnemonic, eliciting emotions and associations that had been long forgotten, giving the patient access once again to moods and memories, thoughts and worlds that had seemingly been completely lost. Faces assume expression as the old music is recognized and its emotional power felt. One or two people, perhaps, start to sing along, others join them, and soon the entire group—many of them virtually speechless before—is singing together, as much as they are able.

"Together" is a crucial term, for a sense of community takes hold, and these patients who seemed incorrigibly isolated by their disease and dementia are able, at least for a while, to recognize and bond with others. I receive many letters about such effects from music therapists and others who play or sing music to the demented. One Australian music therapist, Gretta

Sculthorp, after working in nursing homes and hospitals for ten years, expressed this eloquently:

> At first I thought I was providing entertainment, but now I know that what I do is act as a can-opener for people's memories. I can't predict what will be the trigger for each person, but there is usually something for everyone, and I have a part of my brain that "watches" in stunned amazement what is happening. . . . One of the loveliest outcomes of my work is that nursing staff can suddenly see their charges in a whole new light, as people who have had a past, and not only a past but a past with joy and delight in it.
>
> There are listeners who come and stand beside or in front of me, touching me, for the whole time. There are always people who cry. There are people who dance, and people who join in—for operetta or for Sinatra songs (and *Lieder*, in German!). There are disturbed people who become calm, and silent people who give voice, frozen people who beat time. There are people who don't know where they are, but who recognize me immediately, as "the Singing Lady."

Music therapy for patients with dementia traditionally takes the form of providing old songs, which, with their specific tunes and contents and emotions, call on personal memories, evoke personal responses, and invite participation. Such memories and such responses may become less available as dementia becomes more profound. Yet some sorts of memory and response almost always survive—above all, the sort of motor memory and motor response that goes with dancing.

There are many levels at which music can call to people, enter them, alter them—and this is as true for demented patients as it is for the rest of us. We bond when we sing together, sharing the specific affects and connections of a song; but bonding is deeper, more primal, if we dance together, coordinating our bodies and not just our voices. "The body is a unity of actions," Luria wrote, and if there is no unity, nothing active or interactive going on, our very sense of being embodied may be undermined. But holding someone, making the movements of dance with them, may initiate a dancing response (perhaps in part by the activation of mirror neurons). In this way, patients who are otherwise inaccessible can be animated, enabled to move and to regain, at least for a while, a sense of physical identity and consciousness—a form of consciousness that is perhaps the deepest of all.

Drum circles are another form of music therapy that can be invaluable for people with dementia, for, like dance, drumming calls upon very fundamental, subcortical levels of the brain. Music at this level, a level below the personal and the mental, a purely physical or corporeal level, needs neither melody nor the specific content or affect of song—but what it does need, crucially, is rhythm. Rhythm can restore our sense of embodiment and a primal sense of movement and life.

WITH A MOVEMENT disorder like Parkinson's disease, there is no significant carryover effect with the power of music. The patient can regain a fluent motor flow with music, but once the music stops, so too does the flow. There can, however, be longer-term effects of music for people with dementia—improvements of mood, behavior, even cognitive function—which can persist for hours or days after they have been set off by music. I see this in the clinic almost daily, and constantly receive descriptions of such effects from others. Jan Koltun, who coordinates caregiving to the elderly, wrote to me with this story:

One of our caregivers . . . went home and made the simple intervention of turning on the classical music channel in front of the couch where her mother-in-law had mostly sat watching TV "shows" for the preceding three years. The mother-in-law, diagnosed with dementia, had kept the house awake at night when the caregivers turned off the TV in order to get some sleep. Daytimes, she would not get off the couch for toileting or family meals.

After the channel change, she had a profound behavioral change: She asked to come to breakfast the next morning, and did not want to watch her usual TV fare the next day, and asked for her long-neglected embroidery the next afternoon. Over the next six weeks, in addition to communicating with her family and taking more interest in her surroundings, she mostly listened to music (primarily country and western, which she loved). After six weeks, she died peacefully.

Sometimes Alzheimer's disease may provoke hallucinations and delusions, and here, too, music may provide a solution to an otherwise often intractable problem. Bob Silverman, a sociologist, wrote to me about his mother, who, at ninety-one, had had Alzheimer's for fourteen years and was living in a nursing home when she started to hallucinate:

She told stories, and acted them out. She seemed to think these things were really happening to her. The names of the people in the stories were real, but the action was fiction. In telling many of the stories, she often swore and got angry, which she never did before the disease. The stories usually had a kernel of truth. It was fairly clear to me that there were some pretty deep-seated dislikes, resentments, perceived slights, and so on, that were being acted out. . . . In any case, she was exhausting herself and everyone around her.

But then he bought his mother an MP3 player with about seventy tunes on it that were constantly recycled—these were all familiar tunes which she recognized from her youth. Now, he wrote, "She listens on headphones so no one else is disturbed. *The stories just stop*, and every time a new tune comes on, she will say something like, 'Isn't that marvelous?,' gets animated and sometimes sings along."

Music can also evoke worlds very different from the personal, remembered worlds of events, people, places we have known. This was brought out in a letter from Kathryn Koubek:

> I've read many times that music is a whole other reality. It wasn't until my father's last days, when it became his *only* reality, that I began to understand what that means. Nearly a hundred years old, my father had begun to lose his grip on this reality. His talk became disconnected; his thoughts strayed; his memory was fragmented and confused. I made a modest investment in a portable CD player. When the talk became distracted I would simply put in a beloved piece of classical music, press the "play" button and watch the transformation.
>
> My father's world became logical and it became clear. He could follow every note. . . . There was no confusion here, no missteps, no getting lost, and, most amazing, no forgetting. This was familiar territory. This was home, more than all the homes he had ever lived in. . . . This was the reality.
>
> Sometimes my father would respond to the beauty of the music by simply weeping. How did this music thrill when all other thrills had been forgotten—my mother, young with

a lovely face, my sister and I as children (his darlings), the joys of work, of food, of travel, of family?

What did this music touch? Where was this landscape where there is no forgetting? How did it free another kind of memory, a memory of the heart not tethered to time or place or events or even loved ones?

The perception of music and the emotions it can stir is not solely dependent on memory, and music does not have to be familiar to exert its emotional power. I have seen deeply de-mented patients weep or shiver as they listen to music they have never heard before, and I think that they can experience the entire range of feelings the rest of us can, and that dementia, at least at these times, is no bar to emotional depth. Once one has seen such responses, one knows that there is still a self to be called upon, even if music, and only music, can do the calling.

There are undoubtedly particular areas of the cortex subserving musical intelligence and sensibility, and there can be forms of amu-sia with damage to these. But the emotional response to music, it would seem, is widespread and probably not only cortical but sub-cortical, so that even in a diffuse cortical disease like Alzheimer's, music can still be perceived, enjoyed, and responded to. One does not need to have any formal knowledge of music—nor, indeed, to be particularly "musical"—to enjoy music and to respond to it at the deepest levels. Music is part of being human, and there is no human culture in which it is not highly developed and esteemed. Its very ubiquity may cause it to be trivialized in daily life: we switch on a radio, switch it off, hum a tune, tap our feet, find the words of an old song going through our minds, and think nothing of it. But to those who are lost in dementia, the situation is different. Music is no lux-ury to them, but a necessity, and can have a power beyond anything else to restore them to themselves, and to others, at least for a while.

Acknowledgments

I dedicate this book to three close friends and colleagues, each of whom has played an essential part in its genesis and evolution. Without our conversations over many years on music and much else, this book would have been impossible.

Orrin Devinsky of the New York University Medical School (and founder of its Comprehensive Epilepsy Center), my fellow physician and neurologist, has been unstintingly generous over the years in introducing me to patients and sharing his great clinical knowledge and insight with me.

Ralph M. Siegel, professor of neuroscience at Rutgers University, has been my close associate in various cases—some involving his particular field of vision research, others not—and he has always forced me to consider their underlying physiological basis.

Connie Tomaino—who came to Beth Abraham Hospital when I was working there with my *Awakenings* patients, went on to become President of the American Association of Music Therapists, and then founded the Institute for Music and Neurologic Function at Beth Abraham—has been my co-worker and adviser in all matters musical for more than twenty-five years.

Many other scientists, physicians, therapists, patients, friends, colleagues, and correspondents have generously shared with me their experiences, their thoughts and expertise, and, in some cases, their patients. Among them, I must especially thank Patrick Baron, Ursula Bellugi, Diana Deutsch, Steve Frucht, Daniel Levitin, Bruce Miller, Aniruddh Patel, Virginia Penhune, Isabelle Peretz, and Robert Zatorre. They have each shared their deep knowledge and experience of music and the brain with me, have read and reread drafts of this book, suggested resources, and offered invaluable criticisms, corrections, and additions.

I had the pleasure of knowing Anthony Storr and corresponding with him over many years. We often talked about music, and when he published *Music and the Mind* in 1992, I thought it the best book on the subject I had ever read. I still think so, and I have plundered it quite shamelessly in writing my own book. Indeed, I have to borrow from Storr again to quote what he wrote in his own acknowledgments: "Old men forget, and there may be other people whom I have omitted to thank. To them I can only offer apologies."

And though I will inevitably omit many others who should be mentioned, I would like to express my special gratitude to D.L., Frank V., G.G., Gordon B., Jacob L., John C., John S., Jon S., Joseph D., June B., Louis F. and his wife, Michael B. and his parents, the patients and staff at the Williams Syndrome Clinic of the Children's Hospital at Montefiore, Rachael Y., Salimah M., Samuel S., Sheryl C., Silvia N., Solomon R., Steven, Meghan, Christian and Anne, Sue B., Sydney A., Jean Aberlin, Victor Aziz, Andrea Bandel, Simon Baron-Cohen, Sue Barry, Caroline Bearsted, Howard Brandston, Jerome Bruner, David Caldwell, Todd Capp, John Carlson, Sheryl Carter, Melanie Challenger, Elizabeth Chase, Mike Chorost, Tony Cicoria, Jennifer and John Clay, Jonathan Cole, Heidi Comfort, Richard Cytowic, Mark Damashek, Merlin Donald, Gerald Edelman, Patrick Ehlen, Tom Eisner, Glen Estrin, Leon Fleisher, Cornelia and Lucas Foss, Lawrence Freedman, Allen Furbeck, Richard Garrison, Mary Ellen Geist, Rosemary and Woody Geist, Matt Giordano, Harvey and Louise Glatt, John Goberman, Elkhonon Goldberg, Jane Goodall, Temple Grandin, T. D. Griffiths, Mark Hallett, Arlan Harris, John Harrison, Mickey Hart, Roald Hoffmann, Mark Homonoff, Anna and Joe Horovitz, Krista Hyde, John Iversen, Jorgen Jorgensen, Eric Kandel, Malonnie Kinnison, Jan Koltun, Eric Korn, Carol Krumhansl, Jaron Lanier, Margaret Lawrence, Christine Leahy, Gloria Lenhoff, Howard Lenhoff, Wendy Lesser, Rodolfo Llinás, Dwight and Ursula Mamlok, Robert Marion, Eric Markowitz, Gerry Marks, Michael Merzenich, Jonathan Miller, Marvin Minsky, Bill Morgan, Nicholas Naylor-Leland, Adam Ockelford, David Oppenheim, Tom Oppenheim, Erna Otten, Alvaro Pascual-Leone, Charlotte Pharr, Tobias Picker, Emilio Presedo, Maria Ralescu, V. S. Ramachandran, Leo Rangell, Isabelle Rapin, Harold Robinson, Paul Rodriguez, Bob Ruben, Yolanda Rueda, Jonathan Sacks, Gottfried Schlaug, Gretta Sculthorp, Peter Selgin, Leonard Shengold, David Shire, Bob Silvers, Allan Snyder, Elizabeth Socolow, Steven Sparr, Larry Squire, Alexander Stein, Daniel Stern, Doug Stern, Dan Sullivan, Michael Sundue, Michael Thaut, Michael Torke, Darold Treffert, Nick van Bloss, Erica vanderLinde Feidner, Indre Viskontas, Nick Warner, Jason Warren, Bob and Claudia Wasserman, Deborah and Clive Wearing, Ed Weinberger, Larry Weiskrantz, Ren Weschler, E. O. Wilson, Frank Wilson, Stephen Wiltshire, Rosalie Winard, Michael Wolff, Caroline Yahne, Nick Younes, and Carol Zitzer-Comfort.

This book would not have been completed without the financial support of many universities and organizations which have hosted me over the past years, and in particular I am grateful to the Alfred P. Sloan Foundation, and to Doron Weber there, for providing a generous grant to support work related to aging and the brain.

For editorial and publishing support and advice, I am grateful to Dan Frank, Fran Bigman, Lydia Buechler, Bonnie Thompson, and many others at Alfred A. Knopf, and to Sarah Chalfant, Edward Orloff, Andrew Wylie, and all at the Wylie Agency. And above all, I must thank Kate Edgar, who has spent thousands of hours collaborating with me on the research, writing, and editing of this book—and much else.

Finally, I would like to thank my correspondents, the thousands of people who write to me from all over the world, sharing their lives and especially their neurological experiences with me. I could not hope to see, in my own small practice, a fraction of what I hear about and learn from my correspondents. They often write seeking information; but more often just want to reach a sympathetic ear, or share an interesting view into the human brain and mind. These correspondents form, in effect, a wonderful and exciting extension of my practice, telling me things I would have never encountered otherwise. This present book, especially, is far richer for their contributions.

Postscript

I have made a number of corrections, revisions, and additions for this 2008 edition of *Musicophilia*, including dozens of new footnotes, as well as more lengthy postscripts to several chapters. I am again greatly indebted to friends and colleagues for their helpful criticisms and to the thousands of people who have written to me since the original edition of *Musicophilia* was published, with fascinating comments or descriptions of their own musical experiences. It would be impossible to acknowledge all of these contributors individually, but I must especially thank Liz Adams, Caroline Agarwala, Kyle Bartlett, Kjersti Beth, Eliza Bussey, Nick Coleman, Sean Cortwright, David Drachman, Bob

Daroff, Sara Bell Drescher, Gammon Earhart, Mildred Forman, Cindy Foster, Susan Foster-Cohen, Carleen Franz, Alan Geist, Dorothy Goldberg, Stan Gould, Matthew Goulish, Vladimir Hachinski, Patricia Hackbarth, Madeleine Hackney, Matthew H., Abigail Herres, Kentrell Herres, Paul Herruer, Arlyn Kantz, Philip Kassen, Jeff Kennedy, Ken Kessel, Tracy King, Nora Klein, Louis Klonsky, Jennifer and Karianne Koski, Kathryn Genovese Koubek, Jessica Krash, Nina Kraus, Steven L., Renee Lorraine, Grace M., J.M., Kathleen Mast, Melanie Mirvis, Rebecca Moulds, A.O., Danielle Ofri, John Purser, Gena Raps, Paul Raskin, Annie R., Gary Robertson, Steven L. Rosenhaus, Steve Salemson, Jeremy Scratcherd, Rolf Silber, Bob Silverman, Peter Smail, Dave Weich at Powell's, Ethan Weker, Christina Whittle, David Wise, and Hailey Wojcik.

Bibliography

Alajouanine, Théophile. 1948. The aphasie and artistic realisation. *Brain* 71: 229–41.

Albert, Martin L., R. Sparks, and N. Helm. 1973. Melodic intonation therapy for aphasia. *Archives of Neurology* 29: 130–31.

Aldridge, David. 1992. Rhythm man. In *Don't Think About Monkeys*, ed. Adam Seligman and John Hilkevich (pp. 173–82). Duarte, CA: Hope Press.

Allen, D. A., and I. Rapin. 1992. Autistic children are also dysphasic. In *Neurobiology of Infantile Autism*, ed. H. Naruse and E. M. Ornitz (pp. 157–68). Amsterdam: Elsevier.

Allen, Grant. 1878. Note-Deafness. *Mind* 3 (10): 157–67.

Amedi, Amir, Lotfi B. Merabet, Felix Bermpohl, and Alvaro Pascual-Leone. 2005. The occipital cortex in the blind: Lessons about plasticity and vision. *Current Directions in Psychological Science* 14 (6): 306–11.

Ayotte, Julia, Isabelle Peretz, and Krista Hyde. 2002. Congenital amusia: A group study of adults afflicted with a music-specific disorder. *Brain* 125: 238–51.

Baron-Cohen, Simon, and John Harrison. 1997. *Synaesthesia: Classic and Contemporary Readings*. Oxford: Blackwell.

Bauby, Jean-Dominique. 1997. *The Diving Bell and the Butterfly*. New York: Alfred A. Knopf.

Bayley, John. 1999. *Elegy for Iris*. New York: St. Martin's Press.

Bear, David. 1979. Temporal-lobe epilepsy: A syndrome of sensory-limbic hyperconnection. *Cortex* 15: 357–84.

Beeli, G., M. Esslen, and L. Jäncke. 2005. When coloured sounds taste sweet. *Nature* 434: 38.

Belin, P., P. Van Eeckhout, M. Zilbovicius, P. Remy, C. François, S. Guillaume, F. Chain, G. Rancurel, and Y. Samson. 1996. Recovery from nonfluent aphasia after melodic intonation therapy: A PET study. *Neurology* 47 (6): 1504–11.

Belin, P., R. J. Zatorre, P. Lafaille, P. Ahad, and B. Pike. 2000. Voice-selective areas in human auditory cortex. *Nature* 403: 309–10.

Bell, Charles. 1833. *The Nervous System of the Human Body.* London: Taylor and Francis.

Bellugi, Ursula, Liz Lichtenberger, Debra Mills, Albert Galaburda, and Julie R. Korenberg. 1999. Bridging cognition, the brain and molecular genetics: Evidence from Williams syndrome. *Trends in Neuroscience* 22: 197–207.

Berlioz, Hector. 1865/2002. *The Memoirs of Hector Berlioz.* Translated by David Cairns. New York: Everyman's Library.

Berrios, G. E. 1990. Musical hallucinations: A historical and clinical study. *British Journal of Psychiatry* 156: 188–94.

———. 1991. Musical hallucinations: A statistical analysis of 46 cases. *Psychopathology* 24: 356–60.

Blake, D. T., N. N. Byl, S. Cheung, P. Bedenbaugh, S. Nagarajan, M. Lamb, and M. Merzenich. 2002. Sensory representation abnormalities that parallel focal hand dystonia in a primate model. *Somatosensory and Motor Research* 19 (4): 347–57.

Blanke, Olaf, Theodor Landis, Laurent Spinelli, and Margitta Seeck. 2004. Out-of-body experience and autoscopy of neurological origin. *Brain* 127: 243–58.

Blood, Anne J., and Robert J. Zatorre. 2001. Intensely pleasurable responses to music correlate with activity in brain regions implicated in reward and emotion. *Proceedings of the National Academy of Sciences USA* 98: 11818–23.

Boeve, B. F., and Y. E. Geda. 2001. Polka music and semantic dementia. *Neurology* 57: 1485.

Bossomaier, Terry, and Allan Snyder. 2004. Absolute pitch accessible to everyone by turning off part of the brain? *Organised Sound* 9 (2): 181–89.

Browne, Janet. 2002. *Charles Darwin: The Power of Place.* New York: Alfred A. Knopf.

Brust, John C. 2001. Music and the neurologist: An historical perspective. *Annals of the New York Academy of Sciences* 930: 143–52.

Burton, Robert. 1621/2001. *The Anatomy of Melancholy.* New York: NYRB Classics.

Candia, Victor, Christian Wienbruch, Thomas Elbert, Brigitte Rockstroh, and William Ray. 2003. Effective behavioral treatment of focal hand dystonia in musicians alters somatosensory cortical organization. *Proceedings of the National Academy of Sciences USA* 100 (13): 7942–46.

Chen, J. L., R. J. Zatorre, and V. B. Penhune. 2006. Interactions between auditory and dorsal premotor cortex during synchronization to musical rhythms. *NeuroImage* 32: 1771–81.

Chorost, Michael. 2005. My bionic quest for *Boléro*. *Wired* 13.11 (November): 144–59.

———. 2005. *Rebuilt: How Becoming Part Computer Made Me More Human.* New York: Houghton Mifflin.

Claparède, Édouard. 1911. Recognition et moiité. *Archives de Psychologie (Genève)* 11: 79–90.

Clarke, Arthur C. 1953. *Childhood's End.* New York: Harcourt, Brace and World.

Cohen, Donna, and Carl Eisdorfer. 1986. *The Loss of Self: A Family Resource for the Care of Alzheimer's Disease and Related Disorders.* New York: W. W. Norton.

Cohen, Jon. 2007. The world through a chimp's eyes. *Science* 316: 44–45.

Cohen, Neal J. 1984. Preserved learning capacity in amnesia: Evidence for multiple memory systems. In *Neuropsychology of Memory,* ed. Larry R. Squire and Nelson Butters (pp. 83–103). New York: Guilford Press.

Coleman, Nick. 2008. Life in mono. *Guardian,* February 19.

Colman, W. S. 1894. Hallucinations in the sane, associated with local organic disease of the sensory organs, etc. *British Medical Journal,* May 12, 1894: 1015–17.

Cowles, A., W. W. Beatty, S. J. Nixon, L. J. Lutz, J. Paulk, and E. D. Ross. 2003. Musical skill in dementia: a violinist presumed to have Alzheimer's disease learns to play a new song. *Neurocase* 9 (6): 493–503.

Cranston, Maurice. 1983. *Jean-Jacques.* London: Allen Lane (pp. 289–90).

Critchley, Macdonald. 1937. Musicogenic epilepsy. *Brain* 60: 13–27.

Critchley, Macdonald, and R. A. Henson. 1977. *Music and the Brain: Studies in the Neurology of Music.* London: William Heinemann Medical.

Crystal, H. A., E. Grober, and D. Masur. 1989. Preservation of musical memory in Alzheimer's disease. *Journal of Neurology, Neurosurgery, and Psychiatry* 52 (12): 1415–16.

Cuddy, Lola L., and Jacalyn Duffin. 2005. Music, memory and Alzheimer's disease. *Medical Hypotheses* 64: 229–35.

Cytowic, Richard. 1989. *Synesthesia: A Union of the Senses.* New York: Springer.

———. 1993. *The Man Who Tasted Shapes.* New York: G. P. Putnam's Sons.

Cytowic, Richard, and David Eagleman. 2008 (forthcoming). *Hearing Colors, Tasting Sounds: The Kaleidoscopic Brain of Synesthesia.* Cambridge: MIT Press.

Darwin, Charles. 1871. *The Descent of Man, and Selection in Relation to Sex.* New York: Appleton.

———. 1887/1993. *The Autobiography of Charles Darwin, 1809–1882.* New York: W. W. Norton.

Darwin, Francis, ed. 1892/1958. *The Autobiography of Charles Darwin and Selected Letters.* New York: Dover Publications.

David, R. R., and H. H. Fernandez. 2000. Quetiapine for hypnogogic musical release hallucination. *Journal of Geriatric Psychiatry and Neurology* 13 (4): 210–11.

Davis, John. 2004. Blind Tom. In *African American Lives*, ed. Henry Louis Gates, Jr., and Evelyn Brooks Higginbotham. Oxford: Oxford University Press.

Davis, John, and M. Grace Baron. 2006. Blind Tom: A celebrated slave pianist coping with the stress of autism. In *Stress and Coping in Autism*, ed. M. G. Baron, J. Groden, G. Groden, and L. P. Lipsitt. Oxford: Oxford University Press.

Deutsch, D., T. Henthorn, and M. Dolson. 2004. Absolute pitch, speech, and tone language: Some experiments and a proposed framework. *Music Perception* 21: 339–56.

Deutsch, Diana, Trevor Henthorn, Elizabeth Marvin, and HongShuai Xu. 2006. Absolute pitch among American and Chinese conservatory students: Prevalence differences, and evidence for a speech-related critical period (L). *Journal of the Acoustical Society of America* 119 (2): 719–22.

Devinsky, O., E. Feldmann, K. Burrowes, and E. Bromfield. 1989. Autoscopic phenomena with seizures. *Archives of Neurology* 46: 1080–88.

Donald, Merlin. 1991. *Origins of the Modern Mind.* Cambridge: Harvard University Press.

Down, J. Langdon. 1887. *On Some of the Mental Affections of Childhood and Youth.* London: Churchill.

Dunning, Jennifer. 1981. When a pianist's fingers fail to obey. *New York Times*, June 14, section 2, page 1.

Eco, Umberto. 2005. *The Mysterious Flame of Queen Loana.* New York: Harcourt.

Edelman, Gerald M. 1989. *The Remembered Present: A Biological Theory of Consciousness.* New York: Basic Books.

——. 2006. *Second Nature: Brain Science and Human Knowledge.* New Haven: Yale University Press.

Ellis, Havelock. 1923. *The Dance of Life.* New York: Modern Library.

Fornazzari, L., T. Castle, S. Nadkarni, S. M. Ambrose, D. Miranda, N. Apanasiewicz, and F. Phillips. 2006. Preservation of episodic musical memory in a pianist with Alzheimer disease. *Neurology* 66: 610.

Freedman, Lawrence R. 1997. Cerebral concussion. In *Injured Brains of Medical Minds: Views from Within*, ed. Narinder Kapur (pp. 307–11). Oxford: Oxford University Press.

Freud, Harry. 1956. My Uncle Sigmund. In *Freud As We Knew Him*, ed. H. M. Ruitenbeek. Detroit: Wayne State University Press.

Freud, Sigmund. 1914/1989. The Moses of Michelangelo. In *The Freud Reader*, ed. Peter Gay. New York: W. W. Norton.

Frucht, Steven J. 2004. Focal task-specific dystonia in musicians. In *Dystonia 4: Advances in Neurology*, vol. 94, ed. S. Fahn, M. Hallett, and M. R. DeLong. Philadelphia: Lippincott Williams & Wilkins.

Frucht, S. J., S. Fahn, P. E. Greene, C. O'Brien, M. Gelb, D. D. Truong, J. Welsh, S. Factor, and B. Ford. 2001. The natural history of embouchure dystonia. *Movement Disorders* 16 (5): 899–906.

Fry, Hunter J., and Mark Hallett. 1988. Focal dystonia (occupational cramp) masquerading as nerve entrapment or hysteria. *Plastic and Reconstructive Surgery* 82: 908–10.

Fujioka, Takako, Bernhard Ross, Ryusuke Kakigi, Christo Pantev, and Laurel J. Trainor. 2006. One year of musical training affects development of auditory cortical-evoked fields in young children. *Brain* 129: 2593–2608.

Gaab, N., K. Schulze, E. Ozdemir, and G. Schlaug. 2004. Extensive activation of occipital and parietal cortex in a blind absolute pitch musician. Poster, Eleventh Annual Meeting of the Cognitive Neuroscience Society, San Francisco.

Galton, Francis. 1883. *Inquiries into Human Faculty and Its Development*. London: J. M. Dent.

Gardner, Howard. 1983. *Frames of Mind: The Theory of Multiple Intelligences*. New York: Basic Books.

Garraux, G., A. Bauer, T. Hanakawa, T. Wu, K. Kansaku, and M. Hallett. 2004. Changes in brain anatomy in focal hand dystonia. *Annals of Neurology* 55 (5): 736–39.

Gaser, Christian, and Gottfried Schlaug. 2003. Brain structures differ between musicians and non-musicians. *Journal of Neuroscience* 23 (27): 9240–45.

Geist, Mary Ellen. 2008. *Measure of the Heart: A Father's Alzheimer's, a Daughter's Return*. New York: Springboard Press.

Geroldi, C., T. Metitieri, G. Binetti, O. Zanetti, M. Trabucchi, and G. B. Frisoni. 2000. Pop music and frontotemporal dementia. *Neurology* 55: 1935–36.

Geschwind, Norman, and A. M. Galaburda. 1987. *Cerebral Lateralization: Biological Mechanisms, Associations, and Pathology*. Cambridge: MIT Press.

Gooddy, William. 1988. *Time and the Nervous System*. New York: Praeger.

Gosselin, N., S. Samson, R. Adolphs, M. Noulhiane, M. Roy, D. Hasboun, M. Baulac, and I. Peretz. 2006. Emotional responses to unpleasant music correlates with damage to the parahippocampal cortex. *Brain* 129: 2585–92.

Gougoux, F., F. Lepore, M. Lassonde, P. Voss, R. J. Zatorre, and P. Belin. 2004. Pitch discrimination in the early blind. *Nature* 430: 309.

Gould, S. J., and E. S. Vrba. 1982. Exaptation: A missing term in the science of form. *Paleobiology* 8: 4–15.

Gowers, William R. 1886–88. *Manual: Diseases of the Nervous System.* 2 vols. Philadelphia: P. Blakiston.

———. 1907. *The Borderland of Epilepsy: Faints, Vagal Attacks, Vertigo, Migraine, Sleep Symptoms, and Their Treatment.* London: Churchill.

Griffiths, T. D. 2000. Musical hallucinosis in acquired deafness: Phenomenology and substrate. *Brain* 123: 2065–76.

Griffiths, T. D., A. R. Jennings, and J. D. Warren. 2006. Dystimbria: A distinct musical syndrome? Presented at the Ninth International Conference of Music Perception and Cognition, Bologna, August 22–26, 2006.

Griffiths, T. D., J. D. Warren, J. I. Dean, and D. Howard. 2004. When the feeling's gone: A selective loss of musical emotion. *Journal of Neurology, Neurosurgery, and Psychiatry* 75 (2): 344–45.

Grove's Dictionary of Music and Musicians. 1954. 5th edition, ed. Eric Blom. London: Macmillan.

Hackney, Madeleine E., Svetlana Kantorovich, and Gammon M. Earhart. 2007. A study on the effects of Argentine tango as a form of partnered dance for those with Parkinson disease and the healthy elderly. *American Journal of Dance Therapy* 29 (2): 109–27.

Hackney, Madeleine E., Svetlana Kantorovich, Rebecca Levin, and Gammon M. Earhart. 2007. Effects of tango on functional mobility in Parkinson's disease: A preliminary study. *Journal of Neurologic Physical Therapy* 31:173–79.

Halberstam, David. 2007. *The Coldest Winter: America and the Korean War.* New York: Hyperion.

Hallett, Mark. 1998. The neurophysiology of dystonia. *Archives of Neurology* 55: 601–03.

Halpern, A. R., and R. J. Zatorre. 1999. When that tune runs through your head: a PET investigation of auditory imagery for familiar melodies. *Cerebral Cortex* 9: 697–704.

Hamilton, R. H., A. Pascual-Leone, and G. Schlaug. 2004. Absolute pitch in blind musicians. *NeuroReport* 15 (5): 803–06.

Hamzei, F., J. Liepert, C. Dettmers, T. Adler, S. Kiebel, M. Rijntjes, and C. Weiller. 2001. Structural and functional cortical abnormalities after upper limb amputation during childhood. *NeuroReport* 12 (5): 957–62.

Hannon, Erin E., and Sandra E. Trehub. 2005. Tuning in to musical rhythms: Infants learn more readily than adults. *Proceedings of the National Academy of Sciences* 102: 12639–43.

Harrison, John E. 2001. *Synaesthesia: The Strangest Thing.* New York: Oxford University Press.

Hart, Mickey, and Frederic Lieberman. 1991. *Planet Drum.* San Francisco: HarperCollins.

Hart, Mickey, with Jay Stevens. 1990. *Drumming at the Edge of Magic.* San Francisco: HarperCollins.

Harvey, William. 1627/1960. *De Motu Locali Animalium.* London: Cambridge University Press.

Hécaen, Henri, and Martin L. Albert. 1978. *Human Neuropsychology.* New York: John Wiley & Sons.

Henahan, Donal. 1983. Did Shostakovich have a secret? *New York Times,* July 10, section 2, page 21.

Hermelin, Beate, N. O'Connor, and S. Lee. 1987. Musical inventiveness of five idiot savants. *Psychological Medicine* 17: 685–94.

Hermesh, H., S. Konas, R. Shiloh, R. Dar, S. Marom, A. Weizman, and R. Gross-Isseroff. 2004. Musical hallucinations: Prevalence in psychotic and nonpsychotic outpatients. *Journal of Clinical Psychiatry* 65 (2): 191–97.

Hull, John. 1991. *Touching the Rock: An Experience of Blindness.* New York: Pantheon.

Hunter, M. D., T. D. Griffiths, T. F. Farrow, Y. Zheng, I. D. Wilkinson, N. Hegde, W. Woods, S. A. Spence, and P. W. Woodruff. 2003. A neural basis for the perception of voices in external auditory space. *Brain* 126 (1): 161–69.

Huron, David. 2006. *Sweet Anticipation: Music and the Psychology of Expectation.* Cambridge: Bradford Books, MIT Press.

Hutchinson, Siobhan, Leslie Hui-Lin Lee, Nadine Gaab, and Gottfried Schlaug. 2003. Cerebellar volume of musicians. *Cerebral Cortex* 13: 943–49.

Huxley, Aldous. 1932. *Brave New World.* London: Chatto and Windus.

Huysmans, Joris-Karl. 1884/1926. *Against the Grain.* Paris: Librairie du Palais-Royal.

Hyde, K., R. Zatorre, T. D. Griffiths, J. P. Lerch, and I. Peretz. 2006. Morphometry of the amusic brain: A two-site study. *Brain* 129: 2562–70.

Iversen, John R., Aniruddh D. Patel, and Kengo Ohgushi. 2004. Perception of non-linguistic rhythmic stimuli by American and Japanese listeners. *Proceedings of the International Congress of Acoustics, Kyoto.*

Izumi, Yukio, Takeshi Terao, Yoichi Ishino, and Jun Nakamura. 2002. Differences in regional cerebral blood flow during musical and verbal hallucinations. *Psychiatry Research Neuroimaging* 116: 119–23.

Jackendorff, Ray, and Fred Lerdahl. 2006. The capacity for music: What is it, and what's special about it? *Cognition* 100: 33–72.

Jackson, John Hughlings. 1871. Singing by speechless (aphasic) children. *Lancet* 2: 430–31.

———. 1888. On a particular variety of epilepsy ("Intellectual Aura"). *Brain* 11: 179–207.

Jacome, D. E. 1984. Aphasia with elation, hypermusia, musicophilia and compulsive whistling. *Journal of Neurology, Neurosurgery, and Psychiatry* 47: 308–10.

James, William. 1890. *The Principles of Psychology.* New York: Henry Holt.

Jourdain, Robert. 1997. *Music, the Brain, and Ecstasy: How Music Captures Our Imagination.* New York: William Morrow.

Kapur, Narinder. 1996. Paradoxical functional facilitation in brain-behaviour research: A critical review. *Brain* 119: 1775–90.

Kawai, Nobuyuki, and Tetsuro Matsuzawa. 2000. Numerical memory span in a chimpanzee. *Nature* 403: 39–40.

Kemp, David E., William S. Gilmer, Jenelle Fleck, and Pedro Dago. 2007. An association of intrusive, repetitive phrases with lamotrigine treatment in bipolar II disorder. *CNS Spectrums* 12 (2): 106–11.

Kertesz, Andrew. 2006. *The Banana Lady and Other Stories of Curious Behavior and Speech.* Victoria: Trafford Publishing.

Kertesz, Andrew, and David G. Munoz, ed. 1998. *Pick's Disease and Pick Complex.* New York: Wiley-Liss.

Klawans, Harold L. 1997. "Did I Remove That Gallbladder?" In *Injured Brains of Medical Minds: Views from Within*, ed. Narinder Kapur (pp. 21–30). Oxford: Oxford University Press.

Konorski, Jerzy. 1967. *Integrative Activity of the Brain: An Interdisciplinary Approach.* Chicago: University of Chicago Press.

Kraemer, David J. M., C. Neil Macrae, Adam E. Green, and William M. Kelley. 2005. Sound of silence activates auditory cortex. *Nature* 434: 158.

Lamb, Charles. 1823. *The Essays of Elia.* London: Taylor and Hessey.

Lederman, Richard J. 1999. Robert Schumann. *Seminars in Neurology* 19 suppl. 1: 17–24.

Lehrer, Jonah. 2007. Blue Monday, green Thursday. *New Scientist* 194 (2604): 48–51.

———. 2007. *Proust Was a Neuroscientist.* New York: Houghton Mifflin.

Lesser, Wendy. 2007. *Room for Doubt.* New York: Pantheon.

Levitin, Daniel J. 2006. *This Is Your Brain on Music.* New York: Dutton.

Levitin, Daniel J., and Ursula Bellugi. 1998. Musical ability in individuals with Williams' Syndrome. *Music Perception* 15 (4): 357–89.

———. 2006. Rhythm, timbre and hyperacusis in Williams-Beuren syndrome. In

Williams-Beuren Syndrome: Research and Clinical Perspectives, ed. C. Morris, H. Lenhoff, and P. Wang (pp. 343–58). Baltimore: Johns Hopkins University Press.

Levitin, Daniel J., and Perry R. Cook. 1996. Memory for musical tempo: Additional evidence that auditory memory is absolute. *Perception and Psychophysics* 58: 927–35.

Levitin, Daniel J., and Susan E. Rogers. 2005. Absolute pitch: Perception, coding and controversies. *Trends in Cognitive Neurosciences* 9 (1): 26–33.

Llinás, Rodolfo. 2001. *I of the Vortex: From Neurons to Self.* Cambridge: MIT Press.

Lopez, Steve. 2008. *The Soloist: A Lost Dream, an Unlikely Friendship, and the Redemptive Power of Music.* New York: G. P. Putnam's Sons.

Luria, A. R. 1932. *The Nature of Human Conflicts; or Emotion, Conflict and Will.* New York: Liveright.

———. 1947/1970. *Traumatic Aphasia.* Berlin: Mouton de Gruyter.

———. 1948/1963. *Restoration of Function After Brain Injury.* New York: Macmillan.

———. 1966. *Higher Cortical Functions in Man.* New York: Basic Books.

———. 1968. *The Mind of a Mnemonist.* Cambridge: Harvard University Press.

Luria, A. R., L. S. Tsvetkova, and D. S. Futer. 1965. Aphasia in a composer. *Journal of Neurological Sciences* 2: 288–92.

Lusseyran, Jacques. 1963. *And There Was Light.* Boston: Little, Brown.

Machover, Tod. 2004. Shaping minds musically. *BT Technology Journal* 22 (4): 171–79.

Mailis-Gagnon, Angela, and David Israelson. 2003. *Beyond Pain: Making the Mind-Body Connection.* Toronto: Viking Canada.

Martin, Paula I., Margaret A. Naeser, Hugo Theoret, Jose Maria Tormos, Marjorie Nicholas, Jacquie Kurland, Felipe Fregni, Heidi Seekins, Karl Doron, and Alvaro Pascual-Leone. 2004. Transcranial magnetic stimulation as a complementary treatment for aphasia. *Seminars in Speech and Language* 25: 181–91.

Massey, Irving J. 2006. The musical dream revisited: Music and language in dreams. *Psychology of Aesthetics, Creativity, and the Arts S* 1: 42–50.

Maugham, Somerset. 1931/1992. "The Alien Corn." In Maugham's *Collected Short Stories*, vol. 2. New York: Penguin Classics.

Maurer, Daphne. 1997. Neonatal synaesthesia: Implications for the processing of speech and faces. In *Synaesthesia: Classic and Contemporary Readings*, ed. Simon Baron-Cohen and John Harrison (pp. 224–42). Oxford, UK: Blackwell.

Meige, Henri, and E. Feindel. 1902. *Les tics et leur traitement* (Tics and Their Treatment). Paris: Masson.

Micheyl, Christophe, Stephanie Khalfa, Xavier Perrot, and Lionel Collet. 1997. Difference in cochlear efferent activity between musicians and non-musicians. *NeuroReport* 8: 1047–50.

Miles, Barry. 1997. *Paul McCartney: Many Years from Now.* New York: Henry Holt.

Mill, John Stuart. 1924/1990. *Autobiography.* New York: Penguin Classics.

Miller, B. L., K. Boone, J. Cummings, S. L. Read, and F. Mishkin. 2000. Functional correlates of musical and visual ability in frontotemporal dementia. *British Journal of Psychiatry* 176: 458–63.

Miller, B. L., J. Cummings, F. Mishkin, K. Boone, F. Prince, M. Ponton, and C. Cotman. 1998. Emergence of artistic talent in frontotemporal dementia. *Neurology* 51: 978–82.

Miller, Leon K. 1989. *Musical Savants: Exceptional Skill in the Mentally Retarded.* Hillsdale, NJ: Lawrence Erlbaum.

Miller, Timothy C., and T. W. Crosby. 1979. Musical hallucinations in a deaf elderly patient. *Annals of Neurology* 5: 301–02.

Minsky, Marvin. 1982. Music, mind and meaning. In *Music, Mind and Brain,* ed. Manfred Clynes (pp. 1–20). New York: Plenum Press.

Mitchell, Silas Weir. 1866. The case of George Dedlow. *Atlantic Monthly.*

———. 1872/1965. *The Injuries of Nerves.* New York: Dover.

Mithen, Steven. 2005. *The Singing Neanderthals: The Origins of Music, Language, Mind and Body.* London: Weidenfeld & Nicolson.

Mithen, Steven. 2008. The diva within. *New Scientist* (February 23): 38–39.

Musacchia, Gabriella, Mikko Sams, Erika Skoe, and Nina Kraus. 2007. Musicians have enhanced subcortical auditory and audiovisual processing of speech and music. *Proceedings of the National Academy of Sciences (USA)* 104 (40): 15894–98.

Nabokov, Vladimir. 1951/1999. *Speak, Memory.* New York: Everyman's Library.

Nelson, Kevin R., Michelle Mattingly, and Frederick A. Schmitt. 2007. Out-of-body experience and arousal. *Neurology* 68: 794–95.

Nelson, Kevin R., Michelle Mattingly, Sherman A. Lee, and Frederick A. Schmitt. 2006. Does the arousal system contribute to near death experience? *Neurology* 66: 1003–09.

Nietzsche, Friedrich. 1888/1977. "Nietzsche contra Wagner." In Walter Kaufmann, trans. *The Portable Nietzsche.* New York: Penguin.

———. 1888/1968. The Will to Power as Art. In *The Will to Power* (pp. 419–57). Translated by Walter Kaufmann. New York: Vintage.

Nordoff, Paul, and Clive Robbins. 1971. *Therapy in Music for Handicapped Children.* London: Victor Gollancz.

Noreña, A. J., and J. J. Eggermont. 2005. Enriched acoustic environment after noise trauma reduces hearing loss and prevents cortical map reorganization. *Journal of Neuroscience* 25 (3): 699–705.

Ockelford, Adam. 2007. *In the Key of Genius: The Extraordinary Life of Derek Paravicini*. London: Hutchinson.

Ockelford, Adam, Linda Pring, Graham Welch, and Darold Treffert. 2006. *Focus on Music: Exploring the Musical Interests and Abilities of Blind and Partially-Sighted Children and Young People with Septo-Optic Dysplasia*. London: Institute of Education.

Oestereich, James R. 2004. Music: The shushing of the symphony. *The New York Times*, January 11.

Ostwald, Peter. 1985. *Schumann: Music and Madness*. London: Victor Gollancz.

The Oxford Companion to Music. 1955. 9th edition, ed. Percy A. Scholes. Oxford: Oxford University Press.

Paderewski, Ignacy Jan. 1939. *The Paderewski Memoirs*, ed. Mary Lawton. London: Collins.

Pascual-Leone, Alvaro. 2003. The brain that makes music and is changed by it. In *The Cognitive Neuroscience of Music*, ed. Isabelle Peretz and Robert Zatorre (pp. 396–409). Oxford: Oxford University Press.

Patel, A. D., J. R. Iversen, M. R. Bregman, I. Schulz, and C. Schulz. 2008. Investigating the human-specificity of synchronization to music. In *Proceedings of the 10th International Conference on Music Perception and Cognition*, ed. Mayumi Adachi et al. Sapporo, Japan.

Patel, Aniruddh D. 2008. *Music, Language, and the Brain*. New York: Oxford University Press.

Patel, Aniruddh. D. 2006. Musical rhythm, linguistic rhythm, and human evolution. *Music Perception* 24 (1): 99–104.

Patel, Aniruddh. D., J. M. Foxton, and T. D. Griffiths. 2005. Musically tone-deaf individuals have difficulty discriminating intonation contours extracted from speech. *Brain and Cognition* 59: 310–13.

Patel, Aniruddh, and John Iversen. 2006. A non-human animal can drum a steady beat on a musical instrument. In *Proceedings of the 9th International Conference on Music Perception and Cognition*, ed. M. Baroni, A. R. Addessi, R. Caterina, and M. Costa. Bologna, Italy.

Patel, Aniruddh D., John R. Iversen, Yanqing Chen, and Bruno H. Repp. 2005. The influence of metricality and modality on synchronization with a beat. *Experimental Brain Research* 163: 226–38.

Patel, Aniruddh D., John R. Iversen, and Jason C. Rosenberg. 2006. Comparing the rhythm and melody of speech and music: The case of British

English and French. *Journal of the Acoustical Society of America* 119 (5): 3034–47.

Paulescu, E., J. Harrison, S. Baron-Cohen, J. D. G. Watson, L. Goldstein, J. Heather, R. S. J. Frackowiak, and C. D. Frith. 1995. The physiology of coloured hearing: A PET activation study of colour-word synesthesia. *Brain* 118: 661–76.

Penfield, W., and P. Perot. 1963. The brain's record of visual and auditory experience: A final summary and discussion. *Brain* 86: 595–696.

Peretz, Isabelle, and I. Gagnon. 1999. Dissociation between recognition and emotional judgement for melodies. *Neurocase* 5: 21–30.

Piccirilli, Massimo, Tiziana Sciarma, and Simona Luzzi. 2000. Modularity of music: Evidence from a case of pure amusia. *Journal of Neurology, Neurosurgery, and Psychiatry* 69: 541–45.

Pinker, Steven. 1997. *How the Mind Works.* New York: W. W. Norton.

———. 2007. Toward a consilient study of literature. *Philosophy and Literature* 31: 161–77.

Poskanzer, David C., Arthur E. Brown, and Henry Miller. 1962. Musicogenic epilepsy caused only by a discrete frequency band of church bells. *Brain* 85: 77–92.

The Power of Music: In which is shown, by a variety of Pleasing and Instructive Anecdotes, the effects it has on Man and Animals. 1814. London (Corner of St. Paul's Church-Yard): J. Harris.

Proust, Marcel. 1913/1949. *Remembrance of Things Past.* Translated by C. K. Scott Moncrieff. London: Chatto and Windus.

Ramachandran, V. S. 2004. *A Brief Tour of Human Consciousness.* New York: Pi Press.

Ramachandran, V. S., and E. M. Hubbard. 2001. Psychophysical investigations into the neural basis of synaesthesia. *Proceedings of the Royal Society of London, B* 268: 979–83.

———. 2001. Synaesthesia: A window into perception, thought and language. *Journal of Consciousness Studies* 8 (12): 3–34.

———. 2003. The phenomenology of synaesthesia. *Journal of Consciousness Studies* 10 (8): 49–57.

Rangell, Leo. 2006. Music in the head: Living at the brain-mind border. *Huffington Post,* September 12. http://www.huffingtonpost.com/dr-leo-rangell/.

Rapin, Isabelle. 1982. *Children with Brain Dysfunction: Neurology, Cognition, Language and Behavior.* New York: Raven Press.

Rauscher, F. H., G. L. Shaw, and K. N. Ky. 1993. Music and spatial task performance. *Nature* 365:611.

Reik, Theodor. 1953. *The Haunting Melody: Psychoanalytic Experiences in Life and Music*. New York: Farrar, Straus and Young.

Révész, Geza. 1925/1970. *The Psychology of a Musical Prodigy*. Freeport, NY: Greenwood Press.

Rizzolatti, Giacomo, Luciano Fadiga, Leonardo Fogassi, and Vittorio Gallese. 2002. From mirror neurons to imitation: Facts and speculations. In *The Imitative Mind*, ed. Andrew N. Meltzoff and Wolfgang Prinz (pp. 247–66). Cambridge: Cambridge University Press.

Rohrer, J. D., S. J. Smith, and J. D. Warren. 2006. Craving for music after treatment of partial epilepsy. *Epilepsia* 47 (5): 939–40.

Rorem, Ned. 2006. *Facing the Night: A Diary (1999–2005) and Musical Writings*. New York: Shoemaker & Hoard.

Ross, E. D., P. B. Jossman, B. Bell, T. Sabin, and N. Geschwind. 1975. Musical hallucinations in deafness. *Journal of the American Medical Association* 231 (6): 620–22.

Rothenberg, David. 2005. *Why Birds Sing*. New York: Basic Books.

Rouget, Gilbert. 1985. *Music and Trance*. Chicago: University of Chicago Press.

Russell, S. M., and J. G. Golfinos. 2003. Amusia following resection of a Heschl gyrus glioma. *Journal of Neurosurgery* 98: 1109–12.

Sacks, Oliver. 1973. *Awakenings*. London: Duckworth.

———. 1984. *A Leg to Stand On*. New York: Summit Books.

———. 1985. *The Man Who Mistook His Wife for a Hat*. New York: Summit Books.

———. 1992. The last hippie. *New York Review of Books* vol. 39, no. 6 (March 26): 53–62.

———. 1992. Tourette's syndrome and creativity. *British Medical Journal* 305: 1515–16.

———. 1995. *An Anthropologist on Mars: Seven Paradoxical Tales*. New York: Alfred A. Knopf.

———. 1997. *The Island of the Colorblind*. New York: Alfred A. Knopf.

———. 1998. Music and the brain. In *Clinical Applications of Music in Neurologic Rehabilitation*, ed. Concetta M. Tomaino (pp. 1–18). St. Louis: MMB Music.

———. 2003. The mind's eye. *New Yorker* (July 28): 48–59.

———. 2004. Speed. *New Yorker* (August 23): 60–69.

———. 2006. Stereo Sue. *New Yorker* (June 19): 64–73.

———. 2006. The power of music. *Brain* 129: 2528–32.

Saffran, Jenny R., and Gregory J. Griepentrog. 2001. Absolute pitch in infant auditory learning: Evidence for developmental reorganization. *Developmental Psychology* 37 (1): 74–85.

Schellenberg, E. Glenn. 2003. Does exposure to music have beneficial side effects? In *The Cognitive Neuroscience of Music*, ed. Isabelle Peretz and Robert J. Zatorre (pp. 430–48). Oxford: Oxford University Press.

Schlaug, G., L. Jäncke, Y. Huang, and H. Steinmetz. 1995. In vivo evidence of structural brain asymmetry in musicians. *Science* 267: 699–701.

Schlaug, Gottfried, Lutz Jäncke, Yanxiong Huang, Jochen F. Staiger, and Helmuth Steinmetz. 1995. Increased corpus callosum size in musicians. *Neuropsychologia* 33 (8): 1047–55.

Schlaug, Gottfried, Andrea Norton, Elif Ozdemir, and Nancy Helm-Estabrooks. 2006. Long-term behavioral and brain effects of melodic intonation therapy in patients with Broca's aphasia. *Neuroimage* 31 (suppl. 1): 37.

Schlaug, Gottfried, Sarah Marchina, and Andrea Norton. 2008. From singing to speaking: Why singing may lead to recovery of expressive language function in patients with Broca's aphasia. *Music Perception* 25:4, 315–23.

Schopenhauer, Arthur. 1819/1969. *The World as Will and Representation* (esp. vol. 1, chapter 52). Translated by E. J. Payne. New York: Dover.

Schreber, Daniel Paul. 1903/2000. *Memoirs of My Nervous Illness*. New York: New York Review Books.

Schullian, Dorothy M., and Max Schoen, ed. 1948. *Music and Medicine*. New York: Henry Shuman.

Scoville, W. B., and Brenda Milner. 1957. Loss of recent memory after bilateral hippocampal lesions. *Journal of Neurology, Neurosurgery and Psychiatry* 20: 11–21.

Seeley, W. W., B. R. Matthews, R. K. Crawford, M. L. Gorno-Tempini, D. Foti, I. R. Mackenzie, B. L. Miller. 2008. Unravelling *Boléro:* Progressive aphasia, transmodal creativity and the right posterior neocortex. *Brain* 131 (1): 39–49.

Sforza, Teri, with Howard and Sylvia Lenhoff. 2006. *The Strangest Song*. Amherst, NY: Prometheus Books.

Sheehy, M. P., and C. D. Marsden. 1982. Writer's cramp—a focal dystonia. *Brain* 105: 461–80.

Shenk, David. 2001. *The Forgetting: Alzheimer's—Portrait of an Epidemic*. New York: Doubleday.

Simkin, Benjamin. 1992. Mozart's scatological disorder. *British Medical Journal* 305: 1563–67.

Simner, J., J. Ward, M. Lanz, A. Jansari, K. Noonan, L. Glover, and D. Oakley. 2005. Non-random associations of graphemes to colours in synaesthetic and normal populations. *Cognitive Neuropsychology* 22 (8): 1069–85.

Simner, Julia, Catherine Mulvenna, Noam Sagiv, Elias Tsakanikos, Sarah A. Witherby, Christine Fraser, Kirsten Scott, and Jamie Ward. 2006. Synaesthesia: The prevalence of atypical cross-modal experiences. *Perception* 35: 1024–33.

Slonimsky, Nicolas. 1953. *Lexicon of Musical Invective: Critical Assaults on Composers Since Beethoven's Time*. Seattle: University of Washington Press.

Smith, Daniel B. 2007. *Muses, Madmen, and Prophets: Rethinking the History, Science, and Meaning of Auditory Hallucinations*. New York: Penguin Press.

Smith, Steven B. 1983. *The Great Mental Calculators: The Psychology, Methods, and Lives of Calculating Prodigies, Past and Present*. New York: Columbia University Press.

Snyder, Allan W., Elaine Mulcahy, Janet L. Taylor, John Mitchell, Perminder Sachdev, and Simon C. Gandevia. 2003. Savant-like skills exposed in normal people by suppressing the left fronto-temporal lobe. *Journal of Integrative Neuroscience* 2 (2): 149–58.

Sotavalta, Olavi. 1963. The flight sounds of insects. In *Acoustic Behavior of Animals*, ed. R. G. Busnel (pp. 374–89). Amsterdam: Elsevier.

Spencer, Herbert. 1857/2002. The origin and function of music. In *Music Education: Source Readings from Ancient Greece to Today*, ed. Michael Mark (pp. 47–48). New York: Routledge.

Sparr, S. A. 2002. Receptive amelodia in a trained musician. *Neurology* 59: 1659–60.

Stein, Alexander. 2004. Music, mourning, and consolation. *Journal of the American Psychoanalytic Association* 52 (3): 783–811.

Stern, Daniel. 2004. "Fabrikant's Way." In *A Little Street Music*. Huntsville, TX: Texas Review Press.

Storr, Anthony. 1989. *Freud*. Oxford: Oxford University Press.

———. 1992. *Music and the Mind*. New York: Free Press.

Stravinsky, Igor. 1947. *Poetics of Music: In the Form of Six Lessons*. Oxford: Oxford University Press.

Styron, William. 1990. *Darkness Visible: A Memoir of Madness*. New York: Random House.

Thaut, Michael H. 2005. *Rhythm, Music, and the Brain: Scientific Foundations and Clinical Applications*. New York: Routledge.

Tolstoy, Leo. 1890/1986. *The Kreutzer Sonata, and Other Stories*. New York: Penguin Classics.

Tomaino, Concetta, ed. 1998. *Clinical Applications of Music in Neurologic Rehabilitation*. St. Louis: MMB Music.

Treffert, Darold. 1986/2006. *Extraordinary People: Understanding Savant Syndrome*. Revised ed. Lincoln, Nebraska: iUniverse.

Turnbull, Oliver H., Evangelos Zois, Karen Kaplan-Solms, and Mark Solms. 2006. The developing transference in amnesia: Changes in interpersonal relationship, despite profound episodic-memory loss. *Neuro-Psychoanalysis* 8 (2): 199–204.

Twain, Mark. 1876/1878. "A Literary Nightmare." Reprinted in *Punch, Brothers, Punch! and Other Stories*. New York: Slote, Woodman and Co.

Uga, V., M. C. Lemut, C. Zampi, I. Zilli, and P. Salzarulo. 2006. Music in dreams. *Consciousness and Cognition* 15: 351–57.

Ulrich, G., T. Houtmans, and C. Gold. 2007. The additional therapeutic effect of group music therapy for schizophrenic patients: A randomized study. *Acta Psychiatrica Scandinavica* 116: 362–70.

van Bloss, Nick. 2006. *Busy Body: My Life with Tourette's Syndrome*. London: Fusion Press.

Vaughan, Ivan. 1986. *Ivan: Living with Parkinson's Disease*. London: Macmillan.

von Arnim, G., and P. Engel. 1964. Mental retardation related to hypercalcaemia. *Developmental Medicine and Child Neurology* 6: 366–77.

Wagner, Christoph. 2005. *Hand und Instrument: Musikphysiologische Grundlagen Praktische Konsequenzen*. Wiesbaden: Breitkopf & Härtel.

Wagner, Richard. 1911. *My Life* (p. 603). New York: Dodd, Mead & Co.

Warner, Nick, and Victor Aziz. 2005. Hymns and arias: Musical hallucinations in older people in Wales. *International Journal of Geriatric Psychiatry* 20: 658–60.

Warren, Jason D., Jane E. Warren, Nick C. Fox, and Elizabeth K. Warrington. 2003. Nothing to say, something to sing: Primary progressive dynamic aphasia. *Neurocase* 9 (2): 140–55.

Waugh, Evelyn. 1945. *Brideshead Revisited*. London: Chapman and Hall.

———. 1957. *The Ordeal of Gilbert Pinfold*. Boston: Little, Brown.

Wearing, Deborah. 2005. *Forever Today: A Memoir of Love and Amnesia*. London: Doubleday.

Weiskrantz, Lawrence. 1997. *Consciousness Lost and Found*. Oxford: Oxford University Press.

West, Rebecca. 1957. *The Fountain Overflows*. London: Macmillan.

White, E. B. 1933. The supremacy of Uruguay. *New Yorker* (November 25): 18–19.

Wilson, Barbara A., and Deborah Wearing. 1995. Prisoner of consciousness: A state of just awakening following herpes simplex encephalitis. In *Broken Memories: Case Studies in Memory Impairment*, ed. Ruth Campbell and Martin Conway (pp. 14–30). Oxford: Blackwell.

Wilson, Barbara A., A. D. Baddeley, and Narinder Kapur. 1995. Dense amnesia in a professional musician following herpes simplex virus encephalitis. *Journal of Clinical and Experimental Neuropsychology* 17 (5): 668–81.

Wilson, Edward O. 1994. *Naturalist*. Washington, D.C.: Island Press.

Wilson, Frank R. 1988. Teaching hands, treating hands. *Piano Quarterly* 141: 34–41.

————. 1989. Acquisition and loss of skilled movement in musicians. *Seminars in Neurology* 9 (2): 146–51.

————. 2000. Current controversies on the origin, diagnosis and management of focal dystonia. In *Medical Problems of the Instrumentalist Musician*, ed. Raoul Tubiana and Peter C. Amadio (pp. 311–27). London: Martin Dunitz.

Wittgenstein, Ludwig. 1969. *On Certainty*. Oxford: Basil Blackwell.

Young, Robyn L., Michael C. Ridding, and Tracy L. Morrell. 2004. Switching skills by turning off part of the brain. *Neurocase* 10 (3): 215–22.

Zatorre, R. J., and A. R. Halpern. 2005. Mental concerts: Musical imagery and auditory cortex. *Neuron* 47: 9–12.

Zatorre, R. J., A. R. Halpern, D. W. Perry, E. Meyer, and A. C. Evans. 1996. Hearing in the mind's ear: A PET investigation of musical imagery and perception. *Journal of Cognitive Neuroscience* 8: 29–46.

Zitzer-Comfort, C., T. F. Doyle, N. Masataka, J. Korenberg, and U. Bellugi. 2007. Nature and nurture: Williams syndrome across cultures. *Developmental Science*, in press.

Zuckerkandl, Victor. 1956. *Sound and Symbol: Music and the External World*. Princeton, NJ: Princeton University Press.

Index